The World of My Past

Abraham Hersz Biderman was born in Lodz, Poland, on 20 August 1924. After surviving the Second World War, he was liberated by the British army from the Bergen-Belsen extermination camp on 15 April 1945. All of his immediate family had perished in German concentration camps.

He moved to Belgium, where he met his future wife, and lived there for several years. Then, on 11 January 1949, Abraham Biderman arrived in Australia and started a new life.

In 1951 he established Champs Elysées Models, a ready-to-wear, high-class women's fashion manufacturing company. His designs won many prizes, including the Australian Designer's Award for 1964. He also pursued his interests in the fine arts — especially in acting and painting. In recent years he has written short stories, some of which have been published in the *Melbourne Chronicle*, *Gesher*, and *Generation*. This is his first book.

Abraham Biderman has one son and lives in Melbourne, Australia.

In the absence of tombstones, this book is dedicated to the memory of Shimon-Dov, my father; to my mother, Fradl; and to my brother, Lipek, who were sentenced to death for the crime of being born Jewish. It is also dedicated to the loving memory of Madeleine, who passed away in the prime of her life; and to our son, Simon, so that he will remember and pass on to his children the lesson of the Holocaust.

The World of My Past

ABRAHAM H. BIDERMAN

RANDOM HOUSE
AUSTRALIA

Random House Australia Pty Ltd
20 Alfred Street, Milsons Point, NSW 2061

Sydney NewYork Toronto
London Auckland Johannesburg
and agencies throughout the world

First published in Australia by AHB Publications, 1995Holocaust
Reprinted October 1995

National Library of Australia
Cataloguing-in-Publication data:

Biderman, Abraham, 1924–
The world of my past

ISBN 0 09 183438 4.

1. Biderman, Abraham, 1924– . 2. Holocaust survivors –
Biography. 3. Holocaust, Jewish (1939–1945) - Poland -
Lodz - Personal narratives. 4. Jews - Persecutions -
Poland - Lodz. 1. Title.
940.5318092

Edited by Yvonne Fein and Henry Rosenbloom
Cover design by Phillip Campbell Design
Typeset in 11 on 13.5 Palatino by DOCUPRO
Printed in Australia by Griffin Press

The dark, dark places

The Rt Hon Sir Zelman Cowen AK, GCMG, GCVO

Abraham Biderman, the author of this deeply disturbing book, wrote to me in the latter part of last year, enclosing part of the manuscript, and he invited me to read and comment on it. I found it to be a stark and powerful statement of an appalling personal experience of the Holocaust. He and his family endured long years of privation and suffering in the Lodz ghetto. Living in comfort and security in that flourishing town, they saw it occupied by the Germans in the first days of the war. They saw its rich Jewish life destroyed and its Jews herded into the ghetto. When the Russians entered Lodz in January 1945, barely eight hundred Jews remained out of a pre-war population of 230,000, and plans were in hand for the liquidation of that tiny remnant. Well might his uncomprehending grandmother look out and repeat endlessly, 'The world has gone mad. The world has gone mad.'

By the time the author was liberated from Bergen-Belsen, the family had endured terrible suffering. They had experienced the horror of transportation to Auschwitz where his parents, other relatives and friends perished in the gas chambers and furnaces. It is hard to realise that both parents were then only in their early forties. The author was moved to other camps, which included Dora where German V1 and V2 missiles were under construction, and he was finally liberated from Bergen-Belsen, the camp which British units overran in the last days of the war, in April 1945. I know something of this from the personal account of a friend who was in the British military force which entered Belsen; decades later the hideous sights and smells of that place of horror remained vivid in his memory.

I wrote to Mr Biderman saying that I was deeply moved by the powerful and profoundly disturbing account in those pages. He then sent the complete manuscript to me, and invited me to write a foreword. As do the accounts of such writers as Primo Levi, Elie Wiesel and Samuel Pisar, so too *The World of My Past* overwhelms me with the tragedy and horror of it all. That is expressed effectively in an exchange between prisoners:

'We are *in* the madhouse guarded by crazy people!'

'No,' said a friend of mine softly, and his whispered remark would haunt me forever. 'He's not crazy. That's how they all are. And don't you know? This is how the world always was. How do you think we got here?'

That's how the world always was. The book begins with a brief statement of the words of historic preachers of deicide, of the early saint, St. John Chrysostom of the early church, of Martin Luther in the early days of the Reformation when he called in ferocious words for the destruction of the Jews and their synagogues. It recounts briefly the *acts* of destruction which followed: of the Crusaders, the Inquisitors and of mobs. All this is in recorded history and the charge of deicide was not yet recanted by the Churches when the Nazis overran Europe. And even in the last stages of the story, as Jews, released from the camps, returned to Poland to recover whatever might be recovered, local populations turned upon them with hatred, and committed acts of murder and violence upon them.

The story is told with great effectiveness and simplicity; the book is distinguished by a clarity of style and narrative, and there is a very certain grasp and mastery of the English language which the author could not have had when he was liberated fifty years ago.

I speak with no authority as a Holocaust scholar, but I believe that this book must take a place among the significant personal accounts of that appalling human tragedy. It effectively underlines the point made by Emil Fackenhaim that the Holocaust was unique, in the sense that it was not directed against the Jewish people for acts they were perceived to have done; it was directed against them because they *were*, because their very existence called imperatively and inexorably for their total extirpation. Moreover, that destruction took place with all its horror, its humiliation, its denial of humanity, while the world stood by.

The author's account furnishes an extraordinarily detailed picture; how he has recalled it all, I cannot know. How the human mind can retain and preserve the detail of events long past I also do not know; to the reader it is overwhelming. The accounts of cruelties inflicted by criminals and vicious human beasts, subject to no restraint, no law, are almost unbelievable; yet their veracity can be subject to no doubt.

I first went to Germany in 1947, to Berlin, to prepare some papers for the British Control Commission. There was evidence of terrible destruction all around, and this bore testimony to the disaster which Hitler had brought upon the people he led. In the course of that visit, I saw the Dachau concentration camp in the immediate vicinity of Munich, and I was driven there by a German who told me that he had been at Stalingrad. I talked with him quite freely as we drove to the camp. As we left it, I spoke no more; there was nothing that I wished to say to that German, to any German; they all had responsibility for the horrors which Dachau then exhibited. In the long run we have not sustained that position, because it is not possible to do so, and maybe it is not right. That whole generation is passing. Yet the account of the Holocaust as reproduced in *The World of My Past* is very important for what it tells us about the dark, dark places which lie deep in man.

The tragedy is the more stark because of the reccurrence of Nazi-like manifestations in Germany and elsewhere in the world. How could *any* human being want any part of a world with all of that suffering, with all of that unbridled cruelty, with those manifestations of all that is evil in humankind? What must be unendurable to the author, as it should be unendurable to all of us, is the evidence that it is occurring again in Europe, in Africa, it may be elsewhere. In the hearts and minds of man, the evil that the Holocaust exhibited still lurks — not in you, not in me it may be, but in too many of our fellow men — and it is that which makes this story the more unbearable.

We rejoice in the deliverance of Abraham Biderman, in his subsequent happy marriage, and in his renewal and his success in this good land.

An epistle to the gentiles

Barry Jones, AO

The English historian Lord Acton wrote: 'The falsification of history is the greatest of all crimes because it denies and debases the meaning of human experience ... Truth is ill-served when the strong man with the dagger is followed by the weaker man with the sponge. First, the criminal who slays; then the sophist who defends the slayer.' Abraham Biderman is a witness — and a witness of truth. He writes of a nightmare experience which destroyed every other member of his immediate family. Only he survives.

After fifty years the immediacy and poignancy of his account stands out. I have met and talked with many Holocaust victims, but none has Biderman's power.

His fear that the Holocaust is forgotten and ignored is understandable — but it may be exaggerated. We live in an age of genocide. We have been almost numbed by the extent of recent slaughter in Cambodia and Rwanda. Stalin murdered millions of Russians and Mao even more Chinese. Nevertheless, Hitler's 'final solution' has a unique horror: the industrialisation of mass murder, using the techniques of mass destruction, developed by a country with high levels of literacy, technological skills and a rich culture.

Despite Tom Keneally's book *Schindler's List* and Steven Spielberg's film, the sheer mindless sadism of the Holocaust beggars the imagination because in a comfortable country like Australia it is so remote from our experience as to seem unimaginable. There may be more sceptics in Burwood, Carlton, Vermont and Warrnambool than in Berlin, Karlsruhe, Vienna and Warsaw. In Germany and Poland they have grudgingly come to accept the truth because so many family histories are involved.

This is an important book and it should be read carefully. Its lessons need repeating.

The gift to tell

Phillip Adams, AO

A lifetime of reading has proved to me that many gifted writers have absolutely nothing to say. Whereas, sadly, people with something important to communicate cannot find the words. But from time to time I receive a manuscript where the need to communicate is matched by the ability to do so, when the writer has the gift to tell a vital story.

Abraham Biderman's *The World of My Past* is a work of immense power, not only because it describes some of the most hideous events in human history but because those events are remembered by a person of considerable wisdom. Nothing is exaggerated or overstated (is it possible to exaggerate the Holocaust?) and the clarity of the narrative is unclouded by hatred. Biderman is too wise to hate.

What he does is record, meticulously, the life of one of the handful of European Jews who survived the German death camps. And I say German rather than Nazi because I tire of the evasion in that usual distinction.

As Biderman says on page 344: 'After the liberation, the German population had no knowledge of anything. They had never seen the trains; they had never seen synagogues burning nor had they ever plundered Jewish homes and property. Kristallnacht never happened; in fact, nothing had happened: they had neither seen nor heard anything.'

But something did happen, and that something is now being blurred by the passing of time and denied by anti-Semites masquerading as historians. The ceremonies that took place in January 1995 at Auschwitz showed that historical revisionism isn't limited to the likes of David Irving. It's practised in the upper echelons of the Polish government.

I have walked through the death camps on many occasions, trying to comprehend what happened inside the barbed wire, the barracks and the minds of both the prisoners and the people who brutalised and butchered them. In all my reading, I know of few works that better bring that time to life. Abraham Biderman succeeds all too well. He brings death to life.

Now, throughout eastern and western Europe, the old hatreds are re-emerging. Since the liberation of the camps the world has witnessed other carnages that deserve to be described as holocausts — in China, in Cambodia, in the Soviet Union, in the Balkans, in Rwanda.

Yet what happened in Poland, particularly in Poland, was different, and Biderman explains those differences with an insight that is often profound. This is not a book that anyone will want to read but it is a book that many people need to read.

Contents

Author's note

I wish to express my gratitude and thanks to my friends, Professor Lucjan Dobroszycki, Doba Apelowicz and Heniek Bornsztejn for their encouragement and moral support.

I am a survivor of the Lodz ghetto, Auschwitz-Birkenau, Althammer, Dora and Bergen-Belsen. I have written *The World of My Past* to mark the fiftieth anniversary of my liberation from Bergen-Belsen, in the hope that my memoirs will serve as a legacy for future generations, regardless of colour, creed or gender, so they can learn and remember.

Unless gentile society—above all Church leaders, educationists, teachers and philosophers of today, is willing to come to terms with the historic past of the Church and face up to teachings which have been the cause of the inhuman treatment to which the Jews have been subjected for the last 1600 years, and unless the Church removes anti-Semitism from its teachings, I fear that the world will see more Jewish bloodlettings.

This book is a personal testimony. It is also an indictment of all those who perpetrated the most horrible mass murder in human history and of those who stood by and let it happen.

Abraham H Biderman
Melbourne, February 1995

Foreword

Reverend Professor Robert A Anderson, AM

The harvest was over. The bare fields were waiting to be ploughed and seeded for next season's crop. Next season's crop. Who would be there to see it?

Abraham Biderman was. He was there to witness not only to the harvesting of the crop but, more important by far, he was there, is here, to witness to the awful harvest of anti-Semitism, the Shoah. But he is one of few. That crowded cattle-truck that afforded him his first view of the countryside for 'five long years', his first glimpse of a world outside the Lodz ghetto, had one destination and one only.

The seeds of that other harvest of which I write were sewn throughout the previous nineteen hundred years. It might be argued, with some justification, that certain forms of anti-Semitism existed before the appearance of Christianity, but it may not be denied that it was the particularly virulent strain known as theological anti-Semitism that provided the fertile seedbed for what was to sprout up in the thirties and forties of this century in a Europe that was still the heart of Christendom. As the author has so vividly put it: there was erected 'the largest pagan temple of human sacrifice, the altar of death.'

Much of Europe's history from the early fourth century to the mid twentieth could well have been written in terms of the interaction of Christians and Jews, of Church and Synagogue. But that was not the course that the historians, secular or ecclesiastical, were to choose. Indeed, the latter, along with the Church's theologians, either through ignorance or compliance, kept their silence while the very moral fabric of Christianity and the integrity of the

Church itself were relentlessly being eroded from within. Undeniably, Abraham Biderman is correct when he lays the charge that anti-Semitism is a gentile (Christian) disease from which it is the Jews who die. What we might append to that assertion is this question: to what extent has the Church thereby sewn the seeds of its own collapse?

In his definitive work, *The Destruction of the European Jews*, Raul Hilberg adroitly outlined the process that led to and embraced Nazism's 'final solution', namely, first conversion, then expulsion and, finally, annihilation. In essence, what had been proclaimed to Jews in these three successive stages, wrote Hilberg, was this:

> You have no right to live among us as Jews.
> You have no right to live among us.
> You have no right to live.

Those final words could never have been uttered had they not been preceded by the others. It is not a mere question of assonance and syntax but of inexorability. Conversion failed not only because the arguments of the evangelists were unconvincing but because conversion as such, for Jews, was entirely unnecessary. It was never the aim of Jesus himself to remove even one Jew from his traditional faith. Did he himself not die at Roman hands as a Jew? Did his disciples not continue to worship in the Jerusalem Temple?

Essentially, what the first century of this era witnessed was not the need for Jews to convert, to abandon Judaism, but the possibility of gentiles entering into a knowledge of the God of Israel, not as Jews but as gentiles. The awful tragedy is that the agenda of the historical relationship between Judaism and its daughter faith, Christianity, has been dictated by the complex religious and political context in which the latter arose. Only by a meticulous examination and re-examination of those contingent factors, together with a forthright appraisal of them, may a new and better relationship be put in place. One early step for the Church to take is a clean, unequivocal and public abandonment of any desire to convert Jews.

Expulsion was necessary because conversion did not work and thus the presence of Jews in the midst of Christian Europe tended to erode the confidence of the Church. The Christian 'yes' to the claims regarding Christ is always somewhat muted by the resounding and universal Jewish 'no'. Not even the most strident accusations of deicide and demonisation have been sufficient to remove the unease. Even today, when the nature of our relationship has altered markedly, it is still difficult for the majority of Christians, clergy and laity alike, to come to terms with the Jewish 'no'. It is an issue which Christianity, by its very origin, cannot avoid.

Judaism was and will always be, in whatever way, positive or negative, a part of, indeed essential to, Christian self-understanding. The converse is clearly not the case. In its own self-definition Judaism remains independent. Christian theological exclusivism has repercussions far beyond the merely theological. The Church's historic supersessionist stance towards Judaism must also be abandoned if Jews and Christians are to walk together, sharing their common tasks and responsibilities in a society which not only has room for both but has a need for both.

What of the third stage, annihilation? The schema advanced by Hilberg was in summary form only, and necessarily requires some refining in places. The common history of Synagogue and Church was not without its moments when Christian mobs, often spurred on by viciously anti-Jewish preaching, anticipated the actions of Hitler's henchmen. Nor was it difficult for their leaders and inspirers to find New Testament textual warrant for their actions. Jesus could be made to say, 'But as for these enemies of mine who did not want me to be king over them — bring them here and slaughter them in my presence' (Luke 19:27). Even if these were his words only by implication, who could blame the zealous Polish or Cossack Christian for giving them immediate substance?

In another part of Europe, this time in the sixteenth century, Martin Luther needed to look no further than that text to find dominical warrant for asserting, as he did, that 'we err in not slaying them (that is, the Jews)'. Much later, annihilation was to be rejected by Gerhard Kittel in his *Die Juden Frage* of 1933, not on explicit moral grounds, but because such a course of action had been tried before and had proved to be unsuccessful. If the published opinion of a leading New Testament scholar could show signs of entertaining the possibility of genocide, how much more might such a 'solution' appeal to those whose baser instincts had been fuelled, not only by racial anti-Semitism, but by the perennial charge that Jews were demonic 'Christ-killers'?

It is true that Nazism spawned its own particular form of anti-Semitism, but its leading proponents could not be unaware of the extent of co-operation that might be provided by century upon century of ecclesiastical anti-Judaism and, at times, anti-Semitism, should even they decide, as they did, to implement their Endlösung. Time and again in Abraham Biderman's catalogue of inhuman brutality, the alacrity with which this co-operation was offered, in both Germany and Poland, is only too much in evidence. The admission by the Church, the various Churches, that there is a nexus between Christian proclamation and the Holocaust, is a step that must be taken — not only to create a better relationship between Jews and Christians, but to secure the future of us all.

In his Preface, the author makes the plea that the Church must be 'willing to come to terms with (its) historic past.' I merely add my voice to that plea. But, in doing so, I note that that process has begun. In many churches, world-wide, even before the Second Vatican Council but especially since, clear and forthright statements have appeared which recognise the points he makes and which seek to turn the Church's teachings in a new direction. But, unfortunately, there are still sections of the Church and geographical areas, not least eastern Europe, where the old attitudes still prevail. As already noted, the process has begun. But it is no more than that: a beginning. Moreover, it is one thing to produce and promulgate statements; it is quite another to have them widely studied, accepted and implemented.

Reading Abraham's book, a story of brutally inflicted suffering, of tragic loss but also of courageous endurance, was, for me, an overwhelming experience. I cannot state its effect upon me in a way other than that. It was difficult not to compare his life with mine, at much the same age, and at the same time. The more I read, the less adequate I felt for this present task. Yet, I had promised that I would write this Foreword, and if there is one thing that is highlighted in Abraham's personal testimony it is that — the keeping of a promise. Read what he has to say and you will see what I mean. So I have kept my promise, conscious of the honour and the privilege that is mine in having my name associated with his.

Part One
THE GHETTO

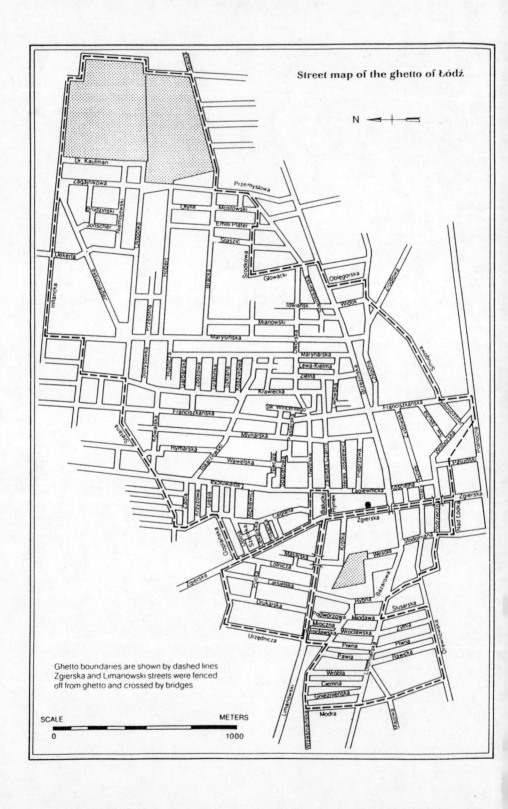

Street map of the ghetto of Łódź

N

Ghetto boundaries are shown by dashed lines
Zgierska and Limanowski streets were fenced
off from ghetto and crossed by bridges

SCALE   METERS
0   1000

The roots of the Holocaust

More than sixteen hundred years have passed since Chrysostom preached his renowned gospel: eight sermons proclaiming hatred toward the Jews. Asserting that 'the synagogue is the work of Satan, a house of prostitution,' he incited his Christian followers against the Jews. He was appointed as the Archbishop of Constantinople. The church later beatified him: he was to be known as Saint John Chrysostom, the 'Golden Mouthed'

Mid July in the year 1099, the crusaders, under the leadership of Godfrey, reached Jerusalem. Upon entering the city, they found the Jews assembled in a synagogue and set it ablaze. The entire population of Jerusalem was put to the sword — babies, children, young and old were slain. For centuries, the burning alive of Jews, and even the slaughtering of entire congregations, towns and villages, had been a familiar feature in Christendom. Christian mobs were continuously fed on venomous hatred against everything Jewish.

> The Christian populace acted as was expected of the disciples of a Gregory of Nyssa, of a Chrysostom, or a Gobard, an Amulo, or an Innocent III, a Capistrano, a Paul IV, not to mention the thousands of lesser luminaries among priests and monks who followed in their footsteps ... The mobs were the least responsible for the massacres; the moral responsibility must be placed squarely on the shoulders of those who taught them, guided them, led them.[1]

For centuries, Christians were reared on the Gospels, made hostile by derogatory references to the Jews such as, 'Ye are of your father the devil, and the lust of your father ye will do. He was a murderer from the beginning' ... (John 8:44); and 'Woe unto you, scribes and Pharisees, hypocrites! ... Ye serpents, ye generation of vipers, how can ye escape the damnation of hell?" (Matthew 23:23 and 33).

Centuries later, their teachings were an inspiration to Torquemada, Isabela and Ferdinand of Spain, Chmielnicki from the Ukraine and, above all, the most notorious Jew-hater, Martin Luther from Germany. Luther poisoned the minds of millions of Germans with his venomous teachings:

> Know, O adored Christ, and make no mistake, that aside from the Devil, you have no enemy more venomous, more desperate, more bitter, than a true Jew who truly seeks to be a Jew. Now whoever wishes to accept venomous serpents, desperate enemies of the Lord, and to honour them to let himself be robbed, pillaged, corrupted, and cursed by them, need only turn to the Jews.

And what were Luther's remedies to the 'Jewish problem'?

> First, their synagogues should be set on fire and whatever does not burn up should be covered or spread over with dirt so that no one may ever be able to see a cinder or stone of it. And this ought to be done for the honour of God and of Christianity in order that God may see that we are Christians, and that we have not wittingly tolerated or approved of such public lying, cursing and blaspheming of his Son and his Christians. Secondly, their homes should likewise be broken down and destroyed ... Thirdly, they should be deprived of their prayer books ... Fourthly, their rabbis must be forbidden under threat of death to teach any more ... To sum up, dear princes and nobles who have Jews in your domains, if this advice of mine does not suit you, then find a better one so that you may all be free of this insufferable devilish burden—the Jews.'[2]

Martin Luther incited his followers and poisoned their minds, and they learned his teachings to perfection. They adhered to every word he wrote and spoke. The Kristallnacht stands as testimony, and proves how well they learned his lessons. To this very day, Martin Luther's venomous teachings are potent, poisonous and lethal. It is obvious that the early fathers of the Church set a precedent of hatred and criminal brutality against the Jews in the name of God. I believe that the flames of the synagogue in Jerusalem set ablaze by Godfrey and his crusaders, and Martin Luther's teachings, were an example and inspiration to Eichmann, Mengele and Hoess. They contained the blueprint for Auschwitz. As an altar of death in the heart of Christendom, Auschwitz stands as a tribute and monument to two thousand years of Christian intolerance towards the Jews.

1

The beginning of the end

ON THE VAST, flat plains of central Poland known as Srodkowopol, beneath tall, whispering pine trees, a few log cabins huddled together under thatched roofs. In the fourteenth century, the cabins stood as if forgotten by the rest of the world. This was the tiny settlement of Lodzia, a little more than 120 kilometres south-west of Warsaw, the property of the bishops of Kujawy. Inhabited by sixty-seven settlers, it was so small that it was not even on the map.

Hundreds of kilometres of sandy soil surrounded Lodzia. The land was poor and unsuitable for agriculture. It had no minerals, no landmarks; nothing to attract settlers — except that land there was cheap. Not even a major road connected this forgotten place to the outside world. Two creeks cut across it: one called Jasienka, the name of a girl; the other, Lodka, after the regional squire, Lodzic. The settlement itself also had the squire to thank for its name. During the summer months the creeks were dry, but they filled up fast in the rainy autumn and froze in the winter.

In 1423, King Vladylav Jagielo granted Lodz a town charter; but for over three hundred and fifty years the town existed on royal parchment only. As late as 1777, the settlement had barely three hundred inhabitants. The historical turning point came with the special decree issued by the Tsar's vice-regent of the Kingdom of Poland on 18 September 1820, declaring Lodz a factory town.

A new era had begun. Large numbers of German weavers began to arrive, bringing their handlooms; new textile workshops opened every day. As production grew, so did the population: between the years 1820 and 1870 the population of Lodz multiplied forty-four fold.

Very early in Lodz's development, the town was off-limits to Jews. Exceptions to this rule were the rich manufacturers and merchants who were granted special permits. As time went on, more Jews were attracted to Lodz and, for a reasonable bribe, they could settle on the outskirts of the nearby town called Baluty. Eventually, Baluty became a suburb of Lodz, densely populated by mostly working-class people.

Lodz grew fast and chaotically. Within the next 120 years, the unsewered, poorly planned town became the largest industrial city in Poland, bearing as its coat of arms a little rowing boat with one oar. Blocks of red-brick factories sprang up almost overnight. They looked like medieval fortresses, grim and sombre. The tenement buildings were huge, grey and overcrowded, without the most basic of facilities. Inhabited by the working classes, they generally provided each family with only one room which in the day-time was a workshop and at night became sleeping quarters. Collapsible beds were erected, taking up all the floor space. The families were large and slept pressed tightly together. Sometimes four people shared one bed.

With the advent of the industrial revolution, Lodz entered yet another epoch. The latest mechanised plant transformed it into one of the largest textile centres of Europe. The skyline was transformed by a myriad factory stacks, belching smoke day and night. The sky itself became a permanent grey cloud, suspended over the city like a storm waiting to break.

In this human beehive, often referred to as 'the Polish Manchester', there lived and toiled a total of 750,000 inhabitants by the year 1939. There were approximately 396,000 Poles, about 60,000 Germans, and between 230,000 and 250,000 Jews. There were also many other smaller ethnic groups from all over the world. They were attracted to the city by its magnetic promise of a better life — a promise created by the combination of German technical know-how and the drive of Jewish entrepreneurial spirit.

The most famous of these European textile magnates were the German families from Lodz: the Scheiblers, the Graumanns, the Biedermanns and the Geyers. As well, there were the most renowned Jewish magnates: Israel Kalman Poznanski, Usher Kohn, the Bukiet brothers, Gedalia Boris, Nachum Ettingon, Laib Mincberg — president of the Lodz 'Kehillah' (the autonomous Jewish governing body) — and many others.

Beautifully designed Renaissance-style palaces, surrounded by large, carefully tended gardens, stood virtually next door to ugly, overcrowded tenements on the busy streets of Lodz.

The commercial centre of the city was predominantly inhabited by Jews. Entire sections of the city were Jewish. On the Sabbath, or on Jewish holidays, the whole commercial centre came to a standstill. The shops and warehouses closed.

The industrial and commercial heart of Lodz pulsated with the vigour and intensity of Jewish enterprise. Graduates of Jewish high schools and technical schools became city leaders. The fast-growing middle class now included yarn merchants, importers, exporters, textile engineers, accountants, doctors, executives and managers of the large textile mills. However, the majority of Jews were still working-class people, squeezed together in overcrowded dwellings. They led very humble lives, adhering to their old traditions, striving, building, and creating a world of their own.

This they did, but not simply by choice. The non-Jewish world around them would not accept them, compelling them to rely upon their own initiative, inventiveness and resources. The doors to higher learning institutions were hardly open to them. Government offices seldom employed them, except in cases where their qualifications were unique. Some government agencies, such as the Department for Public Works, the public transport system and the railways never accepted Jews. Certain positions of employment, such as janitors, chimney sweeps and cleaners of government offices were never open to Jews, nor could they be members of most of the trade guilds. This greatly limited the means by which they could earn their livelihood.

War and surrender

On a beautiful summer's day at the end of August 1939, I came back to Lodz, my exciting school holidays over. The end of the vacation also meant the end of a fifteen-year-old boy's innocent love affair with a beautiful, dark-eyed girl; and the developments of the next few weeks would also see the end of my formal schooling. What I did not then realise was that my education was only just beginning.

Over the next five years I graduated from the Lodz ghetto, after which I just scraped through to qualify for post-graduate degrees from Auschwitz, Althammer, Nordhausen-Dora and, eventually, my final and hardest exam of them all — the German university of hell: Bergen-Belsen.

Within a few hours of the Third Reich's onslaught on 1 September 1939, Poland was thrown into confusion. Hundreds of thousands of refugees flooded the roads and highways, streaming east. Horse-drawn carriages loaded with the sick and wounded, the old and young, were on the run, their exhausted cows and horses dragging behind.

There was no escape. Poland was split in half as Soviet Russia invaded from the east. In the pandemonium, the refugees were cut down like corn under the blades of a harvester as the Luftwaffe sowed death from the sky and the rolling tanks crushed everything in their path on the ground.

Within a few days, the powerful German Panzer divisions decimated the Polish army. The romantic and brave Polish cavalry set out on a suicidal mission, charge after charge collapsing as it was brutally ploughed into the ground by the rolling steel monsters. The Polish infantry retreated in disorder, pursued and harassed by the Germans, absolute masters now of land and sky. The Polish soldiers fought back with determination, but courage was not enough.

On 5 September, the authorities of Lodz evacuated in chaos, handing over the city to a civilian militia. Lodz became like a ghost town — empty, dead, waiting for three long days before finally surrendering to the Germans without a shot.

Late afternoon, Friday 8 September: gloom hung over Lodz. The streets were deserted, silent. In our house there was a strange tension and anxiety. No-one spoke. The dining table was covered with a white table-cloth ready for the Sabbath. The candlestick-holders of sparkling silver held their customary white candles, ready to be lit to sanctify the holy day of rest. I don't remember our home ever being as soundless as on that particular Friday afternoon. Normally, on the Sabbath eve the house was happy and festive, with the lit candles adding just a touch of solemnity; but on that late afternoon they created a strange melancholy, as if someone had died. I stood next to my father near the balcony doors, peeping out through the side of the drawn, heavy drapes. The deathly hush was suddenly rent by the sound of approaching vehicles.

Out of curiosity, I stepped outside onto the balcony. I could see a motor bike with a heavy machine-gun mounted on the side carriage, manned by a German soldier with his finger on the trigger. He was followed by an open army vehicle containing four German officers. A white flag, crested on its bonnet, waved in the breeze as it glided along Zgierska Street towards the centre of the city. These were the first German army scouts to enter Lodz.

With great fear and excitement I stood on the balcony following the German patrol with my eyes. My father pulled me back into the house, saying, 'Come inside and close the door.' I can still see that scene: my grandmother Shayndl standing in front of the lit candles, her hands covering her face, reciting the blessings with tears in her eyes. I had never seen my grandmother cry on the Sabbath, a day when mourning and sadness is forbidden by Jewish law.

Early on Saturday morning, on 9 September, the silence was shattered by the heavy rumbling of German tanks entering the city. There were sixty thousand German inhabitants of Lodz out on the streets to welcome the invaders, waving flags and showering them with flowers. The streets were ablaze with red and white banners sporting the sinister black swastika. From one day to the next, Lodz had changed its face. Where on earth had they obtained so many thousands of Nazi flags overnight? The local Germans were elated, celebrating their victory. Jewish Lodz was in a state of shock.

From the beginning of the German occupation, the Jewish population was singled out for persecution. Jewish holidays were banned. All Jewish bank accounts were closed and the funds confiscated. Jewish factories, offices and businesses were taken over by the Germans. Jewish families were thrown out of their houses, which were then appropriated by Germans.

All Jewish institutions and organisations were banned, including the Kehillah, although the Germans then summoned its representatives, ordering them to form a 'Judenrat', a Jewish Council. At the beginning of December 1939, twenty-four members of the newly formed Jewish Council were shot in the Lagiewnicki Forest near the city. Many Poles and Jews were arrested and locked up in the first concentration camp in Lodz — the textile factory owned by the Jewish family Abe, in Radogoszcz, on the outskirts of town.

Under threat of the death penalty, on 4 November the Jews of Lodz were compelled to wear a yellow armband. This was replaced on 17 November by the yellow star of David, which had to be stitched on the right side, front and back, of the outer garment.

The date of 11 November 1939 is vividly engraved in my memory — it was the day the synagogues of Lodz went up in flames. It marked the beginning of our end, and it took place on Armistice Day, when Poland used to celebrate its independence. In the centre of the city, at Liberty Square (Plac Wolnosci), the proud monument of Kosciuszko, hero and symbol of Polish independence and freedom, was blown up by the Germans; the torso of the statue lay on the ground, a headless corpse. Even so, the Polish inhabitants helped the Germans to round up Jews and put them to work dismantling the air-raid shelters which surrounded the monument. The Germans amused themselves by cutting the beards and earlocks, together with the surrounding skin, of the Jews they had rounded up for work. Jews were knocked to the ground by the Germans, and kicked until their faces were covered in blood. All the while, the Polish population stood around enjoying the black carnival — not realising, or perhaps not caring, that it was the funeral of their own independence and liberty. Alongside the Jews, their own freedom lay in the mud.

My brother, Lipek, who had just turned sixteen, was one of the victims on that day. He was grabbed by a Polish youngster who denounced him to a German soldier. The Germans were not very good at identifying Jews unless they could see beards and earlocks; the Poles, however, had a sixth sense. They could identify a Jew even if he had blue eyes and blond hair. *'Panie'* ('Sir'), they would shout, *'Jude! Jude!'* Lipek resisted the Pole, struggled free and ran. A German soldier shouted that he would shoot. My brother was brought back and beaten with the German's rifle butt. His student uniform was torn and covered with mud. The German cut the silver buttons from his jacket with his bayonet. Late that evening Lipek came home, covered in blood. They had cut off the hair in the centre of his head. He was sick for many days. My mother treated the bruises and cuts on his face and body, but his spirit never really recovered.

The first deportations

A decree issued by Hitler in Berlin on 8 October 1939, and effective from 1 November, caused the city and surrounding provinces of Lodz, as well as the city of Posen with its pre-war perimeters, to form a new province named Warthegau, which was annexed by the Third Reich. Lodz was renamed Litzmannstadt, after a German First World War General, Karl Litzmann. Posen became the capital of Warthegau, and Artur Greiser was appointed as the Reichsstatthalter, the Governor.

From the early days of the German invasion of Poland, the Jews were the prime issue on the agenda of Schutzstaffel (SS) Lieutenant General Reinhard Heydrich, head of the RSHA (Reich Security Main Office, based in Berlin), and Heinrich Himmler's chief lieutenant. According to Heydrich's plans, the newly occupied western parts of Poland had to be cleared of Jews.

From 13 to 17 December 1939, the first mass deportations took place. Fourteen thousand Jews from Nowomiejnska and Zgierska Streets were loaded onto trams, taken to the railway station and carted off in the middle of the night. This action was unexpected, and it took time before people learned to be ready for evacuation at any given moment. The first victims of the surprise deportations were poorly dressed, and winter was at its peak.

At midnight on 17 December, our house at 13 Zgierska Street was surrounded by armed German Schutzpolitzei (Schupo for short). With drawn guns they burst into our home. We were given ten minutes to get out and line up in the street along the tram line. It was bitterly cold, and we hardly had time to dress. As we waited to board the tram, stamping our feet in the snow in an effort to keep warm, a miracle happened. A German police officer pulled up in his car and ordered us back into our homes. We were lucky. From the few who came back after having been deported, we heard gruesome reports. A third of the deportees froze to death or died of hunger before they reached their destination. For days they were hauled about in sub-zero temperatures without food and water. Some of the transports were taken to the outskirts of Krakow, others to Lublin. Then, for reasons beyond our knowledge, the deportations suddenly stopped.

Towards the end of December, Reinhard Heydrich, arguably the chief architect of the Holocaust, completed his plans for the

Polish Jews. Stage One was their relocation to the ghettos. Although the Germans were not supposed to communicate with Jews, those of us in Lodz were informed by 'unofficial sources'. Some of our old German friends were still loyal.

On 10 December, a strictly confidential order was sent from Berlin to the president of Litzmannstadt, Dr Übelhor, instructing him to put in motion all necessary preparations for a ghetto. On 8 February 1940, the order was officially published in all German newspapers. Placards with the identical message appeared on the walls of the city. The Judenrat was informed by the Gestapo that five hundred Jewish families would be removed from their homes into the ghetto area every day.

In the middle of the night of 6 March, the Jewish population of Lodz was shocked by a sudden eruption of bloody massacres organised by the German police. They were assisted by local Germans who had recently joined the SS and the Sturmabteilung [SA]. These killings occurred outside the area designated for the ghetto, but in areas densely populated by Jews. Jewish quarters were attacked, their doors smashed in and the inhabitants shot. In the days that followed, tens of thousands of Jews fled along the streets towards the area where the ghetto was to be.

In our home, countless people came and slept wherever they could find space: on the floor, on chairs. It was open house. Frightened and exhausted, they came with only the bare essentials on their shoulders. Some pushed baby carriages or sledges loaded with their belongings. Others were burdened like donkeys with bundles on their backs. It was a devastating sight. The heavy snow covering the streets was ploughed into mud by the trampling feet of the tens of thousands of refugees.

Thousands of Jews fled Lodz to the provincial villages, as well as to the east of Poland which had been overrun by Soviet Russia. Many, like my aunt, uncle and cousins, left for Warsaw in the hope that, outside the Third Reich, life for Jews would be less dangerous. In the beginning, we received good news from uncle Laib. Our family in Warsaw had welcomed them with much warmth and hospitality, and had set them up in one of their apartments. From time to time they sent us letters; but these ceased by the end of 1942 and, after that, they were never heard of again.

2

The Lodz ghetto, 1940

ON 30 JANUARY, at a top-level secret conference of the RSHA, presided over by Heydrich, with Eichmann at his side, orders were given to resume deportations — at an increased tempo. The minutes of the meeting reported that, up to the present time, seventy-eight thousand Jews had been deported to the Lublin concentration area. Now Heydrich ordered four hundred thousand more to be sent to Lublin within the next month. From the same meeting, Heydrich and Eichmann issued a directive to their SD men (the 'Sicherheitsdienst', the elite security service of the SS) 'to push ahead without the knowledge of the civil or military authorities.'

But opposition to the Heydrich-Eichmann-Globocnik operations was rapidly building up. Heydrich was concerned only with clearing the Jews from the new German state of Warthegau; but they were being dumped in the rest of German-occupied Poland, the area known as the General-Government, under Governor Frank. The public health officials began to point out the inevitable consequences of such 'wild deportations'.

Governor Frank was also becoming increasingly jealous of the way in which the SS and SD officers responsible for the Jewish deportations blatantly ignored not only his authority but also that of every other Reich authority in Poland. The men of Heydrich and Eichmann were rapidly getting above even the Nazi law. He went as far as stating publicly: 'I would draw attention to the fact that there exists in the General-Government no power higher than that of the Governor-General — and that includes the SS. There is no state within a state.' The implications of this statement were obvious in Berlin. Within a fortnight of the Heydrich-Eichmann order to 'ignore the civil and military authorities', Goering intervened.

On 12 February 1940, as the Nazi leader responsible for Jewish affairs, he issued an order forbidding all evacuations until further notice. He confirmed this order six weeks later at the end of March. But Heydrich and Eichmann were quite prepared to defy even Goering — at least by stealth. And although protests were sent as high as Himmler from the joint Polish-Jewish Aid Committee, which was co-operating with Frank, the deportations quietly continued. In fact, they did not stop until the summer of 1940, when Heydrich and Eichmann had more pressing problems to consider.

But deportation of the Polish Jews was not Eichmann's sole interest during the months of the 'phoney war' between the autumn of 1939 and the following spring. His Central Office for Jewish Emigration had been absorbed into the new RSHA. Still, despite the difficulties created by the outbreak of war, Eichmann continued to expel as many Jews as possible from the territories of the Reich itself. Most of them were from Austria. During the winter and spring there was a steady trickle of Jews travelling overseas by way of Italian and Balkan ports.

Eichmann even succeeded in organising a number of illegal convoys down the Danube by boat from Vienna with the final destination designated as British-mandated Palestine. But, as happened in a more historic instance four years later, Eichmann ran into the policies of His Majesty's Government, which declined to grant the visa-less expellees entry. Threatened in the Middle East, the British had no wish to antagonise further the Arab world at that stage of the war, as a result of which only a few of Eichmann's expellees in fact reached the Jewish national homeland.[3]

The spring of 1940 arrived with sunshine and blue skies; but for the Jews of Lodz the horizon was clouded with warnings of an oncoming storm. The Germans had ordered them into a ghetto and, on 1 May 1940, it was closed off — to become the first closed ghetto of a larger metropolis in occupied Poland.

The ghetto was set up in the working-class districts of the Old City (Stare Miasto), Baluty and Marysin near the Jewish cemetery, adjacent to Radogoszcz, where the Germans built a special railway-line to supply it with raw materials for the factories. Later, the line was used for deportations.

When the ghetto was closed off, an estimated 163,000 people were crammed into an area of four square kilometres. The exact figure no-one will ever know; but it is known that the same district, before the war, had housed ten thousand people. It now comprised three separate compounds divided by Zgierska and Limanowskiego Streets which connected the outskirts of Lodz to the main city. The two streets were open to public and general transport, whereas the footpaths belonged to the ghetto territory and were fenced off with barbed wires and planks that were heavily guarded by the Schupo stationed every fifty metres along an eleven-kilometre barbed-wire ring sealing off the ghetto from the rest of the world.

The three compounds were linked by three overhead bridges built of timber — two across Zgierska Street, the first joining Plac Koscielny (Church Square) with Lutomierska Street, the second joining Wolborska Street and Podrzeczna Street, and a third across Limanowskiego Street connecting Masarska Street with Krotka Street. Next to that bridge was a large gate for pedestrians and vehicles. The gate was opened and shut by a Jewish policeman who was, in turn, guarded by a German policeman. Another identical gate was at Dolna Street connecting it to Lotnicza Street.

On the corner of Zgierska and Limanowskiego Streets, opposite the Baluter Market, a three-storey building was occupied by a battalion of six hundred German police assigned to guard the ghetto.

In 1941, the Germans fenced off a small section comprising a few buildings at Brzezinska Street, where the ghetto ended. Behind its fence, five thousand Gypsies from Burgenland in Austria were incarcerated. I witnessed one of the transports when approximately two hundred of them were brought in via the ghetto. There were men, women and children of all ages, heavily guarded by the German police. They looked healthy and were well-dressed, having the appearance of well-to-do, middle-class people. Their suitcases and luggage were of good quality, their bundles tidily packed. They did not have the harassed, fatigued look of the Jewish refugees but seemed, rather, like a group of visitors or tourists. They must have had a lot of musicians amongst them, for many carried musical instruments.

The ghetto population knew very little of what went on behind the fence at the end of Brzezinska Street. Only scant information leaked out and was passed on to us by the Jewish policeman who stood guard at the fence dividing the Gypsy camp from us. It was evident, however, that the Gypsies were maltreated and became undernourished like us. Today we know that most of them were taken to Chelmno where they met the same fate as the Jews. Some of them were murdered with injections in the camp. Many of them died of starvation and typhoid owing to the overcrowded and unhygienic conditions. Only the empty buildings have survived, sole witnesses to the tragedy that befell these people.

Within a short span of time, the Lodz ghetto was transformed into a world of its own: a world of famine, tuberculosis, dysentery and typhus. There was no proper medication. In the first six months of 1940, five thousand dwellers died from famine and sickness.

Organisation under Rumkowski

My family did not have to move as our apartment was already inside the ghetto, on the first floor of 13 Zgierska Street. The barbed wire surrounding the entire area was right in front of our building, and the German guard-booth was directly beneath our balcony so that we were in a dangerous position. Always in fear of being shot at by the guards, we were constantly mindful of not moving too close to the windows or walking heedlessly out onto the balcony. At night, we had to make sure that our windows were completely blacked out. If the slightest gap allowed any light to show on the outside, it was sufficient excuse for the guard to fire into our home.

Along the barbed-wire fence of the ghetto, dwellers were constantly shot at by the guards. Seldom a day passed without victims. I remember one day when nine people were killed by one German policeman guarding the wires. His nickname was the 'Red-Headed Killer'. He just shot at passers-by for the fun of it, to relieve the boredom of his duties.

We in the ghetto were unaware of what was happening beyond the barbed wire. We lived cut off from the rest of the world. The Lodz ghetto was the most hermetically closed and isolated ghetto under German occupation. The fact that Lodz had become incorporated in the Third Reich from the earliest stages of the war was to have disastrous consequences.

On 14 October 1939, the Occupation Commissioner of 'Litzmannstadt' was directed by the Chief of Civil Administration of the German Eighth Army to appoint an Eldest of the Jews who would be responsible for the execution of all orders given by the German authorities. Mordechai Chaim Rumkowski was the one chosen for this position. Even today, nobody has a single, clear explanation of why he should have been appointed; conflicting versions abound.

At the time, Rumkowski was sixty-two years of age, widowed and childless: a man alone. In the past, he had been a merchant as well as a manufacturer, but all his ventures had ended in bankruptcy. He was without friends. His education had been limited to five years of primary school as well as the traditional Jewish religious school ('cheder') and, prior to the Second World War, he had been an insurance agent in Lodz with many contacts in business circles. These helped him in the charity work he involved himself in. Rumkowski was successful in collecting large sums of money for an orphanage for Jewish children of which he became the director. It was built in Helenowek, on the outskirts of Lodz. Before the war, he had also been a member of the Kehillah, and was known by his fellow councillors, as well as by those in his personal life, to be a stubborn and most difficult man — one who was always in opposition to the majority.

Once inside the ghetto, Rumkowski remarried. His new wife, Regina Wainberger, was many years his junior, a solicitor by profession. They adopted a young boy. Rumkowski's brother, Josef, and his sister-in-law, Helena, had always been close to him. He appointed Josef as director of the central hospital at 36 Lagiewnicka Street, and Helena was involved in organising the public kitchens.

Rumkowski meticulously executed all the orders given to him by the Germans. His philosophy was to collaborate with the Germans, believing that by doing so he would save more lives and reduce the bloodshed. He was convinced that by using the Jewish police to execute the German orders he would soften the blows that would inevitably come down upon the Jews. He worked tirelessly, organising the Lodz ghetto according to the plans drawn up by Reinhard Heydrich.

Heydrich was the ultimate prototype of the pure Aryan of Hitler's dreams: tall and blond — and a cold-blooded killer besides. He was Heinrich Himmler's right-hand man, and his first objective was to create a strong Jewish police force of six hundred men. These were eventually stationed in four police precincts, strategically positioned, and functioning from the first day the ghetto was closed off. They were under the leadership of commandant Leon Rozenblat. Another police force, formed on 26 June 1940, was known as the Jewish Sonderkommando.

At a later date, the Germans appointed David Gertler to take control of both the Sonderkommando and the Special Bureau that the Germans set up as an extension of the Gestapo arm in the ghetto. Gertler was the number-one Gestapo informer in the Warthegau as well as in the General-Government, the occupied part of Poland that had not been annexed by the Third Reich. A Jew from Lodz, Gertler was a cunning, uneducated, dubious character who, before World War II, had been an informer for the Polish authorities. In the early stages of the war, he played a leading role as an informer and agent of the Gestapo. At times it seemed as though Gertler was the man in charge, relegating Rumkowski to a secondary position. He commuted frequently between the Lodz and Warsaw ghettos, transferring people back and forth. After Gertler's disappearance on the 12 July 1943, Mordechai Kliger took over his position, which he kept till the final liquidation of the ghetto.

The Lodz ghetto functioned autonomously with German precision. It was run by Rumkowski and aided by a Jewish Council which he appointed and later dissolved, with some of his henchmen being the only members retained. But his real ability to control the ghetto lay in the power of the Gestapo, which used him and built him up to be feared by the ghetto inhabitants. He was also supported by the Jewish police and Jewish Sonderkommando. After these came a hierarchy of dignitaries consisting of the police commissioners, factory managers and technicians. The managers of the bakeries, kitchens and food stores formed the ghetto élite as they had access to the most vital and scarcest commodity in the Lodz ghetto — food.

In early June 1940, a penal system was established with a central prison situated in Czarniecki Street at Marysin. The jail commandant, Solomon Hercberg, became the terror of the ghetto, robbing the population, raiding their homes, pulling up floor-boards, breaking down walls, plundering and looting their possessions.

He divided the spoils between himself and the agents of the 'Kripo' (the German criminal police). For his services in rounding up people in the middle of the night for deportation, or torturing them under interrogation, Hercberg was rewarded by the Germans in their usual fashion. On 17 March 1942, he was thrown into a cattle wagon at Radogoszcz with his wife, three sons and with many other Jews to be deported. Today we know they were all taken to Chelmno and gassed.

The post office in the ghetto worked with great efficiency, and many German Jews found employment there. Amongst them were my uncle Berish and aunt Sarah, who continued to work there until the liquidation of the ghetto. They had lived in Berlin for almost twenty years and were then expelled, together with the Polish Jews, shortly before the outbreak of World War II. They had come to live in Lodz and were eventually locked up with us in the ghetto.

The post office printed its own stamps displaying the head of the ghetto emperor, Mordechai Chaim Rumkowski, but they were never circulated. With his long and flowing silver hair he gave the impression of being a member of the nobility. But the proverb, 'Don't judge a man by his appearance', was especially applicable to him. He had the gentle face of an old man which was a mask only, a disguise, and behind it Mephisto was hidden. At a very early age in the ghetto I learned that people are not exactly what they appear to be. I also learned that, if compassion, love and goodness dwell in the soul of every human being so, too, does evil.

Rumkowski was a classic case of a victim, a hostage, who inadvertently turned traitor. He allowed the Germans to use him as their tool in the destruction of his people. He thought that by doing this, somehow, he could manage to save his own life as well as the lives of a small part of the Jewish community in the ghetto; but the Germans destroyed him once he was of no further use to them.

Rumkowski's own speeches illuminate the leading role he played in the drama of the Lodz ghetto. As well as boasting about his great achievements in the organisation of the factories ('In the ghetto I have forty thousand workers. This is my gold mine.'), Rumkowski constantly bragged about the power the German authorities had given him:

To the workers I forward this slogan — Throw away your party affiliations! Politics, I will without mercy destroy! I broke the powerful fishermen! The butchers! The transport workers! I've closed down the factories because the workers' delegates started to take over! I don't need a Jewish Council that disturbs me in my work! I take from the rich to give to the poor! Those who do not want to surrender their wealth, the Sonderkommando takes care of! The Sonder boys are breaking down walls, searching until they find.

My work awoke in them confidence. My reports to the authorities quote that the ghetto production has reached an income of two million marks per month.

With total confidence in his methods of ruling and controlling the ghetto, he solemnly declared in another of his speeches:

> With my brothers and sisters I will live in peace in the ghetto and may they judge me in the future! Let them condemn me because of the methods with which I have upheld the peace.

Of his achievements for the children, Rumkowski said:

> For the last thirty years and to this very day, I am involved in protecting the children … I steal from the rich and powerful and give it to the children, for they are the most precious treasure that we possess.

This is how Rumkowski spoke of his devotion to the children in the ghetto in November 1941; yet, nine months later, he was to demand that the ghetto population surrender its children to the Germans.

In November 1941, Rumkowski delivered five speeches which were chiefly directed at the newly arrived Jews from western Europe. Using language that was blatantly threatening, he warned them to be obedient and not to resist, or he would be forced to deal with them:

> I have the authority and force to control you! Those who step out of line will be sorry! Watch out! I will break every bone in your bodies. Just do as I say and life will be good for you. I will take care of you and make sure that you are provided for.

In every one of his speeches he called for volunteers to register for work away from the ghetto:

The German authorities need labourers urgently! As in every war, there is a shortage of working hands. They will be well provided for! Those who have already left are very happy. They have it very good.

Rumkowski spoke about deportation as a great opportunity for those who registered:

The first two hundred women who left the ghetto have written wonderful letters. They are working, some on the land and others in factories.

He called a meeting of the German rabbis who had just arrived from the west. 'One of the new arrivals was shot for disobedience and resistance,' he is reported to have said:

The Germans hate the German Jews more than they do the Polish Jews. The shooting is not the first, neither will it be the last. Should I not be able to silence you, somebody else will! The German authorities have requested that I surrender hostages from the newly arrived western Jews for execution as a punishment and a warning to others not to act disobediently. I have declared to the German authorities that I have certain autonomous written rights in the ghetto.

Rumkowski boasted to and warned the newly arrived rabbis of his authority, and of the powers with which the Germans had entrusted him. He finished his speech by saying: 'Silence the young rebels or else it will be very, very bad!' He directed a similar speech towards the newly arrived German Jews, calling them obstinate and arrogant. Then, on 16 November 1942, he spoke at the celebration to honour the first anniversary of the millinery factory. Again, as always, he spoke of his great achievements:

The Kehillah budget has reached over three million marks a month. I worry for the sick, the old and the children. In the ghetto I have 1,650 hospital beds, seven dispensaries, four medical centres and two horse-drawn ambulances. I have one hundred and twenty medical practitioners taking care of the sick. I have a home for the elderly where they can live in peace for the rest of their lives, and are well looked after. Fourteen thousand children are fed by the school kitchens every day.

The figures and institutions used in the above speech were correct; however, nine months later, the Germans had liquidated all the hospitals, and the old and the children had been sent off to the unknown. Then, when a transport of German Jews was sent off soon after, Rumkowski again promised improvements as a means to calm the ghetto: a charity fund for the needy and a milk kitchen for newly born babies; for the western Jews a number of public kitchens that would be run by their own people; and that collectives of western Jews would have the right to elect their own representatives with whom he, personally, would communicate.

Rumkowski's speeches are as fresh in my memory as if I had heard them just yesterday. He never finished a speech without the words: 'I have plenty of food and work for you,' which became the standing joke of the ghetto: 'Plenty of food for himself and plenty of work for us,' we would laugh mockingly.[4]

Rumkowski repeated these speeches again and again, always boasting of the power the German authorities had entrusted in him, never omitting to promise a better future, especially for those who voluntarily registered for 'work' outside the ghetto. The speeches highlight how, in every case, he always said and did only what the Germans dictated. As far as the Jews were concerned, Rumkowski acted recklessly; yet, to the Gestapo, he displayed limitless obedience. They played on his hunger for power and built him up as a man to be feared. With his speeches as his chief tool, he psychologically terrorised and controlled the ghetto population, preparing them for deportation.

The ghetto had its own courts of law, administered by pre-war Jewish lawyers. Rumkowski demanded that the Jewish judges pass death sentences on those found guilty of stealing from the factories or of sabotage at work. This the Jewish judges refused to do and, although threatened, they did not succumb.

The ghetto had its own fire brigade under the leadership of Kaufman, a pre-war professional officer with the Lodz City Fire Brigade. There was also the Department of Labour under the leadership of Sienicki, another Jew from Lodz, and Bernard Fuchs, a German Jew from Hanover. As well as regulating and controlling the labour force in the ghetto, this department was also responsible for drawing up lists with the names of people condemned to deportation. There were many other ghetto institutions, such as the hospitals, the mental asylum, schools, kindergartens, orphanages, the Public Kitchen Department, and the Department of Food and Vegetable Supply, where my father worked as an inspector and where I was employed as a messenger at the head office at 25 Lagiewnicka Street.

The Department of Statistics collected all of the relevant data for the German authorities and Rumkowski instructed the statisticians to register all the important daily events in the ghetto. Of course, they wrote with caution in order to please him, for he kept a close eye on their work; but they did it behind the backs of the Gestapo who wanted them only to note events without comments. Many a time, however, they omitted certain occurrences so as not to expose themselves to danger should the Gestapo discover their chronicles. They called this compilation: *'Biuletyn Kroniki Codziennej Ghetta Lodzkiego'* ('The Chronicle of the Lodz Ghetto'). With the help of some of his friends in Poland, my childhood friend and schoolmate, Dr Lucjan Dobroszycki, a survivor of the ghetto and Auschwitz, succeeded in taking microfilm of these records to the United States. Under the auspices of the Yivo Institute of Jewish Research in New York, he published that very document in the form of a book which is now one of the largest original Jewish documents to survive the Holocaust.[5]

A weekly newspaper was printed in Yiddish under the tight control of Rumkowski and monitored by the Gestapo. The printing of proclamations — usually in Yiddish and German and always signed by M C Rumkowski — was also done under the strict supervision of the Gestapo.

The Department of Finance was organised and managed by a Mr Ser who had been an economist in pre-war Lodz. This department issued ghetto money in the form of bank notes as well as metal coins with Jewish symbols such as the Menorah and the Star of David bearing Rumkowski's signature. This was the only legal tender and anyone found in the possession of Reichsmarks or any other currency was severely punished — usually beaten to death in the infamous red brick villa which housed the Kripo.

The ghetto factories were under the control of Aron Jakubowicz, a protégé of Rumkowski's.

The ghetto administration

At the helm of the ghetto apparatus was the German administration, called the 'Gettoverwaltung'. This was led by Amtsleiter Hans Biebow, a 38-year-old German coffee merchant from Bremen, and a devout Nazi who had found a lucrative niche in the ghetto that gave him wealth and protected him from being drafted into the army. The head office of the Gettoverwaltung was housed in the city at Cegielniana Street. They also had some offices at the Baluter Market.

None of the Nazis realised quite so clearly as Biebow how much the ghetto could benefit the Reich economically. Biebow knew the ghetto's every workshop: its directors, its engineers and the technical staff; and he had precise knowledge of the production capabilities of every factory. The initiative to liquidate the ghetto certainly did not originate with him, although he rarely displayed even the slightest sign that the fate of its inhabitants was of any concern to him. His sole interest was the ghetto's productivity and the profit to be derived from it. On that level, he was able to maintain business-like relations with some of the Jewish workshop directors — although, naturally, he kept a proper distance, and his moods tended to vary. He never forgot that he was a German, and he ruled the ghetto with a firm hand. More than once he beat and bloodied various ghetto-dwellers, including Rumkowski himself.

The fate of the ghetto obviously did not rest in the hands of the local authorities alone. The city authorities, as well as all of the local police forces, had their counterparts both at provincial and at central levels to which they were subordinate. At the very top were Goering, Hitler's deputy and the plenipotentiary for the Four Year Plan; Himmler, the SS-Reichsführer, chief of the German police; and Frick, the Reich's Minister of the Interior. Moreover, because of the goods produced there, a series of other Reich departments and ministries considered the ghetto's affairs to be their direct concern. One example was the Armament Ministry headed by Albert Speer and the Armaments Inspection of the German Armed Forces in the Warthegau. Frequently, the jurisdictions of various city departments — at both provincial or central levels — either overlapped or were at odds with one another.[6]

The Kripo

Apart from the Gestapo and the Gettoverwaltung, the Kripo, the German criminal police, played a most brutal role in the history of the ghetto. They were housed in premises situated on Plac Koscielny where, before the advent of the ghetto, the Diocese of the Catholic Church of the Most Blessed Virgin Mary had been located. Thousands of Jews were beaten to death in the cellars of that building by German interrogators whose sole aim was to extract their last possessions.

The commandant of the Kripo in the ghetto was a brutal killer by the name of Neimann. His chief assistant was Sutter, an ethnic German from the township of Alexandrow, thirty kilometres out of Lodz. This Yiddish 'shtetl' had been famous for generations for its rabbinical court, led by a dynasty of the renowned Alexandrow rabbis. It was a predominantly Jewish township, with a large pre-war German population. The two minorities had lived harmoniously side by side for centuries, trading and working together and respecting one another in a congenial atmosphere.

Sutter had grown up in that environment and spoke Yiddish like a local Jew. He even knew Hebrew blessings and prayers by heart, which he had learned from his childhood friends. Sutter delighted in interrogating and maltreating Jewish manufacturers and merchants whom he knew personally and had dealt with before the war in the textile industry. His knowledge of Yiddish was instrumental in his infamous duties.

Assisting the Kripo in their atrocities were the informers, Akerberg and Wailand — two men who faithfully served the organisation by denouncing their fellow Jews. There were others who assisted them.

At the outset, the Jewish population was locked in the ghetto, deprived of its employment and business activities, without any source of income, its bank accounts closed and requisitioned by the Germans. A grand total of 80 per cent of them were destitute: totally dependant on handouts from Rumkowski. Nine marks per person per month were given to every ghetto inhabitant to enable him or her to pay for the meagre food rations. The first to be deported were those whose names were registered for sustenance.

A small percentage of ghetto people who had succeeded in hiding some of their valuables — jewellery, furs, antiques, paintings, musical instruments or furniture — were allowed to sell them to the 'Einkaufstelle' (purchasing office) organised by Rumkowski. But this was yet another of the many instrumentalities used to rob the ghetto population — the prices paid were a pittance. Until the ghetto money was printed, receipts were given to the vendor in lieu of money and could be used as legal tender.

At its inception, 7,316 people were employed in ghetto administration. Factories at that time were non-existent. The first to register and get work were 3,500 tailors with six hundred sewing machines. At first, only those with their own machines could get work. They were paid twenty marks monthly, barely enough for their own food rations. The rest of their families still had to obtain sustenance from Rumkowski. As time went on, further registrations were made of all trades and professions. There were shoemakers, carpenters, cabinet-makers, electricians, mechanics, fitters and turners, boiler-makers, knitters, textile workers, sheet-metal workers: a total of ten thousand tradesmen registered. It took about ten months before they were all employed.

Slowly the ghetto apparatus gained momentum, developing industries that, by 1 September 1941, employed 40,288 workers.[7]

By June 1944, before the final and total liquidation of the ghetto, the population numbered seventy-nine thousand, out of which 71,711 were harnessed to the ninety factories and various departments that functioned as the autonomous hell on earth called Litzmannstadt ghetto. The above dates and figures derive from an official report compiled and stored in the archives of the Gettoverwaltung.[8]

Rations

Queues! Miles of starving people waiting to collect their meagre food rations, most of the time waiting for nothing: queuing up for days without end. Swollen legs, swollen feet, faces puffed up from starvation, pushing one another, falling over into the mud, some never to get up again. Nobody cared; nobody took any notice of the others. Life in the ghetto was like being on a sinking boat.

It was a life of permanent hunger pangs. My intestines throbbed day and night, sapping my energy. In the beginning, the pain of my hunger drove me to tears. I used to cry as I lay in bed, burying my face in the pillow so that nobody would hear. I could not sleep; the pain was unbearable. It never let go. Yet, as time wore on, I learned to live with it.

The great master has not yet been born who has the genius to portray, in all its enormity, the misery, the agony and fear which the ghetto dwellers had to endure. The Lodz ghetto was a dark inferno of suffering, a never-ending pitch-black tunnel without a spark of hope. The abyss grew darker and deeper, minute by minute; everlasting famine and fear. Five years, five long years in a never-ending macabre dance in the arms of death. All I knew of life at that time was torment.

The rations, always meagre, shrank still further. All food was measured in grams as if it were gold.

The following list is taken from a document showing the theoretical monthly ration for one person for the month of April:

100 g barley	16 kg potatoes
200 g cornflour	4 kg beetroot
600 g brown sugar	6 kg carrots
300 g artificial honey	<u>4 kg kohlrabi</u>
200 g black vegetable oil	30 kg
<u>400 g coffee substitute</u>	
1,800 g	

> 600 g meat
> 200 g sausage
> 80 g margarine
> 2 kg bread for 8 days was the regular ration.[9]

However, even this was more than we really received. Indeed, the margarine ration was never distributed, by the order of the German authorities, and had to be shipped back to the suppliers.

The ghetto fed on rumours, some of which were spread by the Germans to confuse and mislead us. Other rumours were make-believe stories invented by optimists — people who could not go on unless they had something to look forward to. Such is human nature: we needed something to believe in, something to hope for when there was no hope. So we thrived on fantasies, although we had learned many times over that the rumours of good things never came true. Nevertheless, people spoke with great enthusiasm about larger rations, more potatoes, and more bread and fuel to heat the homes. And all the while, the radio news was absolutely appalling. It seemed as though Germany would defeat the whole world.

Events elsewhere in Europe

In April 1940, the German army occupied Norway, Denmark and, within the next two months, overran Belgium, Holland and Luxembourg. With lightning speed, it then invaded France which collapsed and surrendered without a fight. On 21 June 1940, France signed an armistice on German terms.

These events, however, did not deter the optimism of our backyard politicians, nor their military advisers. They stood fast. Within months, most of Europe was overrun by the Germans, who met with hardly any meaningful resistance. They crushed everything and everyone in their path, but they could not crush the spirit of our ghetto optimists. These were soldiers who never surrendered. They kept cheering us up, boosting our hopes. They persistently maintained, 'The Germans must lose the war and this will happen very soon!' They used to say: 'Be patient and you will see! The German tanks will grind to a standstill. The Germans are running out of petrol; they will be unable to feed their huge army. Germany has no raw materials. The front lines are too spread out. The more territory the Germans grab the weaker they will become. Germany will collapse within a few months.' These stories and dreams were what kept us going.

The Germans had their plans ready to destroy the Jews long before they started the war. Wherever their armies invaded, the Jews were easy prey, totally at the mercy of the Third Reich. Hitler's intentions were made clear in a speech he delivered on 30 January 1939, at the Reichstag: in the event of war, he said, the result would be 'the annihilation of the Jewish race in Europe.'[10]

Far from coming to the rescue of the Jews, the local Christian populations in the countries where Jews lived actively helped the Germans in rounding them up by identifying them. In eastern Europe, large numbers of the local population participated in public massacres in front of watching women and children. This happened in Lithuania, Latvia, Estonia, Ukraine and White Russia. In Slovakia the Jews were decimated, with the connivance of the Catholic church which was in full control of the Slovakian puppet government. The same happened in Hungary, where Eichmann had the full assistance of the Hungarian police and was helped by the Hungarian fascist organisation, the Arrow Cross.

Yet Hungary was also the site for the unique phenomenon of Raoul Wallenberg, a Swedish diplomat who risked his own life and saved the lives of tens of thousands of Jews by furnishing them with false papers which identified them as Swedish citizens. When the Russian army freed Hungary from the German occupation, Wallenberg was arrested by the KGB, never to be seen in the West again.

In 1944, Himmler ordered Eichmann to halt the deportations of the Hungarian Jews on account of his secret negotiations with the West: he was trying to swap Jews for army lorries. The negotiations were not fruitful but Himmler's order to Eichmann was never rescinded. Once again, Eichmann acted independently, proceeding with the deportation of the Hungarian Jews against great odds until the last possible moment.

In Romania, some Jews were saved when their government, hitherto anti-Semitic, changed its policy in anticipation of an Allied victory.

In Bulgaria, the case was entirely different. There, out of fifty thousand Jews, 45,000 were saved. The Bulgarian Parliament adamantly refused to allow the Germans to take the Bulgarian Jews.

In Denmark, the whole Jewish population was saved by the Danish people. They mobilised all their strength and evacuated the entire Jewish population, ferrying them across to Sweden, saving 5,500 Jews from death. The Danish King Christian X declared: 'Should the Jews be forced to wear the yellow Star of David, I will be the first to wear one.'

In France, the situation was very grim. Traditionally the French were very anti-Semitic and the Vichy Government, led by Marshal Pétain, collaborated fully with the Germans, especially with regard to the Jews. On 6 July 1942, Theodor Dannecker, an SS officer, and the chief of the Anti-Jewish section of the Gestapo in France, wrote to Eichmann in Berlin:

> The Prime Minister of the Vichy Government, Pierre Laval, has proposed, in connection with the deportation of Jewish families from the unoccupied zone [the Vichy Zone], that the Jewish children under the age of 16 should be deported together with the adults ... I do ask urgently for a decision to be made by the Führer to allow the deporta-

tion of the Jewish children younger than 16 years of age ... from France.[11]

In September 1942, Pierre Laval announced: 'The Jewish children will be deported as well, together with their parents.' The Vichy government wanted 'to purge France of undesirable elements'.

As we learn from other documents in this series, Dannecker, under constant pressure from the French police and the Vichy government, complained many times to his superiors in Berlin. His successor, Heinz Röthke, noted that on various occasions the French police had expressed their desire to have the Jewish children deported to the Third Reich together with their parents. Finally on 20 July, Eichmann telephoned his reply: 'The children may be deported together with the older people.' As a result, six thousand French children of the Jewish faith were deported to Auschwitz and gassed.

Many of the deported Jews were not merely migrants who had never been favourably looked upon by the French; they were members of old, established Jewish communities dating back many hundreds of years. Among them were the descendants of the most prominent French-Jewish families whose forefathers had been heroes of the French Revolution. They were the grandchildren of soldiers and officers who had served Napoleon in his wars for the glory of France. They were Jewish personalities renowned for their contributions to the country in every field: the sciences, industry, the arts and politics. And they were rounded up by the French civic police and the gendarmerie, handed over to the Germans and carted off to Auschwitz. The French authorities made it possible for the Germans to murder eighty thousand French Jews.

However, in a small village by the name of Chambon-sur-Lignon, with a population of five thousand inhabitants, the villagers united, giving shelter and false documents to four thousand Jews, thus saving them from deportation. Chambon-sur-Lignon was inhabited by French Protestants, descendants of the Huguenots, who themselves had been the victims of the religious wars in Europe. They had been mercilessly butchered by the Roman Catholics, and they remembered.

Although Italy was a member of the Axis alliance, there the Jews were helped by the population, as well as by the Italian army, which refused to collaborate with the Germans in the deportations.

In some parts of Europe under Italian occupation, Jews were left in peace and, in many cases, whenever they had to withdraw under orders from their German partners, the Italian army would evacuate the Jewish population, taking them along on their army lorries as they went. This happened in the south of France where the Italian army occupied a large area.

In Belgium, Degrelle, the leader of the fascists called the Blackshirts, assisted the Germans in the deportation of the Jewish population.

In Holland, many of the Dutch people assisted the Jews and helped them to hide. However, the Dutch fascists, who were reasonably numerous, assisted the Germans in rounding up the Dutch Jewish population.

I must qualify all of the above by stating that in some parts of Europe there were many Christians who helped save Jews. Yet, all those who assisted did so as individuals only: no organised help came from any governments or nations except Denmark, Bulgaria and Romania. The majority of Europeans did nothing; many were in fact happy to see Jews deported, being fully aware of what happened to them once they arrived at Auschwitz.

Heroes without medals

Meanwhile, in the Lodz ghetto, in the world of my past, starvation took its toll with ferocity. In that world, a loaf of bread was more valuable than a human life.

Yet within this tragic hell on earth, I saw great human beings. I saw people who chose death rather than the alternatives of compromise and serving the devil. Chaim Widawski was one of these. He was wanted by the Gestapo for radio-listening and feared that, under duress, he might divulge the names of his friends who were also involved. Because the penalty for radio-listening was death, Widawski chose to commit suicide rather than fall into the hands of German interrogators.

These radio-listeners carried on with their self-imposed task of passing on the latest news and keeping the ghetto informed of what was happening on the other side of the barbed wire. They were brave and heroic men, and most of them paid with their lives: among them were Jacob, Joshua and Henoch Weksler, and Isaac Lubinsky. Other heroes were men and women like Dr Szykier, who resigned his position as deputy to Rumkowski; my father who prevented his son from joining the Sonderkommando; and my brother Lipek who chose to take his advice.

There was uncle Berish, who did not accept the position of secretary to Leon Rozenblat, the commandant of the Jewish police in the Lodz ghetto; and my aunty Cerel, the brave, kind-hearted, quiet heroine who shared her food with the needy. There was Dr Wajskop who, with his bare hands, fought Biebow and his assistant, Heinrich Schwindt, when they found him hiding with a small group of Jews after the ghetto was liquidated. Unable to overpower him, the two of them had to empty their pistols into his body. There was my mother, who fought for her family like a lioness, caring for her sick son; she saved his life by selling part of her meagre food ration for medication. She stayed loyal to her children and her husband till the very last, choosing to go with her husband when she could have saved her life by staying back in the ghetto. Beniek Dyzenhaus was another most remarkable man. He tirelessly cared for the sick and dying. In the Lodz ghetto, Beniek was not a person — he was an institution. While others sold medication in exchange for food, he gave it away.

I only mention these few people as examples. There were many thousands of unknown and honourable people who refused to bend or to be degraded. They managed to die with dignity. Of those mentioned above, only Dr Szykier and Beniek Dyzenhaus survived the Holocaust.

Beniek was liberated by the American army at Ebensee concentration camp in Austria on 5 May 1945. He remarried and, soon after, migrated to Australia. Arriving in Melbourne on the SS *Sorrento* on 1 December 1949, he lived and worked there until he passed away on 5 February 1973. He was buried at the Springvale Cemetery; on his tombstone are inscribed the words, 'He lived to help others.' The inscription is as simple and humble as he was.

In the world of my past I saw people larger than life. Amongst them lived one whose name was Shimon. He was humble and quiet — a frail, tall man who carried the heavy burdens of an ordinary ghetto Jew in silence and with dignity. Shimon was my father.

There was my mother, Fradl. As a young girl, she had been the soloist in a Jewish choir called 'The Harp', in a well-known Jewish cultural centre in Lodz. She had a beautiful voice with which she sang a rich and extensive repertoire of many Yiddish songs. I remember many of them to this very day.

My parents met at The Harp. I remember my mother as a young woman, her face justifying her nickname, *Die Sheine Fradl* (the beautiful Fradl). She was a striking woman, of gentle expression and high cheek bones, pale as though sculpted from alabaster, with lips like roses in springtime. Her dark brown eyes, deeply set, never needed make-up, and she wound her jet black hair into a bun that looked as though it had been carved from ebony. Sometimes she wore a large Spanish comb which gave her the appearance of a Sephardic Jewess. I loved her lyrical, soprano voice, and still remember the lullabies and the Yiddish folk songs she sang to us.

There was my brother, Lipek, the young intellectual whom I loved more than my life. Always reading, he was very studious and highly respected and liked, both by our friends and his teachers, for his knowledge and intellect. Gentle by nature, as well as in his looks, he had wavy black hair, dark eyes and olive skin. He was slender and tall. He took after our father physically, as well as in character and personality.

My grandmother, Shayndl, was tall and aristocratic. The traditional wigs she wore were always well-groomed and looked after. She dressed immaculately, as if every day were a holiday. Her house was always spotless, looked after with pride by her servant, Andrzejowa, who had come to her as a very young girl and helped bring up her three children: my father, who was the oldest son; uncle Laib and aunty Sarah — the youngest and the favourite. They all took after my grandmother in physique, all tall, in striking contrast to my grandfather, Itshe Mayer Biderman, who was short in stature but had a compelling personality. He was adored and highly respected by his family and friends.

My grandparents were from a well-to-do, middle-class family, typical Eastern European orthodox Jews who lived piously and strictly by the written law. Shayndl was a true yiddishe grandmother who lived for God and her children only. Andrzejowa, our servant, was actually part of our family. Not only did she bring up my father, uncle and aunt, she brought up every grandchild, including me. She left our house in her late sixties, at which time we booked her into an elderly persons' home. From that time onwards, every Sunday without fail, she visited us after church until the very end of her life. She passed away shortly before the Second World War.

I never had the pleasure of knowing my maternal grandparents personally. My grandfather, Lipman Braverman, after whom my brother was named, died long before I was born — of typhoid, during the First World War. My grandmother, Toba, passed away when I was still a baby; so I have no recollection of her. The faces in my mind's eye come only from the photographs I have seen. They lived in Zdunska Wola where they ran a successful hand-weaving cottage industry.

There were my uncles and aunts: Berish Taglicht, his wife Sarah, my father's sister, with whom we lived together in the ghetto; my uncle, the cantor David Laib Blicblau, his wife Chaya (my mother's older sister); Cerel Zelmanowicz, my mother's cousin whom we called 'aunt'; her husband, known by his nickname Yankev Bolshevik; as well as all my cousins and many more members of my extended family.

As the first year in the Lodz ghetto drew to its end, so too did thousands of lives. Many more had been deported — destination unknown.

Christmas came. The Germans celebrated the birth of Christ as always. The churches overflowed with worshippers as the spirit of Christmas swept across the land. In the silence of the ghetto night I could hear from a distance the singing of the German police in the precinct that was guarding the ghetto. They were drinking and singing carols to the glory of the Jewish child who was born two thousand years before; meanwhile, Jewish children behind the barbed wire were dying in agony from starvation. It was a long night as I lay on my bed listening to their renditions of 'Silent Night' followed by 'Noel, Noel ... He is the King of Israel'. Did they ever stop to think what they were singing?

3

The Lodz ghetto, 1941

TWO HUNDRED and forty-five days had gone by since we were first incarcerated behind these barbed wires. It was 1 January 1941. The Germans celebrated the New Year. Their homes were warm and well lit; their Christmas trees, richly decorated, sparkled with tinsel. For the festive season they were awarded special rations which provided them with an abundance of food and drink. They were ecstatic, drunk with victory, toasting their conquests as Masters of the World.

My brother gets tuberculosis

Early spring, 1941. My brother Lipek became sick with pleurisy and then developed tuberculosis. The shortage of food and lack of medication made him wither away very quickly, and my mother suffered terribly at having no food to give him. Part of the little food we were given I had to exchange for the calcium injections he needed so badly.

Outwardly, our home was calm, as though nothing were wrong. I remember my mother sitting on the edge of my brother's bed, tranquil and controlled, not a tear in her eyes, caressing his limp hands, as his health rapidly deteriorated. He looked as though he would not last much longer, and there was precious little we could do.

I remember my mother asking Lipek one day, 'What can I do to make you happy, my son? Is there anything that might make you feel better? I have no food for you just now. We get the ration tomorrow.'

'Don't worry,' my brother replied quietly. 'I love you just the same. But I love to hear you sing. Please, mama, sing one of your beautiful songs.'

'Which one?'

'Margaritkes.'

It was aunty Cerel who came to the rescue. She was actually my mother's cousin and I will never forget her kind-heartedness. Everything about her was big, though she was softly spoken with a warm smile always shining out of her eyes. Her big arms looked as though they were made to embrace and shelter all the children in the universe.

She worked as a potato peeler in the public kitchen of the Bund (the Jewish Socialist Party). At 3 Lutomierska Street, Cerel used to eat the raw vegetables which she was supposed to be peeling. Thus, daily, she was able to give Lipek her entire portion of soup. At the time, an extra spoonful of soup was very rare, the most precious elixir of life.

Aunty Cerel and Yankev Bolshevik

Aunty Cerel, along with my uncle Yankev and my cousin Luba, lived in one room at 26 Limanowskiego Street. Luba was thirteen. She was hungry like all the other kids in the ghetto. Uncle Yankev was swollen, bedridden and dying of starvation. Aunty Cerel used to say, 'For Yankev it is too late, much too late. Luba, thank God, is healthy. But we must save Lipek, for he is young. We must save the young ones.'

Uncle Yankev was an interesting person; in my eyes, a living legend. His nickname, 'Yankev Bolshevik', was gained during the Russian Revolution. Before joining the revolutionary movement, Yankev studied at the Yeshiva and was known as a very talented Talmudic student. He could recite whole chapters from the five books of Moses by heart, as well as many commentaries from the Talmud, the Mishna, the Zohar and from Rashi, giving his own wise and witty interpretations.

During the crucial days of the Russian Revolution, Yankev was in St Petersburg, rubbing shoulders with the leaders. He knew most of them personally and was on a first-name basis with them. At that time, he was also a private serving in the Tsar's army. Being a talented speaker and devout revolutionary, he was elected as a delegate to represent his army unit in the Soviet. He was entrusted by the revolutionary committee in the crucial hours of the famous

St Petersburg coup to lead a detachment of sailors in storming the Tsar's Winter Palace. It was a most decisive night in the history of Russia; but later, Yankev used to speak with much bitterness and disappointment about his involvement in the revolution and its aftermath that changed the face of Russia.

He had an exquisite and tiny piece of scarlet velvet, taken from the Winter Palace at St Petersburg, that he had kept as a souvenir of the great victory. He had cut it out of one of the carpeted staircases with his bayonet. From time to time, he would take his precious keepsake out of the wardrobe as he reminisced about the revolution. Unfortunately, his dreams of a new communist Russia turned into a nightmare for himself and for many millions when Joseph Stalin came to power. Uncle Yankev fled Russia, settling in Poland.

'I did not trust that ruthless Georgian peasant from the very first moment I laid eyes on him,' he used to say. 'I could see who he was and what he was up to. During the purges of 1937, he killed off most of my comrades. Amongst them were many Jews: Rykov, Zinoviev, Kamenev; I knew them personally in the days before the great night. I used to spend a lot of time in their circle. In Joseph Stalin, I could see not only an enemy of the revolution — I saw in him an enemy of the Jews. I used to tell my comrades behind his back: "Watch that Georgian bastard; he is a vicious anti-Semite." '

In spite of his disappointment with the revolution, Yankev retained his idealism and remained a devout socialist. Before the war, on 1 May, when celebrating Labour Day, uncle Yankev would dress up in all his finery: bowler hat, white starched shirt and collar, black bow-tie, with his black jacket and black pants which had a fine white stripe running through the fabric. Wearing a red carnation in his buttonhole and carrying a black walking stick with a silver handle, he wore his jacket unbuttoned over the black velvet vest which struggled to cover his protruding stomach. This latter was decorated with a heavy golden chain to which was hooked a large golden fob watch — another of his souvenirs from the revolution. All this was finished off with a pair of black, patent shoes around which were wrapped pale beige gaiters. On that day Yankev believed he looked like an English lord dressed for a royal reception.

He would parade in front of his house at 26 Limanowskiego Street, and then in front of the barber shop, which used to be the meeting centre for political and literary discussions and arguments. These were Yankev Bolshevik's 'headquarters', where he would spend his free time debating and discussing with fervour Stalin's purges and the state of affairs in the Soviet Union. With disappointment and bitterness he attacked the communists and their sympathisers. He called them blind fanatics who refused to see the obvious.

'Abraham, these communists are incurable,' he used to say to me. 'They defend Joseph Stalin no matter how criminally he behaves. They are simply fanatics, blind followers.'

As a young boy, I never sympathised with communism, nor could I come to terms with Yankev's views. I could not accept his reasoning that there were true communists and devout socialists who could be virulent anti-Semites as well. How innocent and gullible I was; but my uncle was far older and wiser.

Every day on my way home from school I used to see uncle Yankev across the street, leaning against the wall next to the kiosk, always busy reading a newspaper, a magazine or a book. He was short and broad-shouldered, dressed in a dark brown corduroy suit. His long jacket went right down to his knees, and had two huge patched pockets always full of literature of one kind or another. With his big loose pants tucked into Russian-style boots, he completed his very individual image with a dark brown corduroy cap perched on his big bald head. This is how uncle Yankev looked all year round.

He was a weaver in a textile mill. On his meagre salary he could not afford to buy all the newspapers and magazines he so sorely needed to read, so he would pay five groschen a day to the newspaper vendor, who then allowed him to stand at the kiosk and read all the publications on sale.

In the ghetto, I sat at Yankev's bedside. Day by day, as he became weaker, his bitterness and disappointment grew stronger. His face, parchment yellow, was swollen from starvation. I could hardly see his eyes.

I recall him saying: 'Abraham, look at these German savages. These Nazis of today were yesterday's communists and social democrats. They were our promise and hope for a better world of tomorrow. They were in their millions, but now there is no more sun shining for us in the ghetto. The socialists of yesterday are the

Nazis of today.

'They are the grandchildren of Goethe; they were brought up and educated on his poetry. Nietzsche is their torch bearer; they worship Beethoven. Do you remember the words of the Chorale of the Ninth Symphony? "All people are brothers, all are equal." Today the same Germans are singing songs about Jewish blood spurting from their knives, drowning the world in a sea of blood; and they are doing it easily and with such gusto.

'Abraham, do you remember the Germans from pre-war Poland? For a lifetime I worked with them. We ate and drank together. We lived together side by side as good neighbours. Some of them were communists, social democrats. They had a lot of Jewish friends. They were nice people, friendly and well-educated. They are a highly cultured people. I always looked upon them as a civilised nation. Not like the Poles, the cabbage heads. They are rough peasants, primitive drunkards. The only thing the Poles are good for is making vodka. They're even better at drinking it.

'They used to call me a rich Jew. I was a poor weaver: I had the same salary they had. But in their tradition, the day they got their pay, half of the salary they left in the bars — to come home dead drunk, smashing up their homes, beating their wives and children.

'And do you know what else the Poles are really good at, Abraham? Making pogroms, smashing up Jewish homes and knifing Jews in the streets. Do you remember when the Great Synagogue in the old city was blown up by the Germans? The Poles stood around with smiles on their faces, watching it go up in smoke. They laughed.

'They are betraying us to a common enemy and they do not even see it as treachery. They believe that killing Jews is their holy duty. Jews are the Christ-killers, and for this they must pay with their blood. This is how they were brought up, and this is how they will always be. They are sick beyond curing. They are obsessed.'

As Yankev ranted on about the Poles, in my mind's eye I saw once again how our Polish neighbours incited their children to beat up Jews: '*No czemu sie patrzysz parszywy zydzie?*' ('Well, why do you look, you rotten Jew?'); '*Nieboj sie rambni go w morde.*' ('Don't be afraid, hit them in the snout'). All I could hear were threats and constant swearing: '*Psia krew Zydzie!*' ('Bloody Jew.')

When celebrating 3 May, the day commemorating the Polish

Constitution, they marched down the main streets of the city with songs and slogans: *'Zydy do Palestyny'* ('Jews go to Palestine'); *'Smierc zydom'* ('Death to the Jews'); *'Precz z zydami!'* ('Jews get out!'); or their popular slogan, *'Nasze ulice wasze kamienice'* ('Ours are the streets, yours are the properties.').

'Abraham, listen to old Yankev Bolshevik. Just wait and you will see. This war is not against the Jews only: the Nazis have chosen anti-Semitism, an old tried and true method to excite the masses. The Jews are only the bait. German plans are much further-reaching. Hitler only began with the Jews to get his people warmed up. Next in line, you'll see, will come the Poles, the Russians, the Czechs — the whole of Europe. They'll all follow one after the other. The Germans will turn them into illiterate serfs and harness them up to serve the Third Reich. Hitler is just the megaphone of the German people. They have chosen him as their leader to fulfil their dreams. This sickness of being the master race, they suffered long before Hitler was born.

'You see, Abraham, what goes on is not the doing of one man. He whipped them into a frenzy and has them hypnotised because they wanted to be hypnotised. No other nation has ever before behaved like the Germans do. Look at the Italians, they too have a Führer, a Mussolini. Do they behave like the Germans? Hitler brought out his people's full Teutonic character. The Germans love orders. This is how they have been brought up for generations: they're nationalistic, intolerant, and very aggressive towards their neighbours.'

Yankev stopped speaking as he became exhausted. After a long silence he said, 'Abraham, Abraham, what a shame to see the world go down in blood. And to what purpose?'

I sat on the edge of his bed listening to his words. They scared me; so did his looks. His face was like a death mask, yellow, as though made of wax. As I sat listening, deep in my heart I thought the world was not going down; it was Yankev Bolshevik, the revolutionary, who was going down. It was the freedom fighter who was ready to give up his life for a world of justice.

He lay on his bed, his face blown up with the swelling that obscured his eyes. He was exhausted after his long tirade. They were his last words of protest. He kept repeating, 'Why the bloodletting? What purpose does it serve?'

I still have no answer; I doubt that anyone has. Not even the murderers themselves. They don't know why they kill. Ask the cat, 'Why do you kill birds even when you are not hungry?' Does the cat know? Some people have the killer instinct like a cat. But cats don't attend university, they don't know the Ten Commandments, nor do they claim to live by the Bible.

Yankev had dozed off momentarily and now awoke with a start.

'Abraham,' he said, continuing a train of thought from his dreaming, 'I got away from Stalin and now Hitler has caught up with me. From Hitler I doubt very much if I'll ever escape. In Russia, under the Tsar, the Jews were the enemy of the Motherland. So pogroms were instigated against them. After the revolution, the Jewish leaders were purged, branded as traitors, plutocrats, agents of the capitalists. In Germany, we are the Jewish Bolsheviks — we can never win. Believe me, Abraham, the differences between Stalin and Hitler are mainly in their emblems and their uniforms. Their systems are the same. The Soviets have the NKVD; the Nazis, the SS and the Gestapo. Hitler and Stalin are the most bloodthirsty tyrants the world ever saw.'

That was the last time I spoke to him; he died a little later that day. Running to hospital to see Lipek, I left uncle Yankev by himself, not realising that death was so close. And I did not attend his funeral. By the time I found out that he had passed away, he was already buried. By that time in the ghetto, all forms of civilised life had disintegrated, and ceremony and ritual for the dead had totally disappeared. All that mattered were the few crumbs of bread, or the potatoes and the ration card that had been left by the deceased. Often survivors delayed reporting deaths for days, because it enabled them to collect the bread ration and whatever food was still possible to obtain.

When Yankev passed away, my aunty Cerel was peeling vegetables in the dark, damp cellar at the public kitchen, and my cousin Luba was at work in one of the ghetto factories. Returning home, they found him still holding the golden watch with the chain that used to adorn his velvet vest when he paraded in front of 26 Limanowskiego Street on May Day. Tenaciously he had guarded it for his son, Laibele, who had run off to Russia, unaware of the fate that was to befall the rest of his large family.

Cerel, the potato peeler of 3 Lutomierska Street, together with her daughter, Luba, aged sixteen, perished in August 1944 in the gas chambers of Auschwitz.

Cerel's soup and maybe my mother's singing helped to get Lipek on his feet again. Unfortunately, his recovery was only temporary and, shortly after, he had a relapse. With a great deal of trial and hardship, we managed to have him admitted to the hospital for tuberculosis in Bazarna Street, adjacent to the Jewish Mental Asylum which was located in Wesola Street, in the court-yard of the old Jewish Cemetery.

Barbarossa

It was April 1941 when, in the middle of the night, we were awakened by a rumbling noise in the street. Cautiously, we peeped out from behind the black-out blinds into the street to see columns of army lorries with German soldiers in full battle dress travelling past the ghetto on their way to the east. The heavy guns and tank carriers in battle formation kept rolling and rolling, until night fell on the following day. For five weeks, this procession continued. At regular intervals, heavy anti-aircraft guns were positioned, point-ing into the sky, ready to fire at any moment.

The German army possessed the latest equipment. As a young boy, I had loved to go to the pictures, and I remembered the newsreels showing the French or British armies parading their machinery of war; but never had I seen a motorised army with tanks and heavy guns of such size and quantity. The steel columns kept rolling. And as we watched the massive steel parade with growing apprehension, Berish put his arm around my shoulders and said, 'Abraham, we are lost. The Germans are the mightiest power under the sun. Hitler will destroy us all.'

All the while the steel parade was moving to the east, Reinhard Heydrich had his blueprint of the Final Solution ready. The Führer, without hesitation, ordered its immediate implementation in the imminent Russian campaign. Operation Barbarossa was the plan to destroy 'Jewish Bolshevism'. As the Panzer divisions moved eastward into Russia with lightning speed, the Germans unleashed their accumulated fury and hatred against the Jews.

The actual Führer order for the execution of Jews, Gypsies and Soviet political commissars during the forthcoming campaign against Russia was issued in stages to those responsible. The probability is that Himmler received the order in early March 1941, when the Führer held a conference at his headquarters at which Himmler was given extensive plenipotentiary powers.

At this time, all upper-echelon Nazis were aware of the impending attack on Russia; and, in preparation for the great offensive, dozens of officials from various branches of the RSHA were gathered together at a camp where they set up an academy of murder to train the especially selected three thousand members of the 'Einsatzgruppen' (mobile killing squads). These men had the highest IQs. Amongst them were lecturers, solicitors, and even a pastor. It was located at Pretsch in Saxony, where they underwent special secret training. Heydrich addressed the officers on the dangers of Judaism. Soon afterwards, at a meeting in his office in the Prinz Albrechtstrasse in Berlin, he openly talked of the Final Solution.

Finally, just before the attack on 22 June, Heydrich warned his subordinates of the necessity of including women and children in the anti-Jewish operations to be undertaken in Russia. They must be killed, he said, because they were 'the potential avengers and sources of future corruption'. According to one of those at the meeting, Heydrich stated that the goal aimed at was permanent security, and this could only be achieved if the children, too, were killed. Otherwise, children whose parents had been killed, when they grew up, would constitute no less a danger than their fathers.

On 22 June 1941, without warning, the military might of the German army was suddenly hurled against Soviet Russia. The news was frightening and shattering. The Germans moved with the speed of a tornado, flattening everything in their path. The Russian armies retreated with heavy losses under the pressure of most powerful attacks launched by the German Panzers. Villages, towns and cities were bombed; millions of people lost their lives. Hitler, in speeches full of blistering fury, lashed out against his recent ally with whom he had signed a pact of non-aggression, calling the Soviet government the 'Jewish Bolshevist clique' with a philosophy based on 'vicious and barbarous Jewish doctrines'. The first victims were the Jews. Wherever the Germans invaded, a savage war aided by the locals began against the defenceless Jewish population. Nobody cared; nobody even tried to help.

On 19 September 1941, the day the Germans marched into Kiev, they immediately started forcing Jews into the streets to perform dirty work with their bare hands. Thousands of them were rounded up and deported. On 22 September, placards appeared on the walls announcing that Jews, communists, commissars and partisans were to be exterminated. For denouncing any of the above, the reward would be 200 roubles. On Friday and Saturday, 26 and 27 September, the Germans surrounded the synagogues and killed the worshippers. On 28 September, further placards printed in Ukrainian and Russian appeared, advising Jews from Kiev and the surrounding districts that, on 29 September at 7 a.m., they must assemble with their belongings, money, jewellery, valuables, documents and warm clothing at the Jewish cemetery. Those who did not appear would be punished with death. Hiding a Jew was also punishable by death.

On the critical day of 29 September 1941, large crowds of Jews from all parts of the city converged upon the designated meeting-point. Groups of thirty to forty people were taken to a nearby place called Babi Yar and, at open deep graves, they were made to undress and were then shot in the neck.

In August 1943, when the Red Army was approaching the River Dnieper, an order arrived from Berlin stating that the victims of Babi Yar were to be exhumed in order to wipe out all evidence of the crime. The Germans brought three hundred Russian prisoners of war, officers and junior officers, to Babi Yar to do the work. Chained together, these men dug up the remnants which were then sprayed with petrol and burned. A surviving witness, who was directly involved in the process, gave evidence about this. He stated that the number of corpses excavated reached seventy thousand. Documentation of this event exists in *The Black Book* of Ilya Ehrenburg and Vasily Grossman.[12]

On 29 September 1943, the wiping out of the evidence was completed. Somehow sensing what was to follow, the strictly guarded Russian prisoners of war panicked and ran. The SS sprayed them with machine-guns, killing 280. Twenty managed to survive to tell of the horrors they had seen and, in September 1961, the young poet Yevgeny Yevtushenko first published his famous poem entitled, simply, 'Babi Yar', in the *Literaturnaya Gazetta*.

The hospital

In the early morning of 29 July 1941, a neighbour in the Lodz ghetto gave the alarm that the Jewish Mental Asylum and the Tuberculosis Hospital were surrounded by the 'Rolfkommando' — the mobile liquidation squad operating within the Warthegau region, liquidating the ghettos. I jumped out of bed and, in a flash, raced over to the hospital where my brother was.

All the streets surrounding the hospital and the asylum were cordoned off by the Jewish police, who were out in force. Otherwise, there was not another Jew in sight.

I passed the blockade and walked towards the TB hospital from the rear, opposite Winograd's Timber Toy factory. Walking as though nothing were wrong, I crossed the street, squeezed past the fence and whistled our secret signal. My brother, looking pale and nervous, climbed up to the big window. I told him to get dressed and come down.

Lipek tried to assure me that the administration of the hospital had told them not to panic. They said that the Rolfkommando (Rolf being the name of the police chief of the Warthegau) was here only to take away the mentally ill. I insisted that he get dressed and not listen to the administration's promises. When he came down, we fell into each other's arms and he clung to me, shaking like a leaf.

I held him very tightly and he told me how glad he was that I had come. Fully absorbed in planning how to act in case they moved to liquidate the TB hospital, I had no time for fear. This seemed to have a calming effect on Lipek. I told him that I would just run across to find out what was going to happen once they finished removing the patients from the asylum. I assured him that, no matter what, I would be back and he must wait for my return.

I squeezed past the gap in the fence the way I had come in. The moment I was back on the street, I suddenly heard a bark. '*Du, komm mal hier!*' It was an SS trooper, appearing out of nowhere, who was guarding the rear gate of the hospital. In all my life I never ran as fast as I did then, taking cover in a courtyard across the narrow street. Like an animal in the jungle, I found my way through the escape holes of the ghetto which led from one building to the next. I ran and ran with all my strength. No shots were fired. I heard no sound of boots behind me.

Stopping in a dark corner, I leaned against the wall to catch my breath. As soon as I recovered, I ran on towards Wesola Street, making my way towards the main gate of the old cemetery. On my left arm I wore a yellow and white armband which identified me as a messenger of the Vegetable Department. I walked briskly in the middle of the road towards the gate. I made myself so obvious that it never occurred to any of them that I was bluffing.

The Wesola Street and surrounding area looked like a ghost town. Four SS troopers, armed with submachine guns slung around their necks, sealed off the large wrought-iron gates that led to the courtyard of the old Jewish Cemetery where the asylum was situated.There seemed to be no hope of escape but I kept on walking towards them feeling that, at any moment, I would get a burst of bullets through my body. I tried to give the impression that I was on official business and walked past the SS troopers, taking off my hat as I passed the gate.

On entering the courtyard I was confused for an instant, not knowing where to turn. I approached a man wearing a white coat and a navy cap with a red band in the centre of which was a medical emblem with the sign *'Arzt'* (doctor) on it.

'How far do you think this is going to go?' I asked.

'I know as much as you do,' he replied. 'At this stage, they're taking the mentally ill. Let's hope it stops at that.'

The doctor — I never did find out his name — was very helpful. I told him that my brother was at the TB hospital.

'I'm here to help him escape in case they move further.'

'Young man, you are crazy, just crazy. Watch out that they don't get you. If I were you I wouldn't be here.' I just shrugged my shoulders and said nothing; but I stayed close to him, using him as a cover. He did not seem to mind.

We stood there watching the second and last group of patients boarding the rear of a light grey van that looked like a large ambulance. The doors were wide open, and I could see inside. There were two long benches on either side where the patients were seated. There may have been between twenty and twenty-five of them. Some waved timidly, as though saying goodbye.

Amongst them was a man I knew from my previous visits to the hospital. He used to help at the reception desk and I had spoken to him on various occasions. Middle-aged with grey hair, his Yiddish was cultivated and he had always given me the impression of being someone who was totally normal. The only indications that he was from the mental asylum were the hospital dressing gown, pyjamas and the slippers that he wore. He looked bewildered and boarded the van in silence with a bundle of papers under his arm. They were all very silent, as though in some sort of trance. It occurred to me that they may have been given tranquillising injections, but I never found out. I just stood looking on as the van doors shut. One thing that seemed clear to me, as well as to the other onlookers, was that these patients were all going to their deaths.[13]

The van drove off, followed by a heavily armed escort. The Jewish ghetto police dispersed and the streets surrounding the hospital slowly came to life again. I ran back to Lipek to tell him that they had left and it was all over. But was it? I was worried that they would strike again.

After four months in hospital, Lipek was discharged. His health had improved slightly and his temperature was back to normal. However, he was frail and had to take things slowly. He was still on calcium and glucose injections which I could only obtain on the black market in exchange for food from our rations. Although not fully recovered, he went back to the ghetto high school to continue his studies, and eventually obtained his high school certificate from Rumkowski himself.

Rumours

Meanwhile, most perturbing rumours were circulating in the ghetto. Frightening stories about mass evacuations. Rumours that the entire Jewish population of villages in the Warthegau had been evacuated. Evacuated to the unknown. Soon after, even more frightening stories filtered through into the ghetto about mass executions where thousands of Jews were murdered by firing squad. The rumours were unbelievable. We refused to believe the unbelievable. Unfortunately, the unbelievable was later proved to be true.

These rumours I picked up at work and in the streets in the course of my daily routine as a messenger. I had contacts with lots of offices and people. My school friend, Mendel Feldman, was the liaison between my brother, myself and Skif (the children's organisation of the Bund — the Jewish Socialist Party in Poland). Mendel had access to radio reports from the Wekslers and Bono Wiener who were radio-listeners. For the possession of a radio, hanging was the punishment. Many were found out and executed.

. The Germans countered these rumours with fictions of their own about the evacuated Jews. They spread rumours that the evacuees were well looked after and resettled amongst the peasants, working on the land where they were well provided for and happy — without food shortages.

We now know the facts: only eighty-three kilometres away, the obscure peasant settlement of Chelmno was being prepared by the Germans for the destruction of the Jews from the Lodz ghetto and all the smaller surrounding ghettos situated within the Warthegau.

The secrets of Chelmno

Yes, we know it now. It was more vile than the vilest of the rumours. Jews were brought to the Kazimierz forests on trucks and executed by firing squad. Before execution, the victims had to strip naked, walk to the mass graves already prepared for them, and then stand at the edges, where they were shot. The bodies would roll into the graves and be covered with caustic lime to prevent disease and to speed up the decomposition process. However, this was a costly and cumbersome method, used only in the very early stages of the Holocaust, before the Germans were able to develop more sophisticated techniques.

Euthanasia of handicapped and mentally retarded German nationals began in 1940. A total of 70,277 Germans were given 'special treatment' ('Sonderbehandlung') in five euthanasia institutions. The victims were gassed with carbon monoxide and were dead within six to seven minutes. After the first experiments, carried out under the supervision of the Criminal Commissar, Christian Wirth, Doctor Kallmeyer was appointed, and took over the responsibility for the gassings. In August 1941, Hitler was compelled to revoke the programme due to unrest amongst the population, legal objections and mounting protests by the Church.[14] No such reactions or objections were ever expressed over the gassings of the Jews.

In the autumn of 1941, a special operational police and SS unit was formed, whose task it was to select a suitable place for a death camp to carry out the first experimental actions. Fritz Lange was appointed as the commanding officer of the unit, which took its name from him: Sonderkommando Lange. Later on, when Chelmno had already been established as the place of execution for the Jews of the Warthegau, Lange was replaced by SS-Hauptsturmführer Hans Johann Bothmann. Chelmno, the small village on the banks of the river Ner, a tributary to the Warta, became Sonderkommando Kulmhof (the Germanic form of Chelmno).

In November 1941, twelve hundred Jews from Buchenwald concentration camp were taken to the euthanasia institute at Bernberg and gassed. Soon after, on 8 December 1941, the first gassing of Polish Jews took place in Chelmno.[15]

The distance between Lodz and Chelmno was eighty-three kilometres, with direct access both by road and by the Lodz-Kalisz-Kolo rail-line. From Kolo to Chelmno was only a little over thir-teen-and-a-half kilometres, a distance which was serviced by a narrow gauge railway to Powiercie, and from there the journey was completed by other means of transportation or on foot. The only buildings of any importance in Chelmno were a small two-storey palace still in ruins from the First World War, a church, and the farm buildings on the palace property. Those buildings and the former homes of the village's residents, who had been forced to move, as well as a few newly constructed barracks, constituted the entire expanse of the camp, a total of no more than three hectares. There, the victims were forced into the 'Spezialwagen' (the German code-name for gas vans) — which had the appearance of ambulances.

The gas vans were designed and produced by the German truck manufacturers, Saurer of Karlsruhe, where they still produce trucks to this very day. The motor was turned on, and the exhaust fumes were pumped into the section where the passengers were trapped. The motor had been especially designed to produce an inordinate amount of gas. The victims were asphyxiated by the fumes as they were driven the two-and-a-half miles to the Rzuchowski Forest, precinct 77, where they were buried and, at a later date, exhumed and burned to cover the traces of the crime. When the gas vans were unloaded, the victims who still showed signs of life were finished off with a bullet in the neck. This is recalled by the forest inspector of Kolo County, Heinz May.[16]

The Polish peasants who lived and ploughed their fields hard against the fence of the Chelmno camp knew what went on on the other side. They could see and hear what took place; yet, although they were only eighty-three kilometres from the Lodz ghetto, they never bothered to let the ghetto dwellers know. It was not until two years later that I heard of the Spezialwagen.

An extension railway line was built leading right into the forest where the exterminations took place. The Polish locomotive drivers who drove the trains came back with empty carriages to collect more victims. They had direct contact with the Lodz ghetto Jews who worked at the Radogoszcz railway line where the victims were loaded. They also never dropped a hint of warning.

Hans Biebow was a frequent visitor to Chelmno, keeping close watch on the possessions of the victims so that they would not be stolen by the German police who ran the killing factory. He was also involved in the technical side of things. His offsider, Frederic W Ribbe, in May 1942 ordered Rumkowski to investigate whether there was available within the ghetto a bone-grinding machine, because 'the special commando in Kulmhof is interested in such a grinder.'[17] [to help dispose of the last remnants of evidence]. The funds to cover expenses such as this came from the Lodz ghetto bank account.

Heinrich Himmler, the Reichsführer of the SS, witnessed mass executions by firing squad as well as by gassing, which made him sick to the point of vomiting. On all these occasions he was accompanied by Obersturmbannführer Adolf Eichmann. Himmler's opinion was that gassing was cost efficient, less labour intensive and less demoralising for the SS personnel. In Chelmno, 330,000 Jews from the Warthegau were gassed, of which seventy thousand were brought from the Lodz ghetto.[18]

The year 1941 came to an end. As the calendar turned its last page, another year of famine and misery had passed with no hope for anything better in sight.

4

The Lodz ghetto, 1942

SIX HUNDRED and ten days had passed since we had been hermetically sealed inside the ghetto. We were totally isolated from the rest of the world. The starvation never eased. In the first four months of 1942, a total of 54,979 ghetto-dwellers were loaded onto cattle trains and deported. In the ghetto, we were still unaware of the killing factory the Germans had installed at Chelmno. We heard vague rumours about executions of Jews in the forest near the town of Kolo, but the stories were sketchy and hard to believe.

The Jews from western Europe and the Warthegau
In 1941 and 1942, the Lodz ghetto became the largest transit centre for Jews from western Europe and the Warthegau on their way to be 'resettled in the East'. This was the official code disguising the true intention. Today we know they were all taken to Chelmno and gassed. A total of 15,020 were brought into the Lodz ghetto from the small townships and ghettos in the Warthegau. In August 1942, twelve ghettos in the province of Warthegau were liquidated.

During this liquidation, of the many tens of thousands, only a small number — the fittest — were selected by Hans Biebow, assisted by Günter Fuchs, deputy chief of the Gestapo in Litzmannstadt, to be sent into the Lodz ghetto. In the course of the selection, Biebow personally shot many people, amongst them the Eldest of the Jews of Zdunska Wola, Dr Lemberg.

On 22 August 1942, the SS, with the help of the Schupo, surrounded the Zdunska Wola ghetto. Out of ten thousand Jews in this, the birthplace of my mother, only 1,215 were brought into the Lodz ghetto. A large number of people were massacred in the course of the liquidation, and the killing was merciless. The old and sick were shot in their homes. Many were taken to the Jewish cemetery and shot there. Others were shot as they ran through the streets on their way to waiting vans. Before entering the vehicles, they had to empty their pockets of all their possessions; then they were taken to the unknown.[19]

In late autumn 1941, until mid-1942, approximately twenty thousand Jews from western Europe were brought into the Lodz ghetto, raising its population to 103,996. They were from Vienna, Frankfurt, Munich, Cologne, Berlin, Aachen, Hamburg, Düsseldorf, Luxembourg, Moravia, Brno and Prague. Amongst them were two hundred and sixty Roman Catholics and Protestants. They were Germans whose Jewish grandparents had converted to Christianity. Before their arrest by the Gestapo, some of them had had no idea that they had any connection with Jews. When brought into the Lodz ghetto, they all looked healthy and exceptionally well-dressed; but the drastic change from the reasonably normal lifestyle those Jews had still enjoyed before their 'relocation' had a shattering effect on them, mentally and physically, with the famine and filth causing an extremely high mortality rate among them. They were accommodated in pre-war school buildings within the ghetto, where multi-level bunks were especially constructed in huge dormitories. The toilet and washing facilities were appalling. From the middle of October 1941, until February 1942, three thousand of these western European Jews died of starvation.

The colonel in the ghetto

From time to time, I would drop in on my next-door neighbours, the Majerowiczes. I enjoyed watching their younger son repair spectacles; it helped me to forget my empty stomach. Occasionally I would help him with some work by grinding the lenses to make them fit their frames. This was a tedious and slow process. For many hours I rubbed the glass on a wet sandstone, keeping the speed and pressure constant so as not to chip the glass. It was an old and very primitive method, but the Majerowiczes' automatic glass cutting and polishing machinery, as well as all their latest equipment, had been confiscated by a German soldier before they were brought to the ghetto. He had simply entered their elegant shop in

Piotrkowska Street, the main street of Lodz, and taken whatever he had fancied. He had no written orders and, not only did he rob them, but he had forced them to load it all onto his truck. He was a German; they were Jews. They had no right to defend their property.

One evening, a most interesting elderly gentleman came into their home. His face and bearing were striking, his charisma palpable. In his late sixties, he looked like someone who had once been on the stage: tall, slim, exceptionally good looking and with an erect posture as he walked. His healthy silver-grey hair matched perfectly the long, military, blue-grey cape he wore over his semi-military suit of similar colour. His elongated face with its prominent cheek-bones had a long cut across the right side and, together with the monocle he wore, it gave him the classical look of a German officer. Yet he was well mannered, quietly spoken, and his gentle smile softened the severe lines on his face. If it were not for the yellow Star of David on the front and back of his cape, one could have easily mistaken him for a German; which in fact he was, almost. He was a German Jew from Cologne.

I was intrigued by him and eager to know of his past, so I made sure to be at the Majerowiczes' when he came to collect his reading spectacles. On this second meeting he was rather informal, as though we had known each other a long time. He was a Jew with an ancestry that stretched back many generations in Germany. Although not religious, he was conversant with all the Jewish traditions and holidays. In his younger years, before Hitler's ascent to power, he had been a professional soldier.

'I had a very high position with the German army,' he told me. 'I was a colonel. During the First World War, I was in the cavalry, where I was awarded four Iron Crosses — first, second, third and fourth class — as well as many other orders and medals for gallantry, heroic action in battle, and for leadership qualities on the Russian front line.

'The cut on my cheek is a souvenir from a Cossack,' he continued with an ironic smile. 'I've got many more souvenirs like that all over my body. If it were not for the fact that I was born a Jew, I might now have been amongst the leading German generals.

'Don't think, my young friend, that I am a boaster. I am too old for that. It's what my army colleagues used to say. I am from

Cologne. That's where my wife and daughter still live. My daughter is married. She has two little girls. Her husband has been drafted into the German army.'

He showed me the photos of his family.

'They are all, of course, pure Aryans,' he said with a sad smile, 'although my daughter had a lot of trouble because of me. However, with a lot of hard work, and with the help of some of my old friends, we managed somehow to clear her of her sins and turned her into a pure Aryan. For me, there was nothing that could be done. I am a Jew and I have no regrets. A few days before I was summoned to the Gestapo, I still collected my army pension and the rent for my orders. Then I had to report to the Department of Jewish Affairs at the Gestapo in Cologne. I realised that I would be sent to a concentration camp. On the summons they stipulated that I was to bring my razor, soap, towel and other essentials. One suitcase of twenty kilos was the limit.

'I went to the Gestapo without my suitcase. I didn't even have time to say goodbye to my daughter. My wife pleaded with me to wear my army uniform with all my medals. I refused. I would not make a clown out of myself. However, I took my army book, my orders and my medals with all the certificates and citations I had earned during my years of service. When I entered the office of the Gestapo officer, I walked up to his desk, respectfully clicked my heels, and put all my documents and military decorations in front of him. He stood up angrily and slapped my face. He tore up my army book and ripped all the certificates to pieces. The medals and my orders he shoved into the waste paper basket. And all the while he kept calling me, "*Du Schweinhund! Du dreckiger Jude!*"

' "Who do you think you are! You dirty Jew!" he demanded. "*Du bist ein schmutziger Jude,*" he continued as he raged, hitting me on the face again and again.

'With his anger expended, he ordered an SD man to escort me to my home to pack my suitcase and bring me back. My wife cried as she packed my things. She loved me and I loved her. We were very happy together. She was not Jewish, but every Friday night she lit the candles for my sake. In honour of the Sabbath, she cooked fish in the Jewish style, and for the Passover she never forgot to buy matzos. She did not convert; neither did I. I was always Jewish in the years of my active service and, as a young officer, I enjoyed marching the Jewish soldiers to the synagogue for prayers on Friday nights. Yes, my young friend, I am a Jew, but I must be honest with you. I love my fatherland. I love Germany. It is my country.'

I said nothing. 'They told me I would be resettled in the east,' he went on. 'I was sure they would send me to Russia. As you see, I finished up here.' The old man did not realise that he had not yet been fully resettled, and it wasn't long before he was indeed sent to the 'east'.

Within a few months, the German Jews were reduced from healthy human beings to skeletons. From well-dressed elegant people, they became homeless tramps. They had no facilities to wash and, in exchange for food, they sold most of their clothing to the shady characters who had contacts with the Germans at the Baluter Market or the Kripo. The Polish Jews in the ghetto looked just as bad; their conditions were no better but, somehow, they seemed to cope better.

The Jews from western Europe came from a different environment. Their standard of living had been higher than that of the Polish Jews so they found it more difficult to adjust to the sudden shift in circumstances that had befallen them. Out of desperation they accepted deportation in the hope that, by leaving the ghetto, life would be better. They were people with a different mentality, from a different culture, with a higher education. They were very much like the Germans themselves, with great respect for authority. They used to say: 'The German authorities said so. They have promised,' and this was their downfall. By believing that they were going to be resettled on the land where there would be no shortages of food, and where accommodation would supposedly be much better, they voluntarily registered for deportation. Quite a number of the German Jews, however, committed suicide rather than be deported.

By using lies and devious tricks, the Germans lured the deportees into a sense of security. Victims were given a special food ration of bread, sausage, margarine, jam and sugar for their journey, to entice them into the cattle trains. Every person was supplied with warm underwear, mittens and earmuffs for the colder climate in the east where they were to be resettled to work on the land. Because the use of German money was strictly forbidden in the

Lodz ghetto, those who had no money were given small amounts of Reichsmarks to see them through until they were able to 'start earning'. Such were the means by which the Germans enticed their victims into the gas chambers.

Similarly, back in late 1941, on 17 November, Rumkowski had given a soothing speech to fifteen young couples from the contingent of newly arrived western Jews whom he ceremoniously married. In this speech, he apologised for having requisitioned their solitary one hundred Reichsmarks. He spoke with compassion when wishing them a happy future. Then he announced that ten thousand ghetto inhabitants would be sent out of the ghetto and 'resettled to work in the country'. He revealed his intention of setting up an old people's home for the western European Jews, and appealed to the parents of the young married couples to calm their children. Only disaster and bloodshed could follow should they show hostility to the authorities.[20]

The deportations of the western Jews were now coming to an end. By the end of 1942, most of the Austrian and German Jews had been taken away. But the rounding up of ghetto-dwellers continued nightly as the Jewish police and Sonderkommando dragged people from their beds.

From 1 July till 31 December 1942, 1,100,224.66 Reichsmarks were deposited in the Litzmannstadt Gettoverwaltung account No. 12300. The money was derived from Jewish slave labour. From the above account, funds were transferred to the RSHA to cover the cost of the Sonderbehandlung at Chelmno.[21] The Jews from the Lodz ghetto bore the cost of their own transportation and extermination.

Dreams and realities

An ancient Jewish proverb teaches us that it is better to be a living dog than a dead lion. Those still alive in the ghetto persuaded themselves that somehow they would survive; but the misery and gloom deepened from day to day. The ghetto was covered by a heavy blanket of snow, with an angry frost biting mercilessly at the exhausted inhabitants, penetrating every bone, every joint of the skeletons wrapped in rags. The frost burst the pipes, causing water to leak over the staircases and down the walls.

Inside our apartment, the thick frost covering our walls froze into beautiful designs, inspiring my daydreaming as I floated away to a fantasy land on a distant continent, rich with fruit, flowers and palm trees. The tropics with their lush vegetation became a constant dream.

When not at work, people mostly stayed in bed, fully dressed, to keep warm. I would stare endlessly at the landscapes painted by the frost on the windows. In my dreams I sailed off to the Great Barrier Reef, following the journey of *The Children of Captain Grand* by Jules Verne, and explored the Australian continent. At the time, Australia was only a dream for me. My mother used to say to Lipek and me, 'One day, when you finish your education, we will go to live in Australia.' Only one of us ever made it.

Daydreaming became the most important part of life. My dreams were a blessing, an escape, the only moments of freedom behind the barbed wires. Whenever I wanted something in reality, daydreaming about it first helped me to succeed. The first president of the State of Israel, Chaim Weizmann, said: 'He who is not a dreamer is not a realist.' The truth of this I learned very early in the Lodz ghetto, where I began to understand the meaning of the verses of Papiernikov's song *So What*:

> *Zol zain, az ikh boy in der luft mayne shleser.*
> *Zol zain, az mayn got iz in gantsn nishto,*
> *In troym iz mir heler, in troym iz mir beser,*
> *In kholem der himl nokh bloyer fun bloi.*

> *Zol zain, az ikh vel keyn mol tsum tsil nisht derlangen*
> *Zol zain, az mayn shif vet nisht kumen tsum breg,*
> *Mir geyt nisht in dem, ikh zol hobn dergangen,*
> *Mir geit nor der gang oyf a zunikn veg.*

So what if I'm building castles in the air,
So what if my God isn't there at all,
In my dream things are brighter, they're better,
Dreaming, the sky's bluer than blue.

So what if I never reach my goal,
So what if my ship doesn't make it to shore,
The main thing for me is not to get through,
The main thing is just to journey in sunshine.

These words, and my mother's beautiful voice, still ring in my ears to this day. *So What* was one of the many songs she used to sing to me as a little boy when putting me to sleep.

The year 1942 brought a harsh winter. When eventually the frost surrendered to the spring, the ghetto was suffused with the smell of overflowing latrines. The melting whiteness of the snow was overlaid with big patches of a slimy yellow-brown. The terrible stench made me horribly nauseous.

Hardly anyone had a decent pair of shoes on his feet. The exceptions were the Jewish police officers, the Sonderkommando, and the high-ranking dignitaries of the ghetto. The grey, everyday ghetto-dwellers wore clogs, with their feet wrapped in rags to prevent them from freezing. My feet were always damp from the melting snow that penetrated the canvas of my clogs. At times they bled from the harsh canvas, rubbing my skin.

The faecalists

The most harrowing sight in the Lodz ghetto were the 'faecalists', the toilet cleaners. The majority of them were sentenced to clean toilets as a punishment for breaking the 'law'. Usually their crimes were petty theft: stealing a potato or breaking off a plank from a wall or fence for firewood. Hardly a timber structure survived the winter in spite of the threat of deportation. Most of the fences had disappeared long ago.

The faecalists looked inhuman. Wrapped in rags, their hands, faces and clothes were completely covered with human excrement. With their bare hands they dipped buckets into the toilets, which usually overflowed into the courtyards, spreading typhus, forcing us to walk ankle deep in human excrement. The whole ghetto stank: it seemed to be sinking in filth.

The faecalists filled up their drums, which were mounted on specially constructed carriages, to which they were harnessed like beasts. They pulled these carriages through the ghetto streets on the way to a specially dug disposal pit, at Marysin, spilling the foul liquid as they went. Their exhausted, grey faces wore permanent grimaces of pain and suffering. They were agony incarnate and their life span was very short. They had no means of hygiene; changes of clothes were non-existent, and standing near them was impossible. Their only reward for this work was an extra bowl of soup thickened with a little flour, with a few more slices of potato floating on its surface. This was handed out to them from a special kitchen so as not to have them standing in the same queues with the rest of us.

One of the faecalists had been a business colleague of my father's. His name was Chaim Sobotski, an importer-wholesaler of tropical fruit at the Jona Pilitzers market, a member of a well-known family of wealthy merchants in pre-war Lodz.

In the ghetto, Chaim Sobotski lived with his wife and child in a small room at No. 4 Lagiewnicka Street. For stealing three potatoes he was punished with cleaning the toilets. His young wife, whom I remembered from before the war, had been an attractive, sophisticated woman. She joined her husband in his task, harnessing herself up to one of the drums, emptying the toilets alongside him.

My father and I used to visit them from time to time in their home but stopped soon after they became toilet cleaners. To be in their small room became quite unbearable. They stayed together with their only child, a three-year-old boy, till the day of their deportation.

The death of a Rothschild

A special place in the world of my past was the adjacent neighbourhood at No. 11 Zgierska Street, which housed the millinery factory, employing approximately sixteen hundred people. They produced fashionable hats with the most beautiful trimmings, and slippers for men and women. Looking at the variety of styles and selection of colours, it was hard to believe that we were in a ghetto, dying of starvation.

The courtyard at No. 11 was surrounded by two, three-storey apartment buildings at ninety-degree angles to one another. Zgierska Street from 11 to 17 had the look of a wealthy suburb. The buildings were elegant European apartments. They all overlooked the barbed wires of the ghetto. In the front section at No. 11 on the first floor lived Dr Leon Szykier with his wife, son, daughter and mother-in-law. Dr Szykier was a humble man. When the ghetto was formed he was appointed as the director of the health department and the deputy to Rumkowski.

On 6 May 1941, Dr Szykier had resigned from the position of Rumkowski's deputy. Such a resignation, especially in the early stages of the ghetto, required enormous strength of character. As deputy, he had been a most important dignitary, his position providing him and his entire family with all their needs and desires. His home had had permanent police protection, exempting his apartment from being entered by the Jewish police; a horse-drawn coach with coachmen was always standing by, with a Jewish police officer to accompany him on his trips around the ghetto. Dr Szykier had privileges equal to those of Rumkowski.

His resignation had been in keeping with his character and integrity. He had understood from the very beginning that his position would involve him in activities in which he was not prepared to participate. A far-sighted man with a high moral code, he could see what the Germans were up to, and would have nothing to do with their crimes. From the moment of his resignation, Dr Szykier had become an everyday ghetto Jew practising his medical profession.

On a cold winter night, out of desperation and in need of medical help, I knocked at his door. Without hesitation, he came to see my sick mother. That was the beginning of our friendship. He became our family doctor and, in the course of visiting our home, he befriended my father.

But Dr Szykier is not the only reason that No. 11 Zgierska Street is so deeply engraved in my memory. It was also because of Mr Rothschild, a Viennese Jew in his mid-sixties, who was brought into the ghetto with other western European Jews at the end of 1941. He was a man of medium stature, cultured and softly spoken; a good-natured, gentle person. When I saw him for the first time, he was immaculately dressed and cleanly shaven, the image of an upper class, western European gentleman. It was painful to watch the aristocrat become a beggar. He wandered the streets, begging for a bit of hot soup. The Jewish policeman on duty at the kitchen window urged him to go home, not to make a nuisance of himself.

'But dear sir,' Rothschild answered with tears in his eyes, 'I have no home. Please, officer, just a little bit of soup, just a few spoons. You will save my life.'

The policeman, helpless, repeated: 'Sir, please go home! I have no soup for you. You get yours like everybody else.'

But Rothschild would not listen, insisting that the policeman let him pass. He wanted to see the manager of the kitchen, ignoring the fact that begging in the ghetto was useless.

When I saw Rothschild in December 1941, the frost burned with ferocity, and the courtyard was covered with a heavy snow. He was moving the weight of his body from one foot to the other, trying to keep warm. I could hear the voice of the kitchen manager reprimanding him for behaving like a beggar, but the policeman on duty came to Rothschild's defence, telling the manager not to be hard on him.

'Give him a bit of soup. Don't you know who he is?'

The manager answered curtly. 'Who cares who he is — or who he was!'

But Rothschild persisted until the manager took the rusty pot out of his hand and brought back a bit of hot liquid, handing it to the old man. He praised the manager for having been his saviour, promising him that he would give him his signature and, after the war, the Rothschild family would reward him.

I saw his tears and heard him mumble: 'I am a respectable gentleman. I am not a beggar. I am a man with a name.' Thanking the manager and the policeman, he walked away slowly; but, day after day, he would return.

As time passed, his appearance deteriorated. He stopped shaving and washing. His shirt and tie became grubby, and his shoes fell apart. They had not been made for ghetto winters. His once beautiful grey-and-white herringbone overcoat became filthy, with its right patch-pocket half-torn, hanging down. His pants became too long, falling off his body as he shrank from rapid loss of weight. The cuffs of his trousers became frayed, wet and dirty from being constantly dragged in the mud and wet snow. His elegant hat became dirty and squashed, sitting askew on his head.

Mr Rothschild's smooth gentle face turned into a mask of misery. His voice became weaker as he stood in front of the kitchen window begging for soup day after day. At times, the manager lost his temper, shouting at him: 'Go somewhere else. I can't give you any more soup. I have no right to do that.' Yet the policemen never insulted him nor did they mishandle him. The workers from the hat factory queuing for their soup watched Mr Rothschild in silence.

One day, as I passed the courtyard at 11 Zgierska Street, I saw a body lying face down in the mud of the melting snow near the kitchen window. The policeman on duty was bending over the body, trying to revive him by rubbing his hands and face with snow.

Someone remarked bitterly: 'What are you doing? Why are you trying to revive him? Let him be! Let him die! He's better off dead.'

On that day in the Lodz ghetto, Mr Rothschild from Vienna became just one of the many cadavers waiting to be collected by the large horse-drawn, platform carriage with a big black box mounted on top of it. It cruised the streets, collecting the dead and taking them to the cemetery to dispose of them without a funeral. No gravestone, no marking.

11 Zgierska Street continued in its usual routine. The workers from the hat factory still queued up in silence to collect their daily soup. From time to time, Yankele Herszkowicz, the ghetto troubadour, turned up with his latest compositions about life in the ghetto. Most of his songs were about the Emperor Rumkowski, whom he constantly praised with humour and sarcasm for his great 'wisdom' and 'enterprising genius'. His lyrics also described food rations and the ghetto diet. One of the most popular personalities in the ghetto streets and courtyards, Yankele had a talent for entertainment that brightened up the mood of the hungry inhabitants whenever he performed. He was also a skilled poet and folk singer, able to make us laugh at our own misery. As time went on, Yankele was joined by a Viennese violinist, Karol Rozenzweig, who helped embellish his performances.

Rumkowski, who had no sense of humour, did not take kindly to Yankele's lyrics. He eventually silenced him by bribing him with a job. Yankele became a messenger in one of the offices. His accompanist, Rozenzweig, was deported with all the western Jews, and we missed the fun and the pleasure we had derived from their performances. Yet, although Yankele stopped performing on a full-time basis, he still appeared occasionally, and his songs continued to be sung, becoming part of the ghetto culture.

A popular chorus of Yankele's was:

> *Es iz a brokh zu undz di Lodzher yatn,*
> *Es is a brokh, es helft nisht keyn geveyn,*
> *Nor mir, di lodzher yatn, mir fayfn dokh oyf ale shlek.*

> Woe is to us, the tough guys of Lodz,
> Woe upon woe, no wailing will save us,
> But we're the tough guys of Lodz,
> Still whistling at every blow.

Typhoid fever

The misery in the ghetto grew as the population rapidly shrank. People died in their thousands as another winter began, and I dreaded the miserable cold even more than the hunger. The frost and the wet were silent but merciless killers.

It happened at the beginning of February 1942 that my mother woke up in the middle of the night, and I heard her whisper my name, very softly, so as not to wake the others. I walked over to her bed and put my hand on her forehead. She was burning with a high fever. My cold hand on her forehead seemed to soothe her headache, and she asked me for a drink. Water could not be stored inside the house at night as it froze, so I went downstairs and broke off a few icicles that were hanging from the window ledges. This was the only refreshment I could give her.

From the next morning, I took over the nursing of her as well as the running of our household. Being the youngest and physically the fittest, I was the most suited. Dr Szykier became our ally. Although my mother had typhus, he did not report her case to the ghetto health authorities, because they would have taken her to the infectious diseases hospital — a very dangerous place owing to the surprise visits by the SS on round-up detail. The medication there was very limited and the care very poor. The main objective of hospitalising the contagiously ill was to quarantine them, not to cure them.

I reorganised our household. My mother's cutlery and crockery were separated; her sheets and night-wear I washed and disinfected. All that she used, I separated from the rest of the household's belongings. I got hold of a big bag of chlorine, which I diluted, and washed the floor in our room every night before going to bed, burning the polish off the floor and the skin off my hands. My mother was quarantined as best as possible from the rest of the family but, with my grandmother, father and brother, we totalled five adults in one large room. Except me, nobody in the house came into direct contact with my mother. Dr Szykier explained the disease, its symptoms, its characteristics and how it developed. Apart from disinfecting everything my mother used, he warned me to wash my hands whenever I touched her or her things.

'I have no medication,' he told me. 'We have to leave it to her metabolism to defeat the sickness. She will perspire heavily, but keep her body covered to prevent frost bite.'

On his next visit, Dr Szykier brought me a white coat and left a few pain killers — that was all he had. Before leaving, he called out to me as he stood in the doorway:

'One last thing: don't ever eat anything your mother leaves unfinished.'

Many days and sleepless nights passed. Eventually, the moment came when my mother's temperature shot up to 41 degrees. I kept washing her face and body with cold water. Dr Szykier came late that evening, and checked her pulse and temperature. She was moaning and unconscious, and her temperature climbed to 41.5 degrees.

'Tonight is the turning point in your mother's sickness,' said Dr Szykier. 'Courage, my son. She is very weak. I hope she makes it. Courage, sonny — and keep her body cool.'

He helped me to wrap her in a wet, cold sheet which I kept wet all night. I filled a rubber bottle with ice to keep her head cold. The cold winter, although painful and the cause of a lot of misery, in this instance was kind. The sick who needed the ice had an unlimited supply.

All night I washed her face. Occasionally, she opened her eyes, staring aimlessly; from time to time, her pupils rolled back in her head, making me fear that death was imminent. My fears increased with her rising temperature as it climbed to 42 degrees. That night was the longest I had yet experienced. Sitting next to her, I made up my mind that the moment she died I would go to the wires. I could not face life without her.

Late next morning, my mother's temperature suddenly dropped to below normal. For the first time in many days, her forehead was cool. Slowly, she opened her eyes. They were clear and focussed. She was quite lucid, speaking very faintly, complaining that she felt very weak. Her face looked drawn, her eyes deeply sunken with dark rings under them. I sat on her bed caressing her hands, telling her that she had been saved, that the danger was over, 'You'll be well again. I'll take care of you.'

She slept for many hours. I observed her attentively, watching her breathing. At times I thought it stopped, and I put my ear close to her chest to check if she still had a heartbeat.

I had seen death before, many times over, but when confronted by my mother's mortality I lost my own desire to go on living. I was exhausted and had a throbbing headache. I felt more tired than I had ever felt before. My whole body was wracked with pain, all my joints aching. I lay across the bed near my mother's feet and fell asleep.

It was late in the evening that my brother woke me up when he returned from work. He looked tired. Soon after, my father also came home. Recently he had deteriorated, and I could no longer ignore his swollen face and feet.

I served a bit of soup concocted from whatever I had been able to scratch together. We were all very happy that mother's temperature had dropped. Although I still felt inordinately tired, I did not realise that I was falling ill. I thought it was exhaustion that was making me dizzy. When Dr Szykier came in later that evening, he looked at mother's eyes and, touching her forehead, gave her a big smile.

'You will slowly feel better, Mrs Biderman. You've been in good hands.' Then he looked at me. 'I think you're running a temperature, sonny. Get undressed and let me have a good look at you.'

I lay down on my bed while he looked at my tongue and my eyes. Pressing my tummy he said, 'There is a little swelling building up. You may be developing typhus.'

In a way, it came as no surprise. I had eaten the leftovers from my mother's plate, unable to bring myself to throw away those few bites. My temperature climbed higher. My body ached more and more. My headache was persistent.

Within a few days of my falling sick, mother's temperature rose again. In despair, Dr Szykier shrugged his shoulders.

'A relapse,' he said. 'It happens. But it's usually in a lighter form, and less dangerous.'

He became a daily visitor to our home. Generally he came late, after his long day's work. As he lived next door, he liked to stay over and chat with my father. The two of them had grown fond of one another, and often they talked long into the night. I listened to every word they said. They spoke about the Germans, their culture, their great philosophers, composers and scientists. They could not grasp how a nation that was considered one of the most civilised in modern times could behave like ruthless killers. Neither could I. Not then; not now.

My father spoke about the role the Church played in the eternal tragedy of the Jewish people. He spoke of the Spanish Inquisition and its attendant horrors.

'The difference today, however, is that those Jews who converted to Christianity are not saved. The authorities go back to their great grandparents. Many of these so-called Jews didn't even know they had Jewish ancestors until they were told by the Gestapo. Some of them were devout supporters of Hitler and members of the Nazi Party. Amongst the old German Jews in the ghetto, some of them carry photos around of their grandchildren and children, showing them off with pride in German uniforms. I've seen one of those Jews pointing his finger at a photo of a young German in charge of a heavy tank with the Eiffel Tower in the background. He said with a smile on his face, 'You see, this is my grandson.'

Mr Goldstein, the son-in-law of the optician next door, now worked for the electricity department. He told us a bizarre story in a similar vein. One day, with an order to inspect the electrical installation in a little cottage in a side street off Brzezinska Street, he came across a very young, formerly high-ranking Nazi who was brought into the ghetto and left in the custody of Rumkowski. He had been a führer of the Baltic Hitler Youth, one of the top lieutenants of von Schirach. His deputy, jealous of his position, had investigated him and found out that he was of Jewish descent. It landed him in the ghetto.

Upon his arrival in the ghetto, Rumkowski took special care of his needs, providing him with a comfortable cottage that had everything one could wish for. He even had a housekeeper, a German Jewish lady, who meticulously looked after the cottage and its tenant. For now, I will simply call him 'Siegfried'.

When I first saw him walking down Brzezinska Street, he looked lost and dejected, walking aimlessly. He wore civilian clothing without the Yellow Star of David, which was highly illegal. On his head he still wore his black Hitler Youth cap, but without the swastika.

Mr Goldstein told us, 'The first time I entered the cottage, I got a shock. Suddenly I was confronted by a young German in a Nazi uniform. I just managed to stutter, "Good day, sir" and he jumped up from his couch with an outstretched right arm, clicking his heels in typical Germanic fashion.

' "Heil Hitler!" he replied loudly .

'I nearly collapsed with fear. I apologised for disturbing him, explaining why I was there. He was very formal and spoke with an authoritative voice as though giving me an order.

' "Go ahead! Do your work!" he said.

'He was dressed in a brown Nazi shirt, without the swastika on his arm. His black riding pants were tucked into his black German officer's boots. Around his waist he wore his black Hitler Youth belt with its silver buckle which was engraved with the German Eagle holding the swastika in its claws.

'I did my job as fast as possible so I could disappear. When I said goodbye, he again answered, "Heil Hitler". I was glad to get out of that place.'

From Goldstein I learned that, in the beginning, Siegfried locked himself in his cottage for many months. All he did was lie on his couch and read, day and night. His room was littered with German newspapers and magazines which were delivered to him daily by a Jewish policeman.

Siegfried was slim, of medium stature, and in his early twenties. He wore his silky, platinum-blond hair in Hitler style. He had a slim, pale, face with sky-blue eyes and a pointed nose. He was the classical prototype of an Aryan according to Hitler's dream.

It was many months before he decided to take up an occupation. He accepted a job with the factory that produced military telecommunications equipment. At work he kept to himself, communicating only with the German technicians who visited the factory.

Many months after my liberation, in October, 1945, I visited the Displaced Persons camp at Zeilsheim, near Frankfurt. As I walked past the gate, I ran into my schoolfriend, Levin. We fell into each other's arms and kissed, we were so happy to have found each other alive. Our first questions were about each other's families and relations. Then he took me into his room, where I found a few familiar faces from Lodz. Amongst them was Siegfried, and we shook hands.

'Do you know who I am?' he asked with a smile.

I said, 'Yes, I do.'

He grabbed me and gave me a hug. 'This afternoon I'm getting married,' he said. 'I would very much like to have you as my guest.'

I accepted his invitation and he took me along to another barracks where he introduced me to his fiancée, a petite girl, another survivor from the concentration camps.

Later that day I witnessed their wedding ceremony performed by an American rabbi, an army chaplain. We all drank a *l'khayim* in honour of the young couple, and kissed. The rabbi brought wine, sweets and lots of special kosher food. When I listened to Siegfried repeating after the rabbi, 'Be thou my wife according to the law of Moses and of Israel,' I was overcome by a sense of unreality. Here was Siegfried, a former Hitler Youth führer, returned to Judaism, a survivor of the Lodz ghetto, Auschwitz and other camps.

From our balcony at 13 Zgierska Street, I witnessed another outlandish occurrence that took place regularly near the barbed wires. A German Jew, a sergeant with the Jewish police, came to the barbed wires at the corner of Zgierska Street and Baluter Market once a week, walking up and down nervously. Tension was painted on his face as he looked down the road, as though he was expecting something to happen. Suddenly, an approaching doroszka slowed down. On the carriage were two little boys, aged between twelve and fourteen, dressed in full Hitler Youth uniforms.

'Papa', they called out to the Jewish policeman with his yellow star, standing up and blowing kisses at him from a distance. The Jewish policeman blew back his kisses to the children across the wires. The German Schupo on guard walked in the opposite direction, though of course he was aware of the meeting; it was all pre-arranged. I never saw their mother at those meetings. She was a German but she loved her husband, and so had come from Germany to live in Lodz. In order to save her children from being locked up with their father, she signed a sworn affidavit declaring that the children were conceived by another man who was a pure Aryan. When the ghetto was liquidated, the Jewish policeman was sent off the to the 'east', together with all the other Jews, never to see his wife and children again.

My father's discussions with Dr Szykier continued night after night:

'I was told, doctor, that the Church didn't even try to help the Roman Catholics and Protestants living in the ghetto. I believe that there are nearly three hundred of them, and that some go back two or three generations as Christians.

'When I see them go to the chapel Rumkowski provided for them, I can't help but feel sorry for them. In the eyes of the Germans, they are Jews like us and have to wear the yellow star. The German Christian theologians of all denominations swore allegiance to Hitler. The Pope and the Vatican are silent! In their silence, they are all giving their consent.

'Doctor, even Chmielnicki, that master of the pogrom, was more accommodating towards the Jews than the Germans are today. He spared the life of every Jew who accepted the Cross.'

'In my opinion, Mr Biderman,' said the doctor, 'what we Jews are confronted with today is far more dangerous than anything ever before. Their education and technology make the Germans a far greater danger than the crusaders or the primitive Cossacks. And I do not believe that we have seen the worst.'

'Look at the Poles,' my father said contemplatively. 'They are helping them. And while Germany may well lose the war' — he hesitated for a fraction of a second — 'for us, doctor, for us it may be too late.'

Dr Szykier was pensive as he drew heavily on his cigarette. 'Whenever I have to deal with a mental case,' he said, 'I always find the intelligent, well-educated patient the hardest to handle. He is far more complex and dangerous. The Germans are like that: intelligent, well-educated and so, as madmen, far more complex and dangerous.'

It was late and I had a high temperature, so I went to bed, still able to hear their conversation from where I lay. By nature I am impatient and not a very good listener; however, when the two of them got together, my fascination with their subject made me calm. They were my teachers. They taught me to observe, analyse and understand the world around me as a Jew. Those nights with their lengthy discussions were my university.

Both of them sat motionless, looking down at the floor. It was Dr Szykier who broke the silence.

'This is the third year we have been locked up in the ghettos, dying of starvation and epidemics. But this is still much too slow for them. They are anxious to destroy us faster, in case they lose the war; then, at least, they will have won against the Jews. The less food they give us, the more they feed us with lies and false rumours. And the ghetto population believes them. They have to believe in something. The latest rumours about the deported Jews who live on the land amongst the peasants and how good they have it are fairy tales. Why do you think I resigned as Rumkowski's deputy? The reality is ... ' Dr Szykier stopped as if afraid to say what he had on his mind. Again, he drew deeply on his cigarette and, in a sad, low voice said 'Our situation is very grave.'

Silence fell again.

'You know, doctor,' said my father, 'I have dealt with Poles every day of my business life. Not with the average, simple peasant, but with the educated and well-to-do upper classes. Amongst them were some of the most renowned Polish nobles; they were my suppliers. None of them offered to help.

'I became very friendly with one; we did business for many years. A well-educated young man, he inherited an estate not far from Lodz; he is very wealthy, too. Soon after the Germans invaded, I gave him some of our valuables for safe keeping. Knowing that here in the city the Germans would have taken them from us, I thought they would be safer with him in the country. I see him occasionally driving past the ghetto in his horse-drawn carriage. The first time, I waved my hand to greet him. He poked his coachman who turned his head to look at me. Then they both burst out laughing. He pointed the horsewhip in my direction with a teasing smile on his face, mocking me. Now, when I see him coming, I hide behind the curtains; but he always looks up with a grin, searching for me.

'You know, when the Germans closed the Jewish bank accounts and I was left without the means to pay him for his merchandise, he used to give me unlimited credit — for many thousands of zlotys. He trusted me and I trusted him.'

My father and the doctor both looked tired. Their heads hung between their shrunken shoulders, and their faces were drawn. Their resigned mood irritated me and I lost my patience, sitting up on my bed and saying with anger, 'I know it is bad but we must not give up. We must not surrender. I don't think all is lost.' As I spoke I became very agitated. 'I promised myself that I would see the end of Hitler. You must think as I do. Don't give up. Once you do that you are dead.'

Dr Szykier and my father merely looked at each other, assuming my fever had slightly deranged me. Dr Szykier blew clouds of smoke from his cigarette as he stood up.

'It's time for me to move,' he declared. 'It's getting very late.' Then, turning to me, he said, 'Please, Abraham, calm down. You know you should rest.'

Protekcja

It was the coldest winter I can ever remember. I hoped that the Germans would freeze in Russia and meet the same fate as Napoleon had. My temperature was very high. I felt dizzy, but had to go out to queue up for medication. Standing for hours in the deep snow, my feet became wet and frozen. At times, I was so dizzy that I lost my balance.

'What's the use of your queuing up for medicine that you may not live to have the use of?' Dr Szykier would admonish me.

My father's feet were so swollen that he could hardly walk. My brother, who was constantly sick, could not risk standing out in the cold. I had to be the strong one. Somehow, I was still the fittest of all of them.

While I had typhus, I stayed in bed for a couple of days, at which time my temperature climbed to its maximum — so high that I lost consciousness. Then, overnight, it dropped. I woke up to see Dr Szykier with his hand on my forehead. It seemed like years since I had seen him last, though apparently he had been in to see me many times in the preceding days. In my delirium, I had not recognised him.

'You've turned the corner, sonny,' he told me now. 'But you told me some pretty interesting things while the fever had you.'

It seems I had told Dr Szykier about Limping Laib who, from childhood, had been my very good friend. Now, in the ghetto, he was one of David Gertler's lieutenants: one of the 'strong men'.

For as long as I could remember, Limping Laib had always been very friendly towards me and my family. Before the war, my father and his younger brother managed the family business. It was there, as a child, that I met Limping Laib, at which time he was a battler, trying to get into the wholesale fruit business. A likeable fellow who made friends easily, he became my father's protégé.

Laib was tall, good looking, and somehow always managed to be immaculately dressed. His wooden leg fascinated me. He had a kind face with a soft smile; in his off-white Stetson he looked like the wild-west screen hero, Tim McCoy. I always admired Laib's physique. Even with his wooden leg he could run faster than many who had two legs. Whenever Lipek and I came to visit our father at the store as little boys, Laib would grab me with his strong arms and take me across the street to the sweets shop and let me have whatever my heart desired. This made him my best friend and, in turn, helped him to gain the sympathy of my father.

Our family was influential in the fruit business and our name was highly regarded. My grandfather, Reb Itshe Mayer, was the founder of our family's business. He was a pious Jew of small stature with a patriarchal silver-grey beard, and dressed in the traditional black attire worn by the orthodox Jews in Poland. Reb Itshe Mayer was highly respected amongst the wholesalers in Lodz, and was one of the first merchants in the city to import tropical fruit from overseas. Not only was he one of the oldest wholesalers on the Jona Pilitzer Market, he was also the president of the synagogue. Being his grandson, I was treated with great respect.

Now, in the ghetto, all this seemed so distant, so remote as to belong to another world; but Limping Laib had been on my mind for quite some time now. I was faced with the moral dilemma of whether or not to go to him. His connections, while influential, were also of questionable character. Still, I told myself, this was the ghetto. In order to survive, one had to be prepared to ask for favours: be a protégé of somebody high up. One had to have 'protekcja'. Without it, one was doomed.

Eventually, necessity made up my mind for me. Summoning all my courage, I scrambled out of bed, still wobbly on my feet in the aftermath of the typhus. The need for medication was my driving force. My mother still had a lingering fever from her relapse, and had developed a huge boil on her left hip which was painful-looking and growing larger every day. It grew to the size of a small loaf of bread, and was excruciating for her. She badly needed pain-killers for she hardly slept, constantly moaning and, at times, crying like a child. The only treatment we had was hot salt-compresses to speed up the softening of the accumulated pus.

Dr Szykier was helpless. He had no medication. He told us we would have to be patient until the boil softened sufficiently to lance. He suggested I find some pain-killing injections. The only way to obtain them was on the black market, where I could purchase them in exchange for food. Already we had drastically reduced consumption of our rations, and this was still not enough.

I went to see my closest childhood friend, Rivek Skoczylas, and I told him of my predicament. He, in turn, advised me to see Beniek Dyzenhaus, whom I had known for many years. Before the war, Beniek had worked as a nurse at the Poznanski's Jewish Hospital in Lodz. In the ghetto he was a medical assistant, working in the hospitals. He was well known, especially to those in need. People would knock on his door day and night, and Beniek simply could not refuse to help.

He willingly gave my mother the pain-killing injections she so badly needed. He also managed to get a few calcium injections for my brother and, from time to time, a little bottle of Vigantol for my father. This contained the most essential vitamins, and was the most popular medicine in the ghetto, considered to be a life-saver. Vigantol could only be obtained on the black market for food. Beniek gave it away for free.

Whenever I knocked on his door, he was always ready to come. His wife was not the same. If she answered my knock she would say, 'Beniek is not home. He is at the hospital. Don't come knocking on the door in the middle of the night.' But Beniek would recognise my voice.

'Abraham,' he would call, 'don't take any notice of her. Just wait, I'm getting dressed.' At times he was so worn out that he fell asleep on his feet, but Beniek never refused.

Once, I remember, it must have been three in the morning when I got him out of bed. As we ran through a snow storm, I kept apologising for dragging him from his warm bed in the middle of a frosty night. He cut me off. 'Stop carrying on like an old woman. Get a move on.'

On entering our home, Beniek opened his case and took out a little box of ampoules. Showing them to me he said, 'These are my last few. Before the night is over I will have none left. Medical supplies are drying up. The bastards won't let us have any. Not even the most basic medication. It's going to be tough. Now you will have to procure it from the black market.' And that is what prompted me to go to Limping Laib.

I had not seen him for a long time. His office was on the corner of Lagiewnicka and Pieprzowa Streets where the weighbridge of the Jona Pilitzer Market was situated. In front of the gate was a big crowd of pushing, shouting people; some were falling over, being trampled into the snow. They were all screaming, crying and begging for help. Everybody wanted a favour from the famous Laib. The gates were tightly guarded by the Sonderkommando. To push through was an impossible task, and even after that you had to be allowed to enter. I pushed and shoved for hours in the deep snow, freezing, spending all day without success. It looked as if I would never be able to see him. In the ghetto one had to know how to push and make a path with one's elbows. At this, I was not the best.

After many hours in the street, frozen to the marrow of my bones, I went home empty-handed. My father was already back from work. I felt totally defeated. I suddenly turned to my father and asked sarcastically, 'Please tell me, father, how come your colleagues, the other inspectors at the vegetable department, look so well? They all dress in shining officer's boots and riding pants with their beautiful seven-eighths coats. They dress like kings. Tell me how come?'

I had never confronted him like this before, and he gave me a hard look and walked away in silence. I was very upset with myself. I knew I had offended him, which I had not really intended. I wasn't angry with him. I was exhausted, confused and very hungry. The typhus had drained the last of my energy. I was so tired that I could not control myself and had turned against my father although he was not to blame.

The next morning, my mother called me over to her bedside.

'I don't ever want to hear you speak to your father the way you spoke last night, Abraham,' she said softly and without anger.

I realised I had been wrong, and I was very upset. Although I did not agree with my father's views, I loved him and had great respect for him. He was a very gentle and softly spoken man, always analysing and weighing up every situation. He never acted unless it was in agreement with his code of ethics. A man of great dignity, he unfortunately did not fit into this world. I apologised to my mother, explaining that I had meant no offence.

'Nevertheless,' I said, 'it would have done no harm to anybody in this world if father had tried to get a bonus ration of a few potatoes, a bit of sugar, a little bit of margarine, just anything. He doesn't have to steal like the others do. He should ask for it. He won't even do that! He is an idealist, a man of high principles. There is no room for such men in this world.'

My mother replied, 'If only more men like your father lived in this world, it would be a better place.'

'But what's the good of it?' I demanded. The world is not the way my father would like. It's corrupt, and it's every man for himself. My father acts like the captain who honourably goes down with his vessel. Tell me, mama, is trying to survive a crime? Do you think the few potatoes father would get as a bonus would deprive thousands of their share?'

After a long silence, mother finally said, 'I have pleaded with your father many times. Last time, he said to me, "Fradl, what can I do? What do you expect me to do? Do you want me to become a thief?"

'I said, "Shimon, you don't have to be a thief, but surely you can ask for a little bonus. You meet with Mr Szczeslywy twice a week. You are in contact with Mr Garfinkel every day. He respects you. Why don't you ask him for a bonus? Surely he will not refuse. [Szczeslywy was the director of the department for food supply in the ghetto, and a very close associate of Rumkowski; Garfinkel was the general manager of the vegetable department.]

'You know what your father said? "Fradl, please, you must understand: I can't beg. I can't do it. I can only accept when they offer it to me. Besides, imagine if everybody stole or got bonuses. What will we give to the people?"

' "Shimon," I said to your father, "you are not a beggar; you are a respected man with dignity. Asking is not begging. Others do it all the time. You are not asking for yourself, but for your wife and your sons. It is two years since Lipek became sick; now I'm sick, so is Abraham, and you are shrinking from day to day. Do you realise that in the last two years neither I nor Abraham has eaten the full ration? We have had to trade part of our rations for injections. We sell the margarine, the jam and part of the sugar for medicine. Please be reasonable. Ask your bosses for a bonus!" '

I listened to my mother and made up my mind.

Later that day, I went across again to the gate leading to Laib's office. This time I was determined and aggressive. I pushed and shoved, using my elbows like never before, and eventually found myself inside the gate. Authoritatively, I spoke to the officer in charge of the Sonder guard, practically ordering him to announce my name to Laib.

'Tell him it's his friend who must talk to him. Tell him it's urgent. My name is Biderman.'

'What is it you want?' the officer asked.

'I told you. My name is Biderman. Go and tell Laib I want to talk to him. It's very urgent!'

The officer soon came back, calling my name, and I followed him into Laib's office. Entering, the officer clicked his shiny boots and obediently announced:

'Panie Laib, Biderman is here.'

When the officer left, Laib eyed me quizzically.

'Ah! So it's you,' he said. 'Where is your father? Isn't he in the ghetto?'

'Yes, of course he is.'

'So why don't I ever see him?' Laib demanded.

'You see him, all right. You see him very often. It's just that you don't recognise him any more. And it's no wonder. He's a walking death notice.'

Laib's face became serious. 'Then why doesn't he come to see me, eh?'

I stood silent and motionless. Laib looked tense.

'Well, well,' he chuckled. But there was no smile on his face. 'Of course Shimon never comes to see me! How would it look? The royalty of Jona Pilitzer Market reduced to coming to the Limping Laib! That would be below his dignity, wouldn't it? So he sends you!'

'No, Laib,' I said, 'he doesn't even know I'm here.'

This seemed to upset him even more.

'Laib, please,' I implored, 'don't criticise my father. He has done you no harm. If anything, he did a lot of good for you once, didn't he?'

Laib adjusted his wooden leg sideways. 'Are you well?' he asked, finally.

'Yes.'

'You don't look the best to me.'

'I've just had typhus but I'll be all right. Mother is very sick, though. She has typhus for the second time. She's very weak.' I took a deep breath. 'Laib, I'm here to ask for help. Do it for old times' sake. I'm not the little boy you used to play with. I didn't come for chocolates. I need injections, pain-killers. I need calcium for my brother. My father is run down and sick, too. Maybe a bottle of Vigantol. Can you do something?'

For a moment Laib was silent. Then he said brusquely, 'Have you got medical prescriptions?'

Wordlessly, I handed him a bundle of rolled-up papers. He turned them over and wrote on the back, 'Prosze Wydac' ('Please hand out'), initialling them with his big 'L'.

'Go to the Sonderkommando head office,' he said. 'You will get all you need at their dispensary.'

Gertler's headquarters of the Special Bureau was at No. 96 Zgierska Street, housed in a beautiful villa that, before the war, had belonged to the Jewish family, Gayer, one of the leading yarn-dyers and textile finishers in pre-war Lodz. Now, Gertler was the most powerful man in the Lodz ghetto, Warthegau and the Warsaw ghetto. He was the personal confidant of the Gestapo chief of Litzmannstadt, Dr Bradfisch, and his deputy, Günter Fuchs. He was an associate of Gancwaijch, the chief of the Jewish police in the Warsaw ghetto. Gancwaijch was also the commandant of the infamous 'Thirteen' along with his friends, Heler, the brothers Heinoch, Mailech Cohen, Piekarczyk and many others — the most notorious Jewish Gestapo informers.

The Sonderkommando had its own, well-stocked pharmacy. After Gertler's arrest, Biebow raided the pharmacy, removing all they had; but that was much later.

Before I turned to leave, I thanked Laib and shook his hand. 'Wait, don't go yet,' he said when I had already opened the door. He started to scribble something on his note-pad and then called the officer of the guard. Handing him the note he said, 'Take care of this young man. Look after him well.'

Again I shook his hand and thanked him. As I walked out of his office, he called, 'Abraham, remember me to your father. Tell him it would do him no harm if he came to see me.'

As we walked, the officer asked me, 'Can you handle one hundred kilos of potatoes on your own?'

One hundred kilos! I only hesitated for a minute before I said, 'Of course I can! I live across the road. Give me a minute to bring my sled.'

In a flash, I was back with it, and I followed the Sonder officer across the deserted, snow-covered market that looked like a huge prison yard. As we walked, I remembered the days when Limping Laib played with me, holding me in his arms. This had once been a place full of people, noise, huge trucks, horses, carriages, porters loading and unloading. Thousands of people everywhere, yelling, screaming, haggling, carrying cases of imported fruit from Palestine: mandarins, bananas, oranges, grapefruit. From California: apples, 'Sunkist' oranges. From Italy and Spain: oranges, mandarines and grapes. From Romania and Hungary: plums, apricots, nectarines and beautiful big black cherries. From Canada: the famous 'Red Delicious' apples. The beautiful smell of exotic fruit could make you drunk. Only on the Sabbath and on Jewish holidays was the market place at rest. This was the source of the fruit supply for Lodz and the surrounding provinces, providing for over a million people.

I walked past the stores that once belonged to my family. The signs were still above the doors. I walked closer and closer. As though in a trance, forgetting why I was there, I looked at the signs and felt tears sting my eyes as I read my grandfather's business name: 'I M Biderman and Sons. Established 1892'. The other sign read 'Biderman Brothers'. I stood there, hypnotised, when the loud voice of the officer cut into my thoughts.

'Hey you! Move! It's getting late. I'm not going to wait all day!'

I caught up with him quickly as he walked down the stairs of one of the cellars. He unlocked the heavy padlocks and broke the seal that gave the place the appearance of a secret vault protecting a fortune — which indeed it was. The policeman switched on the lights to reveal a cellar full of potatoes. I couldn't believe my eyes. He urged me on as I stood there, motionless and amazed.

'Come on! Come on!' he growled. 'I haven't got all day! Let's move!'

Picking up an empty bag and grabbing a wooden shovel standing in the corner, he handed it to me, urging me to fill up the bag. The potatoes did not look real. Clean without bruises, not frozen, they were hand-picked. I did not remember ever having seen potatoes as beautiful as these.

I filled up half the bag and the officer helped me put it on the scales. It weighed sixty kilos.

'This will do for now,' he said. 'It will be easier for you if you come back again.'

He helped me up the stairs and tied the bag onto the sled. I was excited and full of energy. I took the potatoes up to our place, pushed the bag under the bed without saying a word to anyone, and rushed out again.

My mother called after me, 'Where did you get all this? Is it for us?'

'Yes it is! I'll tell you later. I must run!'

Finally it was done. When I had finished pushing the second bag under the bed, I sat down on the floor, completely exhausted.

'Is this stolen?' my mother eventually managed to ask, overcoming her astonishment.

'No,' I assured her, 'of course not.'

'But where on earth did you get so much?' she demanded.

I told her the whole story in one burst. She kissed me and smiled without saying a word. Then I showed her the medical prescriptions signed by Laib.

'You see, mother, in the ghetto you must have protekcja or else you are lost.'

I pulled out the smaller bag and picked up a few potatoes, showing them to my mother.

'Look at them!' I said. 'Have you ever seen potatoes as beautiful as these?' I kissed them. 'They look like beautiful girls.'

The Gehsperre

Spring came, and then summer. The pattern of life in the ghetto continued, day in, day out. The deportations became a daily routine. With the western Jews all deported, new volunteers were not forthcoming. Rumkowski carried on with his campaign to fulfil the German quotas, but the police and Sonderkommando had a hard task in gathering more victims. The Germans kept up the pressure, demanding more and more 'volunteers', so Rumkowski instructed the Department of Labour, Sienicki and Bernard Fuchs, to draw up lists with names. For the slightest transgressions one was put on the cattle trains.

Whilst the deportations continued, the rumours became fearsome. People were saying that half the ghetto population was to be resettled, although nobody was saying precisely where. Yet, by now, a large number of people knew what was going on in the forests of Kolo in the vicinity of Chelmno.

I worked at the department of vegetables at 25 Lagiewnicka Street, opposite the Baluter Market and the offices of Rumkowski and Biebow. Now we were ordered to vacate part of the building where our offices were situated, thus reducing our office space. We were very nervous, wondering whether this had any connection with the rumours that the ghetto population was to be cut in half. It seemed plausible enough. We relaxed, however, when we found out that the vacated space was to be occupied by a Jewish museum, but thought it a strange thing to be established in the ghetto.

The director was Rabbi Professor Emanuel Hirszberg who was assisted by his daughter. Once the museum was fully organised, the first exhibit appeared in the display window at the corner of Lagiewnicka and Zawiska Streets, opposite the Baluter Market. The exhibit represented an orthodox Jewish wedding with dolls that were artistically and beautifully made. Their clothing had been sewn in the most minute detail, cleanly and precisely in the traditional eastern European style. The faces of the dolls were lifelike and skilfully made. But why would the Germans need a Jewish museum? Professor Lucjan Dobroszycki provides the answer:

The Research Department was engaged in the production of dolls to be used by the Nazis in anti-Jewish propaganda ... [22]

[It] was really the only ghetto institution that functioned outside the administration of the Eldest of the Jews because it was established directly, by-passing M.C. Rumkowski, by the Lodz branch of the Institute of the National Socialist German Workers Party for Research into the Jewish Question, in Frankfurt am Main. The Lodz branch, directed by Adolf Wendel, a professor of biblical studies from the University of Breslau, was located at 33 Sienkiewicz St. The speciality of the Lodz branch was, as they put it, research into the East European Jewish Question and the agency set up in the ghetto was supposed to prepare specimens for anti-Jewish exhibitions and for 'scientific' study.'[23]

The month of June held many unpleasant surprises for us. Besides the panic caused by rumours of large deportations, the carpentry factory was instructed to build a gallows to accommodate ten people. Once again, Dobroszycki furnishes us with vivid detail:

> The German authorities' demand for gallows was connected with an extensive preventive police action, whose slogan was deterrence. During the liquidation of the ghetto and the deportation of the Jewish population to Chelmno, on instructions from the Reich Security Main Office (RSHA) and from Himmler himself, randomly selected Jews were hanged in order to sow fear and to discourage others from resisting deportation by hiding or fleeing. The German criminal police (Kripo) in Lodz, in a report to the police and security service in Poznan on June 9, wrote: 'Thus far, 95 Jews have been hung publicly here. The measures taken have caused the Jew to understand the severe order here, and from now on he will obey all orders completely and peace-fully.' In another report, on August 15, the Kripo reported: 'All told, and in accordance with the RSHA's instructions, there have been 13 public executions in July, of which 9 were in Warta (Sieradz county), 2 in Lask county, and 2 in the Litzmannstadt ghetto, of those escaping forced labour.'[24]

On 1 September, on the third anniversary of the outbreak of World War II, huge trucks with trailers drove up in front of the hospital at Wesola Street, taking away patients. The same occurred at the hospitals on Drewnowska, Lagiewnicka and Mickiewicza Streets. Some patients fled. The Germans demanded lists of all of them, and a search followed: the Jewish police hunted them down one by one. They were pulled out from under beds, from cupboards, attics and cellars. Nothing could save them. They were all surrendered to the Germans.

We lived with the rumours for many weeks before they were confirmed. Placards appeared on the ghetto walls announcing that on 4 September at 4.00 p.m. Mordechai Rumkowski would address the ghetto population at the Jewish fire brigade's square at 13 Lutomierska Street — the pre-war central bus stop. I went to listen and pushed my way close to where Rumkowski stood. Stanislaw Jakobson, a pre-war lawyer and now one of the ghetto judges, spoke in Polish. He informed the gathering about the order given by the German authorities that all children up to the age of ten and adults over sixty-five would have to leave the ghetto. The same applied to the sick. No mention was made by any of the speakers as to where they would be sent.

Next spoke David Warszawski in Yiddish. He was a personal adviser to Rumkowski, a pre-war textile manufacturer in Lodz. In a few words he introduced Rumkowski, who was then helped onto an office desk. His speech was brief and devastating. He explained to the thousands who had gathered that the German authorities demanded of him twenty-five thousand Jews to be resettled outside the ghetto. The ghetto, he said, would be converted into a labour camp. He repeated that all children under the age of ten and adults over sixty-five would have to be sent away. Only adults capable of working would remain.

The crowd began to shout in anger: 'Tell us where they are sending them!' Rumkowski did not answer, and the angry gathering kept calling and shouting: 'Where are they sending them? We will not give up our children!' Pandemonium broke loose. The huge crowd started to scream and push. Women were fainting and crying. The men were shouting, waving their fists.

Rumkowski was playing poker with the devil. By sacrificing the children, he thought that he could pacify the Germans and save the lives of those who stayed behind by virtue of the hard work they would do for the Germans.

The Jewish police and fire brigade stood around Rumkowski, protecting him. The table started to rock as the mass of people pressed forward threateningly. The noise became louder and louder. People became violent and fights broke out. Rumkowski grew agitated and angry, shouting threats, pointing his finger in the direction of the hecklers, threatening them with arrest, but the Jewish police were unable to contain the angry mob.

Unable to continue, Rumkowski lost control of himself, waving his arms high in the air and shouting in anger, 'I will have you all deported. I know you well. I know who you are. I will deal with all of you. You rabble-rousers! I will hand you all over to the German police!'[25]

I was pushed and shoved, pressed hard against the Jewish police. They surrounded Rumkowski. Eventually he was taken to a nearby office and, as he was pushed hard against me, I heard him mumble to himself as if he were delirious, 'The wolf wants blood! What should I do? What can I do? I have to quench his thirst! I must give up the children!'

Reinforcements of Jewish police arrived with drawn rubber truncheons, and lashed out at the public. The row grew into a vicious riot and I was knocked to the ground. At one point I felt as if I were choking. The mob surged forward, trying to get hold of Rumkowski. I struggled to my feet and somehow managed to get out of the centre of the fight. I ran home and told my mother the news. She was shocked, grabbing me in her arms and crying with fear. I calmed her as best as I could; although I was able to stop her tears, I could not contain her sorrow.

After Rumkowski's speech, placards appeared on the ghetto walls announcing that, 'As 5 September 1942, the Lodz ghetto will be under a general *Gehsperre* (curfew) from 5 p.m. until further notice ....' It was signed by the Eldest of the Jews of the Lodz ghetto.

On the fifth day of September, in the early morning, the SS came into the ghetto, assisted by the Jewish police, the Sonderkommando, and the Jewish fire brigade. They rounded up whoever they could find, building by building, room by room, in cellars and on roof-tops; then they chased the people out into the courtyards, where they were lined up in front of the SS officers who selected them. This was the first time I had witnessed selections, where the sign of a finger, to the left or the right, meant the difference between life and death. Some people were stamped on the palm of their hands.

The children, the elderly and the sick were separated and loaded onto horse-drawn carts that were guarded by the Jewish police who, in turn, were being assisted by the Jewish fire brigade. They were carted off to waiting trucks which had specially constructed high barriers to make it impossible for them to escape.

From our balcony at 13 Zgierska Street I watched the large trucks rushing past with the victims packed on top of each other. An SS man was sitting high above the victims with his submachine gun at the ready. I timed the trucks as I tried to work out where they were going. I saw them travel down Zgierska Street and turn into Limanowskiego Street, heading north towards Alexandrow. It took them about two to three hours to return for another load. At the time, we did not know where they were headed. The Germans spread rumours that the deportees had all been resettled on the land amongst the peasants.

The hospitals were evacuated in the most brutal manner. In the central ghetto hospital, at 36 Lagiewnicka Street, the newly born babies were thrown from the upper-floor windows of the maternity wing into the SS trucks waiting below whilst the SS troopers stood around.

My father and I wore yellow and white armbands identifying us as employees of the vegetable department. These armbands were of some help because the Jewish police turned a blind eye to us even though we had no official exemption. I gave my armband to my mother to wear. She was just recovering from typhus, and was still weak and run down. She looked drawn and pale. With the help of lipstick and make-up we hoped for the best. Luckily, she was never confronted with the selection; I always managed to get her past every blockade. I doubt very much if either she or my father would have passed, if it had come to it. My father looked sick, with swelling under his eyes, but he was always in a different part of the ghetto and managed to get away from the selections. My brother passed and so did my uncle Berish and aunt Sarah. My grandmother was hidden in a wardrobe, and luckily they never looked there. Thus our whole family survived the Gehsperre.

Information withheld

It was 12 September 1942, the last day of the Gehsperre. The ghetto was in a state of shock. My cousin, Tobcia Blicblau, who was twelve years of age, had not passed the selection. She had been put on a horse-drawn cart, watched by the Jewish fire brigade. As she was on her way to be loaded onto the SS trucks, Mendele, her nineteen-year-old brother, a fast-thinking and quick-moving young man, jumped onto the carriage. He urged Tobcia to jump. She was scared and hesitant, but eventually she did, with Mendele following close behind. Had he not succeeded in this daring ploy, the two of them would have finished up in Chelmno. Together they ran and hid, thus avoiding certain death.

My friend, David Rosenberg, who lived at 7 Mlynarska Street, made a similar escape. He was fourteen when he jumped off an SS truck that was on its way to the unknown. His mother was on another of those trucks; for many months, he lost his powers of speech completely, unable to tell his family what had taken place. He survived, but to this day speaks with a severe speech impediment.

13 September 1942: the Lodz ghetto was mortally wounded. Hardly a family was intact. A total of 15,685 of us — children, the sick and the old — had been carted off in a most barbaric manner. In the course of the Gehsperre, the SS were more than usually trigger happy. Their alcohol ration was increased, and approximately six hundred people were shot.

According to memoirs written by Israel Tabaksblat, the author of *Khurban Lodz* (*The Destruction of Lodz*), a letter was brought to the Lodz ghetto by a Jew from Brzeziny who, in turn, had received it from the Rabbi of Grabow, Grabow being a small township near Lodz which had been inhabited by 825 Jews. The letter was written in Yiddish:

Grabow, 19 January 1942

My dearest ones,

The letter dated 8 November I have received, which I did not want to reply to as things were not very clear. Regrettably, now we are aware of our disaster, and we know everything. Today we had a witness who came from the very place — from hell. This is in Chelmno, a small peasant settlement near Dambie. They are all buried in the forest that is called Lochow. The same happened to the towns of Kolo, Dambie, Klodowa, Isbica-Kujawska. Recently thousands of Gypsies have been brought there from the Gypsy camp in Lodz. They have met the same fate. Since last week, they have been bringing thousands of Jews from Lodz. The victims are all destroyed by gas or by shooting.

The heart is like a rock, the eyes have no more tears. Don't think a madman writes to you, but this is the hard, cruel truth. Men, tear your clothing, roll on the ground, run into the streets and cry or laugh from madness. Perhaps the Almighty will take pity and save the last remnants of our people. Help us, O Creator of the universe!

Advise if you are informed about all this.

Signed: Jakub Szulman.[26]

At a meeting of the Zionist Executive Council in the Lodz ghetto, Tabaksblat informed the council about the letter. The council decided to pass on the information to all political parties. According to Tabaksblat's memoirs, two copies of the letter were sent to the Warsaw ghetto by two messengers, Guta Szabinska and Rachel Goldman. There was no reply from anyone in Warsaw; neither were the two messengers ever heard from again.

According to Jacob Nirenberg's *History of the Lodz Ghetto* published in 1948, the letter was also read at a meeting of the Bund committee in the ghetto, after which it was decided to inform Rumkowski as well as all the political parties in the ghetto. However, for some reason, this information never reached the wider public.

People deluded themselves that they would somehow stay in the ghetto. Those working in the factories talked themselves into believing that the Germans needed them for war production. Rumours were constantly spread by the Germans that the deported adults were healthy, well fed and working on the land in good conditions. The children, it was said, had been placed amongst the peasants and were being looked after well. There were even postcards, sent from those who had been deported, and received by their relatives in the ghetto. As we know today, they were written under duress, minutes before their authors were gassed.

Ghetto industry

The Gehsperre was over. The ghetto factories were springing up like mushrooms after rain. Production was increasing. With great enthusiasm and zealous determination, Rumkowski mobilised the pre-war industrialists, manufacturers, technicians and professionals. He set in motion his grand plan. In order to appease the Germans, he decided to transform the ghetto into an industrial centre for war production. More working hands were needed. Rumkowski inspected every office, mustering every able-bodied person into the factories.

He re-organised the clothing factories that employed thousands of tailors. They became army clothing suppliers, turning out tens of thousands of uniforms, boots, underwear, gloves, and fur coats for the Russian front; embroidery factories, producing decorations for German uniforms; large timber factories, turning out millions of ammunition boxes and clogs; and metal factories, producing parts for war machinery, as well as for other industries which had civilian use such as children's toys and household appliances.

The whole ghetto population was harnessed to factories that worked day and night. Every ghetto dweller had to be registered with the Department of Labour and issued with an identity/ working-card. The five-, six- or seven-year-old children who had survived the Gehsperre were taken into the factories, and they worked together with the adults. Of course, there was cheating: all the young ones increased their age. Nobody wanted to be a child.

Through protekcja, I found my mother some work she could do at home. She plaited coloured ropes made from rags for the carpet factory that produced beautiful hand-made rugs. This allowed her to live in the ghetto legitimately. She was registered with the labour department as a working person and she had a working card — the ticket to life.

Lipek is invited to join the Sonderkommando

My brother worked in the laundry at 56-64 Zgierska Street. Lipek was only seventeen months older than I, and very much like our father. Because he was one of the very few young men in the ghetto to have received his high school certificate from Rumkowski himself, he was invited to join the Sonderkommando — the elite unit of the Lodz ghetto police force. On Sunday 11 October 1942, he came home waving a letter and announcing the good news in great excitement.

On the surface, the Sonderkommando had innocent duties such as guarding the food stores, the bakeries and the public kitchens. Behind this facade, however, they were the arm of the Gestapo in the ghetto: arresting and rounding up people for deportation; breaking down walls and pulling up floors in search of hidden possessions, merchandise and valuables; and generally robbing the ghetto population on behalf of the Gestapo.

My parents and I listened very carefully. I became very enthusiastic and congratulated Lipek on his good fortune: it was like winning the biggest-ever lottery prize. More! Much more! There was no bigger prize one could win in this world, in the world of my past. How can anybody in today's world understand what it meant to be one of the Sonder kommando then? It meant a secure position, plenty of food at a time when people were dying from starvation. It also meant being well-dressed, having special privileges and, above all, it guaranteed security and protection for the whole family.

Suddenly, in his usual quiet manner, my father said to Lipek, 'My son, you are very lucky. Indeed, you are most fortunate! But I hope you will not accept this good fortune.'

We were thunderstruck. What was he saying? Had he lost his mind? There was a long silence, then we all started talking at once. I pleaded and debated with my father for hours. Then, for the first time in my life, I dared to oppose him.

'You are wrong!' I shouted. 'You have no right to ask such a sacrifice.'

My father stood firm. He let us talk and argue until he suddenly interrupted us with so much force that it silenced us at once.

'Listen!' he roared. 'I do realise that I have no right to stand in your way.' He turned his face towards my brother. 'So make your choice, Lipman, between your father and the Sonderkommando! But make no mistake. Should you decide to join the Sonderkommando, you are no longer my son. You will leave my house. I will not live with a Sonderkommando policeman under the same roof!' Then he turned towards us and said, 'Maybe I should go and leave you all to this great good fortune!'

My mother broke down and, in the end, with no solution in sight, we were all in tears. Ultimately, it was left to Lipek to choose. The next morning he went back to the damp laundry at Zgierska Street, to carry on shovelling the coal, and loading and unloading heavy bales of clothing.

I was eighteen years old and could not understand my father's thinking. Today, I realise how fortunate I was to have had a father like that. Because of his integrity and high moral standards and his far-sightedness, I can live knowing that none of my family participated in any organisation that assisted in the destruction of my people.

The clothing that Lipek unloaded at the laundry belonged to deportees. The quantities were enormous, far exceeding the number of people who had been deported from the Lodz ghetto. Huge trucks with hundreds of thousands of shoes were brought into the ghetto stores. They all had had their soles and heels torn off in the eternal German search for Jewish valuables.

Clothing! Enormous quantities of it. More storage was made available. Obviously, people from other towns and villages had shared the same fate as the people from the Lodz ghetto. Some of the items were identified by the workers: they knew the people who used to wear them. In the pockets they found photos and personal belongings of their friends and relatives. The clothes were dry cleaned, repaired, sorted and handed over to the German authorities who, in turn, gave them to the philanthropic and charitable organisations in Germany. Some of these organisations were supervised and run by the Church — which was aware where the clothing had come from, and what had happened to those who had worn them.

Masha Rosenberg, my childhood friend's mother who worked with my brother, came up to Lipek one day with a very familiar jacket. The jacket had bullet holes in it, and was covered in blood. In one of the pockets they found a school identity card with a photo. It belonged to our friend Nisek Golusz who, only a few days earlier, had been rounded up with many others and sent away. Upon coming home, Lipek told me what he had seen, thus confirming the reports that had been passed on to us by our liaison from the children's organisation, Skif.

Lipek plans to escape

Nisek Golusz's jacket had a shattering effect on Lipek. From that day on, he thought only of escape. We discussed it hour after hour. Lipek's's view was that here in the ghetto we were all condemned to die; the only hope was escape. Not wishing to desert our parents, I opposed his reasoning.

Lipek replied, 'By staying in the ghetto we cannot help our parents. We can only die together. Escape is our only hope.'

I could not believe that escape was possible. At best, we might succeed in getting past the barbed wire but, once on the other side, we had no hope of hiding. Nor could we count on finding any assistance. Although born and bred in Lodz, with Polish and German connections that stretched back to childhood, we had no door to knock on. The safety of the forest was a pipe dream because of its distance from the ghetto. In the city, we would be denounced by the Germans or the Poles, handed over to the police, and brought back to the ghetto. Thousands of ghetto dwellers, rounded up from the factories and brought to the Plac Bazarny, would then be forced to witness our hanging. This was the fate met by all those who tried to escape.

'Lipek,' I pleaded, 'an escape is doomed to fail. If our faces were not so Jewish, then maybe ...'

My brother and I had jet-black hair, dark-brown eyes and olive skin. In Poland, only Jews had that particular combination; but appearance notwithstanding, the Poles, with their sixth sense in identifying Jews, whatever they looked like, would not hesitate to hand us over to the Germans.

Lipek would not give up his plan, however. He turned to others, one of whom was our school friend, Jack Rosenberg. Jack also did not believe that an escape from the ghetto could succeed. On the other side of the barbed wire was a hostile world. Totally unaware of the existence of Jewish partisans in the Polish forest, we had nowhere to run. As Polish Jews, we were condemned — on the one hand, betrayed by the Poles; on the other, confronted by the most powerful military machine of the time.

The beginning of the winter of 1942-43 was the most ferocious I have ever experienced, and the blizzards and frosts were most decisive on the Russian front line. History repeated itself, and the killing climate helped the Russian army to break the back of Germany's supposedly invincible military might. The most recent radio reports were very encouraging. On 27 November 1942, after many months of door-to-door battles in the suburbs of Stalingrad, the Sixth German Army, under the command of Field-Marshal Friedrich Paulus, finally surrendered after having been encircled for some time. It did so against the orders of its Führer. Paulus, together with seventy thousand of his troops, was taken prisoner.

In the ghetto we rejoiced, but from Stalingrad to Lodz was a long way. The Germans reacted savagely when the signs that they might lose the war became more evident, and their hostility drove them to extremes.

Near the ghetto wires one had to be particularly cautious, especially when the guards were Austrian: they were even more vicious than the Germans. Early one morning I went out onto our balcony and noticed a guard walking past with his rifle in his hands. I shrank back, hiding behind the curtain. Suddenly he raised his rifle, aimed, and a loud bang followed. A young man's life came to an abrupt end. He was just a house painter on his way to work — another Jew dead.

The Austrians formed 75 per cent of the staff managing the concentration camps. Eighty per cent of Eichmann's officers and his entourage were Austrians. He himself was one. To this very day, the Austrians claim they were themselves victims of the Third Reich, but the statistics give the lie to such testimony.[27]

1942 was drawing to its end, but there was neither an end to our suffering nor was there the slightest spark of hope in the darkness of the ghetto abyss.

5

The Lodz ghetto, 1943

NINE HUNDRED and seventy-five days had gone by since we had been first locked inside the ghetto.

Starvation and epidemics had taken a grim toll. The high death-rate and constant deportations had decimated the ghetto community, reducing their numbers to eighty-seven thousand. Passing corpses in the streets became a daily occurrence. For us, the winter was a merciless killer. The frosts and heavy snowfalls created more havoc, pain and suffering. The snow covered the filthy courtyards. The low temperatures froze the toilets, which turned out to be a blessing in disguise: it reduced the stench. It also turned the water supply into a lump of ice. Hand pumps were the only means of obtaining water, and even they were breaking down. Spare parts were not available, and we were forced to walk on the slippery, ice-covered ground, carting water from distant courtyards. Inside the living quarters, the walls were covered with frost.

Experiments with electricity

Heating was non-existent; fuel was rationed out in small quantities, not even enough to boil drinking water every day. The fences and timber structures had long disappeared as sources of fuel. The only alternative was to burn furniture, and this, too, was running out.

The furniture I had salvaged and stored in the cellar from uncle Laib's home after he and his family ran away to Warsaw had been chopped up for firewood long ago. Next in line was our furniture, which slowly disappeared as we preserved only what was essential. Finally, I hit upon an extreme solution. I installed an illegal power point under the bed, connecting the live wire to the power supply and earthing the other to the waste pipe in the kitchen. This installation by-passed the electrical meter, making it possible for us to use an unlimited supply of electricity.

This was a dangerous exercise, electricity being strictly limited to one 40-watt globe per room. I hate to think what would have happened had I been caught. We still possessed an electric kettle that had somehow survived and, eventually, I became more daring and built a home-made electric stove. The coils were from ordinary steel wire, and I only switched this contraption on late at night for limited periods. It made a strange buzzing noise but it managed to produce a lot of heat and make the temperature in our home bearable. I don't know how many watts it consumed, but it was most effective.

It was the freezing temperatures in our home that drove me to this risky venture. It was like being inside a broken down deep-freeze with thick frost building up on the walls. The windows were coated with frost paintings that evoked most unusual fairy tales in my mind's eye. Lying in bed for hours to escape the cold, I used to listen to the traffic on the road outside the ghetto. In the middle of the night, the dimmed headlights of the vehicles lit up the frost-covered walls of our home with millions of diamonds. My mind wandered back to my childhood when life had been good. Returning to 28 Limanowskiego Street, I conjured up all the beautiful food we had eaten. In 1937, after my grandfather's death, we had moved into his apartment at 13 Zgierska Street.

My recollections of Polish anti-Semitism

Most of the neighbours around our former dwelling had been gentiles. Amongst them were many ethnic Germans, including our landlord, Mr Ellsner. This part of Lodz was predominantly built and developed by them. Life for Jews in such a neighbourhood was not peaceful, especially after 1933, with Hitler's coming to power. A wave of hostile and violent anti-Semitism swept across the cities and towns of Poland with pogroms becoming almost a daily occurrence. Walking on smashed glass in the Jewish quarters became commonplace.

Although I was only a young boy in Poland in the thirties, I clearly remember how, leading up to 1939, the anti-Semitic terror had increased from day to day. The Nazi persecutions in Germany fuelled Polish anti-Semitic sentiments, encouraging the Poles to greater violence and more pogroms which flared up all over the country. The Polish fascists took to the streets dressed in uniforms identical to those of the Nazis, swastika included. These brown-shirted hooligans roamed unchecked, encouraged, in fact, by the police who were never present when Jewish quarters were attacked. In our neighbourhood, at 18 Zawiska Czarny Street, one of the Nazi centres was housed. The Nazi flag was always raised in front of it.

The pogroms engulfed Jewish life. In Przytyk, Brzesc-Nad-Bugiem, Chenstochowa, Warsaw, Lodz and all other large cities, Jews were attacked every day in the streets. In the public gardens, Jewish mothers and children who went out for a stroll were beaten up. Such attacks often ended in funerals.

The young and progressive Jewish youth organisations formed self-defence groups. Whenever they repelled their attackers, the police immediately moved in, arresting those who dared to fight back, charging them for disturbing the peace. They were tried and sentenced to long jail terms. The bombing, burning, ransacking and looting of Jewish homes and shops occurred with ever-increasing frequency.

I remember distinctly the Christian holidays and Sundays after Mass. Jews had to take every precaution not to meet worshippers leaving church, for the religious sermons were invariably interwoven with incitement to violence against the Jews. In particular, anti-Semitic anger and hostility would reach a flash point over the Easter period. Jews would disappear from the streets, locking doors and window shutters in panic. Whoever did not disappear fast enough was attacked by the worshippers. Jewish children were not spared; young and old were beaten. Knifing was very common. It is impossible to rid my mind's eye of the bleeding faces of my Jewish neighbours who were beaten up as they ran in panic along the streets, pursued by maddened Poles. The Catholic priests calmly and solemnly continued with the procession as though nothing were wrong.

The pages of Jesuit publications were full of anti-Semitic articles, reminding Christians that Jews were the killers of Christ. Church publications insisted that those schools in which Jewish children were taught together with Christians must segregate the

Jews, so that Christian children would not become contaminated by a morality that was low and unprincipled.

One of the leading anti-Semites in Poland was a Catholic priest by the name of Father Trzeciak. Renowned for his poisonous sermons and speeches, Trzeciak was the Polish Streicher (the editor of the Nazi newspaper *Der Sturmer*). His speeches were published right across Poland in most daily newspapers and publications.

On 20 February 1936, a public letter was issued by Cardinal Hlond, in which he wrote: 'It is true that the Jews are committing fraud, practising usury, and white slavery. It is true that, in the schools, Jewish children have an evil influence on the Catholic children, from a religious and ethical point of view ... But let us be just. Not all Jews are like that. However, one does well to prefer one's own kind.' He preached that, 'In commercial dealings, the Christians should avoid Jewish stalls and Jewish shops in the market, but it is not permissible to demolish Jewish businesses, break windows or bomb their houses.'

Soon after the publication of Cardinal Hlond's letter, massive waves of pogroms swept across Poland. Seventy-nine Jews were murdered and many hundreds injured. In the Polish parliament, anti-Semitic speeches were regularly made. One of the most vocal members was a Mrs Pristerowa, whose vitriolic outpourings were another effective incitement. Thousands tried to emigrate but came up against closed borders everywhere. The world did not want the Jews.

All over Poland, walls were covered with slogans: *Nie Kupoj U Zyda* (Don't buy from the Jew) and *Swoj Do Swego Po Swoje* (Go to your own for your own). The sign *Sklep Chrzescianski* (Christian Shop) was on display in many a window; and there was also the ever-popular, *Zydy Do Palestyny* (Jews go to Palestine).

In pre-war Poland, universities had a *numerus clausus* for Jewish students. Those very few who were admitted had to be exceptionally brilliant. Inside the universities, 'ghettos' were introduced: a separate corner where Jewish students were compelled to sit apart from the others. In protest, Jewish students attending lectures refused to sit in the 'ghetto', choosing to stand near the door instead. With very few exceptions, most of the professors, the Polish intellectuals, the administrators and the university authorities sympathised with and supported anti-Semitic student activities, helping to humiliate and oppress Jewish students. Daily physical attacks and beatings took place, terrorising them and preventing them from attending lectures.

My gentile childhood friends and neighbours

This was the Poland I remember as a young boy in the days before the Second World War.

Whenever it was time for me to go home from school — or from anywhere for that matter — I became tense, like a soldier before battle. Where I lived, on 28 Limanowskiego Street, it was like being on a different planet from the Jewish quarters in which the majority of Jews lived. My heartbeat was faster, my reflexes and instincts were sharpened; I was like an animal in fear of the hunter and always ready to run. As soon as I approached the gate leading to our courtyard, my nerves stretched taut. I could never walk: I had to run as fast as I could. Once I began to climb the stairs leading to our apartment on the second floor, I would start calling out to my mother. She usually called back encouragingly 'Come up! Come up! I'm waiting for you. Don't be scared, I'm waiting for you.'

At 28 Limanowskiego Street the gentiles were never very gentle. I cannot recall a single day of the entire time I lived there that passed without stones being thrown at me or my being involved in a fight with the non-Jewish kids. At best, I was only called names and insulted.

The non-Jewish kids in that neighbourhood believed that Jews were created to be beaten and hated because Jews were dirty and smelly; they were greedy and over-rich, and they all had a lot of money and gold hidden in their pots. Above all, they hated the Jews because we had killed the Lord Jesus Christ — the most unforgivable crime for which we had to be punished forever after; and they were taught by the Church that we were sinners and non-believers. This I learned at a very early age from my Christian neighbours in the courtyard. These and other lessons about the nature of Christianity became deeply engraved in my mind, lessons that were aided in their effectiveness by accompanying knocks and bruises.

The most impressive pedagogues of them all were Rysiek and Zdzich, two six-year-old contemporaries of mine. They made my waking hours miserable and invaded my sleep as well, causing nightmares. Because of them, I could never walk across the courtyard without fear; I could never go down to play in the open air. To me and all other Jewish kids in that tenement, the courtyard was forbidden territory.

Whenever her little boy was playing in the courtyard, Zdzich's mother would watch from her third-floor window, very proud of her son, especially when he attacked me with his fists with the help of Rysiek. She never interfered. Once, in pain from the beating I was receiving from them, I pleaded with her to tell them to stop. She ignored me completely.

The only person apart from my mother who used to protect me was our next-door neighbour, Mrs Safjanowa. Born in the United States to a Polish family, she was a well-educated and cultured woman who, on her first trip to Poland to visit her relatives, had fallen in love with a young Polish gentleman whom she eventually married. Whenever she was around the courtyard, walking her snow-white Samoyed, Eros, she would be my protector and nobody dared touch me. Eros' presence was quite a persuasive deterrent. Zdzich's mother, however, called her a Jew-lover and suggested she leave the children to work out their own affairs.

My mother did very little, out of fear of provoking the neighbours. Whenever I came running home, beaten up and crying, she used to scold me and say, 'Don't come crying to me. There's nothing I can do! Fight back and don't be scared! Just beat back as hard as you can.'

Every morning before school, it was my job to go to the baker with a wire basket to buy the bread rolls and milk for breakfast. One morning on my way there, I noticed Zdzich standing alone at the entrance of his building. I eyed him warily, but I noticed that he suddenly shrank back as if he didn't want to be seen. Somehow I sensed that on his own he was scared of me, and this gave me confidence. I decided that now was the moment to heed my mother's words and teach Zdzich a lesson. I continued walking towards the gate leading onto the street without seeming to pay him any attention. Then, when he was sure I was going to walk right past him, I jumped on him, knocking him roughly to the ground.

Suddenly I felt very calm, and my mind became perfectly clear.

I had no difficulty recalling my older cousin's instructions of how to fight. Shlomo was an amateur featherweight boxer in a Jewish sports club in Lodz and, as Zdzich picked himself up and put up his fists over his face to defend himself, I took up the correct fighting position as per Shlomo's instructions. I feinted to the left, confusing him and, the moment he moved his fists away from his face, I let him have it with a right hook which knocked him to the ground and bloodied his nose.

Zdzich panicked. He picked himself up and tried to run, calling at the top of his voice, 'Mother, mother, help.' I followed him, grabbing his right leg as he ran up the stairs, making him trip and knock his face against the concrete steps. I jumped on top of him, hitting him with the bread basket as hard as I could, my mother's encouraging words echoing in my brain.

When I returned after making the purchases for our breakfast, my mother immediately noticed that I had been in a scuffle. She asked me what had happened; when I told her, she said quietly, 'Good boy, I'm glad you did it.'

Soon after, as we sat at the table having breakfast, Zdzich's mother flung open our door shaking with anger, spouting abuse and insults about Jews in general and us in particular. Mrs Safjanowa came to our rescue, reminding the aggressive mother not to interfere — and to leave the children to their own affairs!

This was the most memorable morning of my life at 28 Limanowskiego Street. My mother's teaching and encouragement had paid off because, from that morning on, Rysiek and Zdzich became my best friends. Now my heart could resume its normal beat; no longer did I have to run across the courtyard in fear. I gained full recognition and rights, and was allowed to play there. Even my friends, who were hesitant to visit me as they were usually intimidated, were suddenly tolerated.

In the winter time, I was allowed to ice-skate or toboggan there as well. Zdzich and Rysiek even took me along to their school to skate. It was one of the most modern schools in Lodz — for Christian children only — named after the president of Poland, Ignacy Moscicky. The school had all the latest amenities, and a large playground with swings and all sorts of equipment for the children. Because of the segregated state-school system, in order to skate on the Ignacy Moscicky rink I had to hide my face under my fur hat, which I used to pull down over my eyes. Zdzich also suggested that I change my name to Janek. The name, Abraham, he reasoned, would lead to trouble. From that time on, outside our courtyard, to many kids around the area, I was known as Janek.

I used to give Zdzich and Rysiek matzo — which they liked very much — as well as many other Jewish specialities that we ate on the Jewish holidays. Yet, although they liked it, they still kept on telling me that the matzo was mixed with Christian blood. No matter how hard I tried to talk them out of it, they still believed what they were told at church.

From them, I learned about the Lord Jesus Christ, the son of God, who could walk on water, bring the dead back to life, make the blind see, feed the hungry and make the lame walk again. I listened eagerly and grew to like the Lord Jesus because he was such a nice person. But these tales created a sharp conflict for me. Why on earth would the Jews kill such a nice man? I couldn't understand it. On the other hand, I had some doubts about their stories. I argued with my two friends, reasoning as best I could with a child's logic.

'If Jesus Christ was the son of God,' I used to ask them, 'how could the Jews have killed him? No-one in the world could kill the son of God as no-one could do anything God would not want to happen.'

I kept arguing with my friends, 'I do not believe the Jews could have killed such a nice man as Jesus Christ. Besides, God would not allow his son to be killed.' To me, this was an irrefutable argument.

I was fascinated by Christ's miracles. His looks impressed me from the pictures and paintings I saw in the homes of my neighbours. He had a gentle and delicate face, and his sky-blue eyes, his silky, blond hair and tall, slim body dressed in a white robe made a deep impression upon me.

One day, when our neighbour's son, Berish Staszewski, came home on leave from the Polish army, I learned an entirely different story about Jesus. My parents had invited Berish to dinner and, as we sat at the table, he told us about his life in the army. The most fascinating part of his story dealt with his colonel, who had commissioned him to paint a portrait of Christ.

Berish Staszewski was a talented young painter. Upon completing the painting, he presented it to his colonel, who almost became apoplectic.

'What is this? What have you painted?' he demanded. 'Is this supposed to be Jesus Christ?'

Berish, standing to attention, answered. 'Yes, sir, this is my Jesus Christ.'

'But you have painted a Jew, a typical Jew!' the Colonel replied angrily. 'Are you making fun of me?'

Berish replied, 'Sir, this is my Jesus Christ. This is how I imagine he looked. This is the way I understand he must have looked at that time when he lived amongst the poor people. He himself was poor.'

At the end of his tether, the colonel burst out: 'But he looks like a rotten Jew!'

'Yes, sir,' said Berish rigidly, 'as far as I know he was a Jew. That's why I painted him to look like one.'

The colonel left the room abruptly, and Berish covered his painting with a canvas, leaving it on the easel. Some days later he was called to the colonel's office and curtly handed an order for fourteen days' leave. When he thanked the colonel, the officer remarked dryly, 'When you come back, I still want you to paint Jesus Christ, but I'd like you to understand that I expect a painting of a more conventional nature. And no further discussions about his being Jewish.'

Berish saluted and took his leave. Upon his return, he obediently painted many portraits of Jesus Christ, serving his two years in the army with his pallet and brushes, eventually being promoted to the rank of corporal.

I was confused and bewildered by Berish's story. I reeled to learn that Jesus Christ had been a Jew, a rabbi, who had lived in Palestine two thousand years ago and was crucified by the Romans for being a rebel and inciting his people against the Roman Empire.

This version of events was unacceptable to Zdzich and Rysiek. They became aggressive and angry, shouting: 'Not only did the Jews crucify Jesus Christ, but to this very day they are still killing innocent Christian children and using their blood in the unleavened bread for Passover.'

I felt guilty to be Jewish

I was shocked and distraught for many days. I was confused and embarrassed, and felt guilty to be Jewish. I went to my mother with my doubts and questions.

'Mummy, why did the Jews crucify Jesus Christ? Why do Jews kill Christian children? Mummy, why are the Jews bad people?' I was panic stricken. My mother used to calm me down and console me. Holding me tight in her arms, she used to say, 'Don't believe what they tell you. Tell your friends we have never killed anybody.' But I was most unhappy. My doubts and fears came and went. I kept asking again and again, 'Mummy, why are we Jewish?' I did not want to be a Jew any longer. I tried to persuade her that we should all be Polish because we had all been born in Poland.

'But we are Polish!' my mother replied. 'Go and tell your friends that you are just as Polish as they are! You are a Polish Jew and they are Polish Christians and there is no difference between you and them. Tell them we are all human beings.'

However, my friends insisted that I was a Jew and a Jew could not be Polish. I pointed out that my father was a Polish soldier and therefore had to be Polish, but my friends were still not satisfied; nor, I was to discover, would they ever be.

To alleviate my distress, my mother began to tell me in some detail about the history of the Jews, their trials and their persecutions over the centuries. At the time, many of the details were beyond my comprehension but, for some reason, one item stayed with me always.

'In the last two thousand years,' she told me sadly, 'the Jews forgot how to fight. They left it all to God. You must understand,' she continued, 'God helps only those who are prepared to help themselves. You must study. You must work and only then will God help you. Should you rely upon God alone to fight your battles for you, your enemies will destroy you.'

At the tender age of six, this was all a bit much for me to digest. She must have known it, but she gave me her words anyway, possibly for future reference.

'There is no glory in death,' she concluded with great emphasis, 'only in life, my son. There is only glory in life. But you should know that in any country ruled by tyrants, where there is no justice, there will always be anti-Semitism.'

Although I listened to my mother's stories, I still wanted to be like the other children. I did not like being different. That was why 13 Lagiewnicka Street became the favourite corner of my childhood, where I could feel free and equal. It was the home of my uncle David Laib and aunty Chaya, my mother's older sister, with their five children: my cousins, Rozia, Lipman, Shlomo, Mendel and Tobcia — they all lived in one large room. There, I could relax and breathe without fear, because I was amongst my own kind.

13 Lagiewnicka Street

13 Lagiewnicka Street was in a most colourful and exciting neighbourhood, the embodiment of a Yiddish *shtetl* village. There were a few Christian children, but they lived and played together with us. Somehow, they became like us: they could even speak Yiddish. They read Yiddish and knew by heart the Hebrew prayers which they learned from the Jewish boys who went to *cheder* religious school.

Amongst them was Vatzek, a big, strong boy we all loved and respected because he would always come to our defence. No matter what, Vatzek would confront the attackers who used to call him 'Rotten Jew-lover'; but he never took any notice of them. He remained steadfast and loyal to his friends.

When the ghetto was first closed off, Vatzek drove a big cart pulled by two draft horses. Risking his own life, he threw parcels of food and medication over the fence for his Jewish friends as he travelled past. I would see him coming, galloping his horses past the barbed wire along Zgierska Street. I would stand at the balcony door in great suspense, watching him operate and, at times, my heart seemed to stop in fear for his safety. Timing was of the essence: the moment the guard turned his back to march in the opposite direction, Vatzek had to throw his parcel over the wires. Time and time again he would risk it. Then, one day in the summer of 1941, I saw him being escorted by a German guard who had caught him in the act. Vatzek was taken away and never seen again.

In my early childhood, however, 13 Lagiewnicka Street was a place where I was never called '*Parszywy Zydzie*' ('diseased Jew') or told to go to Palestine, nor did I hear any offensive swear words. The courtyard was always full of children playing games, singing, dancing, running happily without fear, without insult or harassment. Life buzzed with the activity of a beehive. I loved to visit my aunty Chaya there, who always received me with a great deal of warmth and goodness. I particularly loved her butter-cake for which she was famous. Then there were the five, or sometimes ten, groschen she used to give me, which helped to build up my kitty.

Her husband, my uncle David Laib, was a respected man in the city of Lodz. He was a kosher butcher by trade, but his good name resided in his position of president of the voluntary neighbourhood committee to assist the poor. That meant most of the neighbourhood. As well, he was the president of the Zdunska Wola 'landsmanschaft' in Lodz (the organisation of compatriots from the same village). Zdunska Wola was a Jewish shtetl, approximately sixty kilometres west of Lodz, closer to the German border. My uncle's home was always full of people in need of help, advice or just a little bit of warmth.

He and aunt Chaya also decided to look after the four children next door whose parents had both died of illness within a short time of one another. Their ages ranged from nine to fifteen, and their only living relatives were an uncle and aunt in Australia. My uncle's and aunt's decision to take care of them saved them from being taken to the city orphanage. They were well looked after until they reached an age where they could take care of themselves; eventually, they left for Australia, where they live to this day. In fact, it was thanks to them that I came to this country, where I have lived as a free man for the past forty years.

Above all, my uncle was known in the city of Lodz as one of the finest cantors. When the High Holidays approached, he and his choir rehearsed far into the night, singing the beautiful chants for Rosh Hashana and Yom Kippur. Until the very early hours, people from the neighbourhood and passers-by would gather outside his windows, which faced Berka Joselewicza Street, listening to my uncle's melodic voice singing the prayers.

My aunt's and uncle's home was a very colourful place with exotic plants which my uncle carefully tended. He had hundreds of them. He also loved canaries, which he bred, all of which were beautiful whistlers trained by him. He would sit patiently for hours with special whistles he had fashioned. Each whistle had a small water container attached to it and, depending on the level of the water, the whistle would produce a different pitch. The water created a replica of the canary whistle and it was amazing how the canaries learned to whistle the tunes my uncle played for them. This made them unique but he never sold any of them. Only on rare occasions would he deign to give one of his precious creatures as a gift to a friend whom he felt could be trusted to care for it with the appropriate skill and love. I often recall my uncle coming home at the end of the day and, before even sitting down, opening one of his cages and letting his favourite canary, Matciush, fly out into the room where it would promptly settle on his shoulder. Then my uncle partook of his dinner while, at his feet, his huge faithful Alsatian, 'Looxel', lay proud and watchful.

Once, while playing with Looxel, rolling on the floor under the table, I nearly lost my nose when I tied up his snout and blew into his nostrils for the fun of it. To my surprise, Looxel was not amused. Neither was my aunt Chaya when she saw my bleeding face.

Uncle David Laib, besides breeding canaries, growing exotic plants, and having a great love for singing and music, also possessed a number of musical instruments — violins, flutes, guitars, mandolins and an old Russian garmoshka, a hand accordion, which he brought back from Russia where he had served in the Tsar's army, playing in the military orchestra as a flautist. The flute, of which he had a couple in his collection, was one of his favourite instruments. From time to time, he would sit down and play those tunes that reminded him of his youth. His greatest dream was to see his oldest son, Lipman, become a violinist and his second youngest son, Shlomo, who had a voice like a nightingale, soft and melodious, become a great cantor.

As a young boy, Shlomo was the first soloist in the choir of the great synagogue of Lodz, at the old city Stare Miasto at Wolborska Street. (This synagogue, which was one of the largest and most beautiful in Poland, was blown up by the Germans on 11 November 1939.) In 1942, after two long years working in an RAB labour camp, building the famous highway called Reichsautobahn which Hitler dreamed would connect Berlin to Moscow, Shlomo was among three hundred and fifty men brought back to the Lodz ghetto. Detained for forty-eight hours at the ghetto prison at Czarnieckiego-Marysin, they were taken away by the Germans in the middle of the night — destination unknown, never to be seen or heard of again.

With the liquidation of the Lodz ghetto in August 1944, uncle David Laib, aunty Chaya and three of their children, Rozia, Lipman and Tobcia (Mendele at that time was already in Auschwitz) were put on a cattle train which transported them from the ghetto to Auschwitz. After Dr Mengeles' selection, their fate was sealed in the days approaching the Jewish New Year, 5,704. David Laib, lover of people, birds, nature and music; Chaya, his humble lady; and most of the neighbourhood from 13 Lagiewnicka Street went up in the thick, black smoke that rose from the stacks of the Auschwitz crematoria.

The chants and prayers of the cantor from Lodz were silenced by Zyklon-B and replaced with a new song that rose with a ferocity and an anger that reverberated all over Europe: the infamous *Sturmlied*, carrying a message of death for the Jews. *'Wenn das Judenblut von messer spritzt, Dann geht's noch mal so gut.'* ('When Jew-blood spurts from the knife, things will go twice as well'). The *Sturmlied* was written by Horst Wessel, a young German who eventually became mentally deranged and died of syphilis. Before his death, he achieved the status of a cult figure who was worshipped as a great hero — a hero of the Third Reich.

Food

The harsh winter was drawing to an end. Somehow, I always remember the ghetto in a perpetual winter, enveloped in ice and snow, with frost covering the inside of our home. Our family was still a complete unit. Not many were as lucky as we were, but our strength lay in the fact that we stuck together. We were one for all and all for one.

My mother was in charge of the food. She would cut the bread with great skill, judging every slice and handing out to every one of us the daily ration. She was in charge of every spoonful of soup, and would apportion a little extra for the one most in need. Lipek, usually ill, generally had priority. Next in line came my father. Whenever I managed to organise a few potatoes from Limping Laib, my father would always be very surprised and would caution my mother, saying: 'Fradl, aren't you forgetting your limits, don't you think you are overstepping the line? So many potatoes?'

My mother would reply: 'Trust me. Don't worry. You're not getting too much. Eat! Eat and enjoy!' And, although our bread rations were small, she always managed somehow to hoard a tiny reserve, just a few thin slices, in case of a sudden emergency.

My uncle Berish and aunt Sarah who lived with us, separated their food from ours. We lived together in harmony; we shared our worries and our burdens. But we did not share our food. It upset me at the time, but today I understand it differently. It was the Lodz ghetto, where people were dying of starvation. Most families were torn apart. Everyone had his own food under lock and key. Some would not leave their food rations at home, and took them to work. They even slept with their bread ration under their pillows. Terrible fights broke out amongst families all because of a potato, a piece of bread, a bit of soup. Most of the fights in the ghetto were over food.

The first night of Passover

The snow was melting under the first rays of the spring sun, thawing the frozen toilets that started to flood the courtyards. Heaps of rubbish and dirt surfaced with the receding whiteness of the melting snow. Spring came to the world again, but not to the world of my past. There, gloom and misery was suspended in the air. It was 19 April 1943, the first night of Passover. In our home, the big mahogany table was covered with a white bed sheet — after the second raid by the Kripo, our home had been virtually emptied: not even a tablecloth was left.

I found a couple of empty shoe-polish tins and put a few drops of oil in them, twisted a couple of wicks made from a cotton rag and, in no time, we had a pair of festive candles that created a solemn atmosphere as the whole family gathered around the table to celebrate the festival.

Berish, through some of his connections, had managed to get a few kilos of potato peels, a very rare and precious commodity. They were only obtainable if one had a prescription, and this the doctor would write out only if the person were practically dead. With great care, Sarah washed the peels and put them through the mincing machine. She mixed the brown liquid mass with burned oats that we were given as a substitute for coffee. She added a couple of spoonfuls of cornflour to make the dough bind, and produced the most beautiful coffee cake — the highlight of our supper. It was placed in the middle of the table between the shoe-polish tins, and it made my mouth water. I could not remember a cake as beautiful as this. Next to it lay the white satin matzo-cover, embroidered with a large, blue Star of David. In the centre, embroidered in gold Hebrew letters, was the word 'Jerusalem'. Inside were the three matzos. These were for my grandmother who was the only person in our home who chose to eat matzo, which was available on the ration cards instead of bread. Most of the ghetto people took the bread. It seemed a better choice. The portions looked bigger and were more filling.

The 'Haggadah', the tale of the Jews' historic servitude and liberation, was on the table. We all sat around in silence until my grandmother asked, 'Shimon, who will read the Haggadah?'

'No-one tonight,' my father answered. 'God will forgive us. After the war we will.'

My grandmother stared at the two flickering lights, not uttering a word.

I went over to the double bed and stripped back the eiderdown. Out came the big pot that had been heavily wrapped in paper and woollen blankets to keep warm the soup which I had brought from the communal kitchen at midday. My mother ladled out the watery liquid, stirring with the ladle to fish out a couple of floating potatoes for each plate.

As we sat eating in silence, there came a knock at the door. I ran to the kitchen to open it. One of our neighbours, who was a radio-listener and lived on the third floor in the courtyard, asked for uncle Berish in a nervous whisper. The two of them spoke for a while, standing in the dark foyer. Berish came back with his face flushed, his voice trembling as he gave us the news:

'The Warsaw ghetto is in flames. The ghetto is in revolt. The Jews are fighting! They have guns! They are shooting at the Germans!'

The Warsaw ghetto uprising

We sat as though turned to stone. There was a long silence until my father asked, 'Which radio station?'

'The London News on the BBC,' replied my uncle.

I could not imagine how it was possible for Jews in a ghetto to have weapons. It was beyond my wildest dreams. We were only 120 kilometres from where the battle was raging, but the news had come to us via London. Yet, excited though I was, I remember that my stomach still took priority. I waited with great impatience for my mother to cut the cake.

Later that night, thinking about Warsaw, I could not fall asleep. I was back in the Jewish quarter where, before the German invasion, four hundred thousand Jews had lived — the largest Jewish community in Europe. Before my sleepless eyes appeared the crowded streets with thousands of merchants rushing, running, carrying goods of all descriptions. I walked down Gensia Street, where vendors called at the tops of their voices, advertising their merchandise. On the footpaths, Jewish boys were selling bagels, frankfurters, soda water, lemonade, cakes and all sorts of home-made delicacies. Constantly harassed by the Polish police who used to kick their baskets of merchandise into the gutter, these boys were nevertheless part of the Jewish business centre which was like a beehive.

Neither awake nor yet properly asleep, I walked along Krochmalna and Nalewki Streets. This was the heart of Jewish Warsaw and it pulsated with life. I wandered around Smocha Street, the Jewish slums, the Calcutta of Poland. Children were playing, dressed in rags, neglected, undernourished. The old folk sat on the steps in front of the buildings with sad faces staring into space. I saw their dilapidated homes, inhabited by the most under-privileged people in eastern Europe. It was a degree of poverty that is only comparable to that of the homeless beggars of the Third World. I walked down Pawia Street past the Pawiak prison, where thousands of lives came to a brutal end. Not far away was Mila Street, the famous No. 18 where, in the cellars, the 'Zydowska Organizacja Bojowa' — ZOB: Jewish Organisation of Armed Fighters — had their headquarters.

Lying in my bed, thinking about those in the Warsaw ghetto, I envied them. I would have been ecstatic to have been amongst them, although I knew the fight was lost before it even began. I would just have liked to put my finger on a trigger or throw a petrol bomb at a German tank. It was not that I had a desire to die, nor did I want to become a hero. The heroes I knew were all dead. I would just have been happy to stand, a free man, eye to eye with one of our murderers with a weapon in my hand.

On 20 April, we waited in great suspense for the next bulletin. It was twenty-four hours before the BBC News came on the air again, starting with its usual dramatic drumbeat. The news about the Warsaw ghetto was brief. 'The Warsaw ghetto uprising continues ... The ghetto is in flames.' That first week, the newscast repeated the same thing over and over again with no modifications. The following week, we learned that the Germans were bombarding the ghetto with heavy artillery. The battle raged on.

In the third week we heard: 'The Germans have surrounded the ghetto with a steel ring of tanks. Their artillery and the Luftwaffe are bombing the ghetto to dust!' The Jews fought on behind the collapsing walls.

The fourth week: 'The ghetto fighters battle on till the last, dying under the collapsing walls, jumping from the tall buildings into the flames ... The fight is raging. The Warsaw ghetto is in flames.'

The fight lasted seven weeks; then shooting stopped. Not one building was left standing, only skeletons of burned-out structures smouldering. A haze of smoke was suspended over the ghetto, but it had not fallen. The fighters never surrendered. They battled on until the liberation of Jerusalem. My brothers from the Warsaw ghetto entered a golden page in the history of our ancient people. With fire and blood they engraved a most historic event — an event of biblical magnitude. My glorious Maccabean brothers from the Warsaw ghetto fired the first shot, heralding a new sunrise, the beginning of a new epoch, marking the rebirth of Israel.

Jews on the Aryan side in Warsaw

When the Warsaw ghetto uprising began, my friend, Jacob Celemanski, whom I met at Bergen-Belsen shortly after the liberation, was on the Aryan side.

'Abraham,' he said, 'Can you imagine how I felt when I was standing amongst the Poles on the other side of the ghetto wall? I cannot understand how people could behave the way they did. In the vicinity of the ghetto wall, Luna Park was lit up as usual. The merry-go-rounds turned to the tunes of waltzes whilst, only a short distance away, human beings were being burned alive. The most popular Polish joke of the day was, *'Zydki i pluskwy Sie Smarza'*.

('Yids and bed bugs are being fried.')

Celemanski, a member of the Jewish Labour Party, the Bund, was a liaison officer between the Warsaw ghetto underground and the outside world. He was involved in providing accommodation and false papers for members of the underground who crossed the ghetto wall. He had the face of a typical Pole — high cheek-bones, slightly slanted eyes and pointed nose. His Polish, however, spoken with a strong Yiddish accent, was not very good, so he had to act as a mute. He had all the necessary documents to certify his handicap and, on his left arm, he wore a yellow armband with three large black circles to indicate that he could neither hear nor speak.

He told me many stories about the lives of the concealed Jews outside the ghetto; and about the Szmalcownicks, the blackmailers, who extorted the Jews' last possessions and then, for a bottle of vodka and a couple of kilos of sugar, would denounce them to the Germans.

He told me, too, about the difficulties with which the Warsaw ghetto underground was confronted when trying to obtain weapons and ammunition — apart from the great danger of moving about. The Polish underground was uncooperative. Some weapons and ammunition had to be purchased for exorbitant prices on the black market; and, when the Warsaw ghetto underground negotiated at a higher level via London in an attempt to obtain weapons, the Polish high command of the Warsaw underground thwarted every directive that came from the Polish government in London. The military leaders of the Polish underground were unmoved by the pleas of the desperate ghetto underground organisation, ZOB. Their reply to London usually was, 'We haven't got enough weapons for our men. Besides, the Jews will never use them. They are cowards. They will never fight.'[28]

The Warsaw ghetto smouldered and glowed in its ashes for weeks. Only a handful of the fighters survived the battle and, with their last bullets loaded in their weapons, managed to escape the ghetto through the sewers. From there, they made their way into the forest, where they joined the Jewish partisans.

Partisan Jews in the forest

The situation of the Jewish partisans in the Polish forest was tragic. They had to fight a war on two fronts: one against the Germans; the other against the anti-Semitic Polish underground armies, the 'Narodowe Sily Zbrojne' (NSZ: National Armed Forces) and the 'Armja Krajowa' (AK: Country Army) who waged a treacherous war against their Jewish compatriots, betraying them while desperately fighting a common enemy. The Jewish partisans sustained greater losses of life from the Polish underground armies than from the Germans.

My childhood friend from pre-war Lodz, Juzek Rybowski, survived the war masquerading as a Pole in a small village near Kielce, where he worked as a baker's boy. In the middle of the night in 1942, a heavily armed patrol of the Polish AK underground army paid a surprise visit to his bakery. The commanding officer advised Juzek that, from that moment, he was drafted into the Polish army and must carry out all orders given to him by his superiors. With the Bible in his hand, Juzek took the oath. His employer was told to keep quiet and that he had to allow the boy to leave work whenever he was called for duty. Months passed during which Juzek became an active serving soldier, participating in many sorties against the German army.

His most memorable and traumatic experience occurred when, in the middle of the night, he was ordered to report to headquarters, where he was confronted by his superior officer with the question: 'Are you a Jew?'

'I had two options,' Juzek told me, 'lie or die. That night I was inspected with my pants down by every officer in my battalion, none of whom could decide whether I was circumcised or not. Eventually, I was passed. The next morning I discovered that my brother-in-law had had the same experience and had been detained by the Polish police. He was kept in the police lock-up for two days, constantly interrogated by the senior constable with the assistance of his two policemen. They also could not decide whether my brother-in-law was circumcised. Finally they decided to call the doctor, who immediately stated that he was not, and my brother-in-law was allowed to go home. That doctor must have been an angel.

'During my years of service with the AK, I participated in countless drinking binges, always simulating drunkenness; trying to swallow the least amount of alcohol possible. I could not afford to forget who I was for a moment. For hours I would have to sing anti-Semitic songs and listen to the most offensive anti-Semitic jokes. I often wondered: 'Who are they at war with — the Germans or the Jews?'

In February 1942, Jews from Tomaszow Lubelski organised a partisan group. They fought the Germans for many months, until they were betrayed by the local Polish population. The Germans surrounded the small partisan group in a surprise attack, killing them all in a fierce battle.

Many years later, Mendel Goldberg, who lives in Melbourne, told me: 'I was in the forests near Zelechow with two hundred and fifty armed Jews who had run away from the Zelechow ghetto before the Einsatz-gruppen moved in. We were battling against all odds. Our weapons were primitive; most of the time we had to purchase them from the Polish black marketeers at prohibitive prices. By the time the Russian army arrived, only forty of us were still alive, but not one of our men fell from a German bullet. We could cope with the Germans but we were helpless against the Polish underground armies. They knew the forest as well as we did. They were determined to kill every Jew in it.'

Josef Kermish and Samuel Krakowski, in their commentaries on the historical documentation recorded by Emanuel Ringelblum, write that the commander of the Polish underground army ordered his forces to take active measures against the Jews in the forests.[29]

In the Lodz ghetto, we did not know what was going on on the other side of the fence. In front of our house, the barbed wires were guarded as usual. For us, nothing had changed. Our struggle continued from day to day.

The press in the free world — Jan Karski and Artur Zygielbaum

The press in the free world very rarely mentioned what the Germans were doing to the Jews. Only occasionally would articles appear. By the time they started to tell the full story, it was too late: the majority of central European Jews had been incinerated.

Jan Karski was brought to London in the autumn of 1942, before the Warsaw uprising. He was one of the couriers from the Polish underground in Warsaw to the Polish government-in-exile in

London, and he carried with him a precise report of what he had seen happening to the last remnants of Polish Jewry. He was the first messenger to bring to the West a detailed account of Jews being gassed and burned. Helped by the Jewish underground, and disguised as an Estonian militia officer, Karski was escorted by an SS officer into the Belzec killing factory. He witnessed the most bizarre and frightful scenes of Jews being gassed, and their bodies burned in furnaces to wipe out all the evidence. The brief visit seemed like the longest period of time he had ever endured, and it left a deep imprint on his memory for the rest of his life.

Amongst the very first to be briefed by Karski upon his arrival in London was Shmuel Mordechai (Artur) Zygielbaum, whom I knew personally. He had been my teacher and mentor when I was a twelve-year-old member of Skif. Artur had become the official representative of Polish Jewry, a leader of the Jewish Labour Party, the Bund, and a member of the Polish parliament-in-exile. Karski relayed to him personal messages from friends, as well as the last SOS call from the Jewish underground leaders, pleading desperately that Artur must not rest until world leaders acted to stop the brutal slaughter of the last surviving Jews behind the ghetto walls.

Karski's report of the most brutal and gruesome mass exterminations he had witnessed at Belzec was passed on to world leaders. The first of these to be informed were Winston Churchill and Franklin D Roosevelt.

As we read the excerpts of Artur Zygielbaum's diary, as well as the last letters he wrote before committing suicide, we learn the tragic truth about the indifference of the free world and their leaders.

As early as July 1942, when news of the mass exterminations of Polish Jewry reached Zygielbaum, he relayed a detailed report to the Polish national council-in-exile, requesting them to bring the disaster of Polish Jewry before the world. His plea was ignored. From July to October 1942, three hundred thousand Warsaw Jews perished in Treblinka, and many more hundreds of thousands of Jews were gassed and burned in Auschwitz, Chelmno, Belzec, Sobibor and other extermination camps. He persistently appealed to the Polish government-in-exile to initiate an immediate conference of all Allied powers to protest the German reign of terror, bringing the mass murders to public attention. He insisted that they threaten the Germans with severe reprisals unless they stopped the atrocities. His requests were forwarded to the Allied conference but were totally ignored. They chose not even to reply.

In one of the pages in his diary, Artur writes:

On December 17, 1942, I met with the News Editor of the London *Times*, Assistant Editor of Reuter's Agency, the *New York Times'* London correspondent and Executive-Director of the BBC. Three days later, the London *Times* published large excerpts from the Underground Movement; a feature article appeared on Sunday. Reuter's disseminated the information to numerous newspapers, and an extensive report was cabled to the *New York Times*. The *Daily Telegraph* printed and supported the proposals I had presented at the assembly meeting of the Government-in-exile. However, the BBC broadcast was scant and directed only at its European audiences; there was no mention of the report on local English stations.

Monday afternoon I met again with Raczynski [Foreign Minister of the Polish Government-in-exile] who reported on his meeting with Anthony Eden. Until now, the Government-in-exile has been reluctant to admit Jews were suffering more than Poles, but now they are resolved to deal with the specific Jewish situation.

The British government authorities reacted in a negative manner. They did not accept the reports as genuine, and directed the BBC to minimise the news reports. The British foreign minister firmly denied this. However, that very day, a friend of Artur's on the BBC staff advised him that they had official instructions to broadcast the news briefly and with caution, limiting the newsflashes to a minimum.

Meetings took place at that time in London. Nine governments representing the European countries under German occupation had conferences, with the great powers in attendance as observers. The official expert on Polish affairs briefed the British foreign minister, Mr Eden, with whom Artur Zygielbaum had had various meetings on previous occasions, that reports of the massacres of the Jews most probably were true, although not officially confirmed. This very expert had informed Mr Eden on previous occasions that the reports were correct and verified.

A week later, a friend of Zygielbaum's who worked at the BBC showed him a second directive from the foreign ministry which completely refuted the first. The contents were as follows: the anti-Semitic tactics which Hitler was employing to further his ends should, at this stage, be used against him. The massacres of Jews in Poland should be given broad publicity. Artur wrote:

> Several months ago we were shocked by reports of the systematic and calculated murder of the Jewish population in dozens of Polish cities. It was difficult to believe the figure — 700,000 murdered. In the last few days, a new communication has been received by the Polish Government-in-exile which confirms the previous ones and reports further murders, even more horrible. Out of half a million Jews in the Warsaw ghetto, there remained 120,000 in September; by October, barely 40,000. From July on, 7,000 Jews were deported every day and executed. At the same time, almost the entire Jewish population of Lodz, Minsk-Mazowiecki, Kalisz, Nowy Dwor, Falenica, Lublin, Kielce, and Radom was annihilated. In Belzec, Treblinka, and Sobibor, concentration camps have been established where the murders are executed by means of gas, electrocution and other methods. Huge modern machinery is employed to dig mass graves.
>
> During these past three years, the Germans starved millions of Jews. On Himmler's orders, the entire extermination of a people has begun. We ask the Germans: where are three and a half million Jews? What have you done with them? This question shall be heard for generations to come.

On 21 January 1943, the Jewish underground sent a radio message via the Polish government-in-exile to Jewish leaders in New York:

> We notify you of the greatest crime of all time, the murder of millions of Jews in Poland. Poised at the brink of the annihilation of the still surviving Jews, we ask you to:
>
> 1. Take revenge against the Germans.
> 2. Force the Hitlerites to halt the murders.
> 3. Fight for our lives and our honour.
> 4. Contact the neutral countries.
> 5. Rescue 10,000 children through exchange.
> 6. Send 500,000 dollars for purposes of aid.
>
> Brothers — the remaining Jews in Poland live with the awareness that in the most terrible days of our history you did not come to our aid. Respond, at least, in the last days of our life.

Artur Zygielbaum wrote in his letter to president Roosevelt and prime minister Churchill:

> As the official representative of the Jewish Labour Movement in Poland ... I turn to your governments with the latest desperate appeal of the Jews who are being murdered en masse behind the ghetto walls. The following is an excerpt from the last despatch received from Warsaw, dated August 31, 1942:
>
> 'A savage storm rages over the heads of Polish Jewry, and the terrible storm grows more fierce with each passing day. In recent weeks not only thousands have been killed, but tens and hundreds of thousands — the entire Jewish people is being annihilated ... Not more than one million Jews, or perhaps one and a quarter million out of the 3.5 million Jews in Poland before the war are still alive. And the mass murders go on.
>
> 'The Jews of Poland appeal to you to find ways to save the remnants of Polish Jewry.'

Artur's desperate call for help on behalf of the last remnants of Polish Jewry fell on deaf ears. On 12 May 1943, he committed suicide after hearing the Polish underground radio reporting the massacre of the last Jews of the Warsaw ghetto. In his final testament, addressing himself to the prime minister, Wladyslaw Sikorski, and president Wladyslaw Raczkiewicz of the Polish government-in-exile, he wrote:

> I take the liberty of addressing to you my last words, and through you, to the Polish people, to the governments and the peoples of the Allied States — to the conscience of the world.
>
> From the latest information received from Poland, it is evident that the Germans, with the most ruthless cruelty, are now murdering the few remaining Jews in Poland. Behind the ghetto's walls, the last act of a tragedy, unprecedented in history, is being performed. The responsibility for this crime of murdering the entire Jewish population of Poland falls in the first instance on the perpetrators, but indirectly it is also a burden on the whole of humanity, the people and the governments of the Allied states who, thus far, have made no effort toward concrete action to halt this crime.
>
> By the passive observation of the murder of defenceless millions, and the maltreatment of children, women and old men, these coun-

tries have become the criminals' accomplices. I must also state that although the Polish Government has in a high degree contributed to the enlistment of world opinion, it has yet done so insufficiently. It has not done anything that could correspond to the magnitude of the drama being enacted now in Poland. From some 3,500,000 Polish Jews and about 700,000 other Jews deported to Poland from other countries — according to official statistics provided by the Underground Bund organisation — there remained in April of this year only about 300,000, and this continuing murder still goes on.

I cannot be silent — I cannot live — while remnants of the Jewish people of Poland, of whom I am a representative, are perishing. My comrades in the Warsaw ghetto took weapons in their hands on that last heroic impulse. It was not my destiny to die there together with them, but I belong to them and to their mass graves. By my death, I wish to express my strongest protest against the inactivity with which the world is looking on and permitting the extermination of my people.

I know how little human life is worth today, but as I was unable to do anything during my life, perhaps by my death I shall contribute to breaking down the indifference of those who may now — at the last moment — rescue the few Polish Jews still alive, from certain annihilation. My life belongs to the Jewish people of Poland and I therefore give it to them. I wish that this remaining handful of the original several millions of Polish Jews could live to see the liberation of a new world of freedom, and the justice of true socialism. I believe that such a Poland will arise and that such a world will come.

I trust that the President and the Prime Minister will direct my words to all those for whom they are destined, and that the Polish government will immediately take appropriate action in the fields of diplomacy. I bid my farewell to everybody and everything dear to me and loved by me.

—Shmuel Mordechai (Artur) Zygielbaum.[30]

'Entry strictly forbidden for Jews and dogs'

After the Warsaw ghetto revolt, a silence invaded our home, as though we were all in mourning. By nature, my brother was always quiet; so was my father, but not as quiet as this. I, who was always vocal, became withdrawn. We were all deeply shocked. Only my mother tried to provoke discussions, bringing up any topic to break the silence. Eventually, she would hum a tune and encourage us to join her.

I looked at my brother, wondering if he still wanted to escape. Now I was not so sure that it was not the best plan. Should I encourage his escape and join him? Could we run away and leave our parents behind? This last was inconceivable. It would have been treason. Would we survive if we fled? I doubted it very much. Then I would do a complete turn-around and think: we must run away! Lipek is right! We will all perish!

Ultimately, I returned to my belief that we would survive as long as we stayed together. If we ran, then where to? There was no refuge on the other side of the wires.

Before the war, the Karess family at 25 Limanowskiego Street had always treated us with great friendship and warmth. They had a beautiful grocery-delicatessen, and we used to buy our supplies from them. Mrs Karess always gave me or my brother some sweets whenever we passed her door. She would kiss us whenever we left for or came back from our school holidays. When we were very little, she used to grab me in her arms and show me off to her customers, cuddling my jet black frizzy hair. She admired my dark brown eyes, calling me her 'little black Gypsy'. She was childless but loved children very much, calling us her 'sweet boys', as did Elsa and Hilda, her two young shop assistants.

The day the German army invaded, Otto and Mrs Karess changed. In the beginning, I still went to their store. They would not allow Jews inside, and they had a big sign on their door: *'Juden Und Hunde Eintritt Streng Verboten'* ('Entry strictly forbidden for Jews and dogs'). I took no notice of the sign. I kept going to their store, which was still stocked with everything one could dream about at pre-war prices. They served mainly the Germans of the district. One day Mrs Karess said, 'Abraham, don't you know that you should not come here?'

I looked at her uncomprehendingly.

'I mean not through the front door,' she amended. 'Come tomorrow, after 4 p.m. — through the private entrance at the back. I will have some things ready for you.'

The next day at four I knocked at her door. She did not ask me in. The Karesses were entertaining a house full of German officers, and I could hear them singing their military songs. She switched off the lights in the corridor leaving me to stand in the dark. Soon she came back, handing to me a big bag full of groceries. I could hardly lift it. I asked her how much I owed her.

'Please, go,' she said. 'Go quickly. Come back tomorrow at the same time. Bring 185 zlotys. Don't pay me now. Just go quickly. Should anyone stop you on the way, don't, for heaven's sake, tell them where you got the groceries from.'

When I came home, we unpacked the bags and could hardly believe our eyes. There was sugar, flour, coffee, tea, chocolate, rice, dried figs, almonds, apricots, dried apples, tins of sardines, sprats, fish in tomato sauce and a fair amount of sausage: the most luxurious delicacies, not to be found anywhere else in Lodz. The grocery stores were all empty and closed. Food queues were miles long.

The next afternoon, I went back to the Karesses as arranged. This time the assistant, Elsa, opened the door. She had known me for many years and had always been nice to me, but as soon as she saw me on this occasion, she snapped at me, 'How dare you come here! You little Jew boy, don't you know where you belong?'

With some difficulty I explained to her that Mrs Karess had told me to come but Elsa turned away, shutting the door in my face. I stood in the dark, stunned and upset, not knowing what to do. I waited, hoping Mrs Karess would eventually come. I rang the door-bell again. This time, it was Otto Karess who opened the door. He was tipsy and looked at me with a strange smile.

'Don't you know that we are Germans?' he mocked.

'Of course I know you are Germans,' I stuttered in confusion. 'Please don't be angry with me. It was Mrs Karess who told me to come. Ask her please, ask her. Could I see her?'

'No, not now,' he said. 'Come back a little later. Can't you see we are busy? We have guests.'

I went around to the courtyard, thinking that I would wait for a while. I found a corner to hide, as I didn't want to walk home.

Walking the streets had become dangerous.

Waiting in the dark under a staircase, I suddenly heard the noise of loud laughter and screams coming through the windows of the Karesses' apartment. A raucous-voiced, drunken German voice called out *'Jude, komm mal hier.'* ('Jew, come here!') I saw a man dressed in black with beard and earlocks. He was a neighbour of the Karesses. The Jew walked up to the window as I peeped through a half-closed door leading to the staircase. I could see a German officer grab him and pull him towards the window, slapping him across the face, pulling his beard and earlocks. As he held him, Otto Karess came out into the courtyard with a pair of scissors and, amidst the revelry, he chopped pieces off his neighbour's beard. Finally Karess cut one of his earlocks. The screams and giggles grew louder and louder, approaching hysteria. The women were all participating, their high-pitched, intoxicated screaming able to be heard miles away. The victim was bleeding profusely when another high-ranking German officer came running with his camera, taking photos as the crazy ritual continued.

The officer with the camera ordered the Karesses' neighbour to sing and dance as he took snaps. He finally ordered him to pray. The Jew stood motionless and silent. The German insisted that he pray. When the victim would not move, the officer became impatient and aggressive, punching him in the face. As the man fell to the ground, the officer kicked him and then left him on the cobblestoned courtyard. I stood behind the door, paralysed with fear. I wished the ground would open under my feet and make me disappear. I wished I could become invisible. When the Germans went back into the Karesses' apartment, I ran home as fast as possible. The money I was supposed to pay to the Karesses I handed back to my mother.

The next day, she went to the Karesses. Upon her return, she told us that, although Mrs Karess had still sold her some groceries, she had been distant and, as my mother left the store, Otto Karess had followed her into the street saying: 'Don't come here again, nor should you send your children. We don't sell to Jews.'

Before the war, Otto had been one of nature's gentleman. Softly spoken with a friendly smile, he looked like a warm-hearted country doctor. With the German invasion, however, he seemed to go through a total transformation. For many years, we had been good neighbours and customers of theirs and of the Kalenbachs from 19 Limanowskiego Street, of Schpalle from 54, and of Hesse the Baker, at number 30, whom I had known since childhood.

Old Hesse was a big man with a triple chin, and a huge belly always wrapped in a white apron. Whenever he saw me he would pinch my cheeks and ask how I was doing at school. And he had the best sugar-coated coffee buns in Lodz. Every day after school, my mother would give me twenty-five groschen for one of them, and Hesse would always choose one from the shelves for me saying, 'Abramek, here is a special one for you. It has a lot of raisins.' I knew every one of his family: his sons and daughters and his grandchildren. After the German invasion, they all changed — like people from another planet whose bodies had been invaded by aliens.

One day, as I entered the bakery shop, I was confronted by his oldest son dressed in a black SS uniform. Without a word he showed me out of the bakery, pointing his finger to the sign on the door which read: '*Juden Und Hunde Eintritt Streng Verboten*'.

I knew, therefore, that in any plans of escape I might make, turning to our pre-war German neighbours and acquaintances would be suicidal. To go to my Polish childhood friends, Rysiek, Zdich or Szczepanek, was not a hopeful alternative. The only people I could think of were Mr and Mrs Safjan. Where they now lived, however, was in Radogoszcz, a suburb predominantly inhabited by Germans — too dangerous to risk. Even the political groups had no contacts in the outside world. The Lodz ghetto was the most isolated, the most difficult ghetto of all from which to effect an escape.

Since the invasion of the Germans, Lodz had not only changed its name to Litzmannstadt, it had become a German city. A large part of the Polish population had been expelled and replaced with Germans from the bombarded cities inside Germany. Most of the homes left by the Jews were occupied by German refugees. Those Poles who were allowed to remain in Litzmannstadt were exempt from expulsion because they were essential for the industry and the services the city required.

With the invasion, Litzmannstadt experienced a sudden explosion of 'ethnic Germans' — Poles, actually, who chose to become German, even though they hardly knew the language. Suddenly

everybody wanted to be Volksdeutch. Going back many generations to dig up proof of German ancestry or seeking out distant
relatives who had inter-married, they looked for anything that
would give them this status. While Germany was powerful and
victorious, to be an ethnic German meant one was a privileged
citizen.

Sing Sing

After the Warsaw ghetto uprising, the deportations of Lodz ghetto
inhabitants continued, but Hans Biebow changed his style of
speech-making. He visited the ghetto factories more often, asking
us to be understanding, encouraging us to productivity and obedience. I heard him say once, 'Things are not as good as I would have
liked them to be. You must understand, there is a war.'

The food supply into the ghetto dwindled even further. Our
rations shrank to a bare minimum, with the death rate and sickness
climbing all the time. Production slowed down in the factories. No
raw materials arrived. We were under the distinct impression that
the ghetto was about to be liquidated. More deportations, then a
slowing down. Suddenly, a little more food arrived and raw
materials started to come back into the factories; but the ghetto was
confused, exhausted and weak. In the meantime, we constantly
hoped for Germany's collapse and the war's end. From the radio
we learned of German defeats on all fronts. Biebow appeared more
and more often, with his speeches of encouragement and pleas for
volunteers for deportation.

My father became thinner, ever thinner. His face swelled up
even more and his distended legs bothered him. When he came
home at night, he could not take off his shoes without my help.
Although he had a responsible position in the handling of vegetables, the staple diet of the ghetto, he never tried to help himself. I
could not understand why he did not even put a couple of potatoes
in his pocket, or a few carrots to eat on the spot, just to fill his
stomach. Whenever this subject came up my father would say, 'If
everybody stole, what would we give to the starving people?'

'Don't steal, just save your life,' I would tell him.

My father's answer was, as usual, 'I'm not a beggar nor a thief.
Other people have no more.'

When I said, 'Stop worrying about the others. Try to save your own life,' he would walk away without an answer.

One day, he came home unexpectedly in the middle of the day. He caught me in the act of standing ingloriously with my pants down, and removing potatoes and carrots from my long underwear which I had tied up at the ends to prevent the booty from falling out. I was unloading the few vegetables I had stolen from a store whilst I was out on official business. I would pinch only a few potatoes or carrots at a time, not too often, and only providing it was very safe.

My father was shocked and upset.

'Don't ever do this again,' he said. 'Are you out of your mind? You're risking your life! If you get caught you'll finish up in the hands of Toronczyk. Don't you remember how he smashed up Rosenwald for stealing a couple of beetroots? There was no way to help him either, once he got into the hands of the authorities. They sent him off to Czarniecki Prison and then deported him.'

One day, at the end of November 1943, Mordechai Chaim Rumkowski paid an unexpected visit to the head office, dismissing a large number of people, sending them off to work at the factories. The constant deportations and high death-rate had drastically reduced the labour force, so Rumkowski turned to the office employees as a last resort to increase productivity. My name was called and I entered the manager's office. Behind Mr Frenkiel's desk, Rumkowski peered over his glasses and boomed: 'Who do you come from?' wanting to know my lineage.

In the world of my past, my ancestry was of no significance; I had no pedigree. I was the son of Shimon, a walking 'klapsedra' (death notice), the grandson of the late Itshe Mayer Biderman, president of a synagogue, guardian of the Holy Scrolls.

When I did not reply, Rumkowski became agitated, shouting, 'Who do you come from?' again and again. Finally it was Mr Frenkiel who gave my name and told Rumkowski what my duties were. The old devil kept pointing his finger at me. I was lucky he didn't slap my face, as was his habit. At times he carried on like a medieval despot.

'Tomorrow,' he said, 'you will report to the Department of Labour.' His secretary put my name on the list. The following day, I obeyed orders, asking for Sienicki when I arrived at the department. I knew him from having worked at the Avant Garde Theatre at 3 Krawiecka Street. Sienicki was the theatre's director until its closure by order of the Gestapo. Strangely enough, Sienicki himself came to the door.

'There is very little I can do for you,' he said grimly, and turned me over to one of his assistants. I was given a note with stamps and signatures and told to report for work to the police commissar, Mr L Rosner, the manager of a large timber mill situated at 9 Pucka Street.

The place was nicknamed 'Sing Sing' and Mr Rosner, a nervous red-faced man with shaking hands and voice, assigned me to the machine hall. The sawdust and noise were unbearable. Because it was impossible to hear our own voices, we resorted to sign language. Three thousand people worked on two shifts. None was experienced in using the loud, monstrous machines that swallowed the timber planks, creating a fog of shavings and sawdust. Given just a few minutes of instruction, we were expected to cope. It was hardly surprising that virtually not a day passed without people cutting off their fingers, crippling their hands or losing an eye from flying timber knots. Some people were actually impaled by the planks which were ejected with tremendous force by the screaming machines.

In the end, though, I realised that my chances of survival in this place were slim. If the machines didn't get me, my escapades surely would. I went to see the technical manager, Mr Szwarcowski, and made a request to be transferred to the transport section, explaining that I should not work in the machine hall. There they could employ women or weaker men, I told him. I was strong and fit and could be of better use in transport. Fortunately, my request was granted. After the liquidation of the ghetto, Szwarcowski and I were both together at Althammer concentration camp. During the evacuation, an SS guard emptied his gun into Szwarcowski's body.

The factory turned out millions of clogs every year, which I later discovered were for the concentration camps. As well, we produced crates for all calibres of ammunition. The last order we had was for one million crates which had to be turned out very quickly. The timber yard was not the most congenial place, especially in the freezing winter when everything was covered in snow and frost. For a while, I was assigned to load the kiln to dry the timber. The temperature inside the kiln reached 35 degrees centigrade.

Outside, the temperature was between 12 and 25 centigrade below zero. The contrast in temperatures cut short the lives of many of my friends who worked there. They were under-nourished and feeble, and simply could not take the conditions.

Somehow, I managed to turn Sing Sing to my advantage. Fuel in the ghetto was non-existent but, from the moment I started to work there, our home was never short of boiled water to drink. We even became more hospitable to the occasional visitor who dropped in, at least able to afford to offer them a glass of hot water which, in the ghetto, was a luxury. At any rate, in the ghetto, visitors were very rare and, when they came, they did not expect anything, which was just as well: we had nothing to offer.

For the first time in the ghetto, I could boil the laundry and rid our underwear of lice. Soap was very scarce and we had no detergents or disinfectants. It was no wonder that the ghetto was riddled with vermin and typhus. Although we washed and kept clean, we still picked up lice as we stood squashed together in the queues. I would always take my clothes off in the foyer upon coming home, turn them inside out and brush them thoroughly to get rid of the lice.

The factory yard had a huge mountain of timber offcuts, but to take a piece was strictly forbidden. On their way out of the factory, workers were body-searched and every bit of timber hidden in their clothes was removed. Those found stealing were charged with theft and punished with cleaning toilets. Eventually they were put on the lists and deported.

I worked in a gang of four men — Pelta, Rosenblum, Majteles and myself — and we became close friends, sticking together and helping one another. When one had to jump the fence to run off home because of sickness, the others would work harder to cover for him. We were a well-organised group and worked effectively together. The management looked upon us with respect, and we felt lucky to have found one another.

Pelta came from the Yeshiva. He was an able Talmudic student, bright and interesting. Rosenblum was a good-hearted fellow, big in stature and strong. He had come to Sing Sing from a kitchen where he had worked for the last three years. He still looked healthy. Majteles was a well-read, intelligent young man who had come to Sing Sing from an office. In the beginning, he only spoke

Polish; but, as time passed, he learned Yiddish. He was very good-looking with platinum-blond hair and blue eyes. He could easily have passed as a non-Jew, as could the rest of his family. He was often asked why he didn't try to escape with looks like his.

'You would be surprised how many times I was found out as a Jew,' Majteles would reply. 'It's beyond me how they know. Poles are like bloodhounds: they can smell a Jew for miles.'

With this hand-picked group of boys, I thought that we could organise a scheme that would save us from freezing in our homes. Discreetly, we began to keep an eye on the gates and uncovered a few schemes that were in operation. Of course, they were run by the management. One day, a large quantity of timber loaded onto a horse-drawn cart passed the gate. We went over to the guard-house and bluntly confronted the man in charge. We asked him to let each of us take home one bag of timber. To begin with, he was not very co-operative but, with a little bit of arm-twisting, we convinced him that he should live and let live. Our gang became friendly with the gate-keepers once they realised that we could be of good use. Eventually, we became popular with the management as well. Whenever Szwarcowski or police commissar Rosner needed a cart of timber, we procured its safe delivery to their homes, as well as securing our own share as well.

Once, I decided to take a big bag of timber offcuts home with me. It was a cold December night; the snow was deep and stuck to my clogs, and to walk one-and-a-half kilometres with the heavy load on my back was hard. As I tried to kick the snow off my clogs I suddenly slipped, falling down right opposite the gate leading into the Baluter Market. I struggled with the bag and couldn't get it on my back again. Again and again my efforts failed. Exhausted and nervous, I gave up and sat down on the bag to rest with my head down.

Suddenly, I saw a German guard in front of me.

'Take it easy,' he said. 'Just relax and rest a little; get your breath.'

I was so scared that I could not utter a word. He returned to the guard booth, put his rifle away, came back to me and got hold of the bag.

'You grab the other end,' he said. 'One ... two ... three ... and up!' The bag was across my shoulders again. I just managed to say

'*Danke schön*' and move on.

If he had asked me for a permit, I would have been lost, finished! In many cases, when people were caught stealing from the factories, they were publicly hanged. The lesser punishment would have been cleaning toilets and then being deported on the next transport. This had happened to my school friend, Peretz Zylberberg but, the way I saw it, I had two choices: freeze or take the risk.

The trucks had to be loaded and unloaded at great speed so as not to upset the irritable German drivers who constantly harassed us; but because the work was so hard, we were at least given an extra soup ration. The transport workers numbered about one hundred and fifty men. They were the toughest and roughest lot I had ever met. How the four of us survived amongst them is beyond me; yet, as time went on, they took a liking to us. We became their four kids, and they considered us fine, educated boys. Whenever a confrontation arose between them and the management, they used me as their spokesman.

'Abraham,' they would say, 'you are very good at this. You go and talk to them. To you, they listen.'

At times my task was unpleasant. To negotiate with the police commissar, who was always nervous and smoking like a steam engine, was difficult. Rosner would never talk: he always shouted; it was how he demonstrated his authority. On one occasion, he became so worked up with me that he picked up the phone, shouting at the top of his voice, 'I'll have you locked up at Czarnieckiego.'

Mr Szwarcowski, who had his office next door, came in and, without saying a word, walked over to his desk and disconnected the phone as Rosner was about to speak to the prison requesting my arrest. I was told to leave the office while the two of them proceeded to have a lengthy discussion. After that incident, commissar Rosner became more amenable and I found him easier to talk to. At one stage during negotiations, I said to him, 'Why don't I leave it to you to come to terms with the transport men?' Rosner calmed down immediately and asked me to stay on. All the fights were over a bowl of soup or a slice of bread which the men demanded when they worked longer hours.

Spezialwagen

It was towards the end of December 1943 that four men, who had just arrived in the ghetto, turned up to work at Pucka Street and were assigned to the transport section. They looked well-fed compared to us. They came from an RAB labour camp which was building the Reichsautobahn — the famous highway connecting Berlin to Posen. Hitler's dream was to extend it to Moscow, but it never reached there.

One night, when we were sitting in the shed waiting for the trucks to arrive, they told us about the mobile gassing vans, describing how they looked and how they operated. In the beginning, they were scared to talk about it; then they warmed to their terrible task.

The vans, they said, had the appearance of military ambulances with red crosses painted on them. They had no windows and were hermetically sealed. The carbon monoxide emitted from a specially designed engine was connected to the passenger section. As the van travelled, the passengers were poisoned. By the time it reached its destination they were all dead. They were told by a German road engineer how the Spezialwagen functioned. The 'ambulances' would make regular calls at their labour camp to collect those who, in the opinion of the Germans, were of no further use. These people were never seen again.

I had heard of mass executions by firing squads, but this was the first I had heard of Jews being gassed. On that night I realised, as I never had before, that we were doomed. There was no way out. The Germans would keep us as long as we were of use to them; then it was only a matter of time until we would all finish up in the vans. Little did I know that the news was more than two years out of date: the Spezialwagen had been in use in Chelmno for more than two years (see pages 50–51 above.)

The next morning after work, worn out and confused by my thoughts about what I knew, I came home but did not dare to look directly at anyone. I was scared that my eyes would divulge the terrible news. Still, it was obvious to everyone that my behaviour was unusual.

'What's the matter with you? Please tell me what happened,' my mother asked. I told her I had had a fight at work but she did not believe me. The harder I tried to evade her questions, the less credible I appeared. I kept saying, 'Don't worry. Please don't worry. I will be all right.' What could I tell her? That we were all going to be gassed?

I couldn't go to sleep. I couldn't shut my eyes. The moment I did, terrible scenes would appear in my mind like some bizarre horror film, with one scene more terrifying than the next. I hated it. I became afraid to shut my eyes. I started to read but couldn't concentrate.

I never spoke to any of my family about the gas vans, and only occasionally with some of my friends at work — mainly those who had heard the story from the RAB fellows. The only person whom I spoke to, besides the transport people at Pucka Street, was Rivek Skoczylas, and he knew already, having heard the story from a different source. Rivek was up to date with all the rumours. Working with the tramways, he had contact with lots of people.

As time passed, I calmed down and came to terms with the uncertainty. One can get used to anything. For the last four years we had all been coping with the knowledge of mass executions by shooting. Maybe gassing would be less painful.

The 'Final Solution'

In November and December of 1943, the question of how to carry out the final liquidation of the Lodz ghetto came up again in Berlin. The leaders of the Final Solution Committee, the chief of the RSHA, Dr Ernest Kaltenbrunner, General SS Obergruppenführer Oswald Pohl, Adolf Eichmann and SS Reichsführer Heinrich Himmler were in conference.[31]

As early as 21 May 1943, Dr Kaltenbrunner had cabled Adolf Eichmann, advising him that all Jews from the Third Reich and from the Protectorate must be sent off to the east before the end of June 1943. This meant the gas chambers. Whilst he was in Terezienstadt, he remembered the Lodz ghetto and, in a separate paragraph in one of his memos to his headquarters, he wrote:

> Litzmannstadt ghetto is to be inspected by Obersturmbannführer Adolf Eichmann who will judge on the spot. The decision is to be left to him.[32]

This was an order to Eichmann that he should at once visit the Lodz ghetto to investigate the circumstances and to familiarise himself with the industrial enterprises and bring the conflict which existed between Osti (the industrial section of the concentration camps, run by the SS) and the Reichsstatthalter Artur Greiser to a conclusive end. He was to arrange the takeover of all the manufactured stock, machinery and raw materials that the ghetto possessed.[33]

On 3 December 1943, at Berlin Headquarters, another meeting between Himmler, Kaltenbrunner and Oswald Pohl took place. At this meeting, Himmler authorised Pohl to convert the Lodz ghetto into a concentration camp and not to transport the factories to Lublin as previously suggested by SS General Globocnick. When Pohl moved to execute Himmler's orders, he was confronted again with stubborn resistance from the powerful Reichsstatthalter of the Warthegau, Artur Greiser.[34]

At that time Eichmann, in accordance with Kaltenbrunner's instructions, had to go to Lodz. On 14 December 1943, Eichmann appeared in the ghetto together with important leaders of the Third Reich: Millhorn, government adviser to Posen and a diplomat-merchant from Berlin; and Horn, who was an officer in Globocnick's headquarters, and connected to the activities of the 'Final Solution'. He operated Osti industries, where the Jews were working under terrible conditions, exploited to the very last and eventually disposed of by being transported to the gas chambers in Treblinka.

In the Lodz ghetto, the struggle for survival continued from day to day, minute by minute. In Berlin, at the State Security head office of the Gestapo, the masters of the Final Solution were planning the end of the very last ghetto in Poland with the very last remnants of the Polish Jews who had once numbered 3.5 million — the largest Jewish community in Europe. As 1943 drew to an end, they were discussing how to liquidate the ghetto and bring *Die Juden Frage* — the Jewish question — to its ultimate resolution.

6

The Lodz ghetto, 1944

JANUARY 1944: our fifth winter behind barbed wire. The blizzards hit the ghetto ferociously, covering the dirty courtyards and streets with a heavy blanket of snow. The angry wind punished the starved and frozen people with a vengeance. The frosts saturated every bone, every joint of the emaciated inhabitants, penetrating the walls of the workshops, factories and dwellings. Inside our homes, the frost formed, inches thick, on the walls.

Behind the barbed wires of the ghetto, neither spring nor summer ever came. In my memory, an eternal winter lives on in a world of decay, filth, famine and death. The ghetto people looked as if they had been hewn from rock: their bloodless faces hard, silent and lifeless; only their eyes, deeply sunken into their foreheads, burned with a desire for life. Moving lethargically, dragging their swollen limbs wrapped in bulky rags, they were shadows of shadows, roaming the narrow streets. Like rats in a sewer expecting to be preyed upon by larger rats, when they crossed the streets the ghetto-dwellers constantly looked over their shoulders, fearing capture by the Jewish police and then being handed over to the Germans for deportation.

Those whom the round-ups had missed continued with their daily routine. Queuing up for hours to collect their frozen vegetable rations — a vital component of our intake — was often a task that seemed beyond the strength of many. Only the will to live kept them on their feet. The grim irony of it all was that half of the food was rotten and unfit for consumption anyway.

The flour, sugar and oil rations shrank. Everything was measured in grams as if it were gold. A two-kilo loaf of bread (per head) had to last for eight days. The bread was arguably the most important part of our diet, and those who lost the ability to control their hunger ate up their food upon collecting it, surviving till the next ration only on the watery soup handed out to them every day at work. They were the ones who faded away very fast.

The famine reached frightful proportions. People were hiding the corpses of deceased family members for longer and longer periods in order to collect their food rations. Many froze to death; others slowly expired in their beds, alone and forgotten. Not until the stench of a decomposed body alerted their neighbours were they discovered. In some homes, the dying would be left in a corner unattended, because the others in the house were too sick or too weak to help them. Entire families could be wiped out without a survivor being left to tell what had happened to them.

The Carro family, our next-door neighbours, comprised four brothers — young, wholesome and good-looking men when they came into the ghetto. One was a third-year medical student who had just returned from France for his vacation when the war broke out. He was not to see Paris again.

The Carros were a well-known Sephardic family in pre-war Lodz. Their ancestry stretched back to the Spanish Inquisition, where they had escaped the scourge of the cross. Finally, they fell victim to the broken cross, the swastika, dying of starvation one after another in a short space of time.

Life in the ghetto was full of agony; empty, meaningless and without purpose. Only the next bowl of watery soup and the small, daily portion of bread, made of rye mixed with sawdust, kept us going. And only one who has suffered hunger to the point of starvation will understand how miserable life was in the ghetto when the sole thing that mattered was food. Potato peels were an occasional luxury, going to those who had the right connections. Some people even ate from the garbage heap that contained nothing but rotting filth — anything to fill their stomachs. At 9 Pucka Street, where I worked in the timber mill, I used to chew timber to keep my jaws busy.

In our home, mother made sure that the bread lasted until the next ration. With a steady hand she would slice it without losing so much as a crumb, while the rest of the family sat, hypnotised, watching her. My mouth would water as I observed the bread-cutting ritual which took place every night before bed. The watching was an important part of the meal, lasting longer than the actual eating.

In the ghetto, with life becoming harder, and the misery growing from day to day, we never knew what the Germans were planning and what the next day would bring. There was only one certainty: whatever they were planning was never good for us. We lived in fear.

Profiteers

Artur Greiser was the supreme master of the Lodz ghetto. His goal was always profit, motivated by his thirst for wealth. He was a shrewd manipulator, a German Machiavelli, the main force behind the constant postponements of the ghetto's liquidation. It was largely due to him and his greed that the Lodz ghetto survived till August 1944 — the last ghetto in Poland still in existence. His manipulations revoked three written orders signed by Himmler authorising his men to liquidate the ghetto. His ability to manipulate people always defeated every effort made by Eichmann, Pohl and many other powerful leaders in the SS with direct access to Himmler who were all anxious to grab the accumulated wealth of the ghetto: equipment, materials and slave labour.

Whilst Greiser was busy haggling with Himmler, Hans Biebow was engaged in gathering support from the high-ranking army officers in charge of the army supply, whom the Lodz ghetto was providing with the requirements to outfit five thousand German soldiers per week. With the help of Biebow, Greiser successfully managed to retain full control over the ghetto, its wealth and its profits, fending off the many attempts made by Eichmann and Osti — who were desperately trying to wrest it all from him — until the very last, when the fast-moving Russian army threatened to free most of Poland from German occupation.

On 12 February 1944, SS Reichsführer Heinrich Himmler, in the company of his top men, paid a visit to Posen Government House, where he met with the Reichsstatthalter of the Warthegau, Artur Greiser. At that meeting, Himmler agreed that the Litzmannstadt ghetto should be left under the control of Artur Greiser and remain part of the State. Stock, machinery and all belongings should remain the property of the Litzmannstadt city administration after the Jews had been transported to the east.

In view of the strategic changes and with the approach of the front line, Himmler once again ordered the liquidation of the Lodz ghetto. This time, he referred the logistics of the exercise directly to Greiser, who put the wheels of action into motion, making sure that the raw materials, ready stock and machinery would be taken care of by his faithful cronies. The first spoils he shared with Biebow, as well as the president of Litzmannstadt and a few of his other favourites who had served him loyally. Greiser appointed the Gestapo chief of Litzmannstadt, SS Hauptsturmführer Dr Otto Bradfisch, to the office of Lord Mayor, giving him full control of all civilian and police departments of the city as well as of all the bureaus connected with the Jewish Final Solution. With the help of SS Obersturmführer Günter Fuchs, his deputy, who was in charge of the Bureau of Jewish Affairs 4bII in Litzmannstadt, Bradfisch took full control of the 'Aktion' of the final liquidation of the Lodz ghetto. A conference was called, involving the heads of all the departments of the city of Litzmannstadt. Bradfisch's orders were blunt: 'Shoot to kill whoever resists, disobeys or runs!'[35] However, so as not to provoke the Jews to resist, Bradfisch told his officers not to over-react; they were to pretend that the remaining inhabitants were being sent to Germany to work. What he feared most was having another Warsaw ghetto on his hands.

Greiser, in partnership with Biebow and the president of Litzmannstadt, made fortunes at the expense of the ghetto Jews who slaved for eighty pfennig a day, whilst the German Ministry of Labour allocated six Reichsmarks (600 pfennig) for every working Jew per day. Added to these were the handsome bribes paid to Greiser and Biebow by German industrialists who used Jewish slave labour to manufacture their goods at a fraction of the normal cost. No wonder that they were keen to maintain the starving ghetto in its current form as long as possible.

At the Polish war trials, Greiser and Biebow were found guilty, and were sentenced to death for their crimes against humanity. During the hearings, they accused one another of becoming multi-millionaires through the exploitation and robbery of the hundreds of thousands of Jewish victims whom they sent off to be gassed. This, however, was true of most of the high-ranking German officials who came in close contact with the Lodz ghetto.

The pace of deportation quickens

The food rations had shrunk still further. Potatoes disappeared. All we received was kohlrabi and occasionally a few beetroots. And, as the rations shrank, so did the ghetto population. Through starvation, the Germans aimed at breaking the people's resistance to deportation.

The German tactics changed. The Warsaw ghetto revolt prompted them to act with more caution. They refrained from sending Einsatzkommandos into the ghetto, leaving the rounding-up of the victims to the Jewish Sonderkommando and police.

Rumkowski's constant speeches promised better conditions for those who volunteered to work in Germany; but the soft words and promises were soon replaced with threats. Placards appeared on the ghetto walls:

PROCLAMATION No. 414

WARNING!

IN CONNECTION WITH THE SENDING OF WORKERS OUTSIDE THE GHETTO.

BECAUSE SOME DO NOT REPORT TO THE CENTRAL PRISON, I DEMAND FOR THE LAST TIME THAT THEY SHOULD UNCONDITIONALLY, IMMEDIATELY AFTER THE PUBLISHING OF THIS VERY PROCLAMATION, REPORT TO THE CENTRAL PRISON.

THOSE WHO ARE STILL IN HIDING ARE MISTAKEN IN THE BELIEF THAT, AFTER THE TRANSPORT LEAVES, THEY WILL BE REINSTATED WITH THEIR RATION CARDS. I DRAW TO THEIR ATTENTION THAT THESE BELIEFS ARE TOTALLY FALSE.

AFTER THE WORK FORCE TRANSPORTS DEPART, ALL THOSE WHO HAVE BEEN IN HIDING MUST REPORT WITH ALL THE MEMBERS OF THEIR FAMILY TO THE CENTRAL PRISON.

THOSE REQUESTING THEIR RATION CARDS TO BE REINSTATED WILL BE ARRESTED AND FORCED TO DIVULGE:

WHERE THEY WERE HIDING

NAMES OF THOSE WHO HELPED THEM

NAMES OF THOSE WHO PROVIDED THEM WITH FOOD

IN ORDER TO FIND THOSE GUILTY AND RESPONSIBLE. NOT

UNTIL SUCH TIME WILL THE FOOD RATION CARDS BE REIN-
STATED.

AFTER THIS PROCLAMATION, ALL THOSE IN HIDING WHO
IMMEDIATELY REPORT TO THE CENTRAL PRISON, WILL PRE-
VENT FURTHER ACTION BEING TAKEN AGAINST THEIR FAM-
ILY MEMBERS.

MORDECHAI CHAIM RUMKOWSKI

THE ELDEST OF THE JEWS IN LITZMANNSTADT GHETTO.

3 March 1944.[36]

Rumkowski continued with his speeches in the factories. The
results were not satisfactory: people resisted deportation. He
called an urgent meeting of the factory managers at the
Kulturhaus, ordering them to draw up lists of people from their
factories, primarily of those whose departure would not reduce the
flow of production.

Hans Biebow appeared more frequently in the ghetto factories.
His speeches had a softer tone, his addresses a friendly manner
never heard before. Using words like, 'My dear Jews', and 'Please',
he explained the needs of Germany in the war effort. Praising the
Jews from the Lodz ghetto for the important role they played, and
the hard work and skills they had given to the Third Reich, he
appealed for volunteers for deportation, promising good conditions and plenty of food. Above all, he told them, he was most
concerned for their safety.

'The good workers, young and fit, must be protected from the
approaching war theatre,' Biebow said. 'Soon the ghetto will be
exposed to air raids and therefore must be evacuated. The invading
communists will punish you for having worked so faithfully for
the German war industry. It is for the protection and the well-being
of the Jews from the Lodz ghetto to be evacuated from the invading
Red Army.'

But Biebow's speeches awoke only suspicion and distrust. We
knew his intentions. His sweet promises made no impression. If
anything, they had a negative effect: no volunteers came forward.
The rumours about renewed transports of Jews into the forest near
Chelmno started to spread again.

Fear of deportation intensified. Life in the ghetto was miserable;
but to be deported, worse. In the ghetto we still hoped that we

might survive. We clung to each other for moral and physical support. We were among those very few exceptions of a family being left intact. Having one another was our last hope. Perhaps soon the Russian army would rescue us.

The radio news was encouraging. The Germans were losing on all fronts. The Russian army was fighting on Polish territory, moving towards Warsaw; but the starvation in the ghetto grew ever worse. People were dying at work and in the streets. This I saw every day on my way to and from work. Tuberculosis and typhus were rampant; but the ghetto, under the spell of death, still resisted deportation.

The Jewish Sonderkommando, led by Mordechai Kliger, became more aggressive, grabbing people off the streets on their way to work. Scared to queue up for their food rations, people were being dragged from their beds in the middle of the night.

They take my brother away

In the early hours of 3 March, a violent banging on our door woke us up. This was followed with shouts of, 'Open up! Police!'

The door was shaking with pounding fists and kicking boots.

'Open up! This is the police.'

Our home was silent as the pounding continued. Suddenly my father called out: 'Open the door!' In front of me stood an angry officer of the Jewish Sonderkommando

'Are you deaf?' he shouted. Dressed in my usual night attire — coat, fur cap, shawl, gloves and my last pair of woollen socks which I kept for sleeping only — I said nothing.

The Sonder officer, list in hand, shining his torch into my eyes, snapped: 'Are you Lipman Biderman?'

Still I said nothing.

'Are you Lipman Biderman?' he repeated. 'Answer yes or no.'

He walked into the second room, barking at the top of his voice: 'Which of you is Lipman Biderman? I warn you, whoever you are, you'd better speak up or I will take you all!'

Eventually, my brother said quietly from his bed: 'I am Lipman.'

'You idiot,' the officer roared. 'Why didn't you say so? Hurry up! Get dressed! You're coming with me!'

'Why are you taking him?' I asked. 'And where?'

Without looking at me, the officer snapped, 'I have an order to take him with me.'

'Where are you taking him?'

The officer gave no answer; he just urged my brother to dress more quickly.

My mother switched on the lights. My father, Berish and Sarah came out of their beds, all dressed in their winter clothes as though ready for a walk. They stood around with fear in their eyes. Then my mother walked over to the big mahogany wardrobe with the huge mirror on the centre door. She opened it and took out Lipek's rucksack with the essentials. Every member of our family had his separate rucksack, always ready for the unexpected. Lipek, standing in the middle of the room, looked at mother in silence as he put his rucksack over his right shoulder. She grabbed him in her arms, pressing her body against him, kissing him without a word, without a tear. Then she let go of him and walked over to the corner near her bed. My father put his arms around him, and kissed him with an expression of helplessness on his face; so did Sarah and Berish. None of us spoke. The silence was broken by grandmother's bewildered utterance from her bed:

'God Almighty! God Almighty! Why? What has he done? He is a good boy! Why are you taking him? He has done no harm to anybody. Why are they taking him? God Almighty! God Almighty! Why?'

The second policeman escorting the officer, as if to show his efficiency, suddenly turned to my brother and grabbed his arm:

'Come on! Move! Get going!' he ordered, pulling him towards the door.

I followed Lipek onto the staircase where two more Sonder policemen were guarding the foyer door from the outside. One of them was our neighbour who lived above us on the second floor. He tried to smile, shaking his head with embarrassment as if to say, What can I do?

As Lipek walked towards the stairs I grabbed him in my arms, kissing him goodbye. He descended without turning his head or speaking.

'Don't worry! Everything will be OK,' I called out to him. 'Just hang on. I'll catch up with you in the morning.' Then I just stayed on the landing in the dark, as he walked towards the huge gate leading into the street.

Inside our apartment, the family was still silent. Only my grand-mother kept up her lamenting, 'God Almighty! God Almighty! Why? Why?'

To this day, I ask myself the same question.

We were awake for the rest of the night, saying little. As soon as the curfew lifted, I ran to the Czarnieckiego Prison where Lipek was being held with seven hundred and fifty other men who had also been rounded up that night. They were being kept under heavy guard till further orders.

I ran along the wire fence of the gaol calling Lipek's name. From a distance I heard him answer. He was waiting for me, but the jail was heavily guarded by the Jewish prison police with not the slightest chance of escape.

At the main prison gate, a brisk black-market trade in human beings was going on. Any person could free his relative by provid-ing another man as a substitute. We desperately needed a body, but the going price asked by volunteers was two loaves of bread and one kilo of sugar. This was far beyond our reach.

There were many volunteers — far more lives were for sale than there was bread and sugar to buy them. I ran back home with the news, to be greeted by silence from six adults who between them did not possess the price to save Lipek from being deported. We all went down to the prison and just stood helplessly at the fence.

The only alternative, as I saw it, was for me to take my brother's place. My reasoning was simple. I must replace him because I was stronger and fitter. My parents stood wordless and immobile. What could they say? How could they choose? Uncle Berish was very much against it, arguing that my place was with my parents, to look after the family. After discussing the matter at length, we went back home, frozen, hungry and depressed.

Fully dressed in our freezing home, seated around the big mahogany table, we continued our debate. Then Berish and Sarah stood up and asked me to follow them. The three of us sat down between the two collapsible iron beds near the kitchen window that overlooked the barbed wire. This was the little corner the two of them had for their privacy. Berish repeated his arguments of earlier on, trying to impress upon me that I must not leave. Aunt Sarah supported his reasoning, and I just sat and listened, unable to think straight, incapable of reasoning. At some level, I felt that if I did not take Lipek's place, I would be betraying him.

I was suddenly reminded of how Lipek had planned his escape, and I felt guilty of an enormous perfidy. We should have escaped; we should have. Now I was unable to make a decision, even though I knew it was much too late for regrets. And there was no easy answer. If I went, I realised that my parents would not be able to cope; if I stayed, would Lipek survive?

'Let us hope that in Germany they will feed him better,' Sarah said, trying to console me.

I just shook my head. My parents were both still sitting in the dark at the big mahogany table. My grandmother was in bed talking to herself. From time to time, she would call to my father:

'Shymele, please go to bed. It must be very late. Shymele, please, you must be very tired. Go to bed.'

In the blackness of the night we sat for many hours without saying a word. The walls sparkled with frost and I could hear my heart beat. The regular pounding of my temples drummed out a message: You must go! You must go! No, don't go! No, don't go!

After a while, I went back to the dining room and joined my parents at the table. From time to time, somebody would sigh. In the silence I could hear the squeak of the snow under the boots of the guard walking in front of our building as he hummed the famous German war song: *'Heute haben wir besiegt ganz Polen und morgen die ganze Welt.'* ('Today we have conquered Poland and tomorrow the whole world.')

Waiting for the curfew to lift, my overloaded mind resorted to its usual defence of retreating into the past. It wandered back to the pre-war days when we had had plenty of food, when Lipek and I were both at school and life was good. Our home was always clean and warm, and nobody knew what it meant to be hungry or cold. We went on holidays with aunty Ethel, uncle Laib and my cousins, and there were trips to Vilno and Warsaw with the youth movement, Skif. I remembered the vacations with my mother in the Carpathians, climbing the mountains in Krynica or Szczawnice. The Polish mountains are rich with colourful scenery; the forests unforgettable with their tall pine trees whispering to me as if they were trying to tell me the secrets of times gone by.

The most exciting time of the year had been when uncle Berish, Sarah and my cousin Joe came to visit us from Berlin for Passover.

At my grandfather's big table the whole family would gather: my parents, Lipek, myself, uncle Laib, Ethel his wife, their children Sala, Basia, Heniek, my grandparents and of course our family from Berlin.

I loved to watch my grandmother cover her eyes when blessing the candles in their silver candlestick holders on the white damask table-cloth. There was plenty of food and the most ambrosial wines and liqueurs made by my grandparents. Berish and Sarah always brought presents for everyone. I remember a fountain pen with its golden nib, and a silver pencil in which I could see my reflection in miniature.

Passover meant spring and blossom. It was the season of lilac, my mother's favourite flower. It was a time when we were all bought new shoes, new school caps and new suits. I loved the games with nuts and almonds, cheating, trying to win, fighting, quarrelling with my cousins.

From time to time, flashes of reality intruded upon my day-dreaming, the shock of fear making my heart accelerate. I wondered whether uncle Laib, Ethel and my cousins were still alive after the Warsaw ghetto revolt. I looked at Berish and Sarah. They were tired and sad. My mother had become sick and worn out. Father sat next to her with a worried look on his swollen face, supporting his head with his hands, staring at the table. My jaws hurt from grinding my teeth. I was tense and tired. I remembered the day in 1938 when my uncle Berish had suddenly appeared at our house.

German Jews of Polish origin are expelled

It is 19 October 1938. My uncle Berish is not expected; he just appears in the early morning. He walks from the railway station, not even having the money to pay for a hansom cab. He comes with only the clothes on his back. Excitable and nervous, he paces the perimeters of the dining room, lighting one cigarette after another.

The night before in Berlin, at 77 Friedenstrasse, two Gestapo agents had arrested Berish in his home. He had not even said goodbye to his son, Joseph, who feigned sleep, trembling with fear as he listened to what was taking place in the next room. My uncle had been allowed to take his Polish passport, his hat and coat, nothing else. He had barely kissed his wife goodbye. Having lived in Berlin for more than twenty years, Berish — together with fifteen thousand former Polish Jews — had been taken by train to the eastern border. Being in possession of a valid Polish passport, Berish had been allowed to cross the border into Poland.

For others, the situation is far worse. The border guards do not let them pass. It is the stuff of nightmares. The expelled Jews sit in no-man's-land on the Polish-German border, in a tiny peasant settlement called Zbaszyn, where they are kept for many months in appalling conditions. Jewish representatives in the United States, England and in other countries desperately plead on their behalf, but to no avail.

At the same time, thousands of other German Jews roam the seven seas, unable to find a port that will admit them. Some of them flee to Shanghai and are later locked up in a ghetto set up by the Japanese. They are the fortunate ones. In the first week of May 1939, the passenger liner SS *St Louise*, carrying nine hundred Jews escaping from Nazi Germany, approaches the coast of Florida. On an order given by President Franklin D Roosevelt, the boat is forced to turn back. In consequence, most of the refugees later perish in the Holocaust.

Suddenly, these German Jews of Polish origin are homeless, with no means of support, robbed of everything they possess. They are well-educated, almost all of them having skills in the trades or professions. Many of them are eminent scientists, physicists, mathematicians, doctors, writers, professors, composers, actors, film producers, journalists and teachers. Amongst them are possibly some of the greatest minds of the twentieth century, but only a very few are able to find homes in the United States and Britain.

At this time, the Germans still let the Jews emigrate, but there is no country that is prepared to accept the six hundred thousand Jews from Germany. After many months of pleading and begging by Jewish representatives, small numbers are allowed into England, Australia, Canada and the United States. The rest, about three hundred thousand, perish in the ghettos and gas chambers in Poland.

Recollections of Kristallnacht

While uncle Berish was back in Lodz, aunty Sarah and Joe were still in Berlin, hoping for some change. But the situation only worsened. Three weeks after Berish's expulsion, his knitwear shop at No. 14 Grosse Frankfurterstrasse was ransacked and plundered, the display windows smashed, and the fittings and fixtures thrown in the middle of the road and set on fire. The merchandise was looted by their neighbours and clientele whom they had known for many years and looked upon as their friends.

This was on the night of 9-10 November 1938, when 'Kristallnacht' — the night of broken glass — shattered the last hopes of the German Jews. All over Germany, brown-shirted troopers smashed Jewish shops, offices and homes. Two hundred and sixty-seven synagogues were set on fire, and Jewish books, prayer books and holy scrolls were burned in the streets. Eight hundred Jews were murdered; thousands were injured. Over twenty-six thousand Jewish men between sixteen and eighty years of age were rounded up and sent off to concentration camps. From Austria and South Germany, 10,911 were incarcerated at Dachau; 9,845 from central Germany were taken to Buchenwald; and from Prussia and the north of Germany, 6,000 were locked up at Sachsenhausen. Their treatment was brutal, with many beaten to death. And all this in peace-time, before the eyes of the entire civilised world.

Kristallnacht signalled the beginning of the Holocaust.

Aunty Sarah was desperate to leave Germany, but was not allowed out until she completely repaired all the damage caused to her property. Because the insurance money was confiscated by the authorities, and her private funds were not sufficient to meet the costs, we had to send her the money. She was left penniless after paying for the refurbishment as well as the extra departure tax that was levied on all Jews.

On 19 May my cousin Joe, who was twelve at the time, was amongst a group of three hundred Jewish children from Berlin who were allowed into England. Leaving Germany at the very last minute, he lived in London for a while and was later evacuated to the countryside, where he finished his studies.

Soon after Joe's departure, Sarah joined Berish in Lodz. Leaving Berlin, she had been allowed only one suitcase of personal belongings that was searched many times over by German customs and border police. My aunt and uncle, like all German Jews, had been robbed and turned into beggars overnight. Jewellery, valuables, art, antiques and furniture — whatever they possessed — they were forced to leave behind. Taking up their residence in Lodz, and renting a one-room apartment on the outskirts of the city at Radogoszcz, my uncle and aunt hardly had time to unpack their one and only suitcase when, on 1 September, the war broke out.

Within days, the Germans arrived in Lodz. Sarah and Berish, unwelcome where they lived amongst the Germans, moved into our apartment, their living quarters set up at the end of the long kitchen. Two collapsible iron beds that were usually part of the equipment we used on our summer vacations made up their bedroom. A pale-blue curtain now divided our kitchen and gave them privacy at night. In that little corner, near the big window overlooking the barbed wire, Berish and Sarah shared our home for five years. They had one dream — to join Joe in England.

Berish, a well-educated and cultured man, energetically took up the study of English. It was thanks to him and my father that I could further my education at home for the duration of our time in the ghetto. Berish was an early riser, always the first up to go down to the courtyard where he would pump a bucketful of water. This was the only water supply we had, as the plumbing had been out of order from our very first winter in the ghetto. The pipes had burst and were never repaired. Neither could water be stored inside, as it would freeze in the bucket. But uncle never missed a shave, no matter how cold it became, and he always donned a clean shirt with the right tie to match his suit. Then, because my father could not get used to shaving by himself, Berish would help him with it.

Before the war, the family barber, Mr Nachman Granek, who had his shop at 17 Zgierska Street, would come to our home late at night to get my father ready for the following day. Mr Granek was a very interesting man, well read and politically aware. In his shop he kept all the daily newspapers and monthly magazines, most of which he somehow found time to read. This was part of his business: to be able to debate and discuss current issues of impor-tance with those clients of his who liked to congregate in his shop — the forum where all major problems, as well as all the gossip, was aired. He was not just a barber, but an important personality in town. Not everybody could afford to buy a newspaper, nor did they all have radios in their homes. Without the barber shop, they would have been cut off from the rest of the world.

Once ready with his toilette, looking neat and trim as if ready to go to work, Berish would start his studies. Walking up and down the length of the kitchen, he would blow into his frozen hands, over which he wore hand-knitted gloves whose finger tips had been cut off to enable him to write. He would walk up and down for hours, reciting at the top of his voice the English poems he had learned by heart. He pursued this routine daily and with determination. I will never understand how he was able to study and concentrate in these conditions. Maybe it was what kept him sane, his way of escape.

Before the war, Berish always took an interest in my school work. I was his favourite nephew, and he would encourage me with my studies. He used to say, 'When you matriculate, you will come to live with me in Berlin and study Law.' It didn't matter that I wanted to be an engineer of aeronautics; Berish had different plans for me, and stubbornly adhered to them.

In the early days of the ghetto, going back to 1940 and part of 1941, I always remember his welcoming my homecoming with a smile. At that time, I was involved with the Skif group at Marysin where Rumkowski had allocated us a villa with a plot of land. All the youth organisations in the ghetto were given such plots, where they could continue their political and cultural activities under cover. On these patches of land we cultivated vegetables to supplement our meagre diet. The orphanage was also located there.

The Avant Garde Theatre

At Marysin I got involved with the Avant Garde Theatre when my two older colleagues, Yosl Feldman and Chaim Ajzenberg, nicknamed Mucha, decided to form a theatre. Before the war, the two of them had been interested in acting and were members of Moshe Broderson's School for Dramatic Art. Broderson, a Russian Jew who had settled in Lodz after the Revolution, was a well-known Yiddish poet and writer, as well as the founder and literary mentor of the famous Ararat Theatre in Lodz. This theatre had an international reputation; it had turned out many talented actors and comedians, of whom Dzigan and Schumacher are probably the best known. Broderson made a strong impact on the cultural life of the city.

Although I was much younger than my colleagues, who were already semi-professional actors, they did not object to my joining them. My experience on the stage had been limited to the occasional school show, so I was happy to do whatever was asked of me. Eventually, I took over the technical side and constructed the props for the first performance.

I remember when the first meeting took place at 18 Zagainikowa Street, in the presence of Moshe Pulawer, an Ararat actor and one of Broderson's early students. Pulawer had come from a very poor background. As a young boy, he had lived with his uncle, Yosl the Cobbler, at 38 Zgierska Street. In one little room where his uncle earned his meagre living making shoes, Moshe grew up under Yosl's watchful eye. Besides teaching him to make shoes, Yosl implanted in young Moshe a love of Yiddish literature, art and music. This inspiration and guidance led Pulawer to become one of the finest young Yiddish actors with the Ararat Theatre and, later, one of its stage directors.

Pulawer was excited by the idea of organising a theatre group in the ghetto. He had a great love of acting and Yiddish theatre. By the second meeting, he had brought his large satchel containing scripts and music, and a discussion of the first performance began. By the third, the show took on shape and, soon after, the first variety show, with colourful song and dance, was born under the title *'Yidn Schmidn '* ('Jews are Forging').

It was at the second meeting that Pulawer involved me in a discussion, seeming eager to find out more about me. When he asked how old I was, I cheated by adding a couple of years to the sixteen I had legitimately attained.

He took over the artistic direction of the newly formed Avant Garde Theatre. Although he was always tense and nervous, shouting at the top of his voice during rehearsals, I still liked him: he was a very interesting man. When sitting down for a break, he always found a kind word for me and managed to squeeze a smile from the corner of his eyes. This was his way of saying, 'Don't be upset with me. That's the way I work. I don't mean to be hard.'

Mucha and Yosl mobilised a group of young and talented students from the other youth groups. Some could hardly speak

Yiddish; others came from the Yeshivot. They came from all sorts of backgrounds. Amongst them were the Fred Astaire and Ginger Rogers of the Lodz ghetto — Mietek Rue and his partner, Estusia Berger. Besides attracting young amateur actors, the theatre also drew in professionals: the narrator, Wajnberg; the compere from pre-war theatre in Lodz, Nelken; the ballet dancer, Halina Krukowska, well-known for her fiery Spanish solo dances; and Madam Eliasberg with her ballet school, who staged beautiful performances. We were also joined by the musician and composer of Yiddish folk music, David Baigelman, with his orchestra. The talented, one-legged poet, Szymon Janowski, wrote many beautiful sketches and songs for us, as did Joachimowicz, Szajewicz and many other writers who congregated around the theatre.

Halina Pitel, a young vivacious actress, was the daughter of the first violinist of the Philharmonic Orchestra. My schoolfriend, the red-headed Sarah Bornsztejn; Halina Bitterman; and the alluring Dolly Kotz, with her sparkling black eyes, formed part of the ballet ensemble. There were many others whose names I sorely regret having forgotten. Their faces, however, are clear and vivid in my mind's eye. With their devotion and talent, they all contributed to the success of the Avant Garde Theatre.

The first show was staged in an abandoned school building at Marysin where, with the help of my friend, Kuba Litmanowicz — an electrical engineer by trade — I built a stage of assembled tables. The curtain was patched together from a few sheets. Pinchas Szwarc from Brzezinska Street, a young and gifted painter, was the stage designer, contributing a great deal with his colourful and original stage decorations and costumes. Today Pinchas' name is 'Shahar', and he lives in Soho, New York, where he is a renowned artist. Kuba Litmanowicz never made it, dying in 1942 of tuberculosis.

The day came when the curtain went up for the premiere. Rumkowski turned up for the occasion. At the time I was only a young boy, and it was the most exciting moment in my ghetto life. The show was a huge success. Rumkowski stood up applauding with great delight, shaking hands with Pulawer, the actors, the orchestra and all participants including myself. The highlight of the occasion was when Rumkowski promised that we would be accommodated in a theatre hall. Soon after, No. 3 Krawiecka Street became the home of the Avant Garde Theatre and was shared with the Philharmonic Orchestra under the baton of the well-known composer and conductor, Professor Teodor Ryder, conductor of the pre-war City Philharmonic Orchestra in Lodz, the members of which were all Jewish and most of whom were now locked up in the ghetto.

Mr Senicki, the director of the Department of Labour in the ghetto, took over the management of 3 Krawiecka Street, which eventually became known as the Kulturhaus. Before the war, he had been closely involved with the Ararat Theatre. He engaged a professional technician by the name of Spokojny who took charge of the technical stage requirements. Under his supervision, I continued my work with the theatre.

Spokojny was a colourful character with lots of interesting stories from his past. He used to be on first-name terms with some of the greatest stars from the pre-war theatre, and had worked for many years in the best theatres in Lodz. At times, he would get carried away with his reminiscences, talking excitedly about the famous Julius Adler, Alexander Granach, and Maurice Szwarc; Jacob Waijslic from the Vilner Yiddish Theatre, whom I eventually met up with in Melbourne many years later; Molly Pickon from the USA, and her husband Jacob Kalich; and the greatest of them all — Abraham Morevski. Spokojny spoke with excitement about Ida Kaminska, the daughter of Ester Rochel, the mother of Yiddish theatre. 'Ida always gave me a rose from her bouquet, kissing me on the cheek after the last curtain,' he would say nostalgically.

Later on, Spokojny and I finished up in Althammer concentration camp, where he suddenly took ill with an infected appendix. In desperation, the doctor, a Jewish prisoner from Lvov, operated on him under the most basic conditions of hygiene and without any surgical instruments. He boiled an ordinary knife, washed his hands as best he could and removed the appendix. Within hours, Spokojny showed signs of infection. I saw him that evening as I stood by the half-open window of the sick bay.

'Abraham,' he said, 'I don't know how I survived it. I was only half asleep. They cut me without any anaesthetic. They covered my nostrils with ether to dull my senses. Then they tied me down to an ordinary table and three other prisoners held me. The doctor pushed a piece of timber into my mouth and told me to bite. I screamed until I passed out.'

Spokojny seemed reasonably calm and surprisingly had no pain; but his face was yellow, wearing the mask of death. His unnaturally sparkling eyes were sunk deep into their sockets, leaving black indentations surrounding them. He put his hand under the straw bag, from where he pulled out his bread ration and handed it to me.

'Take it,' he told me quietly. 'I cannot eat.'

'Hold onto it,' I replied. 'You will need it tomorrow.'

'Abraham,' Spokojny said suddenly, 'do you think we will ever work on the stage again?'

'Of course we will,' I answered with bravado. 'We must!'

He was nodding his head. 'Yes, we must, just to spite them, the bastards. We must!' He squeezed my hand when I said goodbye.

'Please come back tomorrow, Abraham, please.'

'You know I will.'

Later that night, on my way to work, I found his body lying next to the latrine, the usual place for the dead. I walked over and stood motionless by the naked, skeletal corpse that had once been a man with dreams. I noticed the bleeding cut in the lower right-hand side of his belly, and I just stood there for a while. Eventually, I pulled the straw mat from under him and he rolled over into the snow. After turning him face up again, I took the mat inside the kitchen/store where I worked as a fire-guard feeding the ovens with coke at night to heat the building that was still under construction. At the beginning of December 1944 in Upper Silesia, the winter was harsh and my striped prison denim gave me little protection; so I hid the straw mat in the cellar and used it to lie down on at night.

For many days I was upset, thinking about Spokojny. It had been wishful thinking to imagine, even for a moment, that one day we would work together on the Yiddish stage again. And to this very day, I distinctly remember regretting that I had not accepted the slice of bread when he offered it to me ...

How could I have known then that, at the beginning of 1946, I would be one of the founders of the Zukunft Theatre Circle in Brussels and that, on 11 April 1948, the curtain would rise in one of the largest theatres of that city for the premiere of The Golem (a famous Yiddish drama written by H Leyvik). To a packed house, I was to play the role of the Golem.

A few days later, I was invited to have coffee with my older friend, Hershl Himmelfarb, a leading member of the Bund and a pre-war trade union leader in Poland. He introduced me to an American visitor who was touring Europe on behalf of the American 'Arbeiter Ring' (Workers' Circle). One of the American's tasks was to find young talent amongst the survivors of the concentration camps. He offered me a three-year stipend to go to New York and attend the Lee Strasberg School of Acting and Drama. When I turned down his offer, he was incredulous, assuring me that I would be very well looked after.

'I can't afford to put my entire life on the line,' I said to him.

'But you're still so young,' he argued. 'You're only beginning your life.'

'Maybe so,' I replied, 'but I feel that I've already lived for hundreds of years. I can't afford to play with my future. I've lost my home and my family; I've got no one to lean on.'

'You'll have the support of the leading Jewish film producers,' he told me. 'They're very willing to help young boys like you.'

I could not see it his way. 'The road to fame on the stage is littered with millions of victims. I don't want to be one of them,' I said.

The Kulturhaus

The Kulturhaus at 3 Krawiecka Street, with its small auditorium, accommodated an audience of approximately four hundred. In the cold winter days, the walls inside were covered with frost. Every morning at 9.00 a.m. the hungry and exhausted musicians sat on the stage, their instruments at the ready. Dressed in coats and hats they would rehearse for hours in freezing conditions. Their only reward was a hot watery soup graciously granted them by Chaim Rumkowski and, occasionally, an extra portion of bread.

There was Mr Pitel, the first violinist and an excellent musician. He used to put his arm around my shoulder after rehearsal and, with a smile on his face, he would say, 'Abraham, don't you think we are lucky to come here and play music every day? This keeps me alive. Mind you, that little bit of hot soup is very nice,' he would concede with a grin, 'but the music is much nicer.' And Mr Rosenzaft, the percussionist, a very likeable middle-aged gentleman, would say, 'When I play, it is as if there were no ghetto.'

Professor Teodor Ryder was a gentleman in his mid-sixties with a very old-fashioned air. Elegantly dressed, he would appear punctually at 8.30 every morning. The silver handle of his black walking cane matched his goatee beard and long silver hair that hung down from under his wide brimmed black plush hat. At exactly 9.00 a.m. I would hear him tapping with his baton on his music stand as, fully clothed in his gloves, hat and coat, he began conducting. As he gradually warmed up he would start to remove his outer wear. I always sat in one of the first rows — my feet up on the chair in front of me to prevent them from freezing — listening to the music, watching the professor, as the steam rose from his back in the sub-zero temperatures.

Rimsky-Korsakov's exotic *Scheherezade* was one of my favourites, with its colourful fairytales of the Arabian Nights transforming my miserable ghetto nights into a world of magic — a world of oriental marble palaces, where I could lose myself in the Casbahs, pushing through narrow streets crowded with exotic people in colourful dress from distant lands. I roamed the oriental markets, hypnotised by snake charmers, and seduced by belly dancers dressed in their transparent harem-pants, rhythmically swinging their hips to the beat of tambourines, waking my desires, setting my blood on fire. Dancers with unsheathed sabres blew flames with every clash of the cymbals. Mr Rosenzaft played the drums with his eyes closed and, when he opened them, just for a moment, they sparkled with the life of a man become young again.

The two initiators and founders of the theatre, Yosl Feldman and 'Mucha' Abraham Ajzenberg, both perished in the gas trucks of Chelmno. Yosl was taken with the children, the old and the sick, during the Gehsperre when the hospital at 36 Lagiewnicka Street was liquidated. Abraham Ajzenberg volunteered for work outside the ghetto and was carted off in one of the cattle trains. Moshe Pulawer survived the concentration camps and settled in Israel. Most of the actors and musicians of the theatre went up in the fires of Chelmno and Auschwitz.

After the Gehsperre in 1942, the Avant Garde Theatre and Philharmonic Orchestra were banned by order of the Gestapo. The Kulturhaus was converted into a factory producing quilted bedding and bedspreads. Still, the actors and musicians carried on with their work on a smaller scale. In private homes, people would gather for an evening of music or to listen to poetry. Sometimes, a small group of musicians would give a chamber recital in a factory or in one of the special kitchens that catered especially to the workers who were rewarded by the commissars or technical managers for their hard work.

Revues were staged on a smaller scale, and appeared in various factories or administrative departments. David Baigelman and his orchestra carried on giving concerts in the factories. Bronislawa Rotsztat continued with her violin recitals accompanied by Professor Ryder. Poets and writers formed a pen club. My school friend, Chawa Rosenfarb, was the youngest amongst them. The renowned painter, Browner, staged a puppet theatre for a short time. His characters offended some of the ghetto dignitaries and, as a consequence, his show was closed and he had to go into hiding. A number of painters and sculptors created and worked underground so as not to draw the attention of the Germans.

There were some very gifted young painters, sculptors and musicians in the Lodz ghetto. Many of them had been born in Lodz, while many others came from Czechoslovakia, Austria, Germany and Luxembourg. Amongst them were virtuosos and composers of international fame: Professor Kurt Berr, Dri Kurt, Birkenfeld, the violinist Wainbaum, Kraft, the singer Rudolf Brandel and his wife Lili Brandel. They all joined the Philharmonic Orchestra in giving regular concerts, their brave and melodic art warming the freezing music lovers.

The Lodz ghetto, although dying of countless diseases, not the least of which was famine, still carried on with a pulsating and creative cultural life. Today, most of the artwork and writings have been lost. Only some of it survived, buried, and was eventually dug up after the war by the few who were lucky enough to survive.

One day, the Gestapo paid a visit to 3 Krawiecka Street with a large film crew and filmed the entire repertoire of the Avant Garde Theatre. Today, somewhere in Germany, in a corner of one of the cellars storing the documentation of the Third Reich, that film must be lying, forgotten. Perhaps at some time in the future it will be rediscovered. It is the only hope that most members of the Avant Garde have of resurrection.

At the theatre, I learned by heart most of the programmes, and had a wide repertoire of songs, recitations and two-act skits.

'Abraham, how about a song?' Berish would say whenever I came home. 'Something exciting! Let's warm up! I'm so hungry. Singing helps somehow, doesn't it?'

He never had to insist. At times, my mother would join in with an old Yiddish folk song, helped along by my father; Berish might also recite some Russian poetry from his student days. His favourite was Lermentov, though occasionally he would recite Heinrich Heine's 'Lorelei', which made him sad. He would turn forlornly to me in these moments and say, 'Don't you think Yiddish poetry, Yiddish music, is much warmer. They penetrate deep into your soul. They are gentle and soothing. The others I like, but lately they sound strange and distant.'

Because of Berish I came to learn about Heinrich Heine's life, and his poetry, prose and lyrics, which are full of irony and pain. They touched me deeply, especially 'The Rabbi from Bacharach'. In that story, I could sense the poet's sadness and feel his suffering: the torment of a human being punished for being born a Jew. Heine's conversion to Christianity did not remove the stigma, nor did it stop anti-Semites from hating him. To this day, Heine's poetry and prose still fill me with wonder, but it is his uncanny prophetic accuracy that makes me shiver. When he left Germany, disappointed and disillusioned, he said: 'A nation that burns books will eventually burn people.' Heine said it a century ago, long before six million Jews went up in flames.

For all my ability to block out the present, the nightmare had not dispersed. Outside was pitch black, a never-ending night, yet time was ticking away. Lipek was still in Czarnieckiego Prison, and there was no rescue in sight. The guard on the street in front of our building was changing. At 7.00 a.m. the curfew lifted and Berish, Sarah and I went to Czarnieckiego. My parents stayed behind: they could not muster the strength to face the ordeal of seeing their son behind the wire fence again.

When Lipek saw us coming empty-handed, he knew his rescue was beyond hope. Berish did the talking while I just stood looking at my brother in silence, pushing my hand through the wire mesh, touching him with my fingers, caressing his hands. I was saying goodbye. None of us cried. Lipek stood calm, listening to Berish, shaking his head as if he were accepting his fate. Sarah and Berish finally said their farewells, but I couldn't. I stayed on for hours, for once unaware of the cold.

By now it was getting late, and the Jewish police started to clear the crowd outside the prison. The detainees were forced into the cells. Lipek and I parted without a word, without a tear. Now, writing these pages, I find that the tears do come.

Later on, in the concentration camp, there was a point at which I made a conscious decision to survive. I had given a promise to my mother that I would look for Lipek and, for that reason alone, it was imperative that I endured. I remembered my grandmother's words when things seemed darkest: 'A Jew must never give up! God will help! A Jew must always believe in the Almighty! With his help we shall survive.'

Early on Monday 4 March 1944, Lipek was carried off together with seven hundred and fifty men, their destination unknown. I came home from Czarnieckiego exhausted, frozen and dejected. Our home was in mourning. Nobody uttered a word, except for my grandmother, who constantly lamented, 'He has done no harm to anybody. Why have they taken him? Why?'

The death of my grandmother

My grandmother was in her late seventies. Always spotless and well dressed, her wigs immaculately combed and cared for, she could not comprehend how it was possible for the Germans to behave as they did. She kept on telling us how polite, reliable and honest the Germans used to be, recalling that during the First World War my grandfather, Itshe Mayer, used to trade with them.

From time to time, she used to take out a bunch of keys from the credenza drawer in the kitchen, pleading with my father to open the stores. 'Surely there must be some business,' she would cry. Telling my father what a shame it was to neglect an old, established business that had been well-known in the city of Lodz, she would say: 'We lived well from that business all our lives. Shimon, you must not give up. A Jew must never despair. A Jew must believe! The Almighty will help. Please Shimon, go and open the store. You will see, God will help. The world is not coming to an end.' But for us in the ghetto the world was coming to an end. And God — where was God?

On those occasions, my father was most understanding and

patient with his old mother who kept clinging to her past, desperately holding on to what had always been most precious in her life. He would take her by the arm, walk her gently to the balcony door — taking care to stand well back — and show her the German policeman in front of our home, guarding the barbed wires.

'Mother, we are locked in a camp. We are shut off from the rest of the world. We are in a prison. Mother, please try to understand.'

She would stand motionless, and then begin to shake her head, sadly murmuring to herself: 'The world has gone mad. The world has gone mad.'

Yet, in a few days time, my father would have to repeat the whole rigmarole. For my grandmother, ultimately, did not want to accept reality; trying to hold on to the past was her way of resisting. We had to be very careful with her all the time, and watch her so that she did not go too close to the windows. She was quite capable of going out onto the balcony. But she was a most resilient old lady, early to rise in the mornings, even in the freezing cold of the winter months.

One morning, shortly after Lipek was deported, Berish, as usual, brought up the water. He spilled a few drops on the floor which he neglected to wipe up and, a little later, my grandmother slipped on the ice, breaking her right hip. She became bedridden, never to walk again. She was taken to hospital and brought back home again; but the swelling built up, spreading all over her body. Late one night, towards the end of March, she passed away with dignity in her own bed, thus avoiding the horrors of Auschwitz.

The next morning, a lady from the Chevra Kadisha came to our place. We unhinged half a door between the kitchen and the dining room, using it as a 'tahara' board to wash the body, which was then wrapped in the white cloth for the dead. She had had it ready in the wardrobe for years.

My grandmother still had her last rites accorded to her by Jewish tradition. We all went to the cemetery, which was covered in deep layers of snow. Hundreds of empty graves, dug in the summer months when the ground was soft, were lined up ready to be filled. The earth next to her grave was frozen solid, and we just managed to break up enough of it to cover her body.

My father recited 'Kaddish'. An old Jew from the Chevra Kadisha was the only person outside our family witnessing the funeral. None of the graves had numbers or name plates; most of the corpses were not even covered with earth.

'Are they going to mark the grave?' my father asked the old man, who simply answered, 'Go home, my friend. Don't worry. The Almighty will take care of everything.'

We struggled across the cemetery, sinking knee-deep in the snow, and went back to a cold and deserted place. The unhinged half-door was still in the middle of the dining room, supported by the two chairs; the water that had been used to wash my grandmother's body was frozen in its container on the floor. Our home looked like a cave in hell. It was hard to believe that once upon a time it had been my grandparents' haven; that in this place my parents had become engaged, as had my aunt Sarah and uncle Laib. Hard to believe that this was once a happy home where all the holidays were celebrated according to Jewish tradition, the table always covered with a white cloth, sometimes with a few drops of white wax from the Sabbath candles, or coloured wax from the 'havdole' candle that my grandfather used to light to celebrate the end of the Sabbath.

Once again I saw my grandfather surrounded by all his children and grandchildren as they sat around the mahogany table singing traditional Hebrew songs. It was a happy home, always full of laughing, noisy children, with the kitchen redolent of the savoury dishes my grandmother prepared. And not only did she cook well, she was also an outstanding pastry cook, baking her own 'khales' for the Sabbath, as well as the most delectable cakes for all occasions.

My grandparents were God-fearing Jews. The poor, some of whom I had known for years, came to their house on a regular basis, to collect their allowances on the same day of every week. So did I until one evening, after Havdola, my grandfather suddenly asked his wife: 'Shayndl, by the time the week draws to an end, I am always short of change. I can't understand it. I count the money at the beginning of the week and it is correct; but by the time Friday comes, there is not enough to finish off the donations for the poor.'

I lit up like a glowing bulb, blushing without uttering a word; yet nothing was said, though my guilt must have been apparent to everyone. The following Sabbath, my grandfather, as was his custom, listened to my reading of the 'sidra' — a chapter from the

Bible for that particular week — and made me an offer. He promised to give me one zloty every week providing I translated the Hebrew scriptures without a mistake. I negotiated a small concession, to which he agreed: allowing three mistakes. From that day onwards, my grandparents were never short of change for the poor, and my translating of the Five Books of Moses from Hebrew into Yiddish improved beyond belief.

Now my grandparents' home stood dark, cold and empty. Most of the furniture had been used for firewood. The silver candle-holders that once adorned their table on the Sabbath and Jewish holidays; the silver wine cup for the blessings, the spice box, Eliahu's big red Venetian wine goblet, engraved with gold lettering, that used to be in the centre of the table when we celebrated Passover; the silver 'chanukiya' that my grandfather used to light for Chanukah; the special silver cutlery, the chinaware, the dinner sets and glassware that were used only for Passover and locked away for the rest of the year in the big mahogany credenza with the crystal panes in the doors — many of these things my grandparents had inherited from their grandparents — had all been taken away by the Kripo in August 1940, when they raided and ransacked our home. They had even taken our sheets, underwear and part of our bedding. My uncle Berish was badly beaten by the Kripo commandant's chief assistant, Sutter. He wasn't fast enough to surrender his wrist-watch. They took my father's golden fob watch with its heavy golden chain that he had inherited from his father — who, in turn, had been given it as a wedding present by his in-laws. I remember how he used to carry it in his waistcoat pocket with the chain hanging across his stomach. My father wore it the same way.

A most interesting watch it was, with a big white face marked with black roman numerals: the lid opened when I pressed the winding button. It was engraved with flowers on the outside, and inside it had my grandfather's initials. As a child I had loved to look at the face of the watch as I sat on his lap, and thus he taught me to tell the time.

My grandfather's large, hand-carved armchair was pushed to the side, standing sad and deserted. This place, once upon a time, was the warmest and most secure place of my childhood. Now, the angel of death hovered over it.

Passover at my grandparents' home

It is the first night of Passover; the mahogany table is covered with a white table-cloth, and six glittering silver candlesticks are lit in full splendour: two for each child of my grandparents. Two more stand on the kitchen table, lit for my grandmother and her husband.

As the youngest grandson, I must spend Passover with my grandparents. With a white yarmulke on his head, my grandfather looks regal in the patriarchal armchair, reclining on two large, white cushions, dressed in a white caftan with his long, silver-grey beard. On this night, he is the king of his home.

'Once you grow up, my son, you too will be the king in your home,' he tells me. 'Every Jew on this night is a king.'

I am seated at his right reclining, according to tradition, on a white cushion, reciting the four questions from the Haggadah. My grandfather reads the story of Moses and the Jews when the Almighty, with an outstretched arm, brought them out of bondage in Egypt and led them to the land of milk and honey.

The Passover table is ready with all the required herbs and traditional foods prepared by my grandmother according to Jewish laws and customs. They are all symbolic: the scorched bone; the bitter herbs; the ground nuts and almonds blended with wine and cinnamon; the hard boiled eggs and salty water symbolising the tears of the Jews in bondage — all surrounded by and placed upon the silver cutlery and chinaware that come out from the locked credenza.

The wine is made by my grandparents and refined in large vats that are stored in our cellar marked *Kosher l' Pesach*. They also supply the whole family with their wines all year round, and take great pride in their products — especially the liqueurs which are spiced with herbs and based on old recipes my grandmother has inherited from her grandmother and would never divulge. The 'Seder' — the meals and ceremonies of the first two nights of Passover — hold a special attraction for me on account of the wine. Traditionally, everyone at the table has to drink four glasses. Of course, this exceeds my capacity and, because of this, I can never remember the end of the proceedings as I am always fast asleep.

Family meals at my grandparents' house were of great significance, and the big mahogany table played a most important role in our lives. If it seems that I refer to it often, it is because around this table the whole family would gather on every important occasion and for every important conference. Over the decades that have passed between then and now, it has become the symbol of the patriarchal home of which my grandfather was master. Seated at its head in his large armchair, he looked the part. Business and family problems were debated there, and no-one would have contemplated finalising a decision without consulting him.

My grandmother, Shayndl, was in charge of the aesthetics of the table, which was richly and meticulously set, and always had upon it a bowl of the most select fruits: the best quality oranges, bananas, grapes, mandarines and beautiful red apples from Canada.

Daily, she would visit our business stores. She had to feed her sons with meals which she insisted upon personally supervising as they were cooked. She would never allow anybody to interfere. Then, only she could carry the two big baskets loaded with the food, plates and cutlery and, whenever I tried to help her, she would always shoo me away. Naturally, the baskets were never empty on her way home. She filled them up with fruit from our stores, and it had to be the best — hand-picked by herself. Not only was grandmother a connoisseur, she was also a good business-woman. All her life, she was involved in her husband's business and knew every detail of it.

Reb Moshe, the porter, was a dignified and pious Jew, highly respected amongst the merchants. They all called him Reb as a mark of respect, although he was only a porter. He worked for my grandfather all his life, and continued to work for our family until he grew too old and slow. Every Friday he would come to our cellar to collect his wages of ten zlotys plus some fruit for his table in honour of the Sabbath. For the winter he was provided with fuel to keep his home warm, the supplies of which were unlimited as we had a lot of timber from the crates in which the fruit was delivered.

This was the rule put down by my grandfather, Reb Itshe Mayer, for it was Poland before the Second World War, when ten zlotys was good money and fuel for the winter was vital. It was a world in which grapes, for example, were so rare, and considered to be so precious, that they were only given to the very sick or the dying. It was life during the Depression and, in many homes, food had to be carefully managed. Every slice of bread mattered, especially to the working classes, where many were unemployed or on strike.

Whenever one is hungry, I have learned, one dreams about food. There was a reel of film in my mind which, often unbidden, started rolling in those ghetto years. As I tried not to think about Lipek, my grandmother's death or the desecrated family home, scenes from colourful Purim festivals — when I and my cousins would come to this place disguised as pirates, kings or clowns — streamed through my imagination. We were given Purim gifts and money by grandfather, while grandmother had prepared the table with plenty of our favourite cakes, cookies and the sweet delicacies that so delight children. We would all sing and celebrate the miracle of Purim, when the Jews had been saved by Queen Esther from destruction at the hands of an evil madman in ancient Persia. We could have used a miracle like that in the ghetto; but it never came, though the villain now was at least as evil, and possibly ten times as mad.

The last spring

In the four years that had gone by since 1 May 1940, when the Lodz ghetto had been closed off from the rest of the world, the population had shrunk from 163,177 to approximately 79,000. The majority of the inhabitants, by now, were Jews from the smaller, liquidated ghettos brought in from the province of the Warthegau. From the original pre-war Jews of Lodz, between thirty- and thirty-five thousand were still in the ghetto; the rest had been sent off in cattle trains. There were still a few Austrian, German and Czechoslovakian Jews left, but most of the western Jews were deported soon after their arrival. The Lodz ghetto was a transit camp, a black inferno of never-ending suffering, a tunnel whose destination was hell.

In our fifth year behind barbed wire, everything stayed the same: there was no news. People were starving but this was not news. Week by week, people were dying in their hundreds. They were being hunted down like animals by the Jewish Sonderkommando and police, carted off by the Germans in cattle trains, never to be seen or heard from again. But this was not news, either. Disaster after disaster, tragedy after tragedy, day in, day out. Not news; the norm.

The ghetto inhabitants desperately resisted the deportations. We hid in attics, roofs, cellars, under the ceilings, in double walls — wherever we could find a hole in which to squeeze ourselves, at times hiding for days without food . People shared their last crumbs of bread and drops of soup with close ones who were on the list, helping them to hide. Rumkowski's threats had little effect. They could not break the will-power of the desperate people in hiding. Nobody wanted to be separated from family and close ones; but the fear of these mass expulsions, always strong, was growing. By now, we all knew what deportation stood for, although only a few would state it outright. The ghetto was in its death throes, but we still hoped that the Russian army would get to us in time. Maybe that would be the miracle that would save us from being carted off to the unknown.

The spring sun, with a dishonest, self-conscious look on her face, shone half-heartedly on the Lodz ghetto, slowly thawing the frozen toilets and heaps of refuse, sending up a nauseating stench. For us in the ghetto, the sun's rays failed to soothe our despair. They did not disperse the winter in our hearts. The icicles hanging from the roofs slowly melted, eventually crashing down with the noise of breaking glass. The snow turned to mud and the ghetto-dwellers, with shrunken yellow faces, shuffled their rag-wrapped, clog-shod, swollen feet through the slush.

It took only a few weeks until the Final Solution reached us; until the last breath of the last survivor of the Lodz ghetto was turned into ashes. To some parts of Europe, the spring of 1944 brought freedom and peace; to my world, that spring never came. When nature re-awakened after a long winter sleep, when the sun took off the snow-woven winter coat from the shoulders of mother earth bowed with cold, when bloom and blossom filled the air with sweet fragrances, the Lodz ghetto blossomed with death and decay.

It was the last spring in my mother's life. She was not yet forty-two, with not even a grey hair in her jet-black waves. It was the last spring for my father: that gentle, righteous man, that thinker, that most humble of men whom, as I grow older, I admire above all men. I realise how immature I must have been at sixteen years of age, when he advised uncle Berish not to join the Jewish ghetto police and, later on in 1942, strongly objected to Lipek's joining the

Sonderkommando. Not only was I immature, I did not even realise how young my parents were. In my eyes, any person over thirty was old. My father was only forty-four years old when he was taken to Auschwitz. I am much older than that now.

It was the last spring for my uncle Berish, the eternal student; for aunt Sarah, his most gentle lady; for the warm-hearted aunty Chaya and uncle David Laib, the cantor from Lodz; for that most kind and gracious Cerel and her beautiful young daughter Luba, only sixteen. It was the last spring for my teachers; my friends, my schoolmates and the closest of them all — Rivek Skoczylas — and the last spring for my neighbours. It was the end of one thousand years of flourishing Yiddish culture in Poland. In the tick of a clock, an entire civilisation was erased from the surface of the earth and fate, with its inscrutable design, chose me to be one of the very few to witness the end of a most complex and, in many ways, splendid chapter in Jewish history.

D-Day

Constant inspections by high-ranking SS officers and officials — Adolf Eichmann among them — occurred daily. The Lodz ghetto's underground radio-listeners were starting to report good news from the front lines: the German army was in retreat. This lifted our morale and bolstered our hopes of the Russians reaching us in time.

On 6 June 1944, the radio news was full of drama. Shortly before midnight, on 5 June, Allied bombers attacked the Normandy coast in heavy assaults that lasted till dawn. Early next morning, Allied task forces under the command of General Eisenhower successfully landed on the beaches of Normandy. Although casualties were heavy, the Germans had been taken by surprise. German coastal batteries were bombarded by 640 naval guns. Early on 6 June, thirteen hundred Liberators and Fortresses aircraft heavily bombed the German fortifications. The RAF sent out one thousand machines to attack bridges, roads and communications behind enemy lines. Four thousand ships of all types, with thousands of smaller crafts, landed fresh troops under strong air cover. More Allied infantry waded ashore. Allied sea-borne and airborne troops had linked up. In the ghetto, we were overwhelmed by the electrifying news. The Allied forces had landed in Europe! Surely liberation must follow soon.

On 7 June 1944, our enthusiasm was suddenly dampened. In the preceding days, round-ups and arrests of large numbers of underground radio-listeners had taken place — amongst them, my school friend's father, Yankel Weksler, his two brothers and many others. A Jewish Kripo informer, by the name of Sankiewicz, had denounced them, and they were interrogated, tortured and taken away, never to be seen again. One of the underground radio-listeners, Chaim Widawski, eluded the police round-ups and managed to hide for a few days. He tried desperately to escape from the ghetto, but to no avail. Trapped, Widawski knew that his only alternative to capture, torture and the subsequent and unavoidable disclosure of other radio users, was suicide. His girlfriend provided him with the cyanide that ended his young life.

The arrests and suicide did not deter other radio-listeners. The sons of Yankel Weksler — Shymek and Karol — carried on unshaken, as did my friends Bono Wiener, Abraham Goldberg and others, who continued to report the latest news to the desperate ghetto-dwellers. And the news was good: the Germans were in retreat. Stalingrad had been the turning point of the Second World War, and the Russian army was closing in on Warsaw, bringing new hope to the ghetto. Allied forces had landed in Normandy. The American, British, French and Polish armies were fighting on Italian soil, and the inexorable German onslaught, begun in 1939, was crumbling on all fronts. We were full of hope.

Suddenly, bad rumours. They were followed by placards on the ghetto walls:

MORE VOLUNTEERS FOR GERMANY URGENTLY REQUIRED. THIS TIME, WHOLE FAMILIES WILL BE ALLOWED TO JOIN THE TRANSPORTS, INCLUDING CHILDREN WHO ARE CAPABLE OF WORK. FAMILIES WILL BE EVACUATED TOGETHER AND WILL STAY TOGETHER.

Rumkowski promised additional food for those who volunteered:

THEY WILL BE ALLOWED TO WRITE LETTERS POSTAGE FREE. THOSE WHO REGISTER WILL BE ALLOWED TO COLLECT THEIR FOOD RATIONS WITHOUT HAVING TO QUEUE UP, IN ADDI-TION TO THE FOOD THEY WILL BE GIVEN FOR THE TRIP. EVERY THOUSAND PEOPLE WILL HAVE A DOCTOR AND ASSISTANT MEDICAL PERSONNEL.

Instructions were published on how to pack personal belongings, giving a detailed list of what was required:

ONE PILLOW AND ONE BLANKET PER PERSON. A THREE-DAY FOOD SUPPLY IS ESSENTIAL. THOSE IN NEED OF RUCKSACKS WILL GET THEM FREE. THOSE WHO HAVE JEWELLERY, FOREIGN CURRENCY OR VALUABLES OF ANY DESCRIPTION, ARE WELCOME TO SELL THEM TO THE EINKAUFSTELLE. THEY WILL BE PAID HIGH PRICES IN REICHSMARKS SO THAT THEY WILL BE ABLE TO BUY THEIR FIRST NEEDS IN THE GERMAN CITIES BEFORE THEY RECEIVE THEIR FIRST PAY.

The first transport of 562 Jews was handled with kid gloves. Their luggage was carried for them to the train on especially assigned horse-drawn carts. At Radogoszcz, Marysin, the Commissioner for Jewish Affairs, SS Hauptsturmführer Günter Fuchs, the deputy chief of the Gestapo in Litzmannstadt, farewelled the victims with a speech apologising for the cattle cars they had to travel in, explaining that, due to the war and shortages of passenger wagons, this was the best he could provide. However, the Gestapo chief promised them good treatment, plenty of good food and excellent working conditions. At Radogoszcz, the families were allocated wagons under similar conditions. Water was provided for every cart. The first transport left without harassment, beatings or coercion. There were no shootings, and Fuchs even offered everyone a chance to return to the ghetto if he or she so desired. He emphasised that anyone who was not willing to go was welcome to stay. The one man who chose to return to the ghetto was taken back and kept at Czarnieckiego Prison, to be sent off with the next transport.

June 1944 started a fresh wave of deportations. More victims were loaded into the cattle trains, hoping for better days. The ghetto shrank by a further 7,176 inhabitants, reducing the population to 71,711. The constant appeals by Rumkowski for more volunteers once again fell on deaf ears. New lists were drawn up by factory management and the Department of Labour, but those on the lists went into hiding. As usual, their ration cards were cancelled.

Eight thousand people went into hiding, and the Germans soon realised that the kid-glove tactics had failed; the polite speeches by

Günter Fuchs and Hans Biebow had had no effect. The ghetto-dwellers had not taken the bait. Resisting deportation at all costs, we had chosen starvation, living like rats in holes, rather than surrender.

The underground radio news continued to be favourable. Within a few days, the Russians took Praga, an outer suburb of Warsaw: 'German resistance weakens,' we heard. Hopefully, soon we would be liberated. The Russians were only 120 kilometres from Lodz.

From our balcony window I could see German civilians evacuating, loading their personal belongings onto the roofs of their cars. The military was evacuating the women and children. They were all running back to Germany in panic, and we rejoiced.

Reprieve

On Saturday, 15 July, Rumkowski cruised the cobblestoned ghetto streets in his brougham announcing at the top of his voice in great excitement, 'The deportations have stopped! It's all over! Life will go back to normal. It's all over! Please go back to work!'

The excitement was great. We would live! The ghetto population was full of joy, crying and dancing in the streets, hugging, kissing one another; but we were unaware that the sudden halt in the deportations was only temporary, due to the dismantling of the killing factory in Chelmno. The demolition had begun on 14 July 1944, motivated by fear that the extermination camp would fall into the hands of the fast-advancing Russian army which was approaching the borders of the province of the General Government. From then on, all the transports were directed to Auschwitz.

On 1 August 1944, the Polish underground radio announced the beginning of the Warsaw revolt. For reasons largely of political expediency, Stalin halted the Russian army, withdrawing it to the east bank of the Vistula until the winter offensive of January 1945 — thus enabling the Germans to choke the Polish revolt that still managed to last sixty-three days. For us this was a deadly blow, as it gave the Germans time to liquidate the ghetto. August 1944 became a symbolic date in the history of the Holocaust, marking as it did the end of the second-largest Jewish community in Europe. It also corresponded with the month of Av in the Jewish calendar, the month in which most of the significant tragedies in Jewish history have occurred.

Biebow visited the ghetto factories more frequently to plead with the workers, trying to convince them that it was in their best interests to be evacuated. Because of the shifting front lines, the entire Jewish population had to be taken to safety; but this time the evacuation was planned differently. The evacuees were told that they were to be moved with their entire families so as not to break them up. The machinery and raw materials were to leave together with the evacuees, so they would be able to continue their productive work as soon as they reached their destination.

These new tactics were an utter failure. More speeches by Rumkowski, Biebow and Bradfisch followed, with rephrased lies. They were desperately trying to fill a quota of five thousand Jews daily. To make the venture appear more plausible, they stressed publicly how important it was to take along one's possessions so that life could continue in reasonable comfort once the destination was reached:

> Fifteen to twenty kilos of personal belongings for every evacuee are permitted. Pots and pans, cutlery and kitchen utensils are essential. Every person should carry a pillow and blanket.

But the population resisted. Food rations were cut. The famine worsened, and still the drastic measures made no impact. According to *The Chronicle of the Lodz Ghetto*, on 30 July 1944 there were still 68,561 people left in the ghetto.

My cousin, Mendele Blicblau, worked at the tailoring factory at 36 Lagiewnicka Street. In order not to expose his entire family to reprisals, he took his rucksack, kissed them all goodbye and went to the Radogoszcz Railway Station. The train was waiting, loaded with machinery and materials. Everything was ready — except the ghetto people, who stubbornly refused to surrender. The cattle train left half-empty. The kid-glove tactics tried by the Germans after, and because of, the Warsaw ghetto uprising, yielded poor results. The Jewish police and Sonderkommando were ineffectual. Their 'Aktions' could not fill up the trains.

The chimneys of Auschwitz

On 6 August, late in the afternoon, my childhood friend, Mendel Feldman, called on me. Mendel, with whom I had spent my school and Skif days, retained close contact with me in the ghetto, never failing to bring me the latest radio news. The reports were hand-written on a little piece of paper rolled up like a cigarette, which he carried between his lips so he could swallow it if the need arose. This time, the message read: *'Kominy Oswiecima Znowoz Dymja Palacymi Zydami Ghetta Lodzkiego'* ('The chimneys of Auschwitz are smoking again with the burning Jews from the Lodz ghetto'). It became engraved in my memory, and I know now that it will always be there. We looked at each other, shook hands, hugged and parted without a word. Within a few weeks we saw each other briefly in Auschwitz-Birkenau, and we met again in Bergen-Belsen some weeks after the liberation.

Fresh placards covered the walls of the ghetto yet again. This time, they were even co-signed by Hans Biebow, but they made no impression. The passers-by did not even bother to read them. The speeches by Biebow and Bradfisch fell on deaf ears. Even Rumkowski's speeches lost their fiery spirit. He must have sensed that the end was coming. The drastically reduced food rations hit hard and created more misery. Nevertheless, fewer and fewer people turned up to the trains as the days passed. The ghetto population endured the misery and famine, and stubbornly refused to be deported. The Russian army was only 120 kilometres from Lodz — approximately one hour by fast train.

On 9 August 1944, SS Hauptsturmführer Bothmann, with his Einsatzgruppe, marched into the Lodz ghetto. Since the Gehsperre in 1942, they had been roaming the Ukraine and Byelorussia, wiping out entire Jewish populations. They were amongst those responsible for Babi Yar. They had just returned from Croatia, where they had been busy purging the district. Assisted by the Schutzpolizei and the city fire brigade, who had been specially armed for the purpose, they now surrounded block after block: every room, attic and cellar was searched. Walls were tapped and tested.

Early in the morning of 10 August, they surrounded 13 Zgierska Street. Our whole block was under siege. Then they were all over the building, smashing down the doors, shouting, pushing and beating. Shots were fired. People were crying. Turmoil, chaos, utter panic broke out. A big fat German waving his pistol rushed into our room, shouting at the top of his voice, *'Alle raus! Alle raus!* You have ten minutes to clear out! Anyone found upon my return will be shot on the spot.' As he ran out of the door he turned once again, shouting, 'Anyone found upon my return is dead!'

I could hear crying and screaming from the upper floors. People were running, falling down the stairs, losing their belongings. Their pots and pans were tumbling down, too, creating a cacophony of rattling as the panic-stricken people were kicked and clubbed by the Germans with their gun butts. They ran to the harsh accompaniment of shouted monosyllables: *'Los! Los! Schnell! Schnell!'*

In the chaos, the last radio report passed on to me by Mendel Feldman kept flashing through my mind. We were trapped. I was terrified. I ran towards the balcony without thinking, ready to jump. My father grabbed me, pointing his finger at the guard down in the street. Had I jumped I would have been shot. Struggling in the arms of my father, I screamed till I thought my vocal chords would burst: 'We must not surrender! We must hide! We must not go! They will kill us all! I know. You must trust what I say. Please listen to me. I know what they are doing with the Jews.'

Holding onto me, my father pleaded: 'Calm down, Abraham, please. Let's act.'

He started to push the huge and heavy double beds away from the big doors connecting our space with our neighbour's apartment. Immediately we all joined in. Opening the double doors we found a mountain of dust and junk wrapped up in cobwebs. For the first time, I began to appreciate the immense height of the doors in our building and the solid thickness of the walls. We all worked frantically under my father's supervision and, in a flash, we had dumped all the bric-a-brac onto our balcony.

My mother, my father and aunt Sarah squeezed in between the doors. Berish and I pushed the heavy double beds back into position against the closed door. We ran next door to our neighbour's place where a heavy, old, classically carved mahogany wardrobe stood obscuring the opening of the door connected to our apartment. Our neighbours, the Majerowiczes, had all been deported. I knelt down, supporting myself on my elbows. Uncle

Berish climbed on top of me, grabbed the top of the wardrobe and pulled himself up. I helped by pushing him. He in turn grabbed my hands and pulled me up. Between the top of the wardrobe and the door opening was a gap of about 1 to 1.5 feet wide, enough for a person to slip through. My uncle slid in first. I followed. Seconds after, the German was back. We stopped breathing. We were pressed together into one mass of tension and fear. We could hear each other's heartbeat. The German kept shouting, ordering the Jewish police to search the place.

In our panic, we had forgotten to hide our rucksacks. Now they lay in the middle of the room, and the German kept shouting, 'You better find them! They must be hiding somewhere close!' The Jewish police were opening cupboards and wardrobes, looking under beds, tapping walls and tearing the place apart. Suddenly, the German opened the door of the wardrobe. From the darkness of the inside we could see him through the tiny gaps in the wall of the wardrobe. Yet, although he was only inches from where we stood, he could not see us. At one point he looked straight into my eyes.

He was big and fat, and the day was warm. His face was damp, glistening with perspiration. He breathed heavily, panting from running up and down the stairs. He unbuttoned his tunic, took off his helmet, opened the window, grabbed an armchair and sat down. Periodically, the Jewish police returned to report that there was no-one to be found. But the German kept insisting: 'You better find them! They are in the building. Search the roof. Check the basement. You will have to find them!'

Again the Jewish police came back, reporting, 'Nobody is to be found in the building.' Another voice said, 'Sir, they must have run away and left their rucksacks behind in the panic.' The German did not move from the armchair. For hours we stood in the dark, scared to breathe, perspiring from fear and heat, achingly thirsty. There was hardly room for two. We were five adults.

The German left. Long hours followed as we stood motionless in the dark, scared to talk, communicating by touch. We lost count of time. Eventually, it was decided that I should find out what was happening outside. The others lifted me out of our hiding-place. With dreadful caution, I moved from corner to corner, crossing the courtyard, stopping, listening and moving on again. There was not a sound. 13 Zgierska Street was deserted. Dead. Everybody had been taken. I ran up to the top of the building, climbed into the attic, and warily approached a small window. I was on the fourth floor and had a perfect view of the whole district. Our part of the ghetto had been completely cleared, and neither Germans nor Jewish police were in sight. I went downstairs moving like a cat so as not to make the slightest noise. Painstakingly, I crossed the courtyard. In a corner behind the toilets were holes cut in the wall connecting our courtyard with those in Lagiewnicka Street. The whole ghetto was interwoven like a net, and these were our escape labyrinths — our only defence.

Slowly, on my hands and knees, I slipped through the holes to come face-to-face with a German Schupo. I jumped back into the dark as if electrocuted. Instinctively, I ran with all my strength. Two gunshots rang out, missing their target. My constant dodging around corners saved my life. The German had no time to aim as I zigzagged past the corners and turns. With all my strength, I dashed back as fast as I could and climbed over the wardrobe back into our hiding hole. I fell on top of my family, speechless, breathless, and I clung to them. They hugged me wordlessly.

Within minutes, 13 Zgierska Street was teeming with Germans, Jewish police, Sonderkommando and Jewish firemen. The building was searched till late afternoon. They came into our rooms time and time again, and it was many hours before we climbed out of our hiding hole. Drained of all our energy, we fell on our beds fully dressed, leaving the double doors open just in case. Our tension and fear made us jump at the slightest noise.

Long days and eternal nights full of fear and anxiety followed, while the Germans carried on with their hunt. Our building was under siege day after day, for hours without end. We developed the skill of moving into hiding even faster. I had found a pair of steps, and hung them on the wall near the wardrobe to facilitate our climbing.

One morning, as we scaled the steps in a hurry, Berish lost his balance and crashed to the floor with all his weight. He lay on the floor in excruciating pain, unable to breathe or pick himself up. I could not move him; he was far too heavy for me to lift. Suddenly, we heard the Germans climbing the stairs. I grabbed Berish, lifted him up and pushed him with all my might to the top of the wardrobe. Fear, not strength, made it possible. I just managed to slide into our hiding-place as the Germans came into our home again with the Jewish police. This time they did not stay very long and, in the afternoon, the blockade was over.

My uncle, badly hurt, went to look for his doctor and found him in his own hiding place. The doctor checked his chest, telling Berish that he had three badly fractured ribs.

'There's nothing I can do,' he said. 'All I can help you with is some pain killers. They're my last few. I can't give you all of them.'

Berish used these tablets only when in extreme pain in hiding, to prevent him from biting his lips. That night I stitched together two towels and bandaged his chest. It eased the pain slightly. Now, with my uncle's infirmity, I had to move the beds on my own, as none of the others was fit to replace him. I dismantled my sled and used a large piece of timber as a crowbar that made it possible for me to move the beds without help. Although our rooms were searched many times, our hide-out withstood every test. Its one great drawback was its lack of space; and it shrank still further when we had to put in a stool for Berish and a bucket of water to revive ourselves and prevent dehydration.

August was very hot, with temperatures at times reaching beyond thirty degrees centigrade. In our hiding hole it became almost unbearable. In the dark, one on top of the other, our perspiration, fear and body-heat fused us into one being. I felt the vibrations and spasms of everyone's nerves; I sensed their reflexes, every twitch of their muscles. I even sensed the thoughts that flashed through their minds. I could hear their racing heartbeats. We all experienced the same sensations, the same agony and fear — unable, after a while, to tell if they were our own or another's. We flinched at the slightest noise.

I was exhausted. My whole body ached from constantly pushing the beds. I became so sore that I could hardly pull myself out of our hide-out. There was tension even when we slept: we would wake with jaws and cheek-muscles that were stiff and sore from having been clenched when we thought we were resting. As time went on, we learned how the Germans operated. The hunt would start in the early morning in the first week, and they searched our building every day. As time went by, they came less frequently, and then mostly in the afternoons. We never knew when they would come again. When out of hiding, we stretched our bodies, walking softly around our rooms without shoes.

In the second week in August, around midday, a Schupo walked into the Majerowiczes' room, took off his boots, helmet and tunic, and stretched out on the bed, his rifle standing by his side. Then he fell asleep. Our hide-out was like a steam bath. We stood mummified, watching through the little holes in the wall of the wardrobe we had strategically drilled to observe every corner of the room. How long he slept, I don't know. It seemed like an eternity. Eventually, he woke up, put his boots and tunic on, slung his rifle over his shoulder and began to search the room.

Before the war, Mr Majerowicz had been a leading optician in Lodz with two of the most modern stores in the centre of the city. Suddenly, the Schupo was attracted by the large mahogany wardrobe with its doors wide open. There, Majerowicz had stored the optical glasses and frames he had salvaged from his stores before he was moved into the ghetto. The Schupo was eagerly searching through the shelves and drawers when, suddenly, his face lit up as he came across a large carton of contraceptives of which Majerowicz had also been a manufacturer. The German poked his head deep into the wardrobe. For one moment his head was right in front of my face and I could hear his breathing. I don't know how he did not hear mine; we were only centimetres apart, divided by the thin, three-ply wall of the wardrobe. To say we froze in that heat is still an understatement.

He wasted no time in stuffing his pockets with the little envelopes. He filled up his knapsack to the brim so that he could hardly button it up. He walked over to the bed, put his helmet on and left. Only seconds passed before he came back again to grab some more, filling up his gas-mask canister. He must have made a fortune out of his loot. The quantity he took was more than one man could use in a lifetime. Eventually he left and, soon after, another German came and made straight for the wardrobe. This time, we were lucky: he took his quantity quickly and left. The first thing I did when it got dark was to remove all the chairs. I dumped the mattress and the carton with the condoms in one of the deserted apartments on the other side of the corridor.

By now we had very little food left. We fetched and warmed up a bit of water in the middle of the night, for in the day-time we could not light a fire; the smoke from the chimney stack would have given us away. To switch on the electric stove would have been just as dangerous, as pots and kettles were always checked to see if they were warm. At that late hour we also washed and changed our underwear and, at daybreak, we went back into hiding. Berish became weaker and thinner from the excruciating pain.

Standing for days in the dark, I thought a lot about Lipek, wondering what had happened to him. We never received news of his transport, but I hoped that he was in a labour camp. I hoped he had food. Hunger hurts. The pain is unbearable. One slowly withers away and finally dies in agony. I had seen it happen to many people, so I knew.

Recollections of uncle Berish

My thoughts took me back to those first days in the ghetto — mid-May, 1940. Certainly, we had feared the Germans and anticipated that life under their rule would be hard. But in my wildest, most extravagant imaginings, could I ever have foreseen what was to follow? Could anyone?

I recalled the day that Berish came home nervous, smoking cigarette after cigarette. I watched him puffing heavily, burning half a cigarette with every draw, and I realised something serious must have happened. Compulsively inhaling every bit of smoke as he walked up and down the long kitchen like a caged lion, he paced for a long time, his cheeks flushed. He steadily filled the kitchen with clouds of smoke, and his face wore an expression I had never seen before. Suddenly, he stopped and said to my father: 'Shimon, I must talk to you. Please, let's sit down.'

They walked into the dining room and sat at the table. I was intrigued; I had to know everything that took place in our home. With the German invasion, my life had changed so radically from one day to the next that I grew up overnight. My father had gone into hiding, unable to walk the streets, as he would have been easy prey. So I took that role, because I was younger and faster. Thinking back, I realise now that I had to act, judge and decide on the most vital of issues. I had to reach adulthood quickly; there was no alternative. I was entrusted with business duties that, under normal circumstances, my parents would never have expected me to undertake, and at times they were complex and burdensome. My good fortune was that I did not realise the full extent of the gravity of the situation. My youth, naivete and energy never gave me time to reflect upon things. I just acted instinctively and luck was on my side. But I was no exception. The ghetto children all matured without having time to age.

'Shimon,' said my uncle, speaking slowly and emphasising every word, 'Shimon, I have accepted the position of secretary to Mr Rozenblat.'

Leon Rozenblat was the Jewish police commissioner in the ghetto, and Berish's announcement was greeted with a deathly silence. The brothers-in-law both sat motionless. I could feel the air between them charged with electricity. Berish was very nervous and he broke the silence first, now speaking very loudly and fast.

'I will be responsible to the police commissioner only and will have nothing to do with anybody else, nor will I be assigned to street duties — only office work. I have insisted and made it a condition that I will neither patrol the streets nor carry a rubber truncheon. Mr Rozenblat was in full agreement.

'He assured me that his secretary would do nothing of the sort, so I accepted his offer. He has promised me excellent conditions: I am to start with the rank of senior constable, with opportunities for promotion.'

Berish stopped for a moment, drawing deep and long on a freshly lit cigarette. Still my father sat without moving, without uttering a sound — in stark contrast to my uncle, whose restless and incessant movements could not contain his tension.

'Shimon, what do you think? What is your opinion?' asked Berish at last.

My father took a series of deep breaths before speaking in a voice that was measured and calm.

'Do you realise what sort of employment you have accepted, Berish? Do you understand what sort of work you will have to do?'

'Shimon,' Berish interrupted, 'I will not be on street duty; only in the office. I will not carry a rubber truncheon. My work will be office work. The only thing I will be using is a typewriter.'

My father shook his head. 'Office work only? What sort of office work does one do for the Jewish police commissioner? Besides, you will not be working for the Jewish police; you'll be working for the

Germans. You'll have to do what they tell you to do. The typewriter will do more harm than the policeman wielding his rubber truncheon. I cannot tell you not to do it, Berish. These are precarious times we're living in, and each man has to decide for himself the best way to get through them. But one thing I know: I would never touch such a job. It's "treiyf" (unclean). If you do such work you, too, become unclean.'

Berish tensed up again. His eyes had become bloodshot, and seemed to glitter in red-flecked anxiety. I had always known he was a heavy smoker but I had never seen him smoke like this. He seemed to eat rather than inhale the smoke with every anxious draw. Once again, silence fell between the brothers-in-law.

'Shimon,' Berish said at last, 'I will talk it over with Sarah.'

'Leave Sarah alone, Berish, please,' said my father, his face troubled. 'Don't bring her into this.'

'Then who do I speak to? Who do I ask?' Berish demanded.

'Ask yourself. You alone must know the answer. Think carefully. Think what you are doing!'

Neither of them spoke for a while. 'Speak to your old party friends, Berish,' my father finally suggested.

As a student, before he went to live in Germany, my uncle had been a member of the Zionist-socialist movement in Lodz, the Left Poale Zion, and somehow he had maintained his connection with them over the years. He also had a number of friends amongst the German Jews who came back to live in Lodz after Hitler's rise to power. It was through them that he was introduced to the ghetto police commissioner.

The debate between Berish and my father excited me greatly. Deep in my heart, I hoped that my uncle would not listen to my father's advice. It would be wonderful to have an uncle as a police officer. I could not understand my father's objections. Why on earth did he call it treiyf ? What harm would my uncle do? He was such a gentle person; he would be the secretary only — an officeworker, nothing more. Besides, we would have protekcja, special favours. We would be amongst the elite. My uncle's position would open all doors for us. In the ghetto, protekcja was a matter of life and death.

Berish was on edge for days, smoking furiously; until, one day, he came back to the apartment exhausted. His face was drawn but calmer. He smoked less. He put his hand on my father's shoulder and invited him to sit next to him at the table.

'I have made my decision,' he said slowly. 'I am not accepting Rozenblat's offer. I will not join the Jewish police.'

My father gazed at his brother-in-law solemnly for a few moments and then asked him for a cigarette. As he was a non-smoker, the cigarette was the pipe of peace, signifying also a moment of great relief. My father took a few puffs of it in a funny, awkward manner, and then offered it to me. I felt very important, fully grown up. My mother, however, became most upset.

'What on earth are you doing?' she protested. 'You're giving him cigarettes? You must be out of your mind.'

'Don't worry, Fradl, it will do no harm,' my father calmly answered. 'I can't give him anything else.' Turning to Berish he said, 'They are young, we must let them have the taste of everything life offers. Time is short, very short.'

'Berish,' he continued, his face becoming suddenly solemn, 'I am glad of your decision. It is better to do anything else: sweep streets or clean toilets. After cleaning toilets you can wash your hands, but those working for the Jewish police — I doubt any of them will ever wash their hands clean again.'

Eventually, my uncle found a senior position with the ghetto post office, and soon after was joined there by aunt Sarah. Five years later, standing in the dark between the wardrobe and the door, I understood what my uncle's role would have been. He could well have been searching for his friends and his neighbours, to betray them.

Berish was tugging at my sleeve, signalling me to climb out. Cautiously, I scouted the terrain, having quickly developed the skill to survey accurately the surrounding empty buildings. My senses were acutely tuned; I picked up every sound, the slightest vibration. I knew every move, every step I would take in advance. Always ready to retreat at any given moment, I knew exactly what my moves should be were I ever to be confronted unexpectedly from the front, the rear, the left or the right. My escape routes were well mapped precisely in my head and had been timed down to the last second. My life, and the lives of my nearest ones, depended on the honing of these techniques.

By now, Berish was in constant pain. His fractured ribs gave him no peace. He could neither lie nor stand, and hiding between the doors became unbearable. He looked up his friend the doctor again, but he and his whole family were gone. Berish searched the room and the cellar where they had been hiding, but they had been taken and had left no trace. Worn out and depressed, he came home.

Later that evening, he looked up one of his friends with whom he had worked at the ghetto post office. They were happy to see each other. Excitedly, his friend informed him that he was moving with his family to the post office. All the post employees would be given protective shelter at the head office and were exempt from deportation. Berish came home to tell us the news. After a short discussion we all agreed that Berish and Sarah should move into the post office headquarters at 4 Plac Koscielny, only a five-minute walk from 13 Zgierska Street. They were both very upset and felt guilty at leaving us, but we encouraged them to take advantage of the chance. Berish would at last get the medical attention he so badly needed. Possibly, they would even have some pain-killers.

I carried my uncle's rucksack. We walked in silence and separated almost wordlessly, saying a brief goodbye and giving one another a kiss. As we parted I wondered if I would ever see them again. It was the middle of the night when I made my way back home again. 13 Zgierska Street was empty: not a soul, not a sound. Death stared out at me from every corner.

A new hide-out

On 17 August, the first proclamation in the ghetto signed only by the Gestapo appeared on the ghetto walls: the ghetto was now to be reduced in size. The west side across the bridge, opposite our apartment, became forbidden territory. Anyone found there would be shot on sight. Looking across the wires, I saw no movement, either by the Germans or the Jewish police. Towards the end of the third week of August, we heard rumours that the east side of Zgierska Street where we lived, was soon to be evacuated and turned into forbidden territory.

The ghetto was shrinking, tightening like a noose around us, and we would be forced out of our well-tested hide-out. I went to see Rivek who worked with the tramways of the ghetto. The tramway workers were protected from deportation, and Rivek told me that his whole family had moved into the leather-goods factory where his father and brother were technical managers. His sister Chana and her child were with them, too. We did not realise that the protective shelters were a new trick: yet another ruse to flush out the ghetto's population in hiding. The Germans gave them brief respite for a few days, and then rounded them up one after the other, loaded them on the trains and sent them off.

Rivek confirmed the rumour that 13 Zgierska Street would soon be excluded from ghetto territory. He advised me to move into his home on the first floor at 24 Pieprzowa Street, where he told me that there was an excellent hide-out in which we would be able to stretch out. Before the war, the building had been inhabited mainly by hand-weavers with rooms exceptionally spacious to accommodate their large handlooms. Rivek's room had properly constructed yarn storage space which was covered with the same wallpaper as the rest of the room. To get inside, we had to crawl on hands and knees into the credenza that was placed against the entrance; by removing a panel, we could enter the hide-out.

That afternoon I checked it out. I knew their home well, and it had never once occurred to me in the five years I had visited them that there was a double wall: it was absolutely invisible. Late at night, we moved into Rivek's home, taking along our rucksacks only. We climbed into the pitch-black hide-out, only to find people inside — a young couple with a boy of ten and a baby, and the parents of the young woman. My nostrils were assaulted by the strong odours of dry urine and perspiration.

Nobody asked any questions. We squeezed in and lay down on the floor that was covered with bales of yarn. The night was long and fearful as we lay virtually on top of each other. The baby cried all through it, and the next morning our building was surrounded. We could hear the shouting of the Germans as they kept coming into the room. We effectively stopped breathing, terrified that the baby might cry or give us away with other sounds. Nobody moved for what seemed like an eternity.

It was late in the afternoon when I decided to see what was going on. The blockade was over. Upon my return, the others were gone. The grandfather of the baby returned briefly to collect their belongings. He told us that his grandchild was dead. While the Germans were searching the room, the father had covered the baby's face with a cushion to prevent it from crying, not realising that the baby could not breathe. He had been trying to protect us. The old man left, and the family never came back again.

The three of us were left alone. Late in the evening I went down Pieprzowa Street to investigate, and ran into my friend Alexander, with whom I had worked at 9 Pucka Street, at the timber factory. He was intelligent and well-spoken and, before the war, had been a leading member of the anarchist movement in Lodz. Now he was pushing a cart on two wheels loaded with a bag of flour and a bag of sugar. I couldn't believe my eyes.

'The food stores at Franciszkanska Street have been broken into and are unguarded,' Alexander told me, and I dashed over there to find the huge cellars wide open. I emptied half of a 100-kilogram bag of flour, so that I could carry it, and returned to get half a bag of sugar, sinking knee-deep in the mixture of loose white powder and crystals. In all my life — before and since — I have never seen so much sugar and flour as had burst out of the bags spread over the cellar floor. I could have drowned in it.

Late in the evening I saw Alexander again, and he asked me to join him in his hiding place with his wife and two children. His hide-out was in a cellar in Pieprzowa Street, well equipped with radio, electricity, water and food stored up to last for many months; but I declined his offer, thinking it safer to be spread out. He told me the latest radio news, warning me about Auschwitz; but it was news I already had. We parted, wishing one another good luck. Before he rounded the corner, he turned and called out: 'Hold on. Don't give yourselves up! You know what happens over there.'

Plans to resist deportation

Alexander and I had developed a close friendship from working together in the timber yard. When the liquidation of the ghetto was already well-advanced, we had a long discussion, culminating in a decision to organise the men from the transport section. Calling a meeting in the stockyard, behind the stacks of timber, we had chosen a time when we knew 9 Pucka Street would be deserted.

I opened proceedings with a brief introduction; then Alexander spoke. He tried to impress upon the men — a tough lot, all in reasonably fit physical condition — the importance of organising ourselves. He suggested we hide in the factory and, if necessary, resist. He was constantly interrupted. Questions were fired at him from every corner.

'What will you do if we're discovered?'

'With what will you resist?'

'What about the women?' someone asked.

'And the children?' another interjected.

The discussion became heated, with everyone speaking at once.

'To kill a few Germans may be possible,' one man conceded, 'But at what price? To see our parents, women and children butchered in front of our eyes?'

Those from the liquidated ghettos in the Wartheland were pessimistic, having witnessed bloody massacres as their ghettos were liquidated. One man articulated the feelings of most of the others. 'I would stand here and fight till the last — but with what? With my bare hands? And to what possible end?'

The meeting became noisy. I tried to stem the tide of pessimism, shouting above the babble, 'Do you know where they're taking us? Have you heard the radio reports? Don't you know that they'll murder us all anyway, one way or another?'

There was a momentary silence which was broken almost immediately by the voice of a man asking, 'Let's assume we kill a few Germans, what do we achieve? How long can we last? One way or another we are condemned. How can you fight against machine-guns and tanks with bare hands?'

'In Warsaw,' said another, 'at least they were armed. We have nothing.'

The discussion became heated and confusing; tempers ran high. Many simply shrugged their shoulders and walked away, deciding to go home and join their families. Some still had children. They called Alexander a lunatic and a dreamer, and soon the meeting dispersed completely.

Dov Lemberg, a member of the Chalutz movement in the Lodz ghetto, was appointed by the organisation to obtain weapons from the Polish underground. Working at the ghetto railway station, Radogoszcz, Lemberg contacted railway workers who belonged to the Polish underground. They promised him some guns, but eventually told him that they had very little weaponry for themselves and none to spare for the ghetto. The Chalutz movement also made plans — which never came to fruition — to steal guns from a German store.[37]

Doctor Wajskop, a well-known personality in the ghetto, called a secret meeting at the headquarters of the Jewish fire brigade at Lutomierska Street. Behaving with dignity and even heroism throughout the entire period, he had refused to accept the privileges extended to him by Rumkowski, and chose to starve with the rest of us. When he called a meeting, people came: the commandant of the ghetto fire brigade, Kaufman, Doctor Wajskop's brother and Doctor Joseph Layder. The meeting was chaired by Wajskop himself, and a resolution was adopted to prepare for an armed revolt.

They drew up a plan. Kaufman was to organise the fire brigade, arm them with axes and iron bars and, on the determined day at the specified time, drive the fire truck to the sixth German police precinct which housed the German ghetto guards. Simultaneously, another group would attack the German sentries stationed around the barbed wire, as well as the guard at the gates leading to the Baluter Market, the Gettoverwaltung and Hans Biebow's offices. Chimowicz, manager of the ghetto metal factory, promised to manufacture hand grenades. Their aim was to disarm every German. The attack would serve as a signal for the population to break out from behind the barbed wires in an open revolt.[38]

Ultimately, however, the Lodz ghetto never rose in an armed insurrection, although the fighting spirit and will to resist were there. One of the major stumbling blocks was the large local German population from before the war — approximately sixty thousand. Lodz had become part of the Third Reich by decree of the Führer and, with the destruction of German towns and cities as a consequence of air raids, large numbers of Germans were brought from their bombed cities into Lodz, replacing the Polish population and swelling the numbers of German inhabitants to one hundred and forty-three thousand. Lodz, now Litzmannstadt, had been virtually transformed into a German city.

The Polish underground in Lodz was small, insignificant and not very willing to help the Jews. Lodz was also strategically disadvantaged by its geographic position. The huge forests, which gave shelter to and protected the partisans and underground fighters, were too distant from the city. Lodz had no sewerage system like Warsaw's, the canals of which had been the secret roads of supply and communication with the outside world. And, finally, the Lodz ghetto was the most hermetically sealed off from the outside world, just like a concentration camp. The streets adjacent to and surrounding the ghetto were completely razed, creating a sizeable and vulnerable no-man's-land that effectively prevented every possible contact with the outside.

The ghetto's last Jews

Within the next few days, at a pre-appointed time, I met Alexander in Pieprzowa Street. He tipped me off as to the whereabouts of bread and other foods; but, although we were close friends, neither he nor I knew the location of the other's hiding places — not because we distrusted one another, but so as not to be burdened with the knowledge and subsequent possibility of betrayal should either of us be caught and tortured.

The ghetto looked like a ghost town. Only shadows occasionally darted across the streets, running from one hole to the next, their faces unshaven, unwashed, their eyes tired and bloodshot. Alexander, too, looked haggard and tired. None of us had washed or shaved for many days.

The last official document, in the form of a placard and signed by Rumkowski — even though his office had been officially closed by the Gestapo on 6 August — appeared on the ghetto walls on 22 August 1944:

REMINDER!
TO THE GHETTO POPULATION!
REGARDING: VOLUNTEERS TO REPORT FOR THE TRANSPORT DEPARTING TOMORROW.

In order to avoid methods of force it is in your own interests to report voluntarily today with luggage for tomorrow's transport.

REPORT TO 3 KRAWIECKA STREET OR THE CENTRAL PRISON.
YOU CAN REPORT ALL DAY LONG AND ALL NIGHT.

Care is taken that all volunteers who do report for the transport will be provided with food at the above centres.

THE ELDEST OF THE JEWS IN LITZMANNSTADT GHETTO
MORDECHAI CHAIM RUMKOWSKI
Litzmannstadt ghetto, 22 August 1944.

The ghetto streets were constantly patrolled by the Schupo and the Einsatzgruppen. Automatic weapons slung around their necks, they stood on the corners half drunk, very relaxed. They had brought in trained Alsatian sniffer dogs. The Jewish police, fire brigade and the Jewish Sonderkommando were not to be seen. They had started to load them on the trains. The ghetto was, by then, practically empty.

Yet another ghetto proclamation, printed in German and in Yiddish, signed by the Gestapo, appeared on the walls, stipulating the remaining areas of the ghetto in which it was still permissible to live; and promising death to those who did not vacate their homes — if they lived outside the designated precincts — by 7.00 a.m. on 25 August.

The next and final proclamation, similar to the previous one, appeared on the ghetto walls on 28 August 1944 and was signed by the Gestapo.

Our hide-out at Rivek's home was excellent. It was roomy enough to allow us to stretch out to sleep. I managed to store up enough food to last us for many months. For the first time, after five long years of famine, we no longer suffered hunger pains.

Lying in the dark for many hours, I realised that the Lodz ghetto had come to its ultimate end. Only the odd few people were still in hiding. In my enforced idleness, lying on the heap of yarn, once again I thought about my brother. Had they taken him to Auschwitz? What had happened to him? I thought about the past, my school years, my friends, my teachers — my mind jumping from one thing to another. Suddenly I thought of my Rabbi Yitzchak Laib. In the dark I could see the silhouette of his pale face and the mysterious glow of his silver grey beard. I could hear his gentle voice whispering:

'Cain, Cain, what hast thou done? Cain, Cain! Where is your brother? And the Lord said to Cain, Where is Abel, thy brother? And he said, I know not: am I my brother's keeper? And He said, What hast thou done? The voice of thy brother's blood cries to me from the ground.'

I fell asleep. I lost count of time, becoming confused about whether it was day or night, exhausted from the many hours in the dark. I woke up thinking about Auschwitz, trying to visualise how it actually happened. How did they kill so many people? My imagination ran wild with scenes of horror.

I could understand natural disasters, I thought — floods, tidal waves and earthquakes that destroy and kill. I could understand carnivorous animals, man-eating crocodiles, poisonous snakes: they kill to feed themselves. But I could not and I cannot — dear God, I cannot — comprehend human beings who murder people day by day, year after year, listen to their agonised cries, see their twisted faces, their intertwined bodies lying on a heap. How could they? How could humans kill children, little babies, beautiful young women, some with the swollen bellies of pregnancy, and then go home to their own women, make love to them, kiss their children and then go back to do more killing? However long I lay in the dark, I knew there was no answer, even if I shouted the questions to the heavens for the rest of my days.

I recalled a story told by my mother which happened during the First World War in Zdunska Wola. A detachment of Cossacks was stationed in my grandfather's house. One night, they were sipping tea around the boiling samovar and having a friendly chat with my grandfather, whom they adored. They especially admired him for his knowledge of the Bible. This night, the eldest of the Cossacks asked him: 'Are there any Jews in this village?'

'I am a Jew,' said my grandfather.

He slapped my grandfather on his back and burst out laughing. 'You've got a good sense of humour,' he roared.

When the old man insisted, the Cossack took off my grandfather's hat and felt his head. 'You can't be a Jew,' he exclaimed. 'You don't have horns! You don't look like a demon. You look like one of us — human!'

The Cossack had never seen a Jew before. All he knew was what he had been taught by the Church: that Jews were the Christ-killers — the children of Satan — worthy to be slaughtered by the Cossacks to enhance the love of their God, their country and their Tsar. They murdered Jews to save their country with the old Russian battle cry on their lips: '*Bee Zydov Spassai Russeiu*' ('Beat the Jews and save Russia').

The Germans, however, were not primitive Cossacks from eastern Europe. They belonged, supposedly, to a higher civilisation. Many years after the war, I read the diary of Rudolf Hoess (the commandant of Auschwitz concentration camp), which peels away the thin veneer of civilisation from his people, exposing their brutality, and displaying their deep-seated and traditional hatred towards the Jews:

> In the summer of 1941 (I don't remember the exact date) I was unexpectedly summoned to the SS 'Reichsführer' in Berlin, directly from his office. Himmler received me without the presence of his adjutant and declared the following: 'The Führer has ordered the final solution of the Jewish question. We the SS have to execute this order …
>
> 'You must keep this order in strictest secrecy even from your superiors. After your talk with Eichmann you must send me immediately the plans of the arrangement. Jews have been the eternal enemies of the German people and must be destroyed. All Jews who will fall into our hands during this war, will be exterminated, without exception. If we do not succeed now, in biologically destroying the power of Judaism, it will in the future destroy the German people.'[39]

The end of an emperor

On 28 August 1944, the emperor of Litzmannstadt ghetto, Mordechai Chaim Rumkowski, along with his wife and adopted son, were loaded onto one of the cattle wagons together with his brother Joseph and his sister-in-law, Helena. The Germans had no further use for him, although Biebow offered him the privilege of staying in the ghetto, at 36 Lagiewnicka Street, with a group of approximately seven hundred ghetto dignitaries. Rumkowski, however, chose to go with his brother and sister-in-law, whom Biebow had denied the privilege of remaining in the ghetto. But the privilege, like all German privileges, turned out to be a dubious one, anyway.

On 20 October 1944, the group of seven hundred dignitaries was loaded onto a train and taken to the concentration camps Sachsenhausen, Oranienburg and Ravensbruck.[40]

Rumkowski could not have changed the history or the fate of the Jews of Lodz. The Germans never asked his advice, nor did they want his opinion. He was a hostage, a pawn, a tool in the hands of a most brutal monster. They gave him orders and he had to obey them, which he did to the letter. Although he was a man with great organisational talents and tremendous drive, he lacked the qualities of a truly great leader, being short-sighted, stubborn and opinionated. He neither asked for advice nor did he listen to the views of others. Too weak to carry the weight with which history had burdened him, he lacked the moral strength and integrity to refuse the kudos and privilege that, for a short time, went with it.

His role was a complex one, which many in comparable positions failed to perform with any greater merit. Although he had been a member of the Lodz Kehillah before the war, he had only ever been on the fringes of Jewish social life. Like the British colonel in the film, *Bridge On The River Kwai,* he was both a builder and organiser who became obsessed with his work to the point of forgetting those he was working for, and what the consequences of this work must ultimately be.

Mordechai Chaim Rumkowski always spoke about 'his' children with great compassion and feeling. In all his speeches he mentioned his immense love of them. Yet, on 4 September 1942, he announced that, by order of the authorities, twenty thousand Jews under the age of ten and over sixty-five had to be resettled outside the ghetto. Those were the instructions he received from the German authorities, and he executed them meticulously. He ordered the Jewish police, Sonderkommando and fire brigade to round up the children, the old and the sick, and load them on German trucks to be taken away to the unknown. (A total of 15,685 were taken away.) But he knew what would happen to them. I remember how, in 1942, he said, 'The wolf wants blood! What should I do? What can I do? I have to quench his thirst! I must give up the children!' A fatal, and unforgivable mistake. Rumkowski had only one way out ... to join his children, like Janusz Korczak from the Warsaw ghetto.[41] Rumkowski turned to the rabbis for advice; they told him to turn to God. Instead, he turned to the devil.

Still, had it not been Mordechai Chaim Rumkowski, the Germans would have found somebody else. They always found their collaborators, wherever they invaded. In the Ukraine, Byelorussia, Estonia, Lithuania and Latvia, they had no Eldest Jew, no Jewish councils, nor did they have the Jewish police. Within a few months of invading these parts, the German Einsatzgruppen murdered the entire Jewish population with the assistance of a large number of the local militia and civilian populations who voluntarily joined in the slaughter. They did it without the use of gas.

Some of my ghetto friends who survived the Holocaust credit

Rumkowski with having saved their lives. They attribute the lon-
gevity of the Lodz ghetto to him. So do some lay historians,
ignoring the evidence that the ghetto lasted as long as it did only
because of the greed for profit and the rapacious appetites of
Greiser and Biebow. It was, above all, the influential
Reichsstatthalter Greiser, who revoked three orders signed by the
most powerful Heinrich Himmler, who delayed the liquidation of
the Lodz ghetto until August 1944.

In the eyes of Rumkowski, as well as in the eyes of many of the
inhabitants of the Lodz ghetto, the factories and workshops created a sense of security. All hoped to be spared because they were
needed for the war effort.

But Hitler had other plans for the Jews. He wanted them neither
as subjects nor as slaves. Hans Biebow was present at the railway
line when Rumkowski was taken to the unknown. Today, I know
his destination was Auschwitz where, upon his arrival, he was
given a special welcome. At the head of the welcoming party were
the underworld characters Moshe 'Chasid' and his brother; Janek
'Tzigan'; and some of the leading thugs of Auschwitz.

Rumkowski was beaten till he was half-unconscious before he
was thrown into an open furnace where bodies were burned when
the crematoria could not cope with the surplus of corpses. The
police commissioner, Leon Rozenblat, and all the other high-ranking Jewish police officers, were beaten to death on the ramp, right
in front of the victims who were just being unloaded.[42]

Were they judges, the Janek 'Tzigans', and his friends, and the
Moshe 'Chasids'? Was Auschwitz the place for justice? It is hard to
be a hero. It is just as difficult to be a judge. I am only a survivor, a
witness telling my story the way it unfolded in front of my eyes.
And my story is a testimony to all those who lived and died behind
the barbed wires of the Lodz ghetto. I leave it for history to judge.

Discovered

In the hide-out, lying on the heap of yarn for many hours, I thought
about myriad events from my past: childhood; kindergarten;
school. I thought about my relatives and my friends, most of whom
were dead by now. In the dark, my feet got tangled up in the yarn.
I felt like a fox caught in a trap and I wondered how long one fox
could survive when constantly hunted by so many hounds and

hunters. I could not fall asleep. Mendel Feldman's last radio message kept flashing through my mind. However hard I tried to stop it, it kept coming back.

Early the next morning, I went down to scout the area. Cautiously, I opened the gate leading onto the street and found myself in the presence of a group of Einsatzkommandos and Schupos who were standing across the street on the corner of Pieprzowa and Mlynarska, casually smoking and enjoying their morning.

Panic-stricken, I turned and ran, pursued by a Schupoman. I was on foreign territory and exhausted from four weeks of playing hide-and-seek with the Angel of Death. Not having planned my escape routes in advance, I was doomed to fail. In my terror, I ran back to the hide-out — an unforgivable, deadly mistake. I bolted the door just before the German came banging on it with his rifle butt. The noise reverberated like thunder through the empty building, with the officer threatening to shoot through the door.

I signalled to my parents to move away from the entrance, in mortal fear that he would carry out his threat. My father disregarded my signalling and walked forward, calling:

'Don't shoot. I will open the door.'

I grabbed my father, struggling with him, trying to prevent his opening the door. My mother began to cry, and it was her tears that disarmed me. I allowed my father to unlock the door.

The German flung it open and rushed at me, knocking me to the ground. He cocked his weapon, and the cold 'ping' of the metal pierced my ears, sending waves of fear through my spine. My father pleaded with him, 'Please don't shoot, I beg you, I am his father. He is young and silly. Please don't.' My mother cried as the German kept clubbing me with his gun. He cursed and yelled, calling me, *'Du Schmutziger Jude! Du Schweinhund!'* ('You dirty Jew! You swine-hound!') But he did not shoot. My father promised him we would depart immediately, so the German left and I heard the nails in the soles of his boots grinding the stairs as he climbed to the upper floors to search the rest of the building. I begged my father not to go, pleading with him to hide again, but he would not listen.

'I am giving up!' he insisted, 'I cannot go on! I can't take it any longer.'

I grabbed him, trying to prevent his leaving. It was the first time in my life that I dared to seize my father and struggle with him. I did not hurt him; I only wrestled with him, trying to prevent his surrender. My mother cried, pleading with me to let go of him.

'Please don't go,' I begged. 'We must hide. We did it before and it worked! Please listen. You know what they will do. They will kill us!'

My father merely stood defeated, hanging his head.

'Yes, I know, I know, I *know*,' he repeated, the tiredness in his voice palpable and desperate. 'I am exhausted! I give up! I cannot go on any longer!'

I turned to my mother, begging her to stop him, but to no avail. My father would not listen. He kept saying, 'I cannot go on any longer. You can both stay if you like.'

'I must go with him!' my mother cried, at which point I became hysterical.

'They will kill you! They will murder us all!' I bellowed.

My mother had tears in her eyes: 'If father goes, I go with him!' she said. 'You are young. Save yourself!'

I turned back to my father. 'Why are you doing this?' I implored him. 'Why? You are destroying us all!'

He kept repeating, 'I'm tired, I give up! I cannot go on any longer! Let it be over and done with!' My mother cried as I pleaded with her not to follow my father. 'How do you expect me to go on living without him? This, never! I must go with him!'

'But mother, they will kill you! They will kill us all! Please stay with me!' I said desperately for the last time, but my parents would not listen: both of them walked down the stairs with their rucksacks on their backs. To this very day, I wonder at the logic of my going with them, even though I knew the destination towards which we were headed. Yet, if I had let them go, I would have been deserting them in the last moments of their lives; so I grabbed my rucksack and followed, trying not to think about what I considered to be my reasonable chances of survival in the ghetto.

The Germans across the road burst out laughing when they saw us and amused themselves by calling us offensive names. '*Raus! Raus! Ihr Schmutzige Juden.*' ('Out! Out! You dirty Jews!') *Los! Los! Schnell! Schnell!* 'And don't stop or you will be shot!'

Never had I felt so powerless and alone as I did when confronted by the half-drunk, heavily armed German hooligans dressed in uniforms decorated with ribbons awarded them for murdering defenceless people. Their submachine guns aimed at our backs sent shivers through my entire body, and I began to experience a strange tingling sensation running over my face and into my brain. Our lives were hanging on a thin hair that could break at any tick of the clock, with the lifeless buildings the only witnesses.

It was late in the afternoon when we got to Marysin, following others in front of us. We reached the railway line where a train, loaded with victims, was ready to leave. There were still some Jewish railway workers and a few Jewish policemen assisting the Germans in loading the last of us. The atmosphere was tense, full of fear, although no screaming, beating or shooting took place.

'You are all to stay at Marysin and report to the train at daybreak,' one of the Jewish police officers announced. 'The next train will be leaving tomorrow.'

We spent the night in a deserted house, stretching out fully dressed on the bare floors.

Although at Marysin there were still some people, it was obvious that the Lodz ghetto was finished. The Jewish police, the Sonderkommando, and the fire brigade no longer existed. They had all been loaded onto the trains the same way they had helped the Germans to load their fellow Jews, and they were destined to meet with the same fate.

Early on Thursday 31 August 1944, we were lined up and loaded onto a cattle wagon. My friend from school and Skif, Heniek Bornsztejn, helped to load water into the cart. He, with his parents and brother, were taken to Auschwitz on the following train, which was the very last out of the Lodz ghetto. We exchanged a few words as I crossed the plank into the wagon. Inside, by sheer coincidence, we met up with a number of friends, amongst whom were Jacob Nirenberg, the chairman of the Bund in the ghetto, with his wife and four-year-old child, Rivcia, his sister and his brother Mayer. There was Mr Dombrowski with his wife, and there were also my childhood and school friends, Motele and Chanele Hauser, with their parents. Our parents had been friends since their own youth. We were all pushed into the same cart — between sixty and seventy people — and a big tin of water was placed in the centre. Although our wagon was crowded, it was not as bad as those which had left before us. The doors were rolled shut. The heavy bolts were pushed into position with a grinding noise and locked. With a sudden jerk, the train moved, throwing its living cargo off balance. I leaned against the wall near the little window and watched the changing landscape.

The train gained speed, emitting long whistles, rushing past farms, villages, peasant settlements and towns. The sky was clear — a warm, bright day with lots of sunshine although the summer was over. Inside the wagon the air was hot and heavy. I felt claustrophobic and tired. There was no room to sit.

It had been five long years since I had seen the countryside, and I had forgotten the look of open fields and trees. The harvest was over. The bare fields were waiting to be ploughed and seeded for next season's crop. Next season's crop. Who would be there to see it?

The train continued to rush towards our destination as the trees flashed before my eyes. Everything looked strange and distant, as if it were from another world, or as if seen a long time ago in another life. I saw flocks of birds in formation heading south and I followed them with my eyes, envying them.

Staring at my mother, I thought that the years of suffering had not completely eroded the beauty of her face. For the most part, however, my mind was in turmoil. I was in panic and fear. I could not believe — nor could I disbelieve — that within a few hours none of us would be amongst the living. What goes on in this world? Why must we die? My father stood near me, silent, with an empty expression on his face, staring aimlessly into space through the little window crossed with barbed wire. He looked tired. His face bore the marks of starvation and pain.

The Polish peasants were out in the fields, and they greeted the train with festive smiles. It almost seemed as though they knew we were coming, as though they were expecting us. They had certainly seen many trains like this before. Some of them made hostile, offensive gestures at us.

Their children were hopping about and clapping their hands with joy. To this day I wonder how they could. They knew who we were and where the Germans were taking us. They knew what would happen once we reached our destination. What sort of people could enjoy the sight of such a train? What sort of people enjoy the sight of a funeral?

The train sped us towards our destiny. Jacob Nirenberg, a carpenter by trade, had his tool kit with him, and pried open a couple of floorboards so we could relieve ourselves. I am still puzzled by his surrender. Better informed than most about the fate of the deportees, he still gave himself up. I can only assume that he, like so many others, fell prey to self-delusion, that self-activating device in the human psyche which leaps into gear when man stares death in the eye. 'It couldn't happen to me!' is probably the most oft-sung refrain in the repertoire of condemned humanity.

The trip was long and arduous as the death train, with a repetitious clatter of its wheels, sped into the dark, rhythmically seeming to warn us of our impending fate. After countless hours travelling in the never-ending night, we passed a little railway station, unattended and scarcely lit. It looked unreal. A lonely kiosk with chocolate boxes on display looked like theatre props on a stage. A sign appeared in big black letters on a white oblong board with a black border: Auschwitz. As the train slowed, my heart-beat accelerated. The driver applied the brakes, reducing the speed even further, and there was a drawn-out, unremitting shuddering of the wagons as, with agonising slowness, their momentum was diminished.

The calendar had turned two pages since we had been locked into the cattle train. It was now in the early hours of 2 September 1944. Our train rolled along ever more slowly on a lonely track leading to a place called Auschwitz. Suddenly, a short railway line branched off, running across flat fields that stretched over many square kilometres. These open areas were covered with grass and had occasional lonely birch trees which shot into the sky of the frosty autumn night. This part of Auschwitz was called Brzezinki — derived from the Polish word, 'brzozy', meaning birches. In German, it was called Birkenau.

The train continued into the dark, its whistling like hysterical cries for help that reverberated far over the horizon, into an endless emptiness. Only the locomotive's wheels replied with their repetitious monotone. Clatter-boom! Clatter-boom! Clatter-boom! And all the while, an indifferent, sleeping world let the train with the last Polish Jews roll on to its point of no return.

There was a sudden squealing of metal against metal as the brakes went into action; and a banging of heavy steel as the buffers struck one another, bringing the train to an abrupt halt, throwing the entire cargo off balance once again. Turmoil and commotion. Exhausted, we fell, one on top of the other. It was very dark and very silent outside. Fear filled my heart, causing the blood to rush to my head and hammer at my temples. My senses sharpened, like an animal in the stockyard smelling blood and death. The wagon was filled with panic. Only lamenting and mourning broke the silence of the night.

EPILOGUE

The Allies' indifference

F rom the very beginning of the Holocaust, the Allied powers and their leaders were well informed about the extermination camps that the Germans had installed in Poland. So, too, were Pope Pius XII, the Vatican, the International Red Cross and the neutral Swiss. They all knew what was happening to the Jews in Treblinka, Sobibor, Belzec, Chelmno and Auschwitz, and they did absolutely nothing. They refused to act. They stayed silent.

Their silence was a green light to the Germans, and they went ahead full speed, annihilating six million Jews.

It must be noted that, long before the killing began, the free world closed its borders and shut its eyes to the plight of those desperate Jewish refugees who were trying to escape. Many might still have managed to do so had they been offered any assistance at all by the West. Instead, vast numbers finished up in the gas chambers and killing factories of Germany.

Every effort made by Jewish refugees was thwarted. The road to the West was blocked off to them.

The president of the United States of America, Franklin D Roosevelt, and all his advisers, secretaries and, in particular, the most anti-Semitic of them all, the secretary of state and his entire staff, did everything possible to prevent the media from finding out what was happening to the Jews in Europe. The same scenario took place in Britain. Winston Churchill, Anthony Eden and all the members of the British cabinet did exactly the same:

In 1940, Jewish representatives in the USA lodged an official complaint against the discriminatory policies the State Department was using against the Jews; the results were fatal. In consequence, the

Secretary of State gave strict orders to every USA consulate worldwide forbidding the issuing of visas to Jews. Jews were declared a security risk. At the same time, a Jewish congressman petitioned President Franklin D. Roosevelt, requesting his permission to allow twenty thousand Jewish children from Europe to enter the USA. The President did not even reply. He totally ignored the petition as well as its sender.[43]

The neutral Swiss, the country that housed the International Red Cross, handed back to the Gestapo thirty thousand Jewish refugees who crossed their borders.[44] They all finished up in the furnaces of Auschwitz. However, the Red Cross stood by with their kindness whenever a train with Jews was leaving. The youngsters were all given a block of chocolate as a farewell gift on their last journey to Auschwitz. Meanwhile, every German deserter who crossed the border to take refuge in Switzerland was given protection according to international law. They were all given asylum. No such consideration was extended to the Jews. They could not benefit from international law.

Jews entering the gas chambers were nobody's concern. It was certainly not the concern of the British. They were mainly interested in Jews trying to enter Palestine. The British navy in the Mediterranean was very efficient. All ships carrying Jewish refugees were forced back or, in the case of the SS *Struma*, sunk with the refugees on board. Most of the refugees finished up in the clutches of the Germans; ultimately they perished in the gas chambers.

The congressmen of the USA did not mind Jews entering their country, providing they did not exceed the tightly controlled quota. The twenty thousand Jewish children who were refused entry were above the quota and were therefore condemned to be part of the 1.5 million Jewish children gassed. This did not bother the congressmen of the USA; neither did it bother the president, Franklin D Roosevelt.

More than fifty years have passed since the events of the Holocaust took place. Slowly, the conscience of the western world is waking up, trying to come to terms with the part it played in the most gruesome bloodletting the world has ever witnessed.

In 1994, the vice president of the United States of America, Mr Al Gore, said, 'All those who stood by with indifference and did nothing to help the Jews during the Holocaust are guilty of genocide'.[45]

Part Two
THE CAMPS

7

Auschwitz-Birkenau

THE CATTLE TRAIN stood in a never-ending night. In its impenetrable darkness I lost my ability to judge time, space and distance. The wagon became a black hole, crushing my body, my mind and my spirit into nothingness. It seemed that it could destroy everybody and everything around me.

Wailing and moaning came from adjacent wagons. The trembling psalms of a man turning to the Almighty for help were all but drowned out by the surrounding clamour of other victims. All I could hear were the sobs of those crying at their own funerals. A woman's weeping made my own eyes fill with tears that seemed to form a lump which hardened in my throat, choking me with pain. I felt my whole world coming to an end.

Once again I took refuge in memory to keep me sane, but my recollections were tainted by the events of the last five years. I remembered how Rysiek and Zdzich, the gentile friends of my childhood, had never come to my rescue. I thought of the Polish neighbours, Mr and Mrs Safjan; the German neighbours, Mr and Mrs Karess; Hesse the baker, and his children; and Herr Valkenberg, the German landlord from Piaskowa Gora from whom we used to rent a villa for our summer holidays. Before the war, Valkenberg's son had run off to Germany, returning as a high-ranking SS officer, after which Fritz, his farm hand, joined the SS as well. Before the war they had all been friendly people. Ultimately, none of them aided us in our hour of need.

Only my old nurse, Andrzejowa, had remained loyal, but she had died long ago. I could still hear her loving voice humming her favourite peasant lullabies, sometimes singing my name as she rocked me to sleep in her arms. One of her favourites had been about a mother singing her son to sleep before he went into battle. Its lyrics were etched in my mind:

Kochany Abrashku Syneczku Moj.
Spij Malutki Spij Kochanie Jutro Wyruszaz
Na Pole Na boj Na Krwawy Na Pole.
A ja bende sie modlila abym ciebie nie stracila
Ali, luli, luli, lu.

My love, little Abraham, son of mine.
Sleep my little one, sleep my love.
Tomorrow you are moving out to the field.
To a bloody battle in the field.
And I will pray not to lose you.
Ali, luli, luli, lu.

As my mind wandered at random, I found myself wondering whether, should daybreak bring my end, Andrzejowa would come to me and rock me to sleep in her arms as she used to. People I had not thought of for many years came floating, unbidden, to mind. Amongst the many, my rabbi, Yitzchak Laib, appeared with the customary book under his arm; this time, the Book of Job.

He sat next to me, swaying rhythmically, his pointer combing the pages as he recited and interpreted Job's tribulations in an old Talmudic tune. To Reb Yitzchak Laib, this world was only a brief passage. It was the world to come that he lived for. His desires were all to do with attaining the purity of a 'Tzaddik', a holy man, and to be one of the 'Lamed Vov', one of the thirty-six righteous men that the world could not exist without. And, in the world to come, he wished only to be seated in the shadow of the Almighty and be blessed with His eternal peace.

In the darkness of the cattle truck, I could see the image of Rabbi Yitzchak Laib clearly, bent forward with his hands supporting his forehead as he swayed over a volume of the Tanakh, the Jewish bible. In 1942, during the Gehsperre in the Lodz ghetto, he had been taken to Chelmno and gassed.

In my fevered state, I found comparisons between Rabbi Yeshua Hanitzri — the Hebrew name for Jesus — and my rabbi, Yitzchak Laib, irresistible. The Romans were the Germans of ancient history, crucifying Jesus as their modern counterparts had gassed Yitzchak Laib. In that wagon of death, where I believed I was spending my final hours, I imagined the two of them together, studying the Tanakh. They would have a lot to discuss, speaking the same language and having been brought up among the same testament and traditions. Ultimately, they had also shared the same fate, dying at the hands of those who may have been separated by time but who were united in their hatred.

With a sense of heightened unreality, crazy speculations about the second coming of Jesus rushed through my mind. For all I knew, he had come to Lodz and been chased by my Polish neigh-bours along the streets as the synagogues were burning. Did they point their fingers at him, pulling the fringes of his prayer shawl, mocking him with the same words they used to mock the people I knew?

'Panie! Panie! Jude! Jude! Tzitzele! Tzitzele!'

And Otto Karess, our German neighbour from across the street at 25 Limanowskiego, did he perhaps cut Rabbi Yeshua's earlocks as the German officer, his guest, filmed him, kicking the Saviour with his boots while the young rabbi lay bleeding on the cobblestoned courtyard? Soon after, was Rabbi Yeshua Hanitzri locked up in the Lodz ghetto and eventually sent off in a cattle train to Chelmno, where he met the same fate as his six million brothers and sisters? And on December's twenty-fifth day at midnight, would Christians once again pray for forgiveness from Rabbi Yeshua, claiming they knew not what they did two thousand years ago, having crucified their master a second time for his crime of being Jewish?

My hallucinations continued through this night of a thousand deaths, the longest night of my life. The wailing had died down, replaced by a silence so profound that the slightest noise stopped my heartbeat. The guards were gone. Gradually, the frosty dawn dispersed the darkness and the cold autumn rays of the sun struggled to pierce through the heavy mist that was suspended from the sky-like veils in a house of mourning.

When the thick mist dissipated, the bright morning light re-vealed Auschwitz, the summit of evil. I did not realise it then, but the place I was about to enter was, in effect, the largest pagan temple of human sacrifice: the altar of death in the heart of Christendom.

Arrival — Dr Mengele's selection

Barbed wires seemed to extend beyond the horizon, further than my eyes could see. Watch towers, search lights and guards at regular intervals surrounded us. Barracks, lined up like army columns on parade, stretched for many miles. My father and I stood next to one another, staring in bewilderment and fear at our surroundings through the little window barred with wires. Trying to keep a note of indifference in his voice, my father pointed his finger in the direction of the barracks and said to Mr Dombrowski, a friend from his youth, '*Dort dreyt zikh di patelnye*' ('Over there the frying pan is turning').

The massive doors of our cattle wagon were unlocked with a grinding noise of the heavy metal bolts. The doors rolled wide open and Hell broke loose. Shouts of '*Raus! Raus! Aussteigen! Aussteigen! Schnell! Schnell! Los! Los!*' echoed in our ears. Strange-looking men in striped uniforms jumped into our cart, calling to us in Yiddish, 'Leave everything and get out!' They were the commando which unloaded the cattle trains, nicknamed 'the Canada'.

People kept asking, 'Who are you? Are you Jewish? Where are we? What's going on here?' But the Canada were not very talkative.

'Don't ask questions,' they replied. 'Just do as you're told. Leave everything and get out.'

When the new arrivals, confused and in panic, persisted with their questioning, the strange-looking people in stripes merely repeated, 'Don't ask questions. Leave everything. You will find out soon. Don't bother carrying anything. Leave everything behind. Just get out!' Pushed to the end of his patience, one of them snapped, 'You're better off not knowing!' These Canada men in stripes looked alien — as though they were from another planet; and, as I soon came to realise, Auschwitz was another world.

The screaming and crying was deafening. The SS dogs tugged at their victims' legs. People were crushed, clubbed with rifle butts, truncheons and sticks while the Germans pushed and shouted. The crowd swayed back and forth like a ship in a storm. The old and sick were trampled underfoot. A panic, a stampede.

We left all our belongings in the train. I grabbed my mother to prevent her from falling. My mind was reeling with all that was going on around me.

The SS separated the women from the men. The children went with their mothers, and the old and the sick were kept apart. Others lay on the ramp and were trampled. Children screamed, clinging to their parents who tried to console them.

The Germans were brutal, savage and vicious, never letting up with their beating and shouting. *'Schnell! Schnell! Los! Los!'* The barking of the dogs, together with the crying and lamenting, still rings in my ears. The wild scenes on the ramp live on in my memory. I can still see my mother's tired and worried face, and her beautiful eyes, and I can still hear her beseeching voice.

'You must look after your father, Abraham. When the war ends, you must search for Lipek, and when you find him, look after each other. Promise you will never part again. Promise!'

I kept repeating, 'Yes mother, yes mother. I will, I will.' The word 'remember' she repeated time and time again.

'Remember, remember what they did to us!' These were her last words to me, her testament. They became my eleventh commandment.

I held her in my arms and cried. My school friend, Chanele Hauser, tugged at my arms, pleading with me.

'Please Abraham, let go. I will look after her. Go across to the men or they'll beat you! Be strong. You cannot afford to act like a child. Please!'

In all my life I have never known such anguish as when I separated from my mother.

I walked across to the men, trying to take hold of myself. I thought it was the last time I would ever cry like that. On the side of the road, on a heap of gravel, a tiny baby wrapped in rags had been abandoned by its young mother. It was hysterical, screaming and waving its little arms. The new arrivals from the Lodz ghetto would not allow the mother to desert the baby and attacked her, the women beating her harshly. As she fell to the ground, a German walked up to her, kicking her in the stomach and face with his heavy jack boots. She struggled to her feet, the blood streaming from her face mixed with tears and dust, her attempt to save her own life thwarted.

'Pick up that shit!' the German yelled. When she picked up her baby, he pushed the mother towards a group of old and sick people, some of them lying on the ground. An SS lorry pulled up.

The young mother with her baby, the sick and the old, were thrown onto it and driven in the direction of the strange-looking brick structures with square solid stacks belching out smoke and fire.

A long queue was moving towards a group of SS officers. One of them, immaculately dressed and wearing white gloves, pointed his finger left, right, left, right. To his left was death; to his right, life. The white-gloved officer was Dr Joseph Mengele, Auschwitz's 'Angel of Death'. He had studied philosophy, graduating from the University of Munich with a PhD before entering the medical faculty from which he emerged as a Bachelor of Medicine. He had arrived in Auschwitz in 1942 with the rank of captain.

Mengele pointed my father to his left; and I, following behind, grasped my father's jacket and pulled him back, calling out to Mengele, 'Leave my father with me, he is a master builder!' I had been tipped off to say this by a man from the Canada, but a fat, red-headed SS officer grabbed my father by his neck with the rounded handle of his walking cane and pulled him so hard that he stumbled and nearly fell. The red-headed German pushed me back to the right. Destiny. He could have sent me with my father, but this was Auschwitz. The luck of the draw reigned supreme.

The selection was over. The young and fit were standing on the loading platform near the train, watching as the majority was marched off in the direction of the towering chimney. Fenced off from outside eyes with withered tree branches and blankets suspended and plaited through the wire fence, thus were the crematoria and gas chambers camouflaged.

I stood confused. Although I saw what was taking place around me, my mind could not fully come to grips with the tragedy that was unravelling. My mother, holding onto my father's arm, leaned her head against him as they walked and were herded away with the others. My parents were only in their early forties. I never saw them again.

Confusion and bewilderment

As we stood on the ramp, I saw a group of young nurses with little children who were dressed in striped clothing. The children looked well-fed and healthy, and numbered twenty-five or possibly thirty. The nurses wore blue-grey aprons over their striped prison garb and nurses' caps on their heads. Some of the children were in the nurses' arms; others were holding onto their hands or aprons. It was very early in the morning and they were all obviously on a peaceful, morning stroll. It was a bizarre sight, out of character with the surroundings, and it added to my confusion. I could not piece together the puzzle. What was going on here? Maybe this place was not so bad. The children on their morning walk had a strangely calming effect.

I found out later that they were part of the stage setting, a decoy to calm the new arrivals. The children were actually Dr Joseph Mengele's guinea pigs: his favourite twins upon whom he conducted experiments. They were mainly Jewish children and, among them, were a few Gypsies.

The young and fit for work were taken to a real bath-house. Before we undressed, we were ordered to empty our pockets. Two SS officers brought up two huge laundry baskets. One of them made a brief speech, warning us that anyone caught hiding valuables or currency would be punished with death. Lined up, we paraded past the baskets, emptying our pockets into them. One basket was for watches and jewellery, the other for money.

Slowly, the bottom of the second basket was covered with all sorts of currencies: US dollars, English pounds and gold coins, some dating back to Napoleon, others from the time of the Tsar. Dr Mengele appeared again with an SS officer as an assistant. Arms above our heads, they made us run naked in a circle: another selection, but this time only a few men were taken, about six or seven. Approximately 90 per cent of the people from our transport had been taken to the gas chambers.

We were kept in the bath-house for many hours. Our bodies and heads were shaven completely, and often our skin was cut too. We were made to walk into an ankle-deep pool of disinfectant while a prisoner, with a rag dipped in the liquid, rubbed the bleeding parts of our bodies. It stung and burned.

The day was long and hot. Dehydrated, we begged for water, but the prisoners in charge of the bath-house took no notice. After what seemed like hours of pleading, one of them finally allowed small groups of us to run across to one of the barracks where we found a tap. On entering, I saw a group of young Jewish girls sitting on boxes with razors in their hands, cutting open the seams of garments that had once belonged to the victims, searching for valuables that might have been stitched into the clothing. When I questioned them about our location they, too, were not very communicative.

'Don't ask, you will soon find out,' was all they would offer, as indifferent to my nakedness as I was. I had just turned twenty, yet felt no embarrassment in front of these girls: the drink of water was of far more urgency. How fast one adjusts. Within hours we were completely dehumanised.

The nearby barracks were stacked with tooth brushes, razors, shaving brushes, dentures, optical glasses, shoes, artificial limbs, surgical belts, crutches and a miscellany of personal belongings that had been the property of the victims. Suitcases, still bearing the names and addresses of their owners, were stacked up to the roof. The names were all Jewish, from all over Europe, even from as far away as the Greek islands. The quantities were so enormous that they could not all be housed indoors. Masses of articles lay under the open sky.

There was a mountain of shoes, a horrifying sight. In a macabre way they seemed to be gaping mouths and silent tongues, which were nevertheless accusing and angry. What were they trying to say? That here murder took place? That this was Auschwitz, where Jews had no right to live?

I stared at the mountain with horror. I saw the stacks belching with smoke and fire. Is this what the largest murder factory of human beings looked like? To avoid what was to come, some people committed suicide by touching the electric fence on the very day of their arrival. When I first saw electrocuted victims hanging from the wires, they reminded me of scarecrows with their outspread arms. I began to shiver uncontrollably. Soon, however, such scenes had no effect. They became the norm.

After many long hours we emerged naked from the bath-house, the blood drying on our skin that had been cut with the razors. We were lined up to receive our clothing: a shirt, pants, jacket and a prison cap. It was civilian clothing, old and torn, painted with red marks. My pants were much too long and far too wide; I could wrap them twice around my waist. An exchange of clothing began at once. I swapped my pants with a tall fellow who was wearing only a jacket. The pants he had been given were too small, and he looked grotesque walking around half-naked.

We all looked like clowns on parade after we had finished adjusting our wardrobes. Looking at each other gave us the giggles, but it was the laughter of hysteria.

In all the commotion and hustle, I was fortunate to run into Rivek and his older brother Srulek. We exchanged news of our families, and I told the boys that my parents had been taken to the gas chambers. I learned that theirs had met a similar fate. Their sister, Chana, had been young and fit, and could have saved her life if she had listened to her mother; but Chana would not part with her seven-year-old son. She joined her parents, holding her little boy in her arms.

A more immediate problem beset me when I realised that I was without shoes. I had to think fast. With caution I moved towards the mountain of shoes and 'organised' a pair for myself — 'organised' being the camp expression which covered all the innovative ways inmates found of obtaining what they needed, whether it was by stealing or trading. For stealing, if one was lucky, the price was a few kicks, punches and knocks from the chief thug, Janek 'Tzigan'. I was learning that nothing you get in this world is free.

Although the day was warm, my feet were cold. I found it hard to come to terms with the shoes I wore. I tried to excuse my taking of another man's property by telling myself that the man was dead; but this was my first day in Auschwitz, and it was still difficult. As time passed, such scruples vanished, and such actions and events had no effect. By the time I was brought to Dora, my third concentration camp, when a Kapo ordered me to remove the corpse of a fellow prisoner who had fallen off the bench as we waited in the bath barracks to be disinfected, I took off his shoes and disposed of him without blinking an eye. His solid Czechoslovakian snowshoes kept my feet dry for a few weeks.

Auschwitz-Birkenau

Thanks to the record-keeping efficiency of the SS, and to the surreptitious diligence of prisoners who worked in the camp offices, I was able to confirm many years later the precise date on which I was brought to Auschwitz from the Lodz ghetto. The following transcript may be found on page 867 in the *Calendar Of Events* at Auschwitz. Some of it survived and is today part of the Auschwitz Museum. The entry is dated 2 September 1944:

A transport of the RSHA [Reich Security Main Office in Berlin] arrived, delivering Jews from Lodz ghetto. After the selection, five
hundred men were retained as prisoners in camp and tattooed with
the numbers B-8603 to B-9102. Most probably the young and healthy,
they were retained in the transit camp of Birkenau. The rest of the
people were killed in the gas chambers. The underground resistance
organisation in camp stated in their report that, during the period
from the 1st till the 20th of September, the SS operating the gas
chambers murdered the rest of the Jews from Lodz ghetto and this is
how the last, still surviving, Polish Jews were liquidated.[46]

Seven to ten days after being admitted to Birkenau BIIe, I was taken
to one of the SS administrative barracks and ordered to sign a pink,
printed form. Reading it was forbidden and whoever attempted it
was hit over the head. I had to give my full name, date and place of
birth, the names of my parents and my last address. Then I was
moved on to the next table and made to bare my left arm. Within a
few minutes, I was a number: from that moment, I became B-8615.
Numbers are not human. They can be erased.

I accepted my number with feelings of uncertainty. I was now
classified as a 'Schutzheftling' (a prisoner in safe custody), and the
alternative was much worse. The veteran prisoners, to cheer us up,
told us,

'You're better off having a number at Birkenau BIIe. You're safer
with one. At least for the time being they'll keep you alive and
eventually you will be assigned to slave labour. Those without
numbers are in line to go up in smoke at any minute to keep the
furnaces going.'

The irony of it all was that the death penalty was in force.
Prisoners were punished by hanging for many 'crimes'. One could
lose one's life simply by ripping a piece of material from a Gypsy
rug or a blanket. In my ignorance, I did exactly that, and wore it
under my jacket to keep warm. If I had been caught, I would not
have been here to write my story.

I was told by other prisoners, who were at Auschwitz, of the
executions which took place in front of them as they lined up and
were made to stand to attention on the roll-call ground. The victims
were left hanging till late at night for the benefit of those inmates
who left the premises to work. Upon their return, they were made
to parade past the gallows, stamping their feet like soldiers in a

procession. Missing a step was another punishable offence as they tried to march in time to the prisoners' orchestra which played regularly twice a day — every morning when they left for work, and at night, when they returned.

The following are excerpts from the memoirs of the commandant of Auschwitz, SS Obersturmbannführer Rudolph Hoess:

Shortly after [1941], Eichmann arrived in Auschwitz and shared with me the secret of the 'actions' planned for several countries ... First came the eastern part of Upper Silesia, the adjacent regions of the General Government and Czechoslovakia. Then, from the West came France, Belgium and Holland. Eichmann also mentioned the approximate number of people in the transports, which again I no longer remember. Next we discussed the way in which the extermination process would be carried out. Gas was the only consideration, in view of the fact that the liquidation of such enormous numbers of people would be absolutely impossible by means of shooting and also because the shooting of children and women could prove to be too stressful for the SS men.

The luggage left at the loading platform was carried to a sorting place called 'Canada', which was situated halfway between an arsenal and a building material storage. The Jews had to undress next to a 'bunker'. They were told that they had to be deloused. The 'Chambers', five in all, were simultaneously filled with people. The hermetic doors were locked and the contents of the poison-filled tins was poured through special openings. Half an hour later the doors were opened. There were two doors in each chamber. The bodies were pulled out, loaded on wagons and driven to pits. The clothes were transported to sorting places by trucks.

All that work: helping the people to undress, filling the chambers, disposing of the bodies, as well as digging the pits and filling up the common graves, was done by the Sonderkommando, consisting of Jews, who were kept in separate lodgings. According to Eichmann's order, they had to be done away with, after every big action.

From the very first transports, Eichmann had an order from the SS Reichsführer to have gold teeth pulled out of the gassed people's mouths. This too was the task of the Sonderkommando.

Selections were conducted the following way: The cattle trains were unloaded one after the other and, having dropped their luggage, Jews had to walk past an SS doctor who decided on their working capacity during that walk. Those found fit were immediately taken to the camp in small groups. The average number of people chosen for work made up about twenty-five to thirty percent of all transports. However, these proportions differed greatly with each separate transport ... Doctors and nurses were without exception sent to the camp.

The temporary Crematorium was demolished when work was begun on building Crematorium II in Birkenau [otherwise known as Crematorium in the Open, or Bunker V]. When activities became more hectic, gassing took place in Bunker V and transports arriving at night were taken care of in Crematorium I to IV. As long as it was possible to burn bodies day and night, the potential of Bunker V was almost unlimited. From 1944, however, activities of enemy aircraft made it impossible to light a fire at night.

I never knew the sum total of the people killed ... All my memory retained are the number of some of the bigger 'actions' ... often given to me by Eichmann or his deputy:

Upper Silesia and the General Government	250,000
Germany and Terezin	100,000
Holland	95,000
Belgium	20,000
France	110,000
Hungary	400,000
Greece	65,000
Slovakia	- 90,000

... Many women hid their babies under piles of clothing fearing that the process of disinfection might hurt them. The Sonderkommando gave special attention to those mothers, talking to them in a friendly manner, until they agreed to take their babies with them. Most little children were crying while being undressed in such strange place but were eventually reassured by their mothers and the friendly attitude of the Sonderkommando men. Playing or teasing each other they walked into the gas chambers, some of them still holding toys in their hands. I noticed that some women who must have had a premonition of what was awaiting them, found it in their hearts (despite the mortal fear in their eyes) to joke or use gentle persuasion with their children ...

I had to look on indifferently as mothers with their laughing or crying children went to the gas chambers. Once, some small children were so absorbed in their play that their mother could not tear them away from it. Even the Sonderkommando did not want to take those children. I'll never forget the pleading look in their mother's eyes. She knew what it was all about. Everyone looked at me. I nodded to the officer in charge and he took the resisting children into his arms. He carried them into the gas chamber, followed by heart-rending cries from their mother, just behind him ...[47]

Hoess showed great talent in developing the mass killing process which he began with a white farm-building situated at Birkenau. He restructured it by bricking up the windows, installing air-tight steel doors and dismantling the walls inside. The structure was meticulously plastered, with all the cracks filled and all the air leaks plugged.

Hoess realised that murdering was only part of the process. The large numbers that could be gassed eventually became too numerous to be disposed of by burial. Soon he had his first crematorium erected next to the gas chamber. This he referred to as the 'Bunker'. In order to develop more efficient gas chambers and crematoria, he involved his colleague, SS General Heinz Kammler, an architect by profession, whom I saw on inspections at a later time when I was in the Dora underground factory. At that time, he was studying the structure of the V2 rocket and was eventually responsible for building the rocket launchers for the V1 and V2 rockets.

As time went by and gassing became more efficient, Hoess installed an elevator at Crematorium V, the largest killing complex, to haul the cadavers from the gas chambers that were below ground level up to the crematoria. Topf and Sons of Erfurt supplied the furnaces.

Inside the gas chamber, the plumbing installations looked real, like any bath-house with pipes and shower rosettes hanging down from the ceilings; but they were only dummies. Any victim showing signs of panic or resistance was mercilessly whipped on the naked body. In extreme situations, the SS would shoot resisters on the spot.

The dressing rooms were set up with hooks and numbers, and the victims told to remember their number so they could reclaim their clothes after the disinfection. The corridors had signs like those in an ordinary, communal bath-house, with posters bearing slogans such as, 'Wash well', 'Use your soap', 'Cleanliness brings freedom,' and so on.

Zyklon-B was dropped through the special openings in the ceiling by an SS man wearing a gas mask. Exhaust fans pumped the gas out once the SS doctor, watching through a thick glass panel in the door, established that everyone in the chamber was dead, usually within a period of twenty-five minutes to half an hour.

Then the doors of the gas chambers were unlocked and the Sonderkommando entered. Cadavers lay in one huge heap, locked together; their faces, twisted death masks expressing agony beyond imagination. They were bleeding from their mouths and rectums, their bodies smeared with blood and excrement, and bearing deep scratches and bite-marks, evidence of the pain and suffering of their last minutes.

The Sonderkommando untangled the corpses, extracted the gold teeth, and inspected rectums and vaginas for hidden jewellery. Once the bodies were loaded on trolleys and transported to the furnaces, the gas chamber was hosed down and scrubbed clean of the blood and human waste. After cremation, the ashes were disposed of in the swamps of Birkenau or driven to the river Sola a few kilometres from the camp. The Sonderkommando was frequently gassed and replaced after large gassings.

For the exhausted, unwashed, starved, thirsty, new arrivals, Hoess introduced a technique to keep them calm and make them undress without undue fright and resistance. A softly spoken member of the SS, usually dressed in a white coat, carrying a stethoscope and playing the part of a doctor, welcomed them with a friendly speech. He inspected their ears and looked into their throats. The real intention behind these actions was to verify those with gold crowns and gold fillings. Those possessing them had their chests marked with an ink pen; thus the Sonderkommando could later identify them without wasting time.

In his polite speech, the 'doctor' apologised for the discomforts of their very long trip, asking the victims to forget all the hardships of the past. From now on, he assured them, everything would be different.

'You will be well looked after. You will get plenty of food. The women who have no trade or profession will do housework. The men without trades will work on the land. Those with trades and professions will be duly employed.' The speeches were so convincing that there were times when the victims actually applauded the speaker.

In Brussels, just after the liberation, I met a Polish Jew who had been one of the last contingent assigned to the Auschwitz Sonderkommando. Whereas all his predecessors had been killed, his contingent survived when the sudden forward thrust by the Russian army caught the SS by surprise. I do not remember his name and I made no record of it at the time, never thinking that I would one day write of my experiences. What he told me, however, became in its way like another tattoo, this time branded on my mind.

'I can speak to you because you were there and you under-stand,' he told me. 'In the beginning, when I told people, they thought I was crazy. Some didn't even want to listen. My stories made them sick. They said I was lying, inventing horror stories.

'Boys from the Sonderkommando would often recognise their fathers or mothers lying on the floor amongst the dead. Some of them found their brothers, sisters, family or friends. Sometimes husbands found their wives or children. I witnessed Sónder boys, finding their nearest of kin lined up to enter the gas chamber, deciding to join them.'

They could not believe nor understand

A justice of the Supreme Court of the United States refused to believe the tragic report brought by Jan Karski to the USA in July 1943. I quote the words of Jan Karski's lecture delivered to the Holocaust Centre in Montreal in 1989:

> It happened at the Polish Embassy in Washington where I was intro-duced by Jan Ciechanowski, the Polish Ambassador in the USA, to Felix Frankfurter, a justice of the Supreme Court. He was a very powerful man. He had the ear of the President. He asked me questions. I remember every word he said to me:
>
> 'Mr Karski, a man like me talking to a man like you, I must be totally frank — so I say I am unable to believe you.'
>
> Ciechanowski, who was a personal friend, broke in:
>
> 'Felix, you don't mean it. You cannot tell him he is lying. The authority of my government is behind him.'
>
> 'Mr Ambassador, I did not say he is lying. I said I don't believe him.'

A friend of mine from Warsaw, who lost his entire family in the Holocaust, and saved himself by running away to Russia, recently visited my home and noticed my manuscript with its heading, *Auschwitz*. He asked me how many pages were contained in this particular segment.

'I don't know yet,' I shrugged. 'Perhaps, after editing, I'll be left with about fifty .'

He was surprised. 'Not very much. How long were you there?'

'About four, maybe five weeks.'

'Is that all!' he exclaimed in surprise. I answered him with silence. What could I say? How long is 'long' in Auschwitz? My parents were there only two, maybe three hours.

At Birkenau, I stared at the crematoria day in and day out. They were situated only a few feet from where we stood for roll-call at Block 11. There was a German Jew who had been brought from the Lodz ghetto, who persistently argued that they were not gassing and burning people in these strange-looking buildings. For him, it was inconceivable that the Germans would do such a thing. Not even the smoke and fire blowing from the stacks day and night, spreading its smell of smouldering human flesh and bones that made us all sick, could change his mind; nor could the open ditches with burning corpses under the open sky. For him they were not there: he simply refused to see. I don't know what happened to him.

At Auschwitz there was a chapel where the SS used to go for prayers. I often wondered whether they went to chapel before or after they did their gassing. Did it ever occur to them that they were reciting ancient, translated, Hebrew prayers to the God of Abraham, Isaac and Jacob? Did they ever stop to think that Jesus lived and died as a Jew?

While the SS guarded the perimeters of the camps and decided the fate of their occupants, the internal organisation and discipline was maintained by the prisoners themselves. In charge was a 'Lageraelteste', a camp Eldest, who was always a German national serving a long sentence for committing a violent crime. They were known as 'Bevauer'. They had a green triangle under their prison number bearing two initials, BV, that stood for 'Berufsverbrecher', a professional criminal. For such a person, transfer from a civil gaol to a privileged status in a concentration camp was very attractive.

Under him were the 'Blockaeltesten', one of whom was in charge of each of the barracks. They in turn were assisted by 'Stubendiensten' and 'Kapos' who were mostly professional criminals of German nationality. Amongst them, also, were social democrats, communists and trade union leaders. 'Stubendienst' literally means 'room service', but in practice it meant 'barracks orderlies'. The duties of the Stubendiensten, however, did not extend to making the guests welcome. Essentially, they maintained discipline in the barracks, making great use of their truncheons and sticks. The word 'Kapo' is related to the Latin 'caput', meaning 'head', and is a slang word roughly equivalent to 'boss'. The Kapos maintained discipline in the parade ground and work places.

Of course, there were some Jews who accepted such positions in return for some temporary privilege, which might be no greater than a few more potatoes. When people are told that they are going to die tomorrow, it is surprising what some will do to put it off until the day after.

Finally, there were Jews who filled positions as clerks, in charge of camp records, and the doctors and nurses who staffed the sick bays. The former often risked their lives keeping the clandestine records which enable us today to reconstruct the true story more completely than we could otherwise have done; while the doctors and nurses did what they could to relieve suffering. For them, I have nothing but respect.

Nothing was wasted in the process of extermination. The hair of the victims was sold off to German mattress manufacturers. Somewhere in an elegant German executive suite one of the leather-covered armchairs is quite conceivably filled with my mother's beautiful black hair. The gold teeth of the victims were extracted and melted into gold bars and sent to the state vault in Berlin. Human skin was used to make lampshades and wallets. Heads of victims were shrunk and used as mantelpiece decor.

The German technocrats were meticulous in making sure that the killing industry functioned profitably. The following document, Z32 from page 302 of the German archives, clearly displays this:

SS PROFITABILITY CALCULATION ON THE UTILISATION OF PRISONERS IN THE CONCENTRATION CAMPS

Daily hiring wage averaging	RM	6,—
minus food	RM	– 0,60
minus cost of clothing	RM	–0.10
Average duration of life		
9 months = 270 x RM 5,30 =	RM 1431,—	

Proceeds from rational use of the corpse:

1. Gold in teeth	3. Valuables
2. Clothing	4. Money

minus cremation costs	RM	2,00
average net profit	RM	200,—

Total profit after 9 months	RM 1631,—	

The clothing was sorted, cleaned, repaired and handed over to German philanthropic and charity institutions, many of which were run by German clergy who were well aware of where the clothing had come from. Their only concern seemed to be that some of the garments still bore the yellow Star of David.

The abandonment of the Jews by the western powers

On a September day during my incarceration in Auschwitz-Birkenau, the sky was cloudless, as though it had been painted in soft azure blue. It was a mesmerising colour, not even to be found among the canvases of the greatest masters; and, gazing skyward, a serenity engulfed my mind. Was there a heaven beyond it?, I wondered. And hell? Where was hell?

My serenity disintegrated. Hell was right here in Auschwitz-Birkenau BIIe. It had been created by the Germans in the midst of Christendom with millions of God-loving people believing that the Jews were being justly punished for their sins. They believed that it was God's will.

Suddenly I noticed a reconnaissance plane cruising above our heads. I wondered whether it had originated in heaven or hell. The anti-aircraft guns fired a few rounds, but they missed their target. It must have been from either the USAAF or the RAF on a photographic mission, but I still hoped that they would come back to bomb the gas chambers. No such luck!

At times, I asked myself, 'Why don't they drop us some weapons?' We would have made good use of them.

As we know today, the high command of the Allied air force was well informed, possessing aerial photographs of the extermination camps. They knew their exact whereabouts; but, to them, the killing factories were not a military target. Although bombing the gas chambers would not have stopped the Germans from murdering the Jews, it would nevertheless have slowed down the extermination process considerably; in consequence, hundreds of thousands of lives would have been saved. The reality was that the entire western world stood by, allowing the Germans to incinerate most of European Jewry. With their indifference, the whole of western civilisation joined in a conspiracy of silence. That silence makes them all guilty.

David S Wyman's *The Abandonment of the Jews: America and the Holocaust 1941–1945*, contains much detailed evidence regarding what action the Allies could have taken, and how very little they actually did. Their designated targets were sometimes within five miles of Auschwitz, but neither the gas chambers themselves nor the railway lines leading to them was ever targeted. The pleas of the Jewish leadership in the United States and in Britain fell on deaf ears. Wyman's evidence is as damning as it is conclusive:

> In early September [1944], pressure built once more for bombing the railroads, this time the lines between Auschwitz and Budapest, where the last large enclave of Hungarian Jews was threatened with deportation ... Rabbi Abraham Kalmanowitz, anxious for the appeal to reach the WRB [World Refugee Board] as soon as possible, telephoned Benjamin Akzin, even though it was the Sabbath ... When Akzin relayed the plea to Pehle ... he pressed for a direct approach to the President to seek orders for immediate bombing of the deportation rail-lines. But the board did not move on the appeal.
>
> On the other crucial bombing issue, the question of air strikes on Auschwitz, the WRB did act, but with hesitation. Near the end of September, members of the Polish exile government and British Jewish groups came to James Mann, the WRB representative in London, with information that the Nazis were increasing the pace of extermination. They urged the board to explore again the possibility of bombing the killing chambers. Mann cabled their plea to Washington. Other

messages then reaching the board were reporting Nazi threats to exterminate thousands of camp inmates as the Germans were forced back across Poland by the Red Army. Pehle decided to raise the issue once more, though not forcibly. He transmitted the substance of Mann's dispatch to McCloy 'for such consideration as it may be worth ...'

McCloy's office thought it worth too little consideration to trouble the Operations Division with it, or even to write a reply to the WRB. Gerhadt recommended that 'no action be taken on this, since the matter has been fully presented several times previously.'

McCloy let the recommendation stand, and the matter was dropped. [John J McCloy was the assistant secretary of the war department of the USA].[48]

Reflections on Vatican complicity

In no other testimony have I read a stronger indictment, condemning the clergy of the Catholic Church for their passive and, in many instances, active participation in the Holocaust, than in Eliezer Berkovitz's, *Faith After the Holocaust*. He also shows that the churches in Germany, Slovakia and Hungary were accomplices of the Nazis.

In 1942, the genocide was well under way. The personal representative of the American president at the Vatican inquired of the Vatican secretary of state whether the Pope had any suggestions as to a practical manner in which the forces of civilised public opinion could be utilised in order to prevent a continuation of these barbarities. The reply to this inquiry reveals the Vatican's complicity in those barbarities. According to the Vatican secretary of state, reports on the measures against the Jews had reached the Vatican, but it was not possible to ascertain their veracity. Another cardinal spoke of 'a great Pope' in Rome, who had given 'unmistakable proofs of a great and undiscriminating affection for all peoples,' who however, 'in order to avoid the slightest appearance of partiality, imposed upon himself, in word and deed, the most delicate reserve.'

Even as late as April 1944, when the fate of over four hundred thousand Hungarian Jews was at stake, the 'great Pope' had still made strenuous efforts to preserve his impartiality. Hungary was essentially a Catholic country. The value of a strong stand taken by the Vatican would have been incalculable. In April 1944, the War Refugee Board, in a direct message to the Pope, asked his intervention in the form of threat of ex-communication of the participants in the expulsion of the Jews to the death camps in Poland. A rather weak message was sent to the Regent of Hungary which, although it contained no threat of spiritual punishment of any kind and was 'characteristically evasive', did have some beneficial results. Unfortunately, by the time it was sent, after a delay of two months, three hundred and fifty thousand of those deported had been gassed.

By its attitude toward the fate of the Jewish people, the Vatican and the other churches lost all claim to moral and spiritual leadership in the world. While, undoubtedly, political considerations played their part, it is hard to believe that politics alone was responsible for this utter failure to respond to what should have been elementary demands of a sane human conscience. There is sufficient evidence to believe that an ingrained theological anti-Semitism that for long centuries had nourished Christianity and was responsible for a tradition of Christian inhumanity toward the Jew was ultimately responsible for the spiritual madness of encouraging acquiescence.

Eliezer Berkovits reports M D Weissmandel's memoirs of his experiences in Slovakia during the war, in which he tells of two characteristic encounters with the Catholic hierarchy in that country. Among the German satellites there had been no puppet government more anxious to get rid of all the Jews than that of the Catholic priest Tiso in Slovakia. Shortly before Passover, 1942, one of the most respected rabbis in Slovakia approached Archbishop Kametko, whom he had known from happier days, to influence his former private secretary Tiso to prevent the expulsion of the Jews from his country. The rabbi spoke of the threat of expulsion only. The archbishop, however, enlightened him regarding the true fate that was awaiting the Jews in Poland. These were his words:

> 'This is no mere expulsion. There, you will not die of hunger and pestilence; there, they will slaughter you all, old and young, women and children, in one day. This is your punishment for the death of our Redeemer. There is only one hope for you: to convert to our religion. Then I shall effect the annulling of this decree.'

As a result of Christian theology, teaching and tradition, the feeling among Christians was widespread that the Jews were receiving what was due to them. No one expressed this more succinctly than the papal nuncio in Slovakia. In the autumn of 1944, Weissmandel together with his family and hundreds of other Jews had been put into a temporary camp prior to their deportation to Auschwitz. Weissmandel escaped and succeeded in making his way to the residence of the papal nuncio. He described to his eminence the conditions of the families in the camp, and asked for his immediate intervention with Tisso [sic]. He received the following answer: 'This, being a Sunday, is a holy day for us. Neither I nor Father Tisso occupy ourselves with profane matters on this day.'

Upon Weissmandel's wondering how the blood of infants and children could be considered a profane matter, he was taught a significant chapter in Christian theology. He was told:

'There is no innocent blood of Jewish children in the world. All Jewish blood is guilty. You have to die. This is the punishment that has been awaiting you because of that sin [meaning the death of Jesus].'

One wonders whether, in the entire history of the human race, the concept of holiness has ever been more degraded and desecrated than in the mouth of that papal nuncio. He was on that, for him, holy day repeating with deep religious conviction the Hitlerite faith that all Jews were guilty. Hitler believed in it on racial grounds, the archbishop and the papal nuncio, for theological reasons. In practice it amounted to the same thing: death to all Jews.

Not all Christians felt that way, but many in high offices in the churches did. The deicide accusation through the ages did its murderous work on the Christian subconscious making Christianity, in many cases, an active accomplice in the Nazi crime and, in most cases, 'a tacit party to the barbarities.'[49]

As recently as late 1992, a briefing document by the Australian Institute of Jewish affairs could fairly summarise the unfinished business of the Vatican with damning succinctness:

The Vatican has failed even to acknowledge, let alone apologise for, any shared guilt for the Holocaust, despite the centuries of Christian anti-Judaism, the silence of Pope Pius XII or the escape routes for Nazi war criminals provided by the Vatican after the war. And the old, anti-Jewish theology of contempt has partially survived, expressed, for example, in renewed charges of deicide against the Jews (made as recently as April 1992, by Cardinal Camillo Ruini, head of the Italian Catholic Church). These and other factors, combined with the Vatican's refusal to recognise Israel formally, indicate that there is still far to go if the brotherhood with Judaism now officially proclaimed by the Church is truly to develop into fraternal love.[50]

The Gypsy Camp

After many long hours of waiting, we were lined up and counted. With clubs and truncheons, a group of Kapos and Blockaeltesten came to take over the new arrivals. The orders were given in German. We were confused and bewildered, like a herd of panic-stricken cattle, pushing one another, turning in circles, not knowing what to do. None of us grasped the meaning of the German orders to line up. Eventually, with the help of the truncheons and clubs, we were marched off to the Gypsy Camp from where, not so long ago, four thousand Gypsies — men, women, children and babies — had been gassed in one night to make room for the fresh victims from the Lodz ghetto. Their red, woollen, Gypsy rugs were the only evidence of their recent existence. Their ashes had been disposed of in the swamps of Birkenau.

We were marched across endless, flat plains. Some people were dressed in striped uniforms, others in civilian clothing with red markings. They all had numbers on their chests under which was a Star of David. One red triangle pointed downwards; the other, in yellow pointing up, was the sign of the Jewish prisoners who constituted approximately 90 per cent of the concentration-camp population.

Some were digging; others were carrying timber logs and stacking them near long ditches. Passing one of the prisoners, I asked, 'What goes on here? What are they building?' He was consumed by anger. 'You fucking bastard. You should have dropped dead before you came here. You should have done what they did at the Warsaw ghetto!'

It was not very long before I discovered exactly what they were digging. It happened one day when I was taken past the compound perimeter with a group of prisoners. From a distance I saw a most bizarre scene. There were corpses burning under the open sky. When the gassing overtook the capacity of cremation, petrol or kerosene was poured on the cadavers and timber logs, and set alight. Dante's Inferno pales in comparison; it is comedy, even farce. In my worst nightmares, I had never seen anything so sinister and frightening.

On another occasion, when I was outside the electrified fence, I saw a group of approximately fifty women. They were naked except for a few whose shoulders were covered with rags. They looked like parading skeletons, their breasts empty sacks of skin hanging down over their rib cages. Their pelvises protruded as they moved forward on their stilt-like legs. With two SS guards following them, they were on their way to the gas chambers, looking like lamps with a last few drops of kerosene, struggling with their last flickers of light.

This part of Auschwitz was called the Birkenau extermination camp, known to the prisoners as 'The Gypsy Camp'. Birkenau was divided into five compounds. The main function of the compound BIIe, in which I found myself, was to feed the four gas chambers and crematoria which were operating at full capacity, belching with flames and smoke twenty-four hours a day. A fifth unit was at Auschwitz, a few kilometres from where we were.

Passing the gate as we entered Birkenau BIIe, we saw on our left the body of a man hanging on the electric wires. His hands, black and grey, were curled up as if suffering from severe cramp, his face twisted in agony. His eyes and mouth were wide open in a silent, deafening scream.

The compound, Birkenau BIIe, was divided by a wide road with barracks lined up on either side. We were stopped in front of Block 11. The Blockaelteste was a short blonde fellow, with a green triangle under his number on the left side of his chest. He wore the letters 'BV'. A Pole from Upper Silesia, he never spoke normally: he yelled and swore in a Silesian-Polish dialect mixed with German, constantly shouting *'Pieronie!'* ('Thunder!'), a favourite swear word.

Marching up and down in front of the five hundred prisoners, the Blockaelteste seemed to enjoy enormously the way he could cut the air with his walking cane as though it were a sword. At the top of his voice he bellowed in German, 'I am your Blockaelteste! Here, I am your master! I am your master of life and death! What I say goes! My word is the law!'

He pointed his cane in the direction of the crematoria that were situated opposite our barracks, across the wires, about six to eight hundred feet from where we stood. At the top of his voice he continued, 'This is the world-renowned concentration camp, Auschwitz! From here, no one comes out alive! This is where those with whom you have arrived this morning are going up in smoke! You will all finish up there! No Jew comes out of Auschwitz alive! You will all join the "Himmelkommando", the sky commando. Here you come in as Jews and leave as smoke.'

Watching the stacks of the crematoria, I was gripped by the strangest confusion of feelings of fear and relief. Relief was stronger than fear. A gradual unburdening from a frightful load, a trauma, I had lived with for five long years seemed to be taking place. The anxiety seemed to be slipping away. Somehow, the smell of the burning human flesh and bones liberated me, in a macabre yet terribly final way, from the fear and worry I had been harbouring for the safety of my family.

All at once, I came to terms with what was going on around me. Confronted so directly by it, death lost its ability to frighten me. As I looked at the chimney stacks, I was fully aware that those very flames were devouring my mother and father, and all those who had come with me from the Lodz ghetto — those who had not passed the first selection.

My thoughts focussed on my father's remark. *'Dort dreyt zikh di patelnye.'* I could hear the voice of my mother ringing in my ears. 'Remember! You must find Lipek! Remember what they did! You must never forget!'

How can I ever? When everything was lost and destroyed, when everybody around me was dead or dying, my mother's words gave me the strength and determination to battle on. As I watched the flames of the crematoria I made a vow to their souls that not only would I never forget, but I would never surrender. My mother's last words made it possible for me to survive.

Srulek, Rivek and I stood next to each other.

'I'm glad my parents are not here any longer,' I said to them. 'They don't feel, they don't see, they don't hear. They don't have to endure the brutalities and pain. They are delivered from evil.'

As if to confirm my words, the Blockaelteste, having finished his welcoming speech, began instructing us in the ways of saluting.

'Now listen, you sons of bitches, you fuckin' Jews, I'll give you a little lesson. Attention! *Mützen ab!*' ('Take your caps off!')

The Blockaelteste's voice rent the air like the shriek of a wild animal. Before we could grasp the meaning of his command, his bamboo stick was in action.

'*Mützen auf!*' ('Put your caps on!')

The beating never stopped. Prisoners with blood streaming down their faces stood to attention, scared to blink an eye while the master of life and death paraded back and forth, slicing the air with his bamboo cane, yelling.

'Your hats must come off with one and only one hit! Your right hand must hit hard against your thigh! May God have mercy on those who miss! Prisoners! Attent-ion! Caps off! You old shit buckets! *Pieronie!* I'll teach you how to put your caps on! It must happen with one hit! Caps on!'

He was not happy yet. He continued like a maniac.

'You old shit buckets! *Pieronie!* I am a patient man but this time I want to hear one and just one thud ... Caps off!'

Suddenly, he jumped into the centre of the column, knocking over prisoners as he ran to attack a man who had missed the beat. He struck his victim savagely.

'Now you better watch out! *Pieronie!* You fuckin' rotten Jews! *Pieronie!* I warn you, this time I want to hear one, and only one, hit. Caps on! Again! Let's try again! Attention! Caps off!'

He was crazy; fuming, swearing with a tirade of the most filthy insults I have ever heard. He was completely mad, but I soon realised that all the people in charge were insane. It was a madhouse run by professional sadists. The beating of people to death was a daily routine. It happened every hour on the hour, minute after minute. They were killing for the pleasure of it.

The saluting exercise went on for many long hours, and was followed day after day for many weeks with variations of knee-bending exercises to break the monotony of the days. With our knees bent and arms stretched out to the front, we had to balance on our toes for long periods of time, which caused many inmates to lose their balance.

One day, a fellow who lost his balance, tried to explain.

'I am a war invalid,' he said. 'My knees and legs are full of bullet holes. I am a Polish officer. I was wounded in the defence of Warsaw in 1939.'

The poor fool was trying to impress the Blockaelteste but it had a reverse effect. Virtually foaming at the mouth, the Blockaelteste roared, 'You old shitbucket! You rotten Jew! A Polish officer! How do you like that? *Pieronie!* A rotten Jew, a Polish officer? I'll teach you how a Polish officer bends his knees. *Pieronie!* And if you can't bend them I'll bend them for you!'

His victim was beaten until he resembled nothing so much as a mass of blood and pulp, and was then left lying on the ground. The Stubendiensten pulled him aside and left him on the ground near the barracks. The saluting and knee-bending continued, filling most of our days.

Selections

Selections took place unexpectedly, sometimes twice or three times a day. We had to strip to the waist with our hands high up above our heads. We then had to stand to attention as an SS officer inspected our bodies; at other times, we had to run past the selecting officer. The selections were for the gas chambers; sometimes they were for slave labour. It was hard to know what the selections were for. One had to use one's instincts to avoid being selected for the gas chambers, but chiefly it was a game of luck.

Some force, some whispered voice, seemed constantly at my ear: turn left, don't step out, don't go to this line. Cool judgement, logic and wisdom were hardly my guides. Pot luck was my wisdom; mere chance was my guide.

Once a day, the 'Blockführer', a junior SS officer, counted the prisoners. This was the famous roll-call that at times lasted for long hours, regardless of the weather. We had to stand to attention till late at night, and sometimes till the morning. Not that they needed a reason, but the rationale behind these prolonged census sessions was that a prisoner was missing. Not until he was accounted for were we allowed back into the barracks.

Entering the barracks through a narrow door wide enough for only one person was a life-threatening experience in itself. Five hundred prisoners were rushed through that restricted opening with the orderlies harassing us from rear. Other orderlies awaited us inside, to beat us upon entry.

The barracks had once been the stables of the Polish cavalry. Inside, at either end, was a fire place, one connected to the other by a brick tunnel that measured approximately seventy centimetres high and one metre wide. The tunnel divided the barracks in two and served as a heating system — which was never lit. In winter, the prisoners froze. The only purpose the tunnel served was for the Blockaelteste to parade up and down mustering the five hundred prisoners who were cramped into a space that could hardly accommodate two hundred.

To lie down for the night we were lined up like soldiers on parade, chins up, chests out. On the command, 'Remove shoes! Bend knees! Spread legs! Fall back!', I fell between the legs of the man behind me with my head on his belly. The man in front of me fell between my legs with his head in the same position. This is how we had to sleep on the bare concrete floor: plaited together in one mass. To get up in the middle of the night in order to urinate was a logistical nightmare. It was impossible to find our places again and, consequently, we had to spend the rest of the night standing. There was a barrel at the end of the barracks for the purpose of urinating which was guarded by a prisoner. Leaving the barracks in the middle of the night was strictly forbidden, an offence for which one could be shot.

At night, the most important thing was to take care of one's shoes, so as not to wake up to discover that they had vanished. To protect my own, I bound them together with my belt, wrapped the belt around my neck, kept the end of the belt between my teeth all night and clutched the shoes under my arm. To lose them in Birkenau was, literally, a death sentence because those who did were barefoot until issued with Dutch clogs. Running in those was impossible; yet, to stay alive in a concentration camp, we could never walk anywhere: everything had to be done on the run. Everything had to be 'schnell, schnell!' Day in, day out, all we did was run and run more. We ran for our lives.

The beating was constant. A storm of clubs and sticks constantly rained down upon our backs and heads. The screaming and crying never ceased. After the Blockaelteste exhausted himself with beating, he left the orderlies to continue while he retired to his corner which he had curtained off from the rest of us with red Gypsy rugs.

I will never forget the first night. The Blockaelteste and orderlies were like savages, jumping on top of the prisoners who lay on the concrete. With all their strength, they hit them over their heads, arms, hands and faces. I could hear the cracking of bones under the impact of the truncheons. Sleep seemed impossible, yet somehow I momentarily dozed off, only to be woken again by the yelling, crying, beating and swearing.

Along with all the others, I found myself being rushed out into the freezing dark. I thought it was the middle of the night, but soon discovered that it was three in the morning. As we were not far from the foot of the Carpathians, I was not too surprised to find that, even in early autumn, the temperature was well below zero.

The nights were unbearably cold. To protect ourselves we formed little groups, like cattle in the rain, pressing close up against one another in small circles of fifteen or twenty men, warming each other with what little body heat we had. We frequently changed positions to give everyone a chance to warm up, those inside the circle moving to the outside. That is how we kept warm in the frosty mornings that stretched on forever.

Daybreak came slowly as the autumn mist dispersed. The sun rose, thawing out our frozen bodies. Late in the morning, the Blockaelteste appeared and we lined up to collect the two hundred grams of bread, as well as the hot black liquid that passed for coffee. It was poured into a rusty, dented dish shared by five men. The loaf of bread was also divided into five. At times we were given a tiny square of margarine or a slice of sausage.

I ate my bread as fast as possible, not relaxing for a second, watching anxiously so that no one would grab it from my mouth. Once the meal was over, we were lined up again and the circus was replayed.

'Now, you fuckin' Jews, we're going to have some fun! Attention! Bend knees! Stretch your arms to the front! Watch it! Watch it!' Once again we underwent the saluting routine.

'Attention! *Mützen ab! Mützen auf!*'

It continued for hours, after which there was another roll-call. We were counted and then lined up for our soup. Of course this, as with all other camp procedures, was accompanied by beating, swearing and shouting. At the same time, we pushed each other forward nervously, falling on top of one another in our desperation to reach the food sooner.

Five prisoners had to share the one rusty, metal dish, and we had no spoons. We ate out of the flat dish, either using our mouths and dipping our noses into the mess, or we helped ourselves with our fingers or a piece of timber. Every man was given his turn to have one sip as the four partners stood with anxious looks in their eyes, occasionally enjoining the one whose turn it was to, 'Take it easy. Don't sip so hard!' I usually paired up with people I knew, and managed to have good partners. Most of the time, I shared my soup with Rivek, Srulek and two other fellows who were no strangers to us.

After the soup, it was back to the saluting again until late at night; then the same routine began all over again: rush into the barracks, fall on top of one another, try to protect one's head from blows.

'Line up! Bend knees! Sit down! Fall back!'

Survival in Birkenau

When I remember Birkenau, it seems to me that those who some-how retained their human dignity and did not turn savage were in the majority. Of course there were many who behaved recklessly, in an animal-like manner, without a thought for their fellow pris-oners; but they were the minority. In spite of everything, we managed to respect one another's rights. Tragically, at later stages in some of the concentration camps, cannibalism was practised — but again, by a minority only.

In the German hell of Auschwitz, every form of civilisation disintegrated. In the jungle of Birkenau, savagery reigned. Yet, in this man-made hell on earth, I still saw some Jews discreetly murmur their daily prayers in the mornings and evenings. Even when the food supplies were at their most meagre, and each tiny morsel could mean the difference between life and death, some very religious Jews would spit out their food if they thought that it could possibly contain meat; nor would they ever eat the slice of sausage they were given, trading it for bread instead. Knowing that the meat could not have been slaughtered in the ritual manner, they preferred to do without.

In some barracks at night, where the Blockaeltesten were rea-sonable men — and not too many of them were — actors and singers would recite or sing Yiddish songs, and poets would recite what they had memorised. Shamaj Rosenblum, well known for his recitations in Lodz, was one such performer. Although totally blind, Rosenblum passed every selection with the help of Moshe Pulawer, the stage director of the Avant Garde Theatre from the Lodz ghetto. Moshe acted as his eyes, always by his side, always vigilant. Somehow, Shamaj survived the concentration camps, together with Moshe; the Germans never perceived his disability.

On Yom Kippur, some Jews fasted. On the Jewish holidays, risking their lives, some gathered in small groups in an inconspicuous corner to say their prayers. While many orthodox Jews became atheists in the camps, there were nevertheless some who, in the very heart of the German wilderness, lifted themselves even higher.

On the third day, before we stretched out on the concrete for the night, a short fellow turned up. They called him 'Shmulekl Magid' (Shmulek the Preacher). A Polish Jew, he spoke to us in Yiddish, running along the brick tunnel like a madman, waving his arms, shaking his fists, yelling at the top of his voice,

'You fucking bastards! You sons of bitches! I hope by now you have learned where you are! So you fucking bastards listen and do as I say! Don't try to be smart or you will be sorry! I know you too well! If you think you can outsmart me, you are very stupid! You see,' he bellowed, pointing to the beams above his head, 'only a few days ago, six men were hanged here. The sons of bitches thought they were smart!

'I know you've pushed your jewellery and money into your arseholes. Some of you keep it in your mouths! But you'll be sorry if you try to cheat! We have the most modern technique of discovering whatever you have swallowed! We'll x-ray your bellies and I promise you, you won't enjoy the way we take it out.

'And now I'll count to three! All those on my left, jump over the brick tunnel to join the others opposite. Stop! Before you go — leave all your possessions on the floor right where you stand! That way, nobody gets hurt! But God help those who try to be smart!'

There was a commotion. We were all on one side, pressed together. The vacated floor was scattered with gold watches, bracelets, chains, rings, coins and bank notes. Shmulekl Magid, piercing us with his glittering, foxy eyes, turned around and stared at us as he burst into crazy laughter.

'Hahah! Hahah! You think you're smart! Is this all you have? I'll give you one more chance! When I count to three, all of you cross over to the other side; and this time, drop *everything* on the floor!'

The process was repeated over and over. Each time, a few more valuables were left lying on the floor, but Shmulek the Preacher was not yet fully satisfied.

'You sons of bitches! Do you think I'm a *schmuck*? I've been here long enough. I know you better than you think. Is this all you have hidden? No dollars? No pounds sterling? And what about the gold coins? Before I start searching, I warn you! Make up your minds! If you want to live, you better drop your things where you stand! This is the very last time! One! Two! Three!'

The exercise took place yet again. Shmulekl, with his foul language and threats, carried on like a lunatic. I had heard rough language before, but this was a new experience, particularly because it was all in Yiddish. I soon learned that whenever a fresh lot of prisoners was brought, Shmulekl gave them this welcome speech.

He shared the jewellery and money which he extorted from the prisoners with the Blockaeltesten and the Kapos. In turn, they traded with the SS, all eager to have a share of the loot. From Himmler down to the lowest-ranking storm-trooper, they were all motivated to kill and rob, and their families enjoyed the lovely things they sent home. At Auschwitz, two high-ranking SS officers from the SD handled the spoils. The rest of them traded with the prisoners, supplying them with vodka, schnapps, cigarettes and tobacco in exchange for valuables and currency.

The unpredictability of concentration camp life was very much brought home to me in my second week at Birkenau. As we stood to attention at roll-call, Rivek complained of a splitting headache. He felt tired, and his body ached all over. His eyes glittered with fever; when I touched his forehead, I could tell that his temperature was very high. Although he managed to struggle through that day, by the following morning he could hardly stand on his feet. Srulek and I had propped him up for hours on the roll-call ground, but he was weakening all the time, becoming dizzy and disoriented. After roll-call, he lay down on the ground near the barracks. He was shivering, and Srulek covered him with his jacket.

On the third day, Rivek's health deteriorated still further. He could no longer stand, and trying to support him under his arms was useless: he simply collapsed. Observing this, the Blockaelteste was amused. 'You've had it. You look finished,' he said, poking him with his stick.

Wobbling with dizziness and almost losing his balance, Rivek struggled to his feet and stood to attention. The Blockaelteste instinctively moved back for fear of contracting the illness, and ordered us to take him to the sick bay. From his symptoms, it was obvious that Rivek had the typhus that was rampant at Auschwitz. He may even have brought it with him from the Lodz ghetto.

We carried him to the sick bay with some reluctance, and had no option but to leave him lying on the floor near the entrance. It was very risky to be there, the constant selections and the proximity to the crematoria making it extremely hazardous. The next day, Srulek found out that the chief doctor at the sick bay, a Doctor Pick, hailed from the same area as Srulek and Rivek. Coming from Zdunska Wola, he knew their families and he promised to look after Rivek. He was helpful and friendly, and was highly respected at Birkenau.

In the second week, a short, fat, Polish prisoner with a shiny, bald head turned up in front of Block Number 11. He was the chief registrar of the Department of Labour. We nick-named him 'Senicki' because he looked like the manager of the Department of Labour in the Lodz ghetto. They were both bald and of similar reddish complexions with white blond eyebrows and lashes.

'Senicki's' job was to select prisoners to fulfil the needs of the German war industry. It was useful to have a trade as it insured one against being selected for work in a coal mine, although even a coal mine was far better than staying at Birkenau. Everybody was anxious to get away from there. The old prisoners used to say, 'In the other concentration camps, life is just as hard, but it is safer to be away from the chimneys.' At Birkenau BIIe, one could be shoved into the furnaces at any moment. Just one more selection and you were a 'fertiger', a goner!

One day, 'Senicki' appeared at our block asking for photographers, lithographers, engravers and printers. Unfortunately, I was not game enough to cheat my way into that group. After the liberation I found out that its members had been sent to Berlin, and had worked in warm and clean conditions. Although their food was not much better, they were treated with less brutality. They were used as forgers of foreign currency in an underground printing and engraving factory, forging passports, documents and all sorts of papers for the German espionage campaign. They produced millions of counterfeit US dollars and pounds sterling, and paid their spies with these products.

In the meantime, Srulek and I kept in touch with the sick bay. In the beginning, Rivek's temperature was very high. His only medication was the bunk beneath him and the roof over his head where he could lie down without harassment and beating. As a protégé of Dr Pick, Rivek received boiled drinking water and the occasional aspirin when in extreme pain. Both these items were luxuries at Birkenau. Entering the washroom or latrines — the only place one could get drinking water — was strictly forbidden without being escorted by the Stubendiensten or Blockaeltesten.

The rule of brutality

Within a few days of Rivek's admission to the sick bay, I fell victim to the Blockaelteste's bamboo stick. Why? This was Auschwitz and the beating never stopped: it was part of the system. Those who did the beating had been beaten before by others, and whoever possessed the stick used it without mercy. Those who beat were the Kapos, Blockaeltesten and Stubendiensten.

The criminals were brought from the German prisons; the political prisoners came from the concentration camps in Germany. Most of the latter had been behind the barbed wires for many years, some since as far back as 1933. There were also homosexuals and people suspected by the Gestapo of being a threat to the security of the state. The political prisoners had received no formal court sentence. In the Third Reich justice, such as it was, was in the hands of the SS and Gestapo.

Some prisoners were marked with a 'Z' that stood for 'Zeitveilig', temporary. Amongst the Kapos and Blockaeltesten were Poles, French, Czechs, Slovaks, as well as Jews. With few exceptions they were, quite simply, a bunch of brutal killers.

The biggest commotion took place every day when the soup was carried in large, heavy, wooden boxes along the main road which divided the compound in two. Some of the most daring prisoners, at great risk to their lives, would jump forward, dip their pots into the hot liquid and run away to eat their spoils — if they were not killed on the spot by the escorts. Not a day passed without victims who never got to enjoy the bit of soup they tried to grab. I made one successful dash, but I never tried again after I saw a young boy's scull literally split in two for the same daredevil stunt. He was dead before he hit the ground.

At Block 11, the Blockaelteste was handing out the soup, and there was the usual big stir. For some reason he went berserk, swishing his bamboo cane left and right, and I happened to be in his way. I was knocked to the ground, and hit the concrete floor heavily. With my hands and arms wrapped around my head, instinctively protecting my head and face, I lost consciousness, fading into a dark silence.

When I came to, my hands and arms were cut and bruised. I do not know how long I had been lying on the concrete but, as I slowly revived, I could hear voices that seemed to be coming from far away. My vision was blurred and everything spun around in circles. My head felt like a block of lead, and I had a sort of whistling in my ears and a constant buzzing in my head. My body was numb, as though paralysed, and I had no control over my limbs.

I tried to get to my feet but managed only to kneel, and then topple, head first, once again to the ground. I heard voices saying, 'He's dying, he's dying!', and I could hear the Blockaelteste's rasping voice ordering me to, 'Get up! Get up!' He kicked me in my side, but still I could not move.

It was dark when two Stubendiensten lifted me up under my arms. I noticed that something was blurring the vision of my left eye but it took a while before I realised I was bleeding. They had to drag me along because, although I tried to walk, I was incapable of placing one foot in front of another. I was carried to the sick bay where a doctor in a white, bloodstained coat came towards us, ordering the Stubendiensten to prop me on a bench against the wall. Then they brought in another man whom they placed along-side me. His face — the little of it I could see not covered in blood — was pale.

'Are you strong?' the doctor asked me. I shrugged my shoulders and watched him examine the other victim, shaking his head and talking to himself. 'Oh boy, oh boy, what a mess. Son of a bitch!'

He turned his attention back to me.

'You're the lucky one. I can't help the other. The bastard scalped him — chopped a piece the size of my palm off the back of his head. He'll bleed to death ... I'll stitch you up.'

Gently touching my head, he slipped a round piece of timber between my teeth and told me to bite it. Next, he pushed a large needle threaded with white sewing cotton into my scalp.

'Bite down hard and scream,' he told me, unnecessarily, as I was already screaming at the top of my voice. I fell to the floor, pleading with him to stop.

He tried to lift me up onto the bench again, at once kind and apologetic. 'My boy, be sensible. Let me help you. This is Auschwitz. This is the best I can do.' He appealed to my common sense, but I was beyond reason. I stretched out on the floor, begging him to let go of me.

'Just let it be,' I implored.

'You'll bleed to death unless I stitch you up.'

'I can't take it. I'm too weak,' I insisted.

'You'll bleed to death; you need stitches,' he repeated over and over again.

'Do you know Doctor Pick,' I asked him suddenly. 'He's supposed to be here.'

He looked at me quizzically. 'Who are you? What is your name?'

When I told him, he said, 'I am Pick. You must be the son of Jankiel or Chaim. I knew your family. My mother was born in Zdunska Wola. In the beginning, I used to see your father and uncle in the ghetto all the time. They were my uncle David Laib's childhood friends.'

Almost to himself, Doctor Pick said, 'They are all dead. They are all gone.' He turned around and left.

When he returned he held a little glass jar in his hand. 'The Germans on the front lines don't get this any more,' he said. 'This is your only hope.' Cautiously, he applied a small amount of the yellow powder to my wound, and left me for a while.

'You're lucky, the bleeding has stopped,' he told me after some time had elapsed and he had once more examined my wound. 'This is a wonder powder.'

While he bandaged my head with paper, I asked him about Rivek.

'He has typhus,' said Doctor Pick. 'He will be okay, but take care of yourself. Get away from here. Don't wait for him. You can do nothing to help him. Have you got a trade? Tell them anything. Be whatever they need: bricklayer, carpenter, electrician, mechanic, anything!

Bluff. But get out of here. The sooner the better!'

I noticed the Blockaelteste standing at the door with the Stubendiensten. Although they scared me, Doctor Pick called them over authoritatively.

'Take him back,' he said sternly and, as they helped me towards the door, Pick, with a light smile on his face, bid me farewell, advising me once again to take care of myself. 'And come back if the bleeding starts again. I will have to stitch you up.'

To the Blockaelteste he said, 'Look after him, he's my cousin.'

It was the middle of the night as we left the sick bay, but still the chimney stacks opposite the electric fence spewed out their ever-lasting flames, lighting up our faces with a fiery glow, staining the sky red. At regular intervals, the beams of the searchlights from the guard towers cut the darkness of the night like glittering knives, gliding over the roofs and walls of the barracks. The exaggerated, elongated reflections of our shadows moved before us like dancing phantoms. And all the while, the Stubendiensten supported me under my arms, my feet unable to connect with the ground, my legs dragging behind, scraping the road, as they hauled me back to the barracks.

Entertainment

At Block No. 11, two low-wattage bulbs threw a dim light on the mass of bodies spread out on the concrete, interwoven like a mat of living ghosts. The Stubendiensten dropped me as soon as they entered the barracks.

'Put the doctor's cousin up on top of the furnace,' the Blockaelteste ordered before retiring to his quarters.

One of the Stubendiensten by the name of Pishta Bachi (Uncle Pishta), was a burly fellow with a childlike face whose head always hung down as if he were embarrassed to look you in the eye.

'Grab that,' he said in a muffled voice, his broken German heavily laced with a Hungarian accent. He handed me a Gypsy rug, so large that I could hardly lift it. Seeing this, he helped me onto the furnace and covered me with the rug. 'Here you will be safer,' he said, not unkindly. 'They won't upset your wound.'

I curled up like a cat and, although warm, I felt my ears block up. My head was heavy, spinning and aching with a constant buzzing that became the refrain of a song that never left me: 'What will I do?

How will I ever find my brother? I have to find him! Will I make it? Yes I will, I must, I have promised.' I felt as if I were on a boat, rocking over the waves, when I was woken out of my dreaming by Pishta Bachi shaking my shoulder and signalling me to follow him. I saw the other victim standing in front of the 'Tagesraum', the Blockaelteste's quarters.

The Blockaelteste himself suddenly appeared by removing the rug which separated his quarters from the rest of us, and ordered us to enter. Standing on my wobbly legs, hardly able to maintain my balance, I observed that the little corner was crowded with Kapos and Blockaeltesten. Cigarette smoke was suspended like a heavy cloud around the electric bulb which hung over a little table that was loaded with sausages, loaves of bread thickly sliced and covered heavily with margarine, glasses filled with vodka, and many bottles of the stuff.

Some Kapos and Blockaeltesten were half drunk, others completely, falling off their stools making sweeping gestures with their arms, wishing one another good health, drinking down entire glasses with one gulp. They were obviously running a thriving business with the SS from the loot Shmulekl Magid collected so assiduously.

The Blockaelteste walked up to us with a strange smile on his face and a glass of vodka in his hand. With amazement in his voice he demanded of my companion, 'What happened to you?'

Confused and scared, my friend shrugged his shoulders and stuttered, 'I ... I ... I d ... don't know H ... Herr Blockaelteste.'

At this, the Blockaelteste burst our laughing, and so did the rest. Turning to me he said, 'Isn't he stupid? He doesn't know what happened to him! What about you? What happened to you? Why do you wear that turban? Are you an Arab?'

Angling back around to his colleagues, he said with a stupid laugh, 'I didn't know we had Arabs in Birkenau.'

'They're all one lot,' another suggested.

'Well, my friend,' the Blockaelteste said, 'what happened to you?'

Hesitantly I said, 'I fell over and hit my head on a stone.'

This pleased him no end. 'Smart guy, aren't you!'

Gulping down the rest of the vodka, he turned to his friends.

'*Mandry Zydek* — a smart little Yid, isn't he?' He poked my chest with his index finger. 'Since you are so smart, you can sing us a song.' Turning to his friends, he shouted at the top of his voice, 'Shut up! Shut up! Dr Pick's cousin is going to sing! What will you sing for us?'

I had already heard that *My Yiddishe Mama* was a great hit at Birkenau. The Blockaelteste silenced the noisy drunkards and, with voice quivering, I began. As I sang, my head spun. Desperately, I tried to maintain my balance as my vertigo increased with every note I sang.

My audience was delighted when I finished, expressing its appreciation with cat calls and whistling. Lifting their glasses of vodka, they all cheered me as the greatest singer in Auschwitz. The Blockaelteste was more than happy. The more he drank the happier he became, but less and less steady on his feet. He pointed his finger at my companion.

'Now is your turn,' he commanded, slurring his words.

My friend was pale and drawn, his eyes deeply sunk and ringed by grey. He looked sick and confused and pleaded with the Blockaelteste, 'Please, I don't know any songs. I'm sorry I can't sing. I don't know, I don't know any songs.'

His voice became fainter, and I could see that the Blockaelteste was displeased. Annoyed, he ordered my companion to sing and not to embarrass him in front of his guests.

'Please,' I interjected, 'I will sing.'

'No! No! He must sing!' the Blockaelteste insisted.

My companion turned to me. 'Can you help me? I don't remember any songs. I don't remember anything. What should I sing?'

'Were you ever a soldier?' I asked him.

'Yes.'

'Don't you know any Polish soldier marches? Any military songs?'

'Yes, but I don't remember any of them. Can't you help me?'

'What about *The Legionnaires Tune*?' I suggested.

'No, I don't think I can remember it.'

'What about, *Hussars Came To The Little Window*?

'Yes,' he said, relieved to recognise the old Polish cavalry song. 'Will you help me?'

I started to sing and my friend mumbled along with me. Another hit. The Blockaelteste was happy and so were his guests, this time showing their appreciation by blowing whistles, clapping their hands, gulping the vodka and puffing on their cigarettes.

With great bravado, the Blockaelteste picked up a large kitchen knife that was lying on the table, cut a whole loaf of bread in two, and slammed a piece of margarine on top of each half with a large piece of sausage as an extra. He handed the bounty to us, showing off his generosity, praising us for our performances. That memorable night at Birkenau was undoubtedly my greatest success as a singer.

Nightmares

Once again I lay on the furnace, my head heavy, my bandage soaked with blood. I was too scared to touch it. I lay down, pressing the bread against my chest, squashing the margarine onto my jacket. My mouth was dry, my tongue a piece of leather. I pinched off a piece of bread and pushed it into my mouth, but I couldn't swallow. Half a loaf of bread with a huge lump of margarine and a big piece of sausage! A fortune, an absolute fortune! What would happen were I to sleep in? It would be stolen from me. My throat locked at the very thought. I was chewing the bread unable to swallow; nor could I go to sleep.

Determinedly I shut my eyes, but the chimney stack kept reappearing. Again, scenes from the past rolled by like a film in my mind that I could not switch off. Suddenly I was back in the Bronislaw Grosser kindergarten on the first floor at 25 Lagiewnicka Street, standing at the sandpit next to my friend, Peretz Zylberberg. He always took my shovel and bucket. When I struggled with him to get it back, he would scratch my face. Where was Lipek? He was in the older group. Why didn't he save me?

I pressed my bread anxiously to my chest, the margarine smearing on my hands and all over my jacket. I was gripped with panic; I feared I would not survive, that I would never see my brother again. Yet the dreaming had helped me to feel better; it had given me courage. It had felt good to be back in my kindergarten. I will find Lipek, I promised myself. I will go on living and find my brother.

Soon, however, that dream was replaced once again by the recurrent nightmare. The crematorium was before my eyes, the disembarkation, the screaming and crying.

Once again, I felt Pishta Bachi shaking me awake.

'What's the matter? How are you getting on?'

'Water, please. Please, some water. I'm so thirsty.'

He came back with a large pot of fresh, cold water. I drank it eagerly, almost choking in my desperation to gulp it down.

My headache did not ease and the buzzing in my ears was constant. Once again I began to chew the bread, swallowing with difficulty, eating out of fear that someone would steal it. Now my thoughts were with my parents. How long had they suffered? I had heard that it took about half an hour. Thirty minutes in the gas chambers was an eternity. Every *second* would last forever. Oh God, where are You? Is this how You treat Your chosen people? They say You are everywhere. Are You in the gas chambers together with the babies? With the tiny babies? Are You the God of this universe? Is Auschwitz, are the gas chambers and the chapel where the SS pray, part of Your realm? Do you listen to their prayers, too? Are You the Almighty who promised to multiply our seeds like the stars in heaven? And You allow *this* to happen? I was at a loss. I could not grasp it.

Lying on the furnace, my mind never stopped. I was feverish and dehydrated, yet I was fortunate to have Pishta to help me. He brought me another pot of water.

'Drink it, you need it!' he told me. 'You lost a lot of blood.'

I finally dropped off into a peaceful doze, only to be woken by screams of *'Raus! Raus! Schnell! Schnell! Bewegung! Bewegung! Los! Los!'*

Outside it was dark and the temperature was below zero. The madness was on again. The prisoners pushed, fought and fell over one another struggling to get out through the narrow door. Pishta appeared from nowhere, signalling to me to stay where I was in the swiftly emptying barracks. He told me to lie down, and I stayed there for most of the day until Pishta came to get me to line up for the roll-call. My bandage was in shreds.

'Take it off,' Pishta said. 'Don't be obvious.'

Quickly I pushed the bloodstained paper into my pocket, wiping my head before the SS men passed the column.

With roll-call over, the soup was brought and the usual commotion ensued. When the Blockaelteste finished ladling it out, Pishta called me over and, giving me a spoon and a pot, told me to scrape out the soup box. I could hardly believe my luck. The bottom of the soup box always contained the thickest, most nourishing ingredients, unlike the substance closer to the top.

Bending over the box, I had vertigo and nearly fell in. Once I had scraped out a large amount, Pishta told me to go into the barracks and eat all of it myself. 'No swapping,' he warned. I offered some of it to him, but he waved me away.

Sitting on the furnace, I began my feast. The more I ate, the more distended my stomach became. It blew up, tight and hard, like a balloon, and I found it difficult to breathe, but I continued eating until the pot was empty. Tomorrow I might have none.

The Hungarian soldier

When the mass of humanity was spread out on the concrete to sleep, Pishta, hanging his head, sat next to me in silence for a long time. Although he looked sad and defeated, he reminded me of nothing so much as a big, calm bear. He was a man of few words, and it took him a while to ask me about my family and the Lodz ghetto.

'I came to Auschwitz with my parents,' I told him briefly. 'Dr Mengele sent them to the gas.'

Pishta pointed in the direction of the crematoria. 'You will all finish up there,' he said. 'You will all go to the Himmelkommando.'

'What about you?' I asked.

'I'm not Jewish.'

'How come you're here?'

'Well, my friend, only a few weeks ago I was brought to Auschwitz in a similar state to the one you are in now. Perhaps I was worse.'

He took off his prison cap and exposed a few long cuts across his skull. As he thrust his face close to mine, I could see it was covered with pinkish-red, half-healed cuts. Somehow, in all the commotion, I had failed to notice them before or, even if I had noticed them, I had failed to be curious. You learned quickly to mind your own business in Auschwitz.

'I am a sergeant in the Hungarian army,' he continued, 'and I was fighting with the Germans against the Russians. It happened when I was on leave from the front line. I stepped out onto a railway platform opposite to where the Germans were loading people into a cattle train. The people were crying and falling, being pushed by the SS and viciously beaten. I was shocked.

'An old lady fell over, and a young SS man stood above her, hitting her with the butt of his gun and kicking her in her stomach. He was wearing heavy boots.

'I lost my temper completely. I was furious. I don't know what came over me, but I ran across and grabbed the German by his throat. I just stopped short of choking him and threw him to the ground.'

I looked at Pishta's strong hands, his powerful arms, and could well believe it.

'Next thing I remember,' he said, 'was lying on the floor in a dark cattle wagon. I was in pain. Every part of my body was bruised and cut. I was only half conscious and it took a long time before I came around. They had taken my rifle, my pistol, my rucksack and my belt. My uniform was in shreds, and so was I. The people in the wagon gave me water; they washed my face and tended my wounds. They were from Budapest. So am I.

'I don't know how long we were travelling in that train,' he sighed, his hopelessness still faintly tinged with disbelief at his predicament. 'At home they will never find out what happened to me. In the army they think I have deserted.'

He paused then, uncertain about whether or not to continue. He seemed to make up his mind all of a sudden.

'I must tell you, I never liked Jews. Don't ask me why. That is how it was back in Hungary, even before the Germans came. Nobody liked the Jews. They were looked upon as cheats, over-rich, dirty and smelly. Very bad things were always said about them. Back in Hungary, it was normal to hate Jews because they were the Christ-killers.'

He was silent again. 'People are stupid,' he said at last, without looking at me. 'They are like sheep; they don't think. Well, am I any different?'

I was no longer sure if he was talking to me or to himself, but I listened, irresistibly drawn by his simple honesty.

'I still can't believe this happened to me.' His voice was a low murmur in the semi-darkness. 'But it's too late for regrets. Besides, I am not sorry. I lost my temper; I so completely lost control over myself, I could have killed the bastard when I saw him kicking the old woman in the stomach. It could have been my mother.'

He shook his head. 'My wife and family would probably say, "Why the hell did you do that? Why do you care what they do to Jews? It serves them right. They've asked for it." If my friends knew how I acted they would never talk to me again. They would have no respect for me. So I had to be beaten like a dog and thrown in to a cattle truck together with the Jews to learn that they are just as human as I am. And then they saved my life. This I will never forget ... How old were your parents?' he inquired abruptly.

When I told him, he said, 'What a crazy thing to do — murdering young people, babies, who've done no harm to anyone.'

'Does it take long before they are dead?' I asked. I had to know. 'I've heard it takes up to half an hour.'

'Oh no, no,' he replied. 'It takes only six to seven minutes. Then they may not be dead, but they don't feel anything any more.'

Once again he refused to meet my eyes, but his tone was grave.

'Get away from here,' he urged me. 'It is very dangerous. At any moment, you can go up the chimney.'

In the following days, Pishta Bachi looked after me with soup, and offered me a few slices of bread. He allowed me to lie on the furnace during the day, and I doubt that I would have made it without his help. He kept giving me plenty of water, constantly reminding me to drink.

'You need it,' he would insist. 'You lost a lot of blood.'

Within a week I began to feel a little better. The buzzing and ringing in my head and ears lessened, although my wound was not healing well. It became infected, and I tore the pockets from my pants to wipe away the blood and pus.

Last meeting with Berish

I tried to get myself into a transport. Whenever 'Senicki' turned up, I was amongst the first to line up. Every day I claimed mastery over another trade, and every day I failed the exams — my answers were simply not good enough. But one day my tattooed number was on his list: he had accepted me as a carpenter. Jacob Nirenberg, a cabinet maker and carpenter by trade, had given me a few tips, and I had managed to produce answers that were credible.

After Rivek went to the sick bay, Srulek sneaked into another barracks. I then joined up with a few men from the Lodz ghetto. We all knew each other from our school years, although we were not all the same age. The younger ones, including me, were from Skif. The older ones belonged to the Bund. They were Jacob Nirenberg, his brother Myer, Shalom Goteiner, Marek Bialkower, Alexander Gelerman, his brother Mendel, Abraham Belzicki, Mr Hauser, in his mid-forties, and his son Motele. Jacob Nirenberg's professional know-how helped us all in getting our numbers registered with 'Sienicki' as carpenters.

One afternoon, standing near Block 11, I heard my name called. Names in camp were virtually never used, 'Hey you!' being the usual mode of address. The only people I knew by name were those in my particular group, but now someone from outside my group was calling me.

I recognised the voice at once. It was Berish, my uncle. He was alive! We fell into each other's arms. He had lost weight but his colour was good.

'Where are your glasses?' I asked him.

'I have them.'

He indicated a spot under his belt, and I realised that he was wise to keep them there. Those who wore them in camp were always picked on; eventually, the glasses were broken in the course of beatings, as their wearers were considered to be too intellectual.

'How is your rib cage?' I wanted to know. 'Any better?'

'It's coming on.'

He asked me about my parents, and I told him in as few words as possible. He shook his head, and then told me how worried he was about his wife, my aunt Sarah, having no idea what had become of her.

'Surely she's in the women's camp,' I said to cheer him up. 'She looked young and fit.'

'Do you really think so?' he asked doubtfully.

My attempts to reassure him seemed to work.

'Here,' he said abruptly, 'have this'. He had taken out his bread ration from his pocket and was offering it.

'Why are you giving it to me?'

'I'm leaving on a transport this afternoon. I may get another ration.

'You'd better keep it,' I said. 'You never know when you might need it.'

'What happened to your head?' Berish noticed the blood stain on my cap.

'It will heal, it's nothing.'

He studied my face. 'You look a bit pale. Take care of yourself. Keep out of trouble. I just learned about you a few minutes ago. Somebody saw you. I better run back to my barracks; I mustn't be away too long. I think they're going to send us to a coal mine.'

We had been walking briskly and talking. Now Berish stopped, and we kissed one another. Then he ran into his barracks, turning around once for a last glimpse, waving and smiling. I never saw him again.

It must have been in the first days of October that we were lined up and marched off to the bath-house outside the camp's perimeter. They took us back to the 'Canada', the same bath-house we had been taken to on our arrival. This was not the routine. Normally, prisoners prepared for transport were disinfected inside Birkenau BIIe. The old prisoners were rather surprised, and began to voice doubts about our destination. When we asked them why, one of them said,

'You never know what the SS are up to. They always come up with a new surprise. It *looks* like you're being sent out to another camp, but you can't be certain until the lorry gets to the first main intersection. If it turns right, *then* you'll know you're not going for Sonderbehandlung' (literally "special treatment", the code word for gassing).

We were disinfected, showered, issued with striped prison garb, and loaded onto lorries. We were approximately five hundred prisoners, mostly Jews from the Lodz ghetto. Amongst us were also a few Jews from Hungary, France, Belgium and Holland. The SS were heavily armed. One of them was an Oberscharführer with two Iron Cross ribbons on his tunic for bravery. I wondered what he had done to get them.

His right leg was shorter than his left and he looked like a ferocious bull dog; but he was tipsy and soon fell asleep, snoring most of the way with his weight crushing me against the wall of the truck. He carried a submachine gun with the ammunition belt locked in the breech ready to fire. Even in his drunken sleep, he held his weapon between his crossed legs, gripping its barrel in his locked palms. Although I willed it countless times, never once did that grip slacken.

I was staring into the emptiness of space when a shooting star marked the sky with a long fiery streak and vanished in the darkness of the night. Was there such a thing as a lucky star, I wondered. Deep in my heart, I hoped there was one for me.

The watchtowers of Auschwitz-Birkenau grew smaller and smaller as the lorries gained speed. We were heading towards the unknown. Only the chimney stacks persistently remained in my mind's eye, their outlines on the horizon crowned with a crimson cloud suspended high above. Their images followed me in the darkness of the night. They followed me in my waking hours and in my sleep. They follow me to this day.

8

Althammer

ON A FROSTY AUTUMN NIGHT, a heavily guarded column of lorries, loaded with five hundred Jewish prisoners from Auschwitz, sped along the highway. Destination: Althammer (Stare Kuznice) in Upper Silesia, approximately ninety kilometres away as the crow flies. After a journey of about three hours, the convoy made a sharp turn onto a gravel road, reducing its speed and gradually slowing to a stop.

Everything was wrapped in darkness. All I could see were SS men with their guns trained on the prisoners; Kapos and Blockaeltesten were everywhere. We were welcomed, as always, with a cacophony of barked orders backed up with truncheons and sticks.

'*Aussteigen, aussteigen! Los, los! Schnell, schnell!*'

Like a herd of sheep, we prisoners turned in circles, huddling against one another, each trying to push himself towards the centre to dodge the blows.

'*Vordermann und Seitenrichtung! Vordermann und Seitenrichtung!*' The shouting and bludgeoning only confused us even more.

'Fodermann?' We looked at one another in bewilderment. 'Who the hell is Fodermann? Why doesn't he come forward?'

After a few blows, we soon realised that *Vordermann und Seitenrichtung* was a command to line up. At Birkenau, the order had been '*Eintreten und Auffallen*'. ('Fall in and line up.') Now we were lined up and divided into groups.

It took me a while to register where I was. The lights suspended over the electrified fence mapped out the perimeter of the camp. Spotlights beaming from the guard towers crossed one another, cutting the blackness of the night with irregular flashes. I had a strange feeling of *déjà vu*; and indeed, in a way, I had been there and seen it all before. One camp was very much like another. Although the chimney stacks were missing, the stench of smouldering flesh and bones lingered in my nostrils — as it does to this day. Even after forty-seven years, it only takes the slightest smell of burning to awaken my deepest fears.

'FORWAAARRRD MARCH!' The camp gate stood wide open with two SS men on either side. We stopped in front of a brick barracks with a large sign painted on it in white: Number Two.

The Blockaelteste was a tall, broad-shouldered, red-faced, fully seasoned prisoner — a Bevauer, with a green triangle under his number. Soon we found out that he was not only a professional criminal but a killer as well. To meet him face to face was danger-ous. Although he was always angry, his enjoyment at slapping prisoners with his wide, red palms that were the size of shovels was clearly evident. Every time he hit a man, he left an imprint of his palm on the victim's face. Blockaelteste Kurt Bayer was feared by everybody, even by the camp élite.

The barracks were divided into four sections with three tiers of metal bunks against the walls. I was allocated a top bunk, an advantageous position, as it protected me from the initial on-slaught of blows by the Stubendiensten and Blockaeltesten. That first night we slept on bare springs.

Five a.m.: A metallic ringing woke me abruptly to the sight of a prisoner using a hammer to repeatedly strike a piece of railing — suspended on a pole near the roll-call ground — to signal the beginning of the day.

'*Aufstehen, aufstehen! Los, los!* Get up, get up!' the Stubendiensten shouted.

Stripped to the waist, we ran to the communal wash house. '*Schnell, schnell! Los, los!*' We were always on the run, never allowed to walk.

The water was freezing. I splashed my face and body and ran back to the barracks, using my shirt as a towel. We lined up to collect the ration — two hundred grams of bread, a slice of sausage, a tiny square of margarine — and we washed it down with a bitter, black liquid they called coffee.

'*Los, los! Schnell, schnell!* Out of the barracks! *In Laufschritt, in*

Laufschritt! Los, los!

We lined up on the roll-call ground, the night lingering into the damp and frosty morning hours.

'Attention! Mützen ab!'

Hats off, the prisoners stood stiffly and motionless to attention as we were counted by the Blockführer who, clicking his heels and with an outstretched arm, saluted the commandant. *'Heil Hitler!'* he roared and, continuing at high volume, reported, 'The number of prisoners on the roll-call ground I have counted and verified. The numbers are correct!'

After roll-call, amid the incessant clubbing and abuse, every prisoner had to fill a bag with wood shavings. Our bags were then inspected by Kurt Bayer. The task of ensuring that the bags — which served as our mattresses — satisfied Bayer's scrutiny was always going to be a task beyond the abilities of some prisoners. So the more able assisted the less, to save them from his wrath. We were given a blanket, a luxury I had never experienced in any of the other camps and, once our bunks were made, we stood to attention in front of them, awaiting the Blockaelteste to initiate yet another inspection.

'Los, los! Raus, raus!'

Again we were lined up on the roll-call ground and divided into work commandos. We were kept there for hours, standing to attention. By the time we were discharged to the barracks it was dark and we were totally exhausted.

'Los, los! Into the barracks!'

The lights were switched off but not my mind, not even while I slept. It seemed I had hardly shut my eyes when the infernal metallic ringing roused me again. Another night had passed with supersonic speed and another everlasting day had begun. It was still dark.

'Aufstehen, aufstehen! Wake up, wake up! *Los, los! Schnell, schnell!'* The routine was on again: the clicking of heels, the removing of caps, the standing to attention. *'Heil Hitler!'* The morning roll-call formalities over, we were lined up in work commandos and the Kapos took over.

'FORWAAARD MARCH! RAM! RAM! RAM! RAM!' Like soldiers on parade we marched, turning our heads to the right when passing the commandant at the gate. His nickname was Tom Mix, an ironic reference to his accurate, trigger-happy habits. He roamed around the camp and the construction site, always with his Luger pistol at the ready. He took great satisfaction in shooting prisoners at a considerable distance from himself as a way of testing his aim, and was always delighted when he scored a direct hit. During the evacuation of Althammer, the first time we were allowed out of the wagon to urinate, he amused himself by aiming at the penises of the prisoners. Thereafter we were content to relieve ourselves inside the wagon.

At the gates, Tom Mix stood three paces ahead of Helmut, the Lageraelteste, a Bevauer, who was yelling at the top of his voice, 'One, two, three, four! One, two, three, four! Heads up, chests out! One, two, three, four! Watch your step! Heads up, the sun is shining!'

The air was damp and frosty, penetrating my striped denims. Stamping my feet, I marched into the night, carrying a burden that pressed on my mind and heart. A constant darkness dwelt in my soul. Inside, I was crying like a child. Helmut's voice followed from a distance: 'One, two, three, four! One, two, three, four! Heads up, chests out! One, two, three, four! The sun is shining!'

Was there still a sun? Would it ever shine again?

Thoughts of escape

The wind blew furiously. We were given picks and shovels, and ordered to work; but, before they told us what to do, the beating was on. Nothing was done without a beating. To this day I still wonder what made those Kapos such cruel sadists.

At Althammer the Kapos, Vorarbeiters and Blockaeltesten were mostly of German nationality. The majority were professional criminals, while some were political. They were the élite of the camp; amongst them were a few Jews, who were as bad as their non-Jewish counterparts. They had all come from concentration camp Monowitz-Buna, a large synthetics factory, producing methanol for aircraft fuel, synthetic rubber and many other by-products from the black-coal basin in Upper Silesia.

The first day on the building site was long and painful. It was dark when we were marched back, and hardly any of us could walk without a limp. Yet, however difficult and strenuous we found the work, it was the beatings that were the worst, the incessant beatings. We worked in the open whatever the conditions — rain, hail, frost — constructing a large power station and, when concrete was being poured, we had to work non-stop throughout the night. The structure grew fast and, at times, I was amongst those chosen for the concrete pouring process. Working on the tenth floor, high above the vast plains surrounded by forests, there was nothing to break the vicious winds. We had to hold on tightly to the railings in order not to be blown off the scaffolding.

Part of the forest had been cut down to make room for the camp and the construction site which stood side by side. The camp site measured approximately three acres and was divided by an electrified wire fence, with watch-towers surrounding the entire complex. Between it and the forest was an empty space of approximately two kilometres. This gave the SS guard a clear view of potential escapes; nevertheless, escape was constantly on my mind. Like a caged animal, I looked through the barbed wires with a yearning for freedom. Oh God! If I could only get into the forest I would be the luckiest man alive. I made mental calculations of how long it would take me to reach the bushes. In my mind, I mapped out the area in detail, trying to estimate my chances of dodging the gunfire should I be spotted.

The machine-guns mounted on the watchtowers were always at the ready but I was still very tempted to take my chances. I was discouraged by an old, experienced prisoner nick-named 'Boxer'. A Jew from Chestochowa, he knew the district well.

'Mark my words, boy,' he said. 'The moment you get into that forest,' he pointed his finger in the direction of the trees, 'you're a dead man! Here, you're still alive. Mind you, the bastards could still shoot us at the last moment and none of us would get out. Still, as long as you're alive, you have hope. But if the machine-guns don't get you out there' — again he pointed his finger — 'the Polish partisans will. Or the villagers and the peasants. They're just as bad. You look too Jewish; they'd give you away as soon as they set eyes on you. One way or another, you're a dead man.'

I never took the chance.

The winter came with frost and blizzards. The forest, as if petrified, was wrapped in a white fairy floss, hardly visible at all when it was snowing. It was my fifth winter behind barbed wire;

my sixth under the threat of German guns, and just the thought of it made me shudder. The cold was a terrible punishment, harder to live with than starvation.

Five in the morning and the familiar metallic ringing signalled another day. Waking up was extremely difficult as, the moment I opened my eyes, reality hit me. Accompanying their actions with foul and obscene language, the barracks orderlies shouted and beat the inmates. Through every waking second, the harassment never ceased. From time to time, in the middle of the night, the half-crazed Blockaelteste would get drunk and we would have to address him as 'Herr Oberleutnant Kurt Bayer', saluting in military fashion instead of our customary doffing of the prison cap. God help the prisoners who mistakenly neglected the salute.

Kurt Bayer beat prisoners for the sheer entertainment of it. There were many times when the wails and screams of inmates resounded through the barracks and, at these moments, my thoughts turned to my mother for courage, her last words never far from my conscious mind: 'Remember! Remember you must search for your brother'. My determination to survive was strengthened.

I had hardly shut my eyes when the metallic ring shook me out of my sleep yet again. Every time I woke up, my heart-rate intensified when I realised where I was.

From the frosty, windswept roll-call ground we could see that the entire landscape was covered with snow: an angry winter at its peak. The temperature was always somewhere between eighteen and twenty-five degrees below zero.

Six a.m., and five hundred living corpses were lined up for another day, another battle. An icy, hounding, blistering wind whistled through the electrified wires, echoing with the cries of baying wolves on the prowl. Every morning I wondered: 'Will I make it through the day?' And, as we waited to be checked and counted, we were frozen to the marrow of our bones. With pale, grey faces, and eyes sunk deep into their sockets, we must have looked as though we had all donned death masks to disguise our human appearance.

During those first days on the building site, the Kapos and Vorarbeiters clubbed the prisoners mercilessly. At night, totally exhausted, we passed the gates into the camp, some of us limping, some injured and having to be helped by our fellow inmates. We looked like a bunch of beaten dogs.

A glimpse of humanity

The second week, Helmut appeared on the building site. Observing from a distance how the Kapos and Vorarbeiters were treating the prisoners, he made some notes and, at night, sent his messenger, Heniek, a young boy from the Warsaw ghetto, to summon the Kapos to his office. He lined them up and, making them stand to attention, gave them a cautionary speech.

From Heniek we learned that Helmut had expressed himself with remarkable forthrightness and humanity. Apparently, he told the Kapos that we were worn out after five years in the Lodz ghetto, while those in positions of power in concentration camps had had it comparatively easy. To conclude his speech, Helmut had asked them to lessen the beatings.

'I'm asking you to slow it down,' Helmut reportedly demanded. 'The way they look and the way you are treating them, they will not last very long. I am cautioning you as fellow prisoners to have a bit of consideration or else I will deal with every one of you individually.'

The Kapos had apparently complained bitterly at such treatment, offended by the way Helmut had spoken to them. Besides, they claimed that the Lageraelteste had no right to interfere with the duties of the Kapos. Helmut silenced and dismissed them.

Only the Oberkapo stayed back. He had been a member of the German Communist Party before Hitler's coming to power and had been locked up in a concentration camp in the early thirties. They had a long and heated discussion during which the Oberkapo tried to explain to Helmut that the new arrivals were green and needed a little training to realise that they were in a concentration camp.

With scant patience for this point of view, Helmut cut him off, insisting that the Kapos calm down and lessen their beatings. Somehow the two managed to reconcile their differing points of view and proceeded to have a friendly conversation. According to Heniek, Helmut offered the Oberkapo coffee, and the two of them sat and talked for a long time. On the following day, the Kapos and Vorarbeiters were less aggressive and, although the beatings continued, they were not as vicious as they had been in the beginning.

Helmut certainly had the welfare of his fellow inmates at heart. He strove against great odds to reduce the violence and brutality, and kept a close check on the distribution of food. From time to time, he would even conduct surprise inspections of the barracks, searching for food that had been hidden from the prisoners by the Stubendiensten.

One night, after the soup had been ladled out at Block No. 3, Helmut came upon a concealed bucket full of potatoes and barley. The Stubendiensten had saved it for themselves, doling out the remaining grey, watery soup to the inmates. Immediately, Helmut distributed the thick and more nourishing contents of the bucket to the prisoners in the barracks, reprimanding the Stubendiensten in front of the other prisoners, and warning them that the next time they would be harshly punished.

The days dragged by interminably. I was always glad when night came, but our exhausted sleep was so brief that each awakening almost seemed a crueller fate than the day which was to follow it. Almost.

'*Aufstehen, aufstehen!* Run, wash; *los, schnell!* Swallow, gulp; stand to attention!' The yelling and swearing, punctuated by the most filthy insults, never ceased. Then morning drill: 'Fall in, line up, attention, hats off!' I would thrust my chin out and straighten my shoulders as Blockführer Olschlager passed, counting the prisoners. Roll-call over, we would line up in our columns of work units, ready to march.

The pious Oberscharführer

On this particular day, my commando was assigned to work outside the electrified fence and continue clearing the stumps of trees which had been felled. Before we moved out, we were briefed by the Oberscharführer in charge of the SS guards: 'Attention, prisoners and beware! Today you are working outside the camp perimeter. The slightest move by any of you, one step outside the limit to the left or right, and you will be shot!' We knew very well that these were not idle threats. On outside duty, the SS shot first and asked questions later.

We soon dragged our feet across an open field, sinking knee-deep into the snow. The wind rose, penetrating my thin, striped denim. I was fortunate to have stolen a discarded paper bag, now empty of its cement, which I wore as a vest under my shirt; while it was a great insulator, it was also a most dangerous garment.

Whenever a prisoner was caught wearing one, the penalty was twenty-five lashes on the backside. After such treatment, it was virtually impossible to sit down or to lie on one's back for many days. A large number of prisoners did not survive it.

The Oberscharführer in charge of the SS guards was a man in his fifties, of medium height, slim and slightly stooped, with a long, skinny neck featuring a hyperactive Adam's apple protruding from the collar of his uniform. He was a tense and nervous old man, constantly angry, shouting and pushing. His submachine gun was slung around his neck and his finger twitched on the trigger. He would walk around the camp, jabbing prisoners with the weapon's cold, hard barrel. Although I tried to keep away from him as best I could, from time to time he still managed to inflict a few bruises on my rib-cage.

It was mid-December, 1944. The winter was harsh and angry, like all the eastern European winters I had spent in the ghetto or the camps. I was starved, underweight and poorly dressed; the frost was a punishment, so painful at times that it drove me to tears. As a child before the war, I had loved the winter with all its excitements: ice-skating, tobogganing, building snowmen with my brother and friends; but during the years of my captivity, winter was a nightmare. The starvation was painful, nagging day and night, yet one could grow accustomed to it and use its pain as a spur to survive. The frost, however, was brutal, seeming somehow to hasten death.

I kept on the move, working all day long, not because I was eager to please, but because the alternative was to freeze to death. Some prisoners did. Hardly a day went by without a few corpses being carried back into the camp at night. It felt like Siberia out there. Whenever I took a deep breath, the frost made my nostrils stick together.

At night, after a long day of hard work, we were given a hot greyish liquid with the occasional vegetable floating in it. The barley and potatoes were still usually eaten by the Blockaeltesten, Kapos and the orderlies. With another cup of the suspect black liquid — the only saving grace of which was its warmth — our quota of calories for the day was filled.

That day, working in the middle of an open field, the cold wind was unbearable. My vision was blurred by tears, and the frost bit my nose and ears. My hands were purple, and my fingers and toes were frozen to near immobility. At times, the numbness was so complete that I felt paralysed. Suddenly, the sound of a gunshot cut the frosty air. I heard the Oberscharführer yell: *'Halt das Feuer!'* ('Hold your fire!') In the distance, I could see one of the inmates stumbling in the deep snow, clumsily struggling to run. Emaciated and totally exhausted, the fugitive could hardly move. Having lost his wooden clogs, he was desperately dragging his bare feet through the icy whiteness.

The old SS man shouted at the top of his voice: *'Stehen bleiben! Stehen bleiben!'* (Stay standing.) Again and again he shouted, but the bundle of striped rags kept stumbling on in the direction of the forest. He moved like a drunkard, lurching, falling, picking himself up and wobbling forward again. The SS man gave chase, somehow managing to move very fast; he was very fit. As he caught up, the prisoner fell.

'Get up,' shouted the SS man, standing over him and waving his arms. 'Get up!' The prisoner refused to move, so the SS man tried to pull him up, but could not.

It was the strangest scene. I could not believe that the SS man did not shoot. Finally, he allowed the prisoner to lie in the snow, standing over him, pointing towards the sky and talking volubly and incessantly. After a while, the prisoner did manage to struggle to his feet, but he could barely stand. The SS man supported him, and the two started back towards us. As they came closer, I recognised the 'Dutchman'.

A Jew from Amsterdam, he had been the registrar in the central camp of Auschwitz concentration camp — death block No. 11, the barracks where prisoners were kept without food or water for twenty-four hours to reduce their will to resist just prior to gassing. There, he and the Oberscharführer had first met. At the time, the SS man was only a private, serving at the gas chambers. His duty was to don a gas-mask, open the Zyklon-B canisters, and empty them through the openings in the ceiling. As a reward for eighteen months devoted service thus spent, he was promoted to the rank of Oberscharführer and put in charge of the SS guard at Althammer. And every evening, after a long day's gassing of Jews at Auschwitz, the pious Oberscharführer-to-be never missed prayers in the chapel.

As the two struggled to rejoin the unit, the SS man helped the Dutchman to sit on a boulder, the latter collapsing with his head hanging between his knees. His hands, purple and swollen from the frost, were limp. The Oberscharführer opened his knapsack, took out his sandwiches and offered them to his 'friend'. The Dutchman sat motionless. The SS man insisted that he take the bread, but still the Dutchman did not move. Suddenly he fell into the snow. The SS man pulled him up, sat him back on the boulder, supporting him so that he would not fall again, and began to berate him in near hysteria:

'You are a sinner! You are a sinner! Pull yourself together. Are you crazy? Eat the bread. You're a sinner! Suicide is a sin! God will never forgive you!'

The Dutchman made no response. The Oberscharführer then ordered us to begin gathering firewood. He lit a fire and we timidly moved closer and closer, incredulous that he did not object. The Dutchman slowly came to, and began chewing the bread in a clumsy manner, the crumbs falling out of his mouth as we stood around watching. My mouth was watering with every bite he took. I repeated his movements as if I were eating. His near-frozen jaws seemed hardly to move; his swollen face became suffused by a strange colour. Even amongst the dead he would have looked terrible. His skin was covered with mushroom-like blotches, and his feet and shins had the wounds of anthrax, oozing pus and blood.

The SS man melted some snow in a container, heated the water and gave it to the Dutchman who dribbled it down his chin and onto his striped vest, where it froze instantly. The SS man kept repeating: 'You are a sinner. Suicide is a sin. God will never forgive you!'

Suddenly, the Oberscharführer straightened his bent body and pointed his long index finger towards the sky. He spoke with the deep voice of a preacher.

'You! All of you! You are all sinners! You are a sinful people! You Jews have sinned against God and God is punishing you! He deprived you of your country. He dispersed you all over the world amongst all the nations to be the eternal wanderers, punished for shedding the innocent blood of the Redeemer — an unforgivable sin! You are the Christ-killers! And for His innocent blood you will pay forever. I know too well that you suffer, and suffer a lot. Nobody in this world can help you. Neither can I. I am only doing my Führer's will. I serve him faithfully because his will is God's will. The Führer is God's messenger, his servant! The Almighty has sent that man to lead the German nation! He will lead us to victory, to a world free from sin. Not until God orders the Führer to forgive the Jews for their unforgivable sins, not until God forgives you for the innocent blood of Jesus Christ, will you ever stop suffering!'

Suddenly the SS man stopped; he had run out of breath. His eyes had the gleam of a hunger-maddened wolf, but his cheeks glowed pink with excitement. We stood in silence.

'Is he human?' I wondered. He looked like a human being, but was he? Had I heard right, or was this an extension of the nightmare I was inhabiting? To this day, I ask myself those questions.

After the sermon, the prisoners remained motionless and expressionless, only their eyes indicating their amazement. One of the inmates muttered, 'He's a madman, a real madman. He should be locked up in a mad house.'

The voice of another interjected: 'We are *in* the mad house, guarded by crazy people!'

'No, ' said a friend of mine softly, and his whispered remark would haunt me forever. 'He's not crazy. That's how they all are. And don't you know? This is how the world always was. How do you think we got here?'

Christmas at Althammer

Long days followed, each one a mirror of the last. The freezing, blistering winds never stopped. The skin on my hands was cracked and my parched lips bled. Every day was a battle to make the dragging hours pass. The constant lining up, the running, loading, unloading, shovelling sand, carrying logs, bricks and parts for the steel structure all had to be done at such speed that our battered bodies protested, yet still managed somehow to perform. At times, I stood for hours in liquid cement up to my ankles, in temperatures that were below zero, trying to spread the heavy mass evenly under the steel structure day in and day out. And all this was done under a hail of clubs swung by the Kapos and Vorarbeiters, themselves always under the watchful eyes of the SS who constantly wielded their machine-guns. In the relentlessly slow passage of time, I never knew the day or the date, except when Christmas came; then the German engineers and technicians were given the day off to celebrate. This was the first time after many months that I could locate myself within a framework relevant to the world as I used to know it.

The morning of 25 December 1944 began with the usual routine. Heniek, Helmut's messenger boy, was beating the morning alarm. Speeding back across the snow-covered roll-call ground from the icy wash-house, I rushed into the barracks wiping myself with my shirt as best as I could, pulling it over my body and allowing its dampness to dry as I wore it. We lined up for the morning ration. No bread? No coffee?

'Raus, raus! Los, los!'

We were made to assemble in the freezing cold, stamping our feet to keep the blood circulating. Helmut stepped forward. 'Attention! *Mützen Ab*!'

The Blockführer Olschlager counted us. Tom Mix the Lagerführer was in good spirits, the morning schnapps having rushed the blood to his face, making his head look like that of a freshly baked pig ready for the Christmas table. His triple chin overhung the stiff collar of his uniform, and matched his fat face to perfection. Dressed in his blue-grey dress uniform, his long pants pressed with knife-sharp creases gave him the look of a man cut from an immense piece of stone. Olschlager clicked his heels: 'Heil Hitler!' The morning *spiel* continued.

Although we waited in suspense, the order to form work commandos never came. Tom Mix wore the cynical smile that usually meant he was in a dangerous mood. He walked up and down in front of the prisoners as if on inspection. Something evil was brewing in his mind as we stood stiffly, afraid to breathe. With the inspection over, he limped back to his stand — the limp, a legacy from the Russian front where he had served with the SS Panzer — and our apprehension increased. Tom Mix handed a note to Olschlager who in turn passed it on to Helmut. The Lageraelteste called out two prisoner's numbers at the top of this voice and two young boys stepped forward: twins from Block No. 3, not much older than seventeen or eighteen. I had known them from before the war when they had been neighbours of my uncle Yankev Bolshevik. Standing next to one another, one was slightly taller, and they both looked pale and drawn.

The Blockführer ordered them into the centre of the roll-call ground, facing Tom Mix. With a contemptuous smile, he handed his whip to the taller of the two, ordering him to flog his twin brother as a punishment for him wearing a cement paper bag under his shirt.

'Give him twenty-five lashes!' he barked.

The taller brother stood motionless, holding the whip in his hand. Tom Mix lost his temper.

'I will teach you! I will teach you!' he screamed and, angrily grabbing the whip, he hit the taller brother, leaving a bleeding welt across his face.

Once again he handed the whip to the prisoner, who still refused to move. Now Tom Mix lost all semblance of control. He grabbed the whip, bent him over, and whipped him with all his might. He kept it up until the poor fellow collapsed into the snow. Still raging, Tom Mix handed the whip to Olschlager who, in turn, unbuttoned his long military overcoat to give himself freedom of movement, and flogged the shorter brother. Olschlager perspired so much from the effort that steam rose from his face and body in the cold morning air. After their ordeal, the two boys were carried back to their barracks.

Whip once again in hand, Tom Mix cut the air with a swish. At the top of his voice he barked: 'Today is Christmas. You will be confined to barracks! No food! Food you get only when you work!' His agitation seemed to increase as he limped up and down in front of us, slapping his right leg with the whip. It seemed that his fun was not yet over.

He stopped in front of a short man with sparkling, very deep-set dark eyes and ordered him to step forward.

'Where are you from?'

'Marmaros-Sziget.'

'Hungarian?'

'Yes, sir.'

Tom Mix snapped at him. 'You are a *Schweinhund*! A dirty dog!'

'Yes, sir.'

'You are an Edd-yeck Medd-yeck!' Tom Mix mocked the Hungarian language.

'Yes, sir.'

'What did you do in Hungary?'

'I worked.'

'What sort of work?' snapped Tom Mix.

The prisoner hesitated. 'I worked as a singer,' he said eventually.

'And where did you sing?'

Once again the prisoner was momentarily hesitant. 'In the synagogue.' His voice seemed to be growing softer and more timid.

'Ah, the synagogue? What did they call you at the synagogue?'

'My name is ...'

'This is not what I want to know!' Tom Mix bellowed. 'What do they call a singer at the synagogue?'

'A cantor.'

'Well, cantor! You are going to sing the morning prayers for us.'

The confused man tried to smile, apologetically rubbing his throat and pointing to his mouth. 'I can't sing, I have lost my voice,' he stammered.

'You have lost your voice? Where did you lose it? You'd better find it!' Tom Mix waved the whip in front of the cantor's face.

Suddenly, Tom Mix unbuttoned the top of the prisoner's jacket and found a shawl around his neck. 'No wonder you can't sing. Just let me help you.' Tom Mix pulled out the coloured piece of material. 'Now you can breathe. On with the prayers!'

'Please, Sir, I can't. I can't, I've lost my voice,' the cantor begged, but Tom Mix would not take no for an answer. He wrapped the rag around the prisoner's neck and began to twist it, tighter and tighter until the face of the victim began to turn purple.

'Now can you sing?'

The poor man squirmed, hardly able to breathe. This game went on for quite a while until Tom Mix suddenly decided to dismiss the rest of us. We ran into the barracks, but the cantor remained on the roll-call ground as Tom Mix maintained his grip on him with the piece of fabric around his neck. Then, Tom Mix left the prisoner standing in the freezing cold as he walked off to have his breakfast. We in the barracks peered anxiously through the windows. Time dragged on as the cantor stood motionless. He was half-frozen when Tom Mix returned, a victim awaiting his executioner. Again the coloured piece of fabric was put around his neck and slowly, very slowly twisted until the prisoner turned blue in the face and fell to the ground.

Holding on to the rag, Tom Mix walked around the camp with his victim dragging behind. From time to time he stopped to check if the man were still alive. Struggling desperately to breathe, the cantor tried to rise to his knees, falling over into the snow as he lost his balance. Tom Mix twisted harder and harder, continuing to drag him like a heavy sack trailing behind him. He stopped, looked at the cantor and spoke to him. There was no reaction. He pushed the cantor's head with his foot; no reaction. The cantor was dead.

Smiling as he walked away, Tom Mix left him lying in the snow. His Christmas dinner was served on time. He had his rest, and was at church punctually for Christ's mass. Both Rabbi Yeshua Hanitzri — or Jesus of Nazareth, as he is known in English — and the Cantor of Marmaros fell victim to an old pagan tradition. They were both punished for their crime of being born Jewish.

The Lagerschreiber

Among the many characters at Althammer, Hertzog was perhaps the most remarkable of all. He was the 'Lagerschreiber', the camp registrar. In the concentration camp, some of the élite prisoners were called by their first names. Hertzog was an exception even to this, for he was addressed by his family name; but it was not merely this which made him so different.

He was a quiet, softly spoken, gentle person. In spite of his prison garb, he still managed to look dignified and striking. He must have been around forty-six or forty-seven, slender, of medium height with an erect posture. His thin, sculptured face with its beautifully proportioned aquiline nose, as well as his fine hands with their long and delicate fingers, all combined to give him the air of an aristocrat. Prisoners in the concentration camp had to have their hair cropped no longer than a quarter of an inch. We maintained it at the correct length by cutting one another's hair with clippers at least every second week. Hertzog's hair was silky and dark, with streaks of grey shooting through it. He was one of three prisoners at Althammer who had received a special exemption from the SS to keep his hair long.

By profession, he was a political journalist. In striking contrast to everybody, particularly to the camp élite, he was polite.

Although he was second in command to Helmut and wore stripes, I never thought of him as a prisoner. His personality set him apart from everyone around him. Spending most of his time inside Block No. I, where he had his bunk and desk, he worked all day running the administrative side of the camp for the SS. He exercised great influence over Helmut, whose attitude towards the prisoners was significantly less brutal than that of other Lageraeltesten.

We knew that Hertzog had been brought to Althammer from Monowitz-Buna but, apart from that, we knew little else about him. According to rumours, he had some very famous rabbis amongst his ancestors, but he himself was actually the product of a mixed marriage, classified as a half-Jew from Vienna. He never involved himself with the élite prisoners, nor did he speak to anyone except when he had to. He was something of a mystery.

He spoke only once to me. It was in the middle of the night, when a truck had arrived from Auschwitz with supplies that had to be unloaded. I will never forget how he woke me. He touched me very gently and I awoke to see his mild face before my eyes. Very softly he whispered, 'I'm sorry to wake you in the middle of the night, son. Forgive me, I had to do it. Please get dressed quickly and follow me.'

This was the first and last time in the concentration camp that anybody in authority spoke to me with such politeness and soft-ness in his voice. Hertzog always struck me as an angel who had inadvertently landed right in the middle of hell.

Helmut was another interesting personality. Of German nation-ality, he was a Bevauer who had spent most of his adult life behind bars and barbed wire. Superficially, he gave the impression of a hardened criminal but, inside, he was a man of warmth and compassion. His dark eyes sparkled with intelligence; his smile projected concern and kindness. The moment any member of the SS was present, his face turned sombre and angry and his voice became threatening, like the bark of a ferocious dog. He always put on a good act.

There were few, if any, Lageraeltesten — the highest-ranking prisoners in the concentration camps — who behaved towards their fellow inmates with as much consideration as Helmut did. Appointed by the SS, Helmut had authority over all the lesser wielders of power in the camp. According to regulations, every prisoner had to salute him, doffing his cap, clicking his heels, stating his prisoner, block and commando numbers, as well as what he was doing at that given moment. With Helmut, all these formalities were not necessary, providing the SS were not present. He was liked and respected by all the prisoners. The German camp élite, however, was not always as approving of some of his methods. Above all, he was not popular with the Kapos because, in their opinion, he interfered in their affairs.

Ultimately, Helmut was a person of integrity. Although he was a criminal who had lost his freedom, having been locked away in jails and in concentration camps for many years, he had lost none of what must have been an innate compassion. This made him a great man in my eyes.

Then there was Kapo Walther, also of German nationality and also a Bevauer, a criminal with a colourful past, to say the least. By profession he was a safe cracker, having broken into some of the most complex safes in the largest banks in Germany. Before he came to Althammer, he had been jailed in the most escape-proof prisons in Germany; over the years, he had managed a number of escapes, but none to date from the concentration camp.

Walther shared with us his prison wisdom and experience. He lectured us on how to preserve our energy and how to survive. He used to say, 'In concentration camp you work with your eyes; you use your intelligence, not your muscles. You only act as if you are working when the SS is watching.'

One day, as he lectured us at the top of his voice, an SS man came up behind him and overheard his advice. We tried to signal to Walther to shut up, but he did not realise what we were getting at. We tried whispering words of caution, but he was stone deaf from the beatings he had received during many police interrogations. His broken face resembled Auguste Rodin's bronze, *Man With The Broken Nose*.

The SS man gave Walther a terrible beating. He tore off his armband with the sign Kapo, and took him to the guard house where he was brutally beaten again, discharged from his duties as Kapo, and given a further twenty-five lashes on his backside. The following day Walther was put to hard labour under SS supervision, breaking up large stones with a sledge hammer from early morning till late at night.

Kapo Kutscher

One morning during the roll-call, Kapo Kutscher noted down the numbers of some particular prisoners. Mine happened to be one of them. It was simply the bad luck of the draw, but now I had become a member of his work commando.

One of the most feared characters at Althammer, this Kapo Kutscher was in charge of the constructing and brick-laying commando No. 9, which was erecting a building inside the camp to house the camp kitchen. He was tall, broad-shouldered and strong, the favourite of Tom Mix. Apparently, before Hitler's coming to power, Kutscher and Tom Mix had been next-door neighbours. Although they were both Germans, they had opposing political views: Tom Mix was an SS man, and Kutscher was a leader of the Communist Party. Kutscher was arrested and locked up in Hitler's early days, when the Gestapo, on searching his house, discovered a printing press and large quantities of forbidden literature in his cellar. Kutscher had been the editor of a communist newspaper.

The two former neighbours, whose political affiliations drove them to extremes, became political enemies. The one thing they shared, however, was an obsessive desire to kill Jews. Now that Tom Mix had become a concentration camp commandant and Kutscher his prisoner, they fulfilled their ideological imperatives — the commandant with his gun and the Kapo with the oak handle of a shovel.

Kutscher's favourite diversion was making speeches in front of the prisoners on the building site. His preferred topic was 'Judaism and the Old Testament.' Even though he was an atheist, he had an obsessive fascination with the Bible, and he loved making speeches. 'You Jews are a unique people,' he would say. 'Your devotion to and love of your God in the face of reality is an enigma beyond my comprehension.'

He spoke at length about Moses, his Ten Commandments, and about Jewish laws and ethics. In his opinion they were the pillars of modern, Western civilisation. 'You Jews,' he would continue, 'gave birth to the greatest minds that ever lived: Moses, Jesus, Marx, Freud, Einstein ... the list is endless. They left a deep imprint upon humanity.'

We were always glad whenever Kutscher was in a talkative mood. This made him ease off with his oak handle. To keep him going, prisoners made favourable comments and asked questions, complementing him on his knowledge and showing interest in his opinions. It was enough to ask him, 'What do you think of the contribution of the Jews to modern civilisation?' for him to oblige with one of his lectures.

'Yes my friends, the Jewish laws, the spirit of the people for freedom and justice were, from time immemorial, an inspiration in the struggle against tyrannical empires. You revolted against the ancient Greeks; you fought the Roman empire, but you were too small in numbers, so you were defeated. And strangely enough, although the Jews were devoted to the cause of freedom and justice, they never won the hearts of the enslaved nations. The dark masses let themselves be brainwashed by their oppressors, who blamed the Jews for their misery. The illiterate mob always believed them.

'For over sixteen hundred years, you've been victimised by the Church. They had an absolute hold on the masses and they turned them against you. The Church attached a dreadful stigma to you, slandering you as the Christ-killers, the children of Satan, users of Christian blood. You've been the eternal scapegoats, having the evil eye, poisoning the water wells, bringing the black plague. All disasters have been blamed on the Jews, and illiterate, superstitious fanatics have accepted it blindly.

'Nothing will change their attitude towards the Jews because they need someone to blame for all the wrongs and ills that besiege society. You Jews were always guilty. One way or another you were guilty, the eternal scapegoat. It matters not at all that you gave them the son of God, the ancient Hebrew scriptures their religion is based upon, the twelve apostles and the teachings of the prophets which are an eternal source of wisdom and justice. They still hate you because Christians cannot come to terms with history and their past!

'But my boys, listen and remember. All the ancient empires that were out to destroy the Jews finished up as dust, buried under the sands of the desert. All that is left of them is some broken pottery and gods made of stone and clay, and the rest you can read about in the libraries. The Third Reich will have the same end.'

From time to time, when Kutscher was in an exceptionally good mood, he loved singing a popular little song, *'Alles Geht Vorüber,*

Alles Geht Vorbei. Nach Jedem September, Kommt Wieder Ein Mai'. ('Everthing passes, everything comes to an end. After every September, May comes round again.')

He also had different verses which we all enjoyed singing when the SS was not around. *'Alles Geht Vorüber Alles Geht Vorbei. Erst Geht Der Hitler, Dann Seine Partei!'* ('Everything passes, everything comes to an end. First Hitler goes, and then his party.') But you Jews will go on living. You are an eternal people, the symbol of eternity.'

At times Kutscher got carried away with his loud voice, and acted as if he were speaking to massed thousands. It was the fashion of the time to emulate the Führer. He spread out his arms like an eagle in flight, holding onto his favourite oak handle from which he never parted.

Kutscher was loud and pompous. 'You Jews are the only true aristocrats, a nation of noblemen with an undivided devotion to God — a God who abandoned you. They are throwing you into the fires. They murder you in His name for His glory. The German people happily accept Hitler and his lies. What they don't realise is that the German banks, the steel industry, the large factories and German enterprise never belonged to the Jews. The German armaments and military power that caused the great disaster engulfing the world today had nothing to do with the Jews; but when Hitler blames them, Germany believes him.'

Kutscher was a typical example of a non-Jewish prisoner who had spent many years in concentration camps. In spite of his being well educated and knowledgeable, a man of ideals and intellect, he behaved barbarously towards Jewish prisoners. Although he spoke with great admiration about Jews, he could suddenly turn around and beat us to pulp. I was never able to work out what sort of a man he was; nor, I think, could the most skilled psychoanalyst. If it was a love-hate ambivalence, then his love for us made him an orator, while his hatred made him a murdering madman.

Listening to his speeches, I was reminded of the words of my uncle Yankev Bolshevik: 'There are good and devout communists who have no difficulty in being anti-Semites,' he told me in my youth. At the time, although I never had sympathy for communism, I was quite tolerant of Soviet Russia. It took a while for me to understand that Hitler and Stalin were alike, both leaders of evil empires, both murdering millions of people, and both of them anti-Semites. Not until Althammer did I fully understand Yankev Bolshevik's thinking. In Kutscher's voice, I realised, I was hearing the voice of the world, a sick world that could not cure itself of anti-Semitism.

Smuggling

Shortly before the New Year, Kutscher lined up his commando, looking everyone in the eye with a quizzical expression. 'Which of you is smart? Step forward,' he called out. There is no shortage of fools in this world; a few inmates stepped forward. Kutscher had fun with them, gave them a few knocks and dismissed them back into the line. Again he made his inspection, this time pointing his finger at a few specific prisoners, one of whom happened to be me. He ordered us to step forward.

'Listen carefully,' he declared. 'How would you propose to bring two, one-litre bottles of vodka into the camp without getting yourselves caught?'

Questioned one by one, none of the men volunteered a suggestion. As he approached me I hesitated, desperately unsure as to whether I should offer the scheme that was forming in my mind. Although I was scared, there was the chance that he might like my idea; that, as well, there might be some compensation at the end. Focussing on the possible piece of bread or those few potatoes, I brushed aside my fears. I did not even consider Tom Mix, nor that my mission might well be my end. When I suggested to Kutscher that I put the two bottles in a cement box and cover them with tools, he accepted my plan.

'Do you know what to say should they catch you?'

'Yes, sir. I'll say that I found them.'

It was then that the consequences of capture and discovery dawned upon me with full force.

The box was ready. It was so heavy that Kutscher had to help me lift it. Once it was on my shoulder, having made sure that my legs would support the load, I gathered all my energy and shakily started for the guard house. Olschlager was on duty. As he opened the little sliding window, I reported to him in my best German according to regulations. The Blockführer signalled to the guard and the gate opened. I could not believe my luck.

Suddenly, out of nowhere, Tom Mix appeared, walking straight towards me. My heart seemed to stop. As he closed in on me, I dropped the load to the ground. He scrutinised it critically. It was my good fortune that the bottles did not break, and that he did not search underneath the tools. Before he had a chance to question me, I straightened up, clicked my heels and snatched off my cap.

'Prisoner B-8615, commando 9, I report obediently by the order of Kapo Kutscher that I am delivering tools to the building site.'

With his customary mumble under his nose, Tom Mix muttered, '*Weitermachen! Weitermachen!* Get on with it!'

I bent down, picked up the box and somehow managed to lift it back onto my shoulder without assistance. As I walked away, I could not believe that I was still alive. With my last breath, and with my heart racing painfully, I lowered the box onto the sand near the cement mixers. In the space of a moment, I slipped the two bottles into the sand pit and sat on top of them, trying to catch my breath. I had had many encounters with the 'Malekh Hamovess', the angel of death; but this had been one of the closest. I am still not sure why I risked it. No man in his right mind would have done what I did. And for what? I did not even know what I would get for risking my neck. But starvation is a painful experience; it can drive a man to take insane risks. Fear is a powerful motivator as well. How else can I explain lifting the heavy cement box full of tools onto my shoulders without help?

Kutscher appeared soon after, but he would not come near me for a few days. From a distance he snapped, 'You just made it by the skin of your teeth. Where are the bottles?'

'I buried them in the sand.'

'Take them to Block No. 7 and hand them over to the Blockaelteste.'

Although I was inside the camp, I still had to be cautious not to be caught at the last moment. The Blockaelteste, expecting the delivery, gave me a whole loaf of bread which I pushed under my jacket, bidding him goodbye with a big '*Danke Schön*.' Back at my commando, I discreetly enjoyed my wages of fear and, by the time we were discharged into the barracks, the entire loaf had disappeared. The safest place for the bread was my stomach.

The following day, Kutscher still kept his distance, but managed to communicate that I should go back to Block No. 7. There, the

Blockaelteste gave me a large sausage, approximately two kilos in weight.

'Nobody must see what you have,' he cautioned, 'and remember, should they catch you, you know the answer, don't you?'

'Of course,' I said with a smile, 'I found it.'

'You are a lucky devil, you just made it,' he said. 'Run along and enjoy the sausage; but remember, nobody must ever find out.'

The bonus was far beyond my expectations. I ran to my barracks, hopped onto my bunk and slipped the sausage into my mattress, deep within the wood shavings. The moment I left, Kurt Bayer came along, having noticed me from a distance. There was another prisoner inside the barracks who had not seen what I was up to. When Bayer questioned him, the prisoner said fearfully, 'Sir, he was cold. He came to warm up. I told him to leave.' Bayer searched my bunk but did not find my treasure.

At night, before the lights were switched off, I ran along to see my friend Marek Bialkower, a Stubendienst at Block 5. When I asked him who would be the best to trade sausage for bread, he pointed to a German Kapo. 'He's a bastard but he won't cheat you.'

I spoke to the Kapo and made the deal: two loaves in exchange for half the sausage. As down payment, he gave me half a loaf, and the balance in three lots within the next few days. Before New Year's Day arrived, the bread and sausage were gone and my festive nights were over.

Fortunately, on New Year's Day itself, the German engineers and supervisors were not given a day off. As a consequence, we worked and got our food ration. The day did not go uncelebrated, however: the management of the company we were slaving for gave every prisoner three cigarettes as a New Year's present. This was a gesture of great generosity that had never happened before; nor did it happen again. It was not too difficult to trade my cigarettes for bread. There were always some prisoners who would rather smoke.

Tom Mix and the man from Glowno

In the years of my captivity, I witnessed terrible scenes of sadism and plain, cold-blooded murder. What I found so remarkable was that those committing the murder did it with such ease. Tom Mix was one of the most callous killers I ever came across. Whenever he was in my proximity, my heartbeat increased, making me lose my breath. For him to kill a prisoner was an amusement, a kind of game. His sombre, expressionless face, perpetually wearing its mask of depression, would only light up with a grimace that faintly resembled a smile when he fired his Luger. His grumpy moods and the way he mumbled made me very nervous. Whenever he spoke to me I panicked, afraid that I might misunderstand him and provoke his anger. It was impossible to predict his reactions.

He constantly roamed around, sneaking up when least expected. He would stop prisoners at random and search them, and would beat them up for the slightest transgression, write down their numbers, and flog them on the roll-call ground in front of all the other prisoners. Flogging at Althammer was a daily routine. He once stopped and searched a Kapo, a Jew from Warsaw, by the name of Tamborin. Finding a packet of tobacco on him, Tom Mix gave him a savage beating and then hit him over the head with the butt of his hand gun. In addition, he punished him with twenty-five lashes on the roll-call ground.

One day, my commando was assigned to unload a train-load of bags of cement, each one weighing fifty kilograms. To carry such a load on snow-covered ground was risky, as well as being a task beyond the capacity of most prisoners. We were all worn out and looked like walking skeletons. Suddenly, as if from underground, Tom Mix appeared, his face wearing its habitually miserable expression.

At the top of his voice he demanded, 'What sort of work is this! Where do you think you are! Kapo! What goes on here!' Even more loudly he barked, 'Two bags of cement per prisoner at a time! *Los, los! Schnell, schnell!*'

I was in the queue to take my turn when, in front of me, an inmate who could not sustain the load dropped one bag. The bag burst, spreading its grey powder over the white snow, and Tom Mix exploded with fury. His Luger was immediately out of his holster.

'Sabotage! Sabotage! I will shoot you like a dog!'

With his drawn gun, Tom Mix ran after the prisoner until he had unloaded the second bag that remained on his shoulders, poking him in the ribs as he tried to run back for the next load. Tom Mix pushed him over to the side, yelling insanely, 'Stop here! Next prisoner pick up your load! *Los! Weitermachen! Weitermachen!* Continue!'

The prisoners followed one after another. One actually stepped out of the queue. '*Herr Lagerführer,*' he pleaded, 'I cannot, please, I cannot carry two bags.'

Tom Mix barked at him, '*Kannst du nicht oder willst du nicht? Ich helfe dir gleich!*' ('Can't you or won't you? I'll help you straight away!') He pushed that prisoner — a man so emaciated that he could hardly stand on his feet — to the side as well.

My turn came. I braced myself, taking a deep breath as the second bag settled on my shoulders. Every bone in my body felt as though it were cracking under the tremendous weight. I have never, before or since, carried a 100-kilogram load on my back. My legs were shaky. All I could think of was Tom Mix's index finger on the trigger. Moving with caution, I tested my first step. With all my willpower I concentrated on sustaining the pressure that came down from the top, making me feel as though my thighs were penetrating into my pelvis. I took a couple of steps. It worked. I moved slowly and carefully, my legs and knees trembling. With every additional step, I gained confidence. 'Yes I will, I must, I must.' I kept encouraging myself. 'Keep going! Keep going! You can do it. You can do it.'

I was glad when the load came off my back and that, by the time I walked back for my next round, Tom Mix and the two 'Muselmänner' had left. (This was a name, which literally meant 'Moslems', that we gave to prisoners who were so skeletal that we knew they were close to death.)

On the way back to the camp, Tom Mix shot dead the prisoner who had dropped the bag. The second one he put to cleaning the camp latrine, amusing himself by kicking him as he knelt scrubbing the floor. When I entered the latrine the next day, the poor man was crying in fear. 'I'm in trouble, I'm in trouble. He'll shoot me. I'm a dead man. Help me! He comes in here threatening me that he will shoot me.'

I tried to cheer him by reassuring him that, had Tom Mix really intended to shoot him, he would have done so yesterday. 'You'll see,' I told him, 'one day you'll laugh when you remember it.'

'Do you really believe that?'

'Of course I do. We'll both have a good laugh about it.'

I knew I was lying. What else could I do? What does one say to somebody in such a situation? The following day, his body lay outside the latrine, waiting to be picked up by the supply truck from Auschwitz on its daily round. At the back of his head was a bleeding wound.

I had known him from school vacations that I had spent at Glowno, a Jewish shtetl in the vicinity of Lodz. Although I do not remember his name, the vision of his swollen, yellow face with eyes full of fear is still in my memory as I write these lines. His words still ring in my ears as he cried, 'Do you remember me? I am from Glowno. I remember you as a school boy when you came with your grandmother to the market place holding onto her hand. What happened to us? What happened to the German people? What happened to the world?'

Evacuation from Althammer

The dreaded clanging of the frost-covered piece of steel on the roll-call ground brought another night to an abrupt end. I always awoke with a thumping heart. The mere thought of the snow-encrusted, slippery scaffolding suspended high above the empty, wind-blown stretches terrified me. The waking moments were the hardest to cope with when reality intruded upon sleep. In the depths of my soul I wondered whether this nightmare would ever end. The shouting of the barracks orderlies soon brought me back to reality. This was not the place nor the time for contemplation. I had to run, run for my life; be alert and watchful. There was no time for thinking. Thinking was dangerous, even deadly: it could have driven me to madness or suicide.

'*Aufstehen, aufstehen! Los, los! Alle raus!*' Run, run for your life.

Back from the freezing wash house, we lined up to collect our ration. The tiny piece of bread lasted but a few moments. I swallowed it before I had time to appreciate its taste. Only when I finished eating did my hunger pangs start to nag with a painful persistence. It was always when finishing the last bite that the craving for food was fully aroused.

We were lined up on the roll-call ground waiting for Tom Mix in the vicious frost of the lingering night. The striped skeletons stamped their feet to keep warm. I felt the angry wind piercing my face, ears and limbs with a million needles. We seemed to stand there for a long time, waiting without knowing why. The Kapos and Blockaeltesten were gathered in small circles, whispering. Something mysterious was afoot.

The last few nights, the horizon had been lit with flashes that had become brighter with each passing night. The thundering noises of the approaching front line were becoming louder and more frequent. In the distance, we could hear the heavy thuds of the artillery fire. In the middle of the night, we heard the roar of aeroplanes flying above our camp. Flares came floating from the sky. They looked like Christmas trees hanging upside down with hundreds of glowing lights, drifting towards the ground, illuminating the dark night with the brightness of lightning. Bundles of silver foil would also come floating down from the sky, dropped by the aircraft to confuse the German air defence.

And still we stood, freezing to numbness, waiting for Tom Mix. Olschlager was walking back and forth with a nervous expression on his face. After a long wait, Tom Mix finally appeared. The roll-call routine was brief. Helmut stepped forward to announce, 'Attention, prisoners! Today you will not go to the building site.' He discharged us with the remark, 'Stand by for further orders!'

The window panes on the watch towers were pushed wide open. The heavy machine-guns were moved forward, their barrels poking through the gap. The SS were tense, their short submachine guns slung over their necks at the ready. A group of Kapos tried to strike up a conversation with one of the guards on a tower, who responded by pointing his gun at them with a loud click of the safety catch. The Kapos dispersed.

Tom Mix came back into the camp and, once more, we were lined up. Without raising his eyes he announced: 'Today you will be evacuated. Those prisoners who are not fit for long marches, step forward.' Nobody moved. Again he repeated, 'Prisoners who are in no condition to sustain long marches need not fear. Nothing will happen to them! They will be allowed to stay back in camp. They will be provided with food.' His assurances had no impact.

We stood on the roll-call ground awaiting further instructions but, when the order came to march, no food ration had been issued. We left the camp, soon joining up with long columns of prisoners evacuated from the surrounding concentration camps. These columns seemed to stretch for miles without end. Exhausted, emaciated, starving shadows of humanity, with eyes sunken deeply into their skulls, scarecrows with their striped rags flapping in the wind, they dragged their feet through deep snow across the windblown fields.

From the inmates we met, we learned what had happened in other camps: on 7 October 1944, the Sonderkommando at Birkenau had staged a revolt, blowing up one of the gas chambers and a crematorium, thus killing a few of the SS team. I was told how the dynamite had been smuggled into the camp and passed on to the Sonderkommando by a group of girls who had worked at the Auschwitz ammunition factory. After the liberation, I actually met some of them in Bergen-Belsen and heard the story in detail.

The revolt had been short-lived: the SS staged a massive counter-attack, assisted by the local German army garrison which was stationed in the district. Two hundred and fifty prisoners managed to break out from the camp, after which a brief gun duel followed in a nearby forest. The overwhelming strength of the Germans brought the resistance to a swift end, with most of the prisoners falling in battle. Only a few were brought back to the camp and hanged.

I knew neither the day nor the date of our leaving Althammer, until one of the prisoners plodding alongside me said, 'Today is a lucky date; it's the eighteenth of January.' He was referring to the fact that the alphabetical equivalents of the number 'eighteen', when written in Hebrew, are a *chett* and a *yudd* which, together, spell the word, *chai*. In Hebrew, *chai* means 'life'. For us, however, the eighteenth of January 1945 marked the beginning of a journey that was to leave a trail of death across Upper Silesia, Czechoslovakia, Austria and Germany, as well as leaving ineradicable imprints on the minds of all those who survived it.

To keep the highways free for the German army, we were forced to march in knee-deep snow across the fields, without food or water, leaving behind a trail of blood and urine. Night fell, and we were marched on through all the hours of darkness. In captivity, I had learned many strategies for survival; now I learned another: to sleep whilst marching, helped by comrades who supported me under the arms. This we took in turns so that eventually all had a chance to rest. Anyone who stopped or stumbled was shot, which meant that we had to urinate as we marched.

Twenty-four hours had passed since we left the camp: another day began. We marched on non-stop, harassed by SS guards, and without food and water. In one sense, we were fortunate that it was winter, for there was an unlimited supply of snow. It became our only sustenance. Dragging our feet through the depths of it across the fields, sinking into it until we lost sight of our knees, we hauled each other onward whenever one of us fell. We knew that if we did not support one another as much as possible, we would all perish.

The second day drew to a close without our having passed one village or settlement. They were leading us along a route designed to avoid the civilian population. After a gruelling thirty-six hour march, they stopped us at Nikolajew, a Polish peasant settlement in Upper Silesia. We were allocated barns in which to sleep. The Russians were not far behind, their artillery pounded the Germans relentlessly. At night, approximately thirty to thirty-five miles from the front line, we could see the fires of the battle. The German army was in turmoil, leaving behind its own wounded while the SS held on to us with great determination; but the obsessive counting of the prisoners had stopped.

The Death March continues

After a few hours rest, we were chased out into the early morning frost to continue our march: destination unknown. It was 20 January 1945. A glacial wind almost blew our feet out from under us, piercing our faces, ears and toes, and making our hands purple and swollen from the cold. We were barely dressed, our striped denim offering no protection against the bitter winter. We were lined up on the snow-covered country road, stamping our feet, clapping our hands so as not to freeze to death. Those who stood motionless turned purple, and collapsed. A bullet in the neck put them out of their misery.

Suddenly, three prisoners climbed out of one of the barns and came running to join the ranks. Amongst them was Emile, the orderly from Block No. 2 at Althammer where I had been housed. A Frenchman from Paris, Emile was the son of Polish Jewish migrants, and his slight knowledge of Polish might have saved his own life and the lives of his friends. They had been trying to hide in the hay, with no intention of rejoining our march, but Polish peasants had put paid to their scheme.

Emile was furious. 'You wouldn't believe it unless you saw it,' he exclaimed. 'They came at us with hay forks. I was nearly perforated. They meant business. Unbelievable! I've never seen savages like that. Crazy people! Why would they want to kill me? They don't even know who I am. Now I understand what my father was trying to tell me about the Poles and their obsession with Jew-hating.'

The peasants had emerged, swearing with anger, 'The place stinks of Jews. Those bloody Jews are a curse. We'll never get rid of that rotten plague.' The Blockführer, SS Obersturmann Olschlager from Althammer, stood next to me watching the scene.

'They're crazy,' he said. 'They're real *schmucks*!' As they joined the ranks he abused them. '*Schmuck Schticks*! Idiots! Why did you come back? You should have stayed where you were. You would have been free within a few hours! Don't you see what's going on? You stupid shit-buckets!'

But Olschlager was no angel; I had, in fact, seen him shoot many prisoners. An ethnic German from Romania, he was a ruthless killer. On the building site at Althammer, he had walked up to a prisoner one day, a Muselmann who could hardly stand on his feet, and abused him for having ears that were supposedly dirty. The prisoner was a French Jew, a medical student from Paris; and Olschlager, picking up some snow and rubbing the prisoner's head with it, mocked him:

'Let me give you a wash, you dirty Jew!'

When he had had enough of playing with his victim, Olschlager took the young prisoner to one side and shot him in the neck.

'That will teach him to keep clean,' he chuckled. Tom Mix stood smiling nearby as he witnessed his subordinate's heroic action.

The motivation behind Olschlager's sudden friendliness and concern was obvious. If the Russians were to catch up with us, he was hoping for a word or two from us in his defence.

After a long wait, the order came to march onward. Standing was a painful punishment, and I was glad to be on the move again; but to be struggling once more in the deep snow for endless hours, with prisoners collapsing everywhere, made me wonder about the relative merits of marching. We had to watch our step not to trip over the bodies that were strewn in our path. Those still showing signs of life were shot in the neck, their corpses then loaded on horse-drawn carts that followed at the rear. Neither food nor water was given. Only the snow and the will to live kept us going.

By the third day, we seemed to be marching aimlessly, getting progressively weaker with every kilometre. Suddenly, some prisoners began singing a Polish military march. The rest of us joined in, and its effect was magical in the way it raised our spirits. Most of the prisoners were Polish Jews, and we sang for a long time. As we ran out of Polish songs, we continued with Russian military marches we had learned from the Russian POWs. Ordinarily, this would have been strictly forbidden; but now the SS did not mind. They needed it as they, too, were getting tired — strong, well-dressed and well-fed though they were. They suffered no shortage of warm drinks and schnapps to boost their morale.

The third day without food was drawing to a close. We had no idea where we were. Driven off the beaten track in order to avoid settlements and country towns, we passed between artillery placements where I saw young kids, no older than fourteen or fifteen, in Hitler Youth uniforms carrying artillery shells and setting up rocket launchers. Eventually, late at night, we arrived at a familiar scene. Electrified wire fences, surrounded by watch towers and machine-guns at the ready, the gates were wide open as we were marched into concentration camp Gleiwitz III. Allocated to brick barracks, we were still given no food. Most of us fell, exhausted, to the concrete floor, lying one on top of the other, tightly squeezed together for warmth. I don't know for how long I slept, but it was still night when they woke us. '*Alle raus, alle raus! Schnell, schnell!*' We were chased out into the freezing cold. Day four without food and water was beginning. Once again, we had only our will-power and the snow to keep us alive.

We moved out in the middle of the night but, by early morning, they were marching us through the city of Gleiwitz. People were on their way to work carrying their lunch boxes under their arms. They simply stared. Not one person tried to help with food. An old woman standing on the porch of her house, horror in her eyes, made the sign of the cross, covering her face with her hands. 'Jesus Maria, Jesus Maria!' she cried.

With the rising of the sun, we were taken into the railyard on the outskirts of the town and loaded into cattle wagons. We were so tightly pressed together that we could hardly breathe. They counted us: one hundred and sixty-eight prisoners. Many hours passed, and still the train stood motionless. To cheer ourselves up we invented our own news: 'There are no locomotives. They are surrounded by the Russian army.' With no rational basis, our hopes began to soar. 'We may be liberated at any moment!' As darkness descended and the day drew to a close, they counted us again and again as though we were gold. A sudden jerk shook us out of our lethargy as the train began to move. So beguiled had I become by fantasies of liberation that the movement at once horrified me and made me desolate. Inside me, my heart was crying.

The Death Train

The Germans carried us off in front of the oncoming Russian army. We were transported through Czechoslovakia, Austria and Germany from one concentration camp to another — all of which were over-filled with evacuated prisoners from the east. Not one of them would accept our transport.

In my wagon were my school friends, Shalom Goteiner and Abraham Belzycki, whom we called 'Bella'. We kept close, supporting one other physically and emotionally. Dehydrated and exhausted, we craved water with an intensity that was becoming unbearable. My lips were parched, my tongue and mouth were dry. The thirst drove some of us to insanity, absolute madness. Prisoners drank their own urine. I tried it, swallowing a couple of sips, but it made me sick.

After a few days of travelling without pause, the train pulled up in the middle of nowhere, on an open, snow-covered field. We remained there, stationary, for a while; it was then that Shalom asked me to help him climb to the top of the wagon. Having hoisted himself up with the support of my shoulder, dish in hand, he begged the guard to fill it with snow. The SS man's response was to aim his gun at Shalom. His nerves — like the nerves of all of us — wearing thin, Shalom lost control.

'You criminals! You murderers! Your days are numbered! You will pay for this!' he burst out, shouting and waving his clenched fist at the SS man.

Instantly, a shot rang out, the bullet hitting Shalom directly. It seemed to tear off the entire left side of his face. Unconscious, he crashed down on top of me and, in a moment, I was covered with his blood. His wound was huge but there was nothing with which to bandage him. Bella and I tried to make a little room for him, arguing with the other prisoners, pushing them back, so that they would not stand on top of him. I actually got into a fight over it, but Bella broke it up.

'Leave it, Abraham. There's no use in fighting. He's dead.'

At the next stop, when the wagon doors were opened, the SS ordered the unloading of the dead. Just as Shalom's body was being thrown out, I heard him mumble, 'Leave me. Leave me. I will go by myself.'

I was shocked and incredulous that he was still alive. Bella and I tried to stop them from taking him, but they would not listen. They grabbed his legs and pulled him along. With his head dragging behind, he left a trail of blood in the snow. Then he was gone. In Hebrew, Shalom means peace.

Within our wagon, there were a few men I had known from back home. I had worked with one of them — a cabinet-maker by the name of Mendel Gelerman — in the Lodz ghetto at 9 Pucka Street. His younger brother, Alexander, had remained behind at Althammer, hardly having been able to stand on his feet. His face had been yellow and swollen from starvation.

Many years after the war, I met Alexander in Melbourne. 'Three days after you left the camp,' he told me, 'an Einsatzkommando turned up to finish us off. From my hiding place under the roof of a barracks I saw them come through the camp gate. They turned back to the guard house and spent some time on the telephone. Suddenly, Russian soldiers surrounded the camp. It was like a miracle. The Einsatzkommando panicked and fled. Two of them were caught and taken away. To this very day, I still cannot believe that I made it. But, for a long time, my liberation was no joy. I was too sick and exhausted. I could hardly stand, and just managed to drag myself to the nearest hospital where I collapsed. It was many weeks before I could walk again.'

Alexander's brother, Mendel, died in the cattle train, standing next to Bella and me. In his last moments he begged, 'Please help. *Rateve*. Abraham, Bella, save me, I'm dying. Please help me. Don't let me fall. *Ikh shtarb. Bite helft mir. Lozt mikh nisht faln.*'

He managed to say, '*Ikh shtarb*' — I am dying — once more before his head dropped for the last time, his mouth and eyes remaining open. I shut his eyes. That was all I could do for him. He died standing, with no room for his body to fall. His corpse stayed erect for some time, held up by the pressure of the people around. Eventually, it slid slowly down to the floor. Only a few minutes before he had been a human being; now he was merely a body lying on the floor, with others standing on top of him. A corpse did not matter much. Neither did the living.

The longer we travelled, the more aggressive and violent we became, and fights broke out for no apparent reason. Many prisoners became completely crazy from the thirst and attacked those standing near them. Beside me was a man I remembered from childhood, a most gentle Yeshiva student. He lost his mind. We were travelling across Austria and he decided that he had to get off the train. As he began to climb, I pulled him back and tried to reason with him, but he would not listen. I persisted because I knew he would be shot if I let him go. He drew a homemade knife, the length of a bayonet, from under his jacket. Bristling with hostility, he began shouting at me in Hebrew mixed with Yiddish.

'In the name of God,' he cried, 'let go of me or I'll cut your throat!'

I pleaded with him, 'I'm not your enemy, I'm a Jew, a prisoner like you. I'm trying to help you.' Amazingly, he trusted me and let me have his knife.

Over a few nights, we began to hear suspicious gurgling noises and, with the dawn, we would discover that some of the dead had blood coming from their mouths and noses, and bore blue-black finger marks on their throats and necks. They had been strangled to death. The following night we kept a vigil and saw that three Russian POWs were struggling with an inmate, attempting to strangle him for the tiny piece of bread he had hidden under his shirt. Their trial was brief, their execution swift. No more dead bodies with marks on their throats would be found.

The death train continued rattling along until I lost count of the days. Hunger is painful; thirst is worse: it drives one to madness. We scraped every bit of frost from the metal bars and, necessity being the mother of invention, we developed a method of gathering snow by suspending a dish from a rope while the train was in motion. The rope we fashioned from strips torn off the shirts of the dead.

Early in the journey we had crossed Czechoslovakia, where the population must have known we were coming. People were waiting on the railway overpasses and, as we went by, they threw food into the wagons. On their way to work, people threw us their lunches. The Czechs were brave and determined, ignoring the SS who were firing their guns. My wagon was out of luck; not one parcel landed in it.

I could not help noticing how different it was after we crossed into Austria and then Germany. There, no such gestures were made by the population. All they gave us were cold looks, our presence spurring them to anger, making them hostile and insulting. Instead of food they threw stones.

As we passed the Austrian Alps, I looked with wonder at the majestic snow-covered peaks reaching towards the clear sky. The little chalets down in the valleys were like pictures from a book of fairy-tales, their red roofs, white walls with green shutters looking like toys. Skiers were gliding down the slopes and the tall pine trees stood erect, covered in snow like soldiers wrapped in white fur coats.

The contrast was devastating. Here in the wagon people were dying, killing one another. They were delirious, half-crazed from dehydration and exposure. Only a few hundred metres away there were homes and people, warmth, food and water; there was life. Little villages were huddled together in the valleys with tall church spires towering above them. Did God dwell there? Was God nearby, in those churches, perhaps, and merely indifferent? Where were His servants, those preachers of love and compassion?

Was this God's will? Was there a God at all?

The problem of overcrowding lessened with every day as more and more corpses were transferred to the front carts. I was lucky they never chose me to load the dead, for it was a dangerous job: many were shot after they finished stacking the bodies. It was dangerous to do most things, even to get off to pass water, so we urinated inside the cart.

One day, as the train stopped in a siding, a locomotive moved slowly onto the line alongside us. Holding a hose connected to the boiler, an SS man sprayed piping hot water over the heads of the prisoners. As everyone tried to collect a little of it, a commotion broke out, with everybody pushing. I managed to harvest a few drops into a dish as it splashed out, burning my hands. Some of it ran up the inside of my sleeves and, desperate to retain the liquid, I did not shake it out. It scalded my skin, immediately creating blisters; then, within minutes, my wet sleeves froze, stiffly rubbing against the blisters on my elbows and forearms, making them bleed. But I had a couple of sips — my first water in many days.

For two days, our wagon could not unload its accumulated corpses, and we had to lie on top of them. The stench, mixed with human waste and blood, was sickening. Everything reeked of death; even the snow had a smell that was nauseating. From eating it I became ill and shivery, and I began to run a temperature. As time drew on, I became weaker and less aware of my surroundings. Lying on top of the dead no longer bothered me. Nothing mattered any more.

With every day, our wagon became emptier. Those still alive took the clothing off the corpses to keep warm. Soon they themselves would be dead.

9

Dora

IT WAS THE FIRST week in February 1945. Ten days had passed since we had been crammed into the cattle truck without food or water. I had spent most of the final two days of the journey in a stupor from cold, hunger and dehydration. I was too weak even to gather snow as the train rumbled onward. In our wagon, Bella and I were the sole survivors from Althammer; the carriage was almost empty. From the one hundred and sixty-eight prisoners who had boarded at Gleiwitz, only fourteen or fifteen were still alive.

Finally, the hell on wheels pulled up at its final destination. The grinding noise of the sliding doors shook me out of my lethargy.

'*Alle aussteigen, alle aussteigen! Los, los! Schnell, schnell!*'

I could scarcely stand: my legs refused to obey. There was no ramp, and I rolled out of the wagon, landing in the deep snow, where I lay, unable to rise. I saw the SS shooting those prisoners who were lying prone and helpless, and it seemed as though I must be next. But the adrenalin coursed through my body and, with my last strength, I dragged myself to my feet.

Seven or eight hundred metres ahead of me stood the gates. I stumbled forward with the last of my strength, but the distance ahead of me did not seem to be shrinking. All I could think of was that I had to keep going, keep going. I had to get there. That short distance felt like a journey of a thousand miles, but eventually I managed it. I was inside the camp.

But where was I? I kept hearing the name, 'Dora', uttered by various Kapos. It reminded me of a young girl, but there were no young girls anywhere in sight.

I was soon to find that Dora was a code name masking one of the most important secrets in Germany. For the moment, however, it was just another camp. But, unlike the barren flatness of Auschwitz and Althammer, this camp was in a valley, crouched against the side of a mountain. Later, I discovered that we were very close to the central-German town of Nordhausen.

We were directed to the bath-house. My face was burning from the cold; my feet and hands were numb and frostbitten; and my lips were parched and bleeding. I looked in at the window of the bath-house and, instead of taps and rosettes, I saw the reflection of a stranger. Who was this person, this corpse emerging from the grave, eyes deeply sunken, mouth and tongue black? I was covered in filth, blood and human excrement. My striped denim was saturated with urine, permeated with the stench of the decomposed bodies who had so recently been my travelling companions. The reek of it all penetrated deep into my pores, and for months the smell of death followed me as if it were under my skin.

The moment we entered the bath-house, the prisoners threw themselves at the water. Those who fell over never got up again: they were trampled to death. Others drank so deeply that the shock of it produced a heart attack. The floor of the bath-house was littered with so many corpses that there was no alternative but to walk on them.

We were kept endlessly in the bath-house while we were shaved, disinfected and showered. Finally, in the middle of a frosty night, we were chased out, naked, to stand totally exposed and barefoot in the deep snow. It felt like walking on hot coals, the pain of which made the prisoners hop. After a long wait in that darkest of cold nights, we were given our prison garb. It had come out of a steam boiler and was still dripping wet. We helped one another to wring out our clothing, and pulled on the wet garments with great difficulty. Within minutes, the material froze to our bodies. Finally, we were counted and marched off to the barracks.

I was assigned to Block No. 136. Although I was glad to be under a roof again, the barracks were hopelessly overcrowded: the inmates lay three or four to a bunk designed for one. Fights broke out between Russian prisoners, who were in the majority, and the others who were weaker. The Russians ganged up against the rest, pulling them off their bunks so that only those with stronger fists retained their places while the weaker had to sleep on the floor. This, too, became complicated, as the passages between the bunks had to be kept clear so that the barracks could be patrolled. The orderlies came down the passages with their truncheons, striking those prisoners not fortunate enough to have found themselves a bunk. One alternative was a spot under a bunk, but this was not the best place as some prisoners were extremely ill and could not control their motions. I found a corner on the floor.

It seemed that I had hardly slept at all before I was woken again at five a.m. *'Alle raus! Schnell!'* Within minutes, we had to clear the barracks and run towards the huge, snow-covered roll-call ground. Outside, thousands of prisoners were lined up and we were made to stand in a blistering frost till late at night. Many fell over from exhaustion while others froze to death. After fourteen hours of standing to attention, we were made to run back to the barracks.

We lined up to collect the ration — a slice of bread and some black, warm liquid. It was our first food in fifteen days. In the dormitory, the prisoners waged a war against one another. Where the law of the jungle ruled, I learned fast to defend my rights. Only the fittest would survive. I found Bella and the two of us joined up with other inmates to secure our bunks. With our clogs and shoes, we fought as hard as we could. Anyone who tried to pull us off the bunks was hit over the head. I learned an extensive repertoire of Russian swear words which I was soon able to reel off without difficulty. Only brute force and coarse vulgarity were valued. Those who could pound and curse the hardest were respected.

Registration

Following a long battle that second night, lights were switched off; then, after what seemed like only moments of repose, the orderlies were chasing us out into the frosty night again. This time they took us to large offices where we were lined up in long corridors for many hours. Other prisoners were registering the new arrivals; when it was my turn, I registered as an electrical engineer, on the advice of a Polish prisoner who worked in the office.

'Tell them you're a qualified electrical engineer or else they will send you to Ellrich,' my new-found Polish friend told me. 'What a shame you look so Jewish, otherwise I might have advised you to register as a Pole. Maybe you should declare yourself a Gypsy. At Dora, it's very bad for Jews; they don't last very long. Ellrich is even worse. That's where new tunnels are drilled. You're dead within a few days.' Tunnels? I still had no idea what the tunnels were for. Mines? Railway tunnels?

The registration took the rest of the night. It was a re-admission to the human race. When we had left Auschwitz, we had been recorded as leaving for an unknown destination. Our existence had, for the purposes of the meticulous German records, been cancelled. Those who had died on the train had not been identified or recorded, simply joining the endless lists of those who disappeared without trace during that infamous period.

Those of us who had survived now had to have our existence un-cancelled; a new record, a new name. Mine was 107,978. My Auschwitz name, B-8615, was tattooed to my forearm — and still is — but to the administration of Dora I was a new creation, 107,978.

At daybreak, we were lined up on the roll-call ground, and I was assigned to Sawatzki Commando 147. Beside the main gate of the camp, there was assembled the camp's brass band, which struck up a cheerful military march. In a place where atrocities beyond imagining took place, the Germans forced the emaciated musicians to perform, and we had to march past them in time with the music.

Before they were brought to the concentration camps, these musicians had been members of the renowned opera, theatre and symphony orchestras of Europe. Now, thirty-five to forty of them, dressed in striped prison garb, were standing by the roadway, a band of living corpses, playing the swaggering marches of Berlin and Vienna for a march-past by a regiment of ghosts.

The secret of Dora

We tramped out of the gate and down to the railway tracks. Here we turned left and marched along the tracks towards the side of the mountain. Two tunnel mouths gaped at us from under a roof of camouflage netting. From the air, it would have seemed that the railway tracks simply terminated at the base of the mountain.

We were directed into the right-hand tunnel. As we entered, we were met with a sight which defied belief. The tunnel stretched away into the distance (over two kilometres, I was later to discover), brilliantly lit throughout its length. A railway track ran down the right side; a wide roadway ran down the middle, on which electric vehicles ran smoothly and silently. On the left side

was a conveyor belt, on which the products of this bizarre underground factory were being assembled. Near the mouth of the
tunnel, an overhead crane was taking the completed products and
transferring them across to freight wagons on the railway.

It was not difficult to guess what the product was: it was clearly
a missile, and the stubby wings and rocket-like motor indicated
that it was self-propelled. I soon came to know it as the V1,
'Vergeltungswaffe 1', Retaliation-weapon 1. The name was significant: they were Hitler's great hope for victory or, failing that, at
least retaliation for the damage being done in air-raids on German
cities.

Numbered boards down the conveyor belt indicated the positions to be occupied by each commando. Commando 147 was in
the final assembly stage, and my job was to install just one component into the virtually completed missiles. The components arrived, like all other components, on the electric trucks, and were
offloaded and stockpiled at workstation 147. My job was to insert
a box into a cavity in the side of each fuselage as it passed slowly by
on the conveyor, and fix it in place with two bolts. The next member
of the commando then connected some wiring, and a third fixed a
cover plate over the cavity.

The spanners I used were the finest precision instruments I had
ever seen, made of chrome steel and perfectly forged to fit the
heads of the bolts. They were equipped with ratchets to cut the time
required for tightening the bolts to the absolute minimum, and
each stage in the job was perfectly timed so that it was just possible
to complete it before the missile reached the end of my workstation
and moved into the next. The production rate had to be maintained, as failure to keep up was an act of sabotage. Sabotage was
punished by immediate execution by hanging.

Precisely what I was installing I was not told. However, I was
told to be very careful not to drop or jar the boxes in any way.
Sounds from inside the boxes suggested that they contained radio
receivers, from which I concluded that they were the guidance
systems. This has since been confirmed, though the sounds I heard
were probably those of an operational gyroscope rather than a
radio.

Once again, there was music. The camp symphony orchestra
was installed beside the main road in the tunnel, playing a Mozart

violin concerto. A few metres away, in one of the side chambers, three Russian prisoners were hanging from the steel superstructure, executed for some alleged act of sabotage.

The reference to tunnels which I had heard earlier now became clear. Some time later, when I was imprisoned in the Bunker with Russian prisoners, one of them gave me more detail about the conditions at Ellrich. Ellrich was the base for the construction of extensions to the tunnel system. The prisoners were expected to sleep in the damp and dusty tunnels where the drilling of the rocks was taking place. When one shift ended, the next carried on. Sleep was impossible, as the blasting of the rock, together with the constant vibrations of the compressors and jack hammers, never abated. The trains came and went, carting rocks and constantly ringing their warning bells. Because there was no electricity, carbide mining lanterns were used. There was no ventilation.

Worst of all was the total absence of protective clothing: the prisoners were given no helmets, and hundreds of them were injured by falling rocks. Neither was there a sick bay. The injured were not treated and, in most cases, were condemned to die from infection and loss of blood. Ellrich prisoners had no latrines. Instead, they used the barrels in which the carbide was delivered, thus spreading a terrible stench. Such miserable food rations as existed had to be brought from Dora and, at times, it never even arrived. There was no drinking water, but prisoners were always wet from the water dripping from the rocks.

At Ellrich, the prisoners saw no daylight. Those few who survived had damaged vision; for most, death was their salvation. They were replaced by a continuous flow of fresh victims from the countries under German occupation. There was no shortage of slaves to drive the German war machine: Poles, Czechs, Belgians, Russians, French and Dutch, and Italian soldiers from General Badoglio's army who had refused to fight with the Germans. Amongst them were the last Polish Jews who had survived the Polish extermination camps; but the majority were Russian prisoners who were treated like the Jews.

The V2 underground factory
After a short time, I was transferred to Kommando ZBV, which stood for 'Zubesondereverfügung'' ('to sundry assignments'). It

was moved around all over the tunnels to work wherever reinforcements were required. In this way, I came to see most of the underground factory.

If the first tunnel looked like an elaborate set from a science-fiction film designed by a mad director with background music by Mozart and Beethoven, the second tunnel was a realisation of a nightmare. The second tunnel was the assembly factory for the V2, the first long-range military rockets.

It is difficult for me to describe my reactions to our first sight of these monstrous weapons. I had of course seen bombs and shells before, some of which seemed to be of obscene size. Compared with these, the V1 had looked menacing enough; but the V2 rockets looked totally diabolical. The diameters of their bodies were large enough for me to stand up in them. Resting horizontally on their cradles, their fins towered above our heads to the height of a two-storey building. Standing vertically on their fins, which they did in other parts of the tunnel, they stood as high as a five-storey building. The prisoners next to me were equally shocked, hypnotised by the sight. I heard whispers: 'Germany will destroy everything and everyone on this earth. These monstrous bombs will flatten the world.'

We now know that the rockets were less devastating than they appeared. Most of the size and weight was devoted to propulsion; the actual warhead was approximately a tonne, the same as the V1, and much less than the bomb-load of each of the hundreds of Lancasters, Halifaxes and Flying Fortresses which were by then raiding German targets around the clock. But a one-ton nuclear warhead would have changed the face of the war.

The rocket factory was under the management of Albin Sawatzki of the Mittelbau Gesellschaft. The Germans had hollowed out the Mount Kohnstein and had built a vast industrial complex inside for the production of secret weapons. Construction had begun as early as 1933, with Hitler's coming to power, when Germany began to arm itself, preparing to take over the world.

Each tunnel was initially eight hundred metres long and was wide enough to accommodate one railway line, a road for trucks and, beside it, the assembly lines. There were eighteen side chambers. The drilling continued until the tunnels were extended another eighteen hundred metres and housed a total of forty-six side chambers. By the time the factory was in full production, tunnels A and B were nearly three kilometres long, fourteen metres wide and ten metres high. Some chambers even reached thirty metres in height; these were the ones used for the testing of the immense V2 missile.

Air pumps supplied a constant change of air, the temperature of which was an even eighteen degrees centigrade above zero. Electrical generators installed in the tunnels supplied the power and — an unheard-of luxury — the toilets were beautifully finished with white tiles and kept very clean.

The V2 was developed from a prototype called A4, which stood for 'Aggregate 4', meaning Device 4. It was designed by the brilliant young professor Werner von Braun. On 3 October 1942 he successfully launched the first V2 missile, which marked a turning point in the history of modern warfare. The V2 was the first self-propelled missile to break the sound barrier, roaring into the sky above the Baltic Sea in a 185-kilometre test flight. It fell only four thousand metres short of its target.

Professor von Braun played the leading role at Dora in the mass production of his invention. He was the chief executive, managing the technical side of the production, and was thus deeply involved in the brutalities and misery which destroyed thirty thousand lives. A devout member of the Nazi Party, von Braun, together with the blueprints of his invention and his technicians, was taken to the United States by the American authorities immediately after the defeat of the Third Reich. Von Braun and his team all worked and lived in luxury, the professor becoming one of the chief technical designers at Cape Canaveral, where he continued to design the ballistic missiles and outer-space rockets for NASA. Werner von Braun was never tried for his crimes against humanity; neither was any of his staff. They lived as free citizens of the United States, showered with wealth and honour.

The V2 missile became the hope and promise for the realisation of Hitler's dream of world domination, injecting new hope of German victory after their disaster at Stalingrad when the invincible German Panzers began to lose the Blitzkrieg.

The components were made in factories all over the Third Reich, with several sources for each so that production would not be curtailed by the loss of any one factory. The parts came together at

Dora, under the protection of a roof of hundreds of metres of granite, the most bomb-proof factory in the world. The railway lines within the tunnels were linked directly to the German railways system. As the wagons were loaded, they were covered in tarpaulins to conceal their cargoes, and then despatched directly to their destinations in northern France, Belgium and Holland, well within range of London.

After a number of reconnaissance missions to photograph the area, the Allied air force bombed the factory area in late February 1945, only managing to damage a few structures on the surface. I was not even aware of the bombing until after I emerged from the tunnel, but even I could see that the raid had had virtually no effect. The factory was installed too deeply under the rock, and was beyond penetration: within, we had heard nothing. The sum total of the damage was a few large craters and some fallen trees; after two air raids, the Allies concentrated on bombing the railways and highways. The underground factory was beyond their reach.

The air raids aimed at the disruption of transport became so prevalent that they prevented us from changing shifts. We had to go on working until it was safe for the next shift to make its way across and come to relieve us. Those who were in camp were marched back to the barracks.

The camp
Dora was surrounded by two electrified fences with guard towers manned by the SS holding heavy machine-guns at the ready. They patrolled the tunnels and the surrounding factory grounds with Alsatians — huge, vicious beasts specially trained to hate the sight of those dressed in prison garb. They never growled at German officers nor at those dressed in civilian clothing.

The camp was about seven hundred and fifty metres from the tunnels. Green weatherboard barracks, in which tens of thousands of starved prisoners were crowded like cattle, were spread over the mountainside and down the valley. With the arrival of the evacuees from the east, the camp population swelled from sixty thousand to one hundred and fifty thousand, filling the barracks well beyond their capacity. According to information from prisoners who worked at the 'Arbeitsamt' (Labour Office), at times the numbers reached well above two hundred thousand.

Dora had all the facilities of the most efficient German concentration camp. The crematorium was well-run, dealing swiftly with its daily intake — victims of cold, disease, starvation and execution. The high mortality rate made room for the constant stream of new arrivals.

As in other camps, the operation was in the hands of privileged prisoners. To boost their morale, Dora had a sports ground, a swimming pool, and even a brothel. The girls were recruited from female concentration camps. For a little extra bread and soup, they accepted their fate and hoped that it would save their lives.

Dora had no gas chambers. Instead, a huge barracks, known as the Kino Barracks — the Cinema barracks — was employed, filled to capacity with thousands of dying prisoners incapable of work. The Kino Barracks served as a warehouse for prisoners to be stored until they joined the Himmelkommando (that is, died). They were hardly fed, and were left to lie for days without water until they died. There were no bunks. Thousands of prisoners lay on straw mixed with excrement and urine, the straw rotting under their bodies. To get to my block, number 136, I passed the Kino Barracks twice a day. Unfailingly, I would see a fresh stack of corpses in front of its wide open gates.

My cousin Mendele found himself in the Kino Barracks at one stage. He and I had actually run into each other on our arrival from the east, but we had hardly recognised one another. He had come to Dora from the 'Furstengrube', a coal mine in Upper Silesia. On his arrival, he was a Muselmann, having lost half of his weight. He seemed shrunken to the size of a child, and I remember thinking that he would not last very long.

He had been placed in Barracks No. 137, adjacent to mine. However, this had become infected with typhus and diarrhoea, and had consequently been quarantined, its windows and doors boarded up, reminiscent of the Dark Ages. Nobody was allowed out and nobody volunteered to go in. The prisoners were left without medication, without food, condemned to die. Soon after, in the middle of the night, Mendele escaped with two other prisoners, breaking away the planks that sealed the windows. The only place they could escape to was the Kino Barracks.

He told me the Blockaelteste was a crazy criminal who trampled the prisoners as he walked, swinging an iron bar and hitting them over the head. This was his chief amusement, usually at night before he retired to sleep, when he would go on a killing rampage with the help of the orderlies. By a stroke of good fortune, Mendele escaped from this hell, too, because a Kapo wanted to use him as his personal tailor. The Kapo gave him accommodation in his barracks, where not only did Mendele have a bunk to himself, but a blanket and a pillow as well.

This barracks was only for the camp élite. Referred by the Kapo to the SS officer in charge of the laundry and clothing store, Mendele was given a job as a tailor and set up in a workroom where he catered to the needs of the SS officer alone. This miracle saved his life. From that day on, he had plenty of food, more than he could eat. He gave the surplus to his friends, unsuccessfully searching for me amongst the prisoners in order to share his bounty. Eventually, he gave up the search — it was almost impossible to find somebody in Dora, among the multitudes of prisoners — and concluded that I had most probably been sent off to Ellrich or Nordhausen, Nordhausen being another concentration camp in the vicinity.

The most frightening place at Dora was the Bunker, the jail, 'The House of No Return', where prisoners were locked up in small overcrowded cells. They were kept there for weeks for the purposes of interrogation, at which time the SS carried out their most brutal tortures. Many prisoners died during the interrogations. Others were beaten beyond recognition and left to die in agony. The fortunate ones were put out of their misery on the gallows, but their fate was the prerogative of the individual interrogator. Every SS man was the master of life and death, and could do with the prisoner as he chose.

Arrest and interrogation

The camp and the tunnels of Dora teemed with informers, some of whom were prisoners recruited by the SD, the security service. While SS officers disguised as prisoners worked in the tunnels, the German 'Abwehr' — military counter-intelligence — had its own independent network of agents working as technicians. Every move of every prisoner was under constant surveillance.

Among many 'crimes' a prisoner could commit was to be found in the possession of money. The camp regulations, printed in large block letters in every barracks, stated:

THE POSSESSION OF REICHSMARKS AND FOREIGN
CURRENCY IS STRICTLY FORBIDDEN. THOSE IN
POSSESSION WILL BE PUNISHED BY DEATH.

In practice, the punishment was worse than death. Possession of
money was seen as *prima facie* evidence of connections with the
outside world — that is, espionage. So being caught with money
meant a one-way ticket to the Bunker: interrogation and torture,
with execution as a merciful release at the end.

The informers were instructed to take particular note of any
evidence of possession of money, and supplied with goods for sale
to gain the evidence.

I had made a new friend at Dora, David Garfinkel. David told
me he had some American money, and I confided to him that I had
200 Reichsmarks. In fact, I had 2,200 Reichsmarks, which I had
found one morning under the table when we were waiting to get
our daily rations. The notes had been wrapped in a sock, probably
thrown away by a prisoner who realised that in Dora they could
only buy the noose.

David said he knew someone through whom we could buy
food. The person in question was a prisoner from Czechoslovakia,
approximately our age, about eighteen or nineteen, who worked as
a lorry driver. David was the first to make a deal, paying with a
couple of American bank notes. As well, he still managed to retain
a couple of American gold coins and some gold teeth from
Auschwitz. Although very young, David was an old and experienced prisoner, having survived two years in Auschwitz and
sundry other camps. I trusted his judgement.

I was naive enough to believe that the money would help me
buy some food. Eventually, late one night, after many days of
waiting impatiently, I received a small parcel from David that
contained four cigarettes, a few lumps of sugar, a few pieces of
dried fruit and about twelve sweet tea biscuits with the English
inscription 'Canada' in the centre. The biscuits originated from Red
Cross parcels intended for the prisoners who, of course, never saw
any of them. The tea, coffee, rice, chocolates, sugar and other
delicacies no longer available in Germany were enjoyed by the SS.

With great excitement, I unpacked my parcel as I sat on the bunk
next to Bella. The moment he noticed the imprint on the biscuits,
Bella remarked, '*Abraham, du bist oyf groyse tsores. Du bist a*

farlorener.' ('You are in big trouble. You are lost.') I realised I was. It hit me like thunder. Too late to regret my foolhardiness, I gave Bella a few bits and pieces; although I was worried, I ate up the rest, retaining the four cigarettes which I thought I might trade for bread. Then I lay back on the bunk. I could not go to sleep. Of all the sleepless nights, this was one of the worst.

Sure enough, early next morning they came looking for me. I was picked up in the tunnel by a patrol of four SS men, led by an Oberscharführer from the SD. I was suspected of spying and being connected with organised sabotage. They paraded me along the centre of the tunnel as if I were a most dangerous criminal, the crunching noise of their jack boots drawing the attention of the prisoners working at the conveyor belts. Their sad, knowing eyes followed my progress towards the exit. Bella, in the middle of fastening a rocket to an electric crane when he noticed me, became confused and forgot to lock the arms. He pressed the button, the bomb rose above his head, and inevitably it came crashing down onto the conveyor belt, missing him by a only a few centimetres. He was lucky that the rocket did not suffer damage or he would have been hanged on the railing structure above his working place.

I was never involved with any underground espionage or resistance group. I had no connection with spying for Allied Intelligence, as was suggested by my interrogator. In the Bunker, I discovered for the first time that organised espionage was, in fact, going on, and that there were four groups in existence operating independently of one another: Polish, French, Russian and Czech networks. Their objective was to pass information to the Allies and sabotage the production of the rockets. There was also a group of German political prisoners whose task it was to organise self-defence and be prepared for the final showdown at Dora. It was common knowledge among the prisoners that the SS would eliminate us at the very last minute to wipe out all the living evidence of their abominable crimes.

Because our investigator was not, as yet, fully satisfied that he had extracted all possible information, David and I were held in the Bunker for further interrogation. Things looked very bleak. I was extremely fearful because I knew that nobody left the Bunker alive. The purpose of keeping prisoners there was to break their spirit, make them talk and extort any and all information possible. The moment the investigation was terminated, the victims were taken to the tunnel and hanged on the rail structure above the machine at which they had worked. Their corpses were left hanging for twenty-four hours so that they would be seen by both shifts.

My interrogator was a skilled and professional SS officer: he knew his vocation to perfection. On the left sleeve of his uniform he wore a narrow black ribbon with the letters 'SD' embroidered in silver, identifying him as an officer of the Sicherheitsdienst, the élite corps of the SS.

He was not very impressed with my story; in fact, he did not believe a word of it. The truth of it was that I had found the money under a table wrapped in a sock in Block No. 136, but the SD interrogator kept patiently probing, 'Tell me the story again. But this time you will tell me the truth.'

For the entire day and far into the night, I kept repeating exactly what I had told him before. Eventually, I lost count of the number of times I said the same thing over and over again. At a small desk behind me, a man dressed in a striped prison outfit typed every word I said on a shorthand machine. I became completely exhausted, hardly able to sit up in the chair. Finally, the SD man stopped the interrogation.

'I like you,' he said. 'You're a clever young man. You're too intelligent not to comprehend that you can't fool me with your fairytale of "I found it". I've been doing this job a long time, and I can't tell you how often that "I found it" nonsense comes up. They all find things! Is it just luck? Tell me, 107,978, how come I never find anything? And where did you get the American dollars? I hope you are sensible enough to realise that you are in a very precarious situation. Remember, I am your friend and I would like to help you, but you must help me or you might find that I can be very hard. Be sensible, my young friend. Tell me who the prisoners were who gave you the money and what you did to get it.'

'I found it under a table wrapped in a sock in Block 136,' I repeated dully.

'Show me your hands,' he said suddenly. I obeyed.

'Now move your fingers,' he ordered. Once again I obeyed, but cautiously, not sure of the reasons behind his request.

'Does it feel good?' he asked.

'Yes, Herr Oberscharführer,' I answered.

He then brought a bookbinder's hand press over to his desk. When I saw its two metal plates with spikes protruding from both the upper plate and the base, my tiredness gave way to renewed fear. He ordered me to put my hands on the lower plate, but I was too frightened to obey.

Calmly he kept repeating his order until, at last, trembling, I complied. Very slowly, he began to crank down the upper plate, gradually reducing the opening. In panic, I pulled away my hands and, once again, he made me put them back. I shut my eyes and screwed up my face and waited for the pain. But, although I did not realise it at the time, the SD man was only playing with me, the way a cat may tease a mouse he has caught and is not yet ready to eat.

The game continued for quite some time until, without warning, it stopped and he ordered me to get up. My legs were so wobbly that I could hardly stand. The room seemed to be going around in circles.

'It's been a long day,' he said. 'Go back to your barracks and report to me early tomorrow morning. I hope you realise that I'm offering you my friendship. Should you decide to be *my* friend, I will take care of you, I will look after you and I promise that you will never be hungry again. Think it over. Tomorrow I expect to know who gave you the money and who organises the sabotage in the tunnel. It's not difficult. You just have to give me their numbers.'

I was about to leave when he called me back. 'Look at him,' he said, pointing to the man seated at the typewriter. 'Remember his face, take note of his number. Very early tomorrow morning you will go to Block No. 6 and give him the numbers of two prisoners who are involved in organising sabotage. Those two numbers will save your neck. If you do as I say, you won't have to come back here. And remember I also promised you that you would never be hungry again. I am a man of my word. I always keep my promises.'

It was late at night when I finally returned, exhausted, to my barracks. Coloured spots seemed to be floating through the air in front of me, and my sense of direction was confused. As I staggered out of the 'Politische Abteilung', the Gestapo's political department in the camp, the first person I saw was David. My relief was short-lived, because he immediately began to abuse me, calling me a 'tzinker', an informer, and he accused me of having denounced him. My efforts to calm him were to no avail. All he seemed able to repeat was that the interrogator had told him that I was the one who had pointed the finger at him. Tired as I was, I refused to accept this indictment, especially after all I had endured.

'Where is the Czech guy who brought the parcel?' I demanded. 'Your supplier — where is he? Why isn't he in trouble? And how come my interrogator knew exactly what I should have had in *my* parcel? I received only four cigarettes and he actually told me that I should have been given six. Tell me David, who took the two cigarettes? You or the Czech? Don't you understand? Can't you see? This is a trap. That bastard Czech is a mole, an SS plant. They're trying to turn you against me so we'll fight each other. You think I'm a tzinker? Maybe I should accuse *you*!'

David was tired and nervous. The moment we entered the barracks, he called out angrily to the men, 'He is a tzinker. He denounced me to the SS.'

Without hesitation, they grabbed me and knocked me to the floor. Fortunately, Bella and another fellow — who had known me from our school days before the war — came to my rescue. By reasoning with the men, they stopped them from beating me. An informer was usually dealt with very promptly; in the morning, there would have been one more corpse on the heap outside the barracks.

'You'd better watch that Czechoslovakian guy!' Bella said to the men when they had all calmed down. 'Use your brains. He's the SS plant: he's the informer. Keep an eye on *him*. Why wasn't he even there to be interrogated? If they knew about David and Abraham, and questioned them, why not him? It only makes sense if he's the informer.'

The common sense of the argument caused their anger to cool and they all climbed onto their bunks as the lights were switched off.

That night I did not sleep. I told Bella about the interrogation and the Oberscharführer's proposition. The way I saw it, one way or another, I was a dead man. I had spent enough time in the Lodz ghetto and the camps to know what the Gestapo did with their informers. All night long, I tossed restlessly, thinking about my interrogator and what awaited me. I was scared of being hanged. I wanted to live more than ever. I had experienced fear many times before but never so intensely, never so agonisingly. When I spoke, Bella listened but did not reply. What could he say? Early the next morning we parted wordlessly, and I made my way to the Politische Abteilung. What concerned me most was that, in the course of interrogation, I might divulge the numbers of my friends.

Recently, I had given two hundred Reichsmarks to Franek, my Kapo, and another two hundred to his foreman, Jendrek. Fighters from the Polish Warsaw uprising, they were both decent men. Jendrek kept assuring me that he would get some potatoes, if I would just be patient, and Franek was trying to persuade one of the German technicians to bring him some food in return for the money. The two of them must have had sleepless nights worrying that I would reveal their identities.

Early morning I met up with David in front of the Politische Abteilung. We shook hands.

'David,' I said, 'I know they have propositioned you to work for them. They made me the same offer, but I'm sticking to my story. After all, I'm not hiding anything. I've told them the truth. There's nothing else we can do. We have to stick it out and hope for the best.'

We parted in the corridor as we walked towards our respective interrogation rooms. When I came into the room, my interrogator welcomed me with a smile, and ordered me to undress. I stood naked in front of his desk and saw that the press was just where it had been left the night before. He took out his pistol and laid it on the table in front of him. Again the same questions; again the same answers, endlessly repeated. Every time I looked at the press, the rate of my heartbeat increased, and it rose further still as I sensed that the Oberscharführer was becoming restless as he walked around the room questioning me relentlessly. Eventually, he stopped pacing and returned the pistol to its holster. Looking at his watch, he ordered me to stand against the wall with my hands stretched above my head, after which he simply left the room.

The man in the striped prison uniform behind the desk began to talk to me. In a friendly manner, he advised me to be sensible. 'Tell the truth. The Oberscharführer is a good man. He will take care of you. You will never be hungry. Don't be stubborn. Tell the truth. You will never regret it.'

'I told the truth,' I replied. 'I have withheld nothing. He thinks I am involved with espionage or saboteurs. I have no contacts. I don't belong to any group. I have no knowledge of espionage nor do I know who is organising sabotage. I have never participated in anything of the sort.'

The man stopped talking to me. I became dizzy and I lost my balance once or twice; standing naked with my hands up, facing the wall for many hours, was painful. Then I became very tired. My back felt as though it were breaking in two, and the room started to spin. When I put my hands against the wall to support myself, the man in prison garb told me off. 'Stand straight! Let go of the wall!' he ordered, so peremptorily that I suspected he was an SS man disguised as a prisoner.

Late in the afternoon, after many hours had elapsed, the SD man came back. Without asking me any further questions, he ordered me to dress and sit down next to him. He offered me a cigarette, lit it for me and watched as I became dizzy from the inhaled smoke, nearly falling off my chair. When I asked for a drink, he brought me a cup of water himself. He continued in this friendly and soothing manner. That was his style: he never hit me — he left the beating to the others — but he scared the life out of me.

He picked up his phone. I tried to listen in but he spoke too softly. Putting the receiver down, he ordered me to follow him, and we walked towards the Bunker. He put his arm on my shoulder. 'My boy, you are young and intelligent,' he said. 'You seem to me to be from a good background. Where are you from?'

'Lodz, Poland.'

'How is it that you speak German so well?'

'I learned it at home.'

'What a shame. I would have liked to help you, but you are of no help to me.' He spoke to me with regret, in a tone that was almost fatherly.

'Herr Oberscharführer,' I pleaded, 'I swear to God I told you the truth. I have nothing hidden. I am not a spy; I have never taken part in sabotage and I don't know of any prisoners who do. Please believe me. I beg you. Please! I am telling you the truth.'

He smiled at me. 'I'll send you for a little rest,' he said. 'There you will have time to think. What a shame. You are young, the spring is coming. Can you hear the birds singing? The sun will shine, but not for you. You, my boy will finish up high! *Du kommst hoch.'* He meant I would be hanged or go to heaven.

I pleaded, and begged him again and again: 'Herr Oberscharführer, please let me live. I have done nothing wrong. I want to live. I can still work. Please let me live. Spare my life, please.'

He simply walked on, saying, 'Now you are going for a little rest, and there you will realise that I was good to you. The others are rather a rough lot.'

Now, as I write these lines, I am happy that I withstood the pressure and implicated nobody. I was not a hero. I was filled with fear all the time because I wanted to live — and I wanted it so strongly that the force of it was painfully intense. I had tucked the balance of sixteen hundred Reichsmarks safely away between some rocks in the tunnel near the place where I worked. For all I know, they may still be there. David never knew exactly how much I had, and I never told him about Franek and Jendrek either, out of fear that perhaps he would weaken under duress and talk. How could I trust David? I did not trust myself.

The Bunker

The executioner met us when we were half-way to the Bunker. This gave me a terrible fright: I saw myself hanging in the tunnel above the conveyor belt. He was a German Bevauer by the name of Killian and had volunteered for the job when Kapo Kuntz, a former member of the Reichstag before Hitler's coming to power, had refused to do the hanging. For his disobedience, the SS broke each of Kuntz's fingers, one by one — probably with the same hand press with which my interrogator had terrorised me — and then took him to the Bunker, where he was savagely beaten and left to die in agony.

When he saw us, Killian obediently removed his prison cap, halting at the appropriate distance and clicking his heels together.

'You will take special care with him,' the Oberscharführer quipped. 'Be gentle; he is my friend.'

Killian was tall and slim with a red face and a hoarse voice. *'Jawohl! Jawohl!'* he kept saying as he walked a few feet behind us, heaving from side to side as he struggled uphill, wheezing asthmatically. I thought my own heart would stop beating from sheer terror; but I was given the chance, yet again, to learn that one does not die of fear, one only suffers the agony of it.

As we walked uphill, my mind seemed to fade in and out. I was overcome by a strange feeling, losing every notion of reality, as though I were in a trance. My eyes were open, I could hear and see, but my mind was blank and my body was numb — as though it were not mine. I had become aware of a similar sensation as I stood facing the wall for hours in the interrogator's office. Now, once again, transfixed in a nightmare from which there was no escape, some other self entered another world where everything stood still. I was completely detached from myself.

We walked up to the Bunker. The Kapo, a German criminal, welcomed me with an empty expression on his face. His name was Jumbo, and it suited his looks. Grabbing me by the collar, he pulled me through the gate, and I saw the SD man farewell me with a cynical smile as he turned and walked away, followed by the executioner. I was relieved to see them go. It seemed my end was not to be immediate.

I was taken to the guard room, and made to undress and stand in the corner with my face to the wall. I was not interrogated. Not much time elapsed before Jumbo introduced me to his professional boxing skills, using my face and my head as a punching bag. His nose was flat from the many years he had spent in the ring. He spoke with a muffled voice and, at times, he was hardly audible. At that moment, however, Jumbo was shouting. I could hardly understand what he was saying, but I managed to make out that he was upset because I had marked the wall with blood. Two SS men holding black electrical cables gave me a thrashing. I never got back my prison garb nor my shoes. All they gave me was a shirt that hardly covered my navel.

The two SS men escorted me through a long and narrow corridor flanked by iron doors with locks and long bolts to keep them secure. They pushed me into cell No. 18. The door slammed behind me, reverberating like thunder in the empty concrete space of the building. Jails have a sound of their own. The clashing echo of my exit being blocked sounded as though it had travelled from an alien space; the bolts were pushed into position with a clamorous grinding. Locked into a new world, I soon realised that life in concentration camp had had some merits.

David was already there, his face badly bruised and covered in blood, his eyes bloodshot and swollen, his upper lip split. We stared at each other in silence, but there was no room to move, no privacy to be had. Crowded on top of one another in a standard single cell approximately five feet wide by ten feet long, we were nineteen prisoners in all. During my imprisonment in the Bunker, I did not once stretch out my body. Although living skeletons don't take up much room, we could nevertheless only sit leaning against the wall with our knees drawn up. At all times, some of us had to be standing up. Consequently, we worked out a roster that enabled everyone to rest.

From the moment of our incarceration, David and I were disliked by the cell Aelteste, a German Gypsy, and his two German helpers. Our names 'David' and 'Abraham' did nothing to endear us to them, even though the Germans treated Gypsies the same way they treated Jews. Making us even more unpopular was our command of German. Our presence posed a threat to the three because we understood everything they said. Until our arrival, they had had absolute control over the fourteen Russian prisoners whom they had terrorised, robbing them of their rations. The Russians could neither speak nor understand even the most basic German words. Now we could interpret for them.

I don't remember how long I was locked up in the Bunker. In that dark cell, I lost count of time. At times I did not know whether it was day or night. The only thing that kept me busy was the constant physical abuse. The moment I came into the cell I was given a thrashing. It was probably my bleeding, bruised face that provoked the Gypsy to attack me, causing him to react like a savage animal to the smell of blood.

That was my formal initiation, immediately after which I was awarded the honourable position of 'Sheisskubelmeister' — master of the shit bucket. My job also determined my position in the cell: I had to sit on the big tin when it was not in use. Amidst the cell's bare walls and concrete floor, it was the only item of furniture.

The cell Aelteste informed us of the rules: 'Here, I am your Lord. For the first three days, you don't get any food. After that, you will miss your food ration every fourth day.'

By the second day, I was already familiar with the jail routine. Early in the morning, the light came on and the prisoners turned around to face the door, waiting for it to be unlocked. The moment it was opened, we charged forward like race horses released from a starting box, hardly waiting for the command, ' *Alle Raus! Los!*' The corridor leading to the washrooms at the other end of the prison was long and narrow. Lined up on both sides, holding rubber truncheons and rubber-covered electric cables, the SS whipped us mercilessly as we ran past. I was always last so as not to obstruct the others as I carried my large container — which had no handles — with inordinate caution for fear of spilling its contents.

The first couple of times I was very slow. By the time I got to the washroom I had collected lashes from every guard in the corridor. My whole body was covered in welts. I soon learned how to dodge some of the guards but the dogs were unavoidable. Going for my feet, they scared the life out of me. By the time I had cleaned and disinfected the container, I had to run back, having missed out on my chance to wash and, even more importantly, the chance of a drink I so desperately needed. Although drinking whilst washing was strictly forbidden, the prisoners disregarded the punishment and kept on drinking as the SS yelled, '*Trinken ist Verboten, Schweinhunde!*" ('Drinking is forbidden, you dirty dog!')

Roll-call followed our return to the cell. The cell Aelteste stepped forward, straight as a rod, and recited his own number, the cell number and the number of prisoners in the cell. The commandant checked the numbers and ordered the jail service to hand out the food rations.

I counted nineteen slices of bread, one slice for each prisoner; one dish of greyish liquid (which was the soup) per two prisoners; and hot, black, bitter water (which was the coffee). The portions in the Bunker were half the size of the camp rations. No spoons were given: we had to eat out of the metal plate like animals. I had to share my soup and coffee with David, who anxiously watched every sip I took, worrying that I might deprive him of a few precious drops of this fare. When it was David's turn, I watched him with equal anxiety.

Once the door was shut, the Gypsy handed out the food. David and I were not given any. At the top of my voice I started to shout, 'I want my bread! I want my food!'

Without a word, the Gypsy attacked me with the help of the two

Germans. One looked very Jewish, although he denied that he was; the other looked like a character out of a circus. His whole body was covered with tattoos from head to foot. Even his ear lobes had earrings tattooed onto them and, around his eyes, he had lines tattooed like a woman's make-up. I had never seen anything like him before. A hardened criminal, he had spent most of his life in jail, and was now under a life sentence, most probably for murder.

They continued beating me and I continued to shout: 'My bread! My bread! I want my bread! I am entitled to my food.'

'They will kill you. Be quiet!' David pleaded with me, begging me to stop.

I refused to listen. 'Unless we stand up for ourselves right from the beginning, we will be dead before they hang us.'

The Russians immediately reacted in my favour, encouraging me, calling out, "*Davay! Davay!*" Good on you, keep it up. They do it all the time! Every fourth day they deprive every one of us of a day's ration! We can do nothing! None of us speaks German! They steal our food all the time!'

As they beat me, I covered my face with my hands. 'I will report you! I will report you! I must get my food! In here, you are the same piece of shit as I am,' I shouted, still sitting on the container. They would not stop raining their blows down on me. In desperation, I started banging on the doors, my thumping on the metal echoing thunderously. This brought an SS guard, demanding to know what was happening.

'I want to speak to the commandant! I want to report to him personally,' I roared. The Gypsy and his cronies panicked, and immediately stopped beating me.

'You better shut up or else I'll deal with you!' the SS man cautioned us.

The next morning, at roll-call, the cell Aelteste stood to attention and reported according to regulations. When he had concluded, the commandant asked, 'Is there anything else to report?'

'No, sir.'

The commandant slapped his face, knocking him to the floor. He got up and stood to attention. The commandant asked again. 'Have you anything else to report?'

'Yes, sir. This dirty Jew,' he said, pointing at me, 'is a trouble maker.'

Without hesitation I stepped forward, obediently quoted my number, and requested permission to speak. The commandant nodded his head.

'Herr Kommandant, Prisoner 107 978, Cell 18,' I recited in my best German, in strict accordance with camp rules for addressing the SS. 'I report obediently that the cell Aelteste is stealing the prisoners' food. He refused to give me the ration to which I am entitled as a prisoner.'

'Are you the cell Aelteste?' the commandant demanded of the Gypsy.

'Yes, sir.'

The commandant hit him again. 'Are you in command here?'

'Yes, sir.'

'So you make sure this cell is trouble-free and is run according to the rules. Is that understood?'

With a red mark on his swelling face, the Gypsy stood to attention repeating, 'Yes, sir! Yes, sir!'

The commandant turned to the jail service. 'No food for Cell 18,' he ordered. Pointing his finger at the Gypsy he said, 'If you are unable to control this cell I will deal with you! There must be order!'

Once the door was shut and bolted, the three infuriated Germans started to abuse me, blaming me for the penalty. I sat on the bin in silence while the Gypsy, in particular, cursed and threatened me but, when they became violent, I spoke out.

'Unless you stop beating me, I will report you again,' I warned them. It was like magic; they stopped immediately. Still afraid, but with growing confidence, I persevered.

'From tomorrow on,' I told them, summoning every last ounce of courage, 'everybody gets his ration every day. You are not going to rob us of the food we are entitled to. If you try, I will report you again no matter what. You can beat me, but I will report you for that, too.'

'For God's sake, be quiet; they'll kill you! They'll murder you!' hissed David.

I ignored him. 'One more thing. From now on, during the day, the prisoners in this cell will talk to each other. You are not going to stop us from talking.'

In my limited Russian mixed with Polish, I translated to the Russians what I had said. They were all behind me and, quite unintentionally, I had become their spokesman. I was not looking to be a hero or a leader; I was simply desperate to survive.

From that moment, conditions in the cell changed. Actual speaking was out of the question as it had been forbidden by the SS; but, during the day, prisoners now whispered softly amongst themselves. The following morning, everyone received his food, and the stealing of rations became a thing of the past. The Russians volunteered to work out a roster to share the carrying of the container to the washroom; but this, the Gypsy would not allow. I was compelled to continue hauling the load myself.

The fugitive

The population of the cell fluctuated. Prisoners were constantly being brought in and taken out. At times, there were as many as twenty-one and we could hardly find room for our feet on the floor, especially when the three Germans stretched out their bodies to sleep, reducing the floor space to a minimum. Once, in the middle of the night, the cell door opened and a prisoner, still wearing his prison garb, was thrown in on top of us. He lay curled up near the door with his face resting on my feet, over which I soon felt his warm blood flowing. He was begging for water, faintly moaning.

'I'm dying. Water, please. I'm dying. Help me,' he said in Polish.

I tried to console him but I felt helpless. All I could do was whisper to him, 'I have no water, there is none in the cell.'

He kept crying, 'Please help me. Water, water, please.'

'What happened to you?' I asked him. 'Were you shot? Are you in pain?'

'I don't know,' he moaned. 'I don't know. I tried to run away. They were shooting ... they were shooting. I could hear the gunfire behind me. It's the dogs! It's the dogs!'

He kept begging for water that I could not give until, eventually, he calmed down and was able to mumble, 'Remember my name. I'm a Gypsy from Poland. I was born in Vilno. I know they will hang me. Should you ever meet Gypsies from Poland tell them what happened to me. Maybe some of my family are still alive.'

He told me his name but I have since forgotten it. I think it might have been 'Stephann Kwiek', but I cannot be certain. As time drew on, his face became colder and his voice softer. By morning he was silent. Before roll-call, they removed his body, leaving a big puddle of blood on the floor.

One more night had passed and another day began.

Running through the corridor with the shit bucket was the hardest part, and I was always glad to be back in the cell. As soon as we reached it, I placed the tin in its usual corner near the door, replaced the lid and sat on it with relief, to recover from my ordeal. The tin's steel cover was buckled, with sharp edges that cut into my bare flesh. I used to put my hands under my buttocks to protect them from having the skin torn off them.

The first time I was taken to the bath-house, I noticed that I had sores on my legs, as did the other prisoners. Some had wounds all over their bodies. We were all infected with anthrax. No wonder the cell stank of puss mixed with the smell of excrement and urine emitted from the tin. Soon, however, my sense of smell adjusted and I ceased to notice the stench: one can get used to anything. But I was running out of hope very fast now. The seemingly endless store of optimism that I had nourished and treasured was being eroded by the eternal darkness that pressed upon my soul. Fear of death was eating away at my flesh and my life. I felt as though I were withering like a tropical vine mistakenly planted in the desert. Nothing is as disabling as the fear of death.

In the dark cell, sitting on top of the container, my only escape became my ability to drift off, sometimes, to a land of fantasy as my mind wandered back to my childhood. In the face of my bleak and hopeless prospects in the Bunker, this was my only respite; for a short while, it could even make me feel good.

In my dreams, I was a child again, running back to my mother. In her arms, I felt safe and good; she gave me confidence. In her arms, the fear dispersed. I begged her for help. Her calm face was full of goodness but her eyes looked sad and tired. I told her that I was scared, that I was condemned to be hanged.

'No,' she said. 'You will live. You must live. Have you forgotten your promise?' Her voice was firm and full of confidence as she made me repeat my vow.

'I will search for Lipek. I will search for Lipek, I promise. I will not forget. I will search for Lipek,' I said over and over again.

Suddenly, I was shaken out of my dream by Ivan, one of the Russian prisoners, who stood over me from his position against the wall.

'Abrashka! Abrashka!' he whispered. 'What are you talking about? What are you saying? Who is Lipek?'

'Lipek is my brother.'

'I, too, have a brother,' he said.

Revolt and reprisals

In jail we were naked. This measure had been introduced after the Bunker revolt when, on the evening of 9 March 1944, the SS went to have their supper, leaving one SS guard on duty. In desperation at the mass hangings that were taking place every day, the prisoners organised a break-out. The majority of them were Russians. An Austrian Jew, with whom I stood under the shower, told me most of the story.

They had simulated a brawl in one of the cells. When the SS man opened the door to investigate, he was hit over the head with the leg of a bunk which was suspended from the wall, and knocked unconscious. They took his keys and opened some of the cells. Commotion broke out as the prisoners rushed out into the yard. The jail guard soon recovered and fired his pistol, alerting the guards on the watch towers which faced the prison yard. The two heavy machine-guns, one at either end of the jail, opened fire. Escaping prisoners were hit. Most of them retreated. A few managed to scale the fence, finishing up inside the camp. They were soon rounded up in a massive hunt by the SS with their dogs.

The revolt was short-lived and brutally suppressed. Reprisals followed in the form of mass executions. The victims struggled, kicked and shouted as the SS beat them viciously and tied their hands and feet with electric cables. Prisoners were gagged with pieces of timber shoved in their mouths and secured by being tied behind their necks with wire. They were hanged on the roll-call ground and left hanging there to be seen by both shifts as they came marching to and from work to the tune of military marches played by the camp brass orchestra.

The reprisals continued with what they called a 'Zehntling'. Cell after cell was opened, and every tenth prisoner was taken out and hanged. The Austrian Jew told me that he had been the tenth in his cell chosen for execution.

'I begged for my life,' he said. 'The SS officer stopped and listened. I told him I was a musician, a composer, that I was young, and could still compose some beautiful music. I pleaded with him to spare my life. He asked me where I was from and I told him, Vienna. I must have impressed him; possibly it was my good German, or maybe he loved music. He sent me back to the cell. I still don't know why.'

There were executions every day. The cell doors were constantly opening and closing at irregular intervals as prisoners were taken out to be hanged. Every time they came to get the victims I begged in my heart, 'Please, not me. Please, not me.' I wanted to live. Although life in the cell was atrocious, I had come to terms with it. I was prepared to go on just to be left alive. A profound force beyond my control, from an unidentifiable source inside me, urged me on. 'Just one more minute, just one more hour, just one more day.' I was holding on with all that remained of my strength and determination.'

Late in the afternoon of 4 April 1945, the Bunker suddenly came to life with feverish activity. The shutter outside the little window of our cell high up under the ceiling was closed, and I heard the pounding of jackboots. From outside, I could hear the roaring of a motor bike. Then the lights in our cell were switched off. The boots of the SS tramped up and down the long corridor. Cells were unlocked and locked. Every time the metallic clang of the bolts reverberated in the concrete building, my heart froze. I could hear the calling of prisoners' numbers.

Their executions took place in the prison yard, directly under our cell window. They were seven of the leading German communists who had been imprisoned from the early days of Hitler's rise to power, all of them Oberkapos. I heard the words clearly as SS officer, Obersturmbannführer Sander read the order, and I can still recall each one of them: 'By the order of the SS Reichsführer Heinrich Himmler, you are found guilty of activities against the Third Reich and punished with death. Prisoners, kneel down!'

Seven shots rang out, followed by a long, pain-filled moan. One more shot, and then silence. I could hear the heartbeats of everyone in the cell. My blood curdled in my veins. This was the first time in a concentration camp that I had been present at an execution by firing squad. The routine had always been hanging in the past. In a strange sense, I was relieved to know that I would be shot. The thought of being hanged scared me beyond all else. I kept telling

David that I had a feeling we would be shot, but nothing happened; our cell remained silent.

I could hear my heartbeat ticking my life away. I felt hot and dizzy; my mind was spinning. I wondered what would happen to Lipek. I would never see him again. He would be deserted and lonely. A heart-pounding sweat covered my body. Although the sensation of fear was no stranger to me, on that late afternoon I experienced it as an excruciating pain that paralysed my mind and body. My tongue became numb. I lost the ability to speak. I learned that the pain of the mind is more disabling than the pain of the body. I did not want to die. In the years I had spent behind the barbed wires, I had always had a premonition, however faint, that I would survive. Now it seemed that this had only been wishful thinking.

'Abraham, it's the end,' David was whispering. 'Six long years. So many camps. I've passed so many selections. I survived two years in Auschwitz. I survived the evacuations. I was certain I would make it. Abraham, Abraham! We must pray.'

'Leave me alone.'

'Before death, a Jew must ask the Almighty for his forgiveness. Abraham, you must do it,' he insisted.

I was too terrified to speak; I could hardly think. Shivers ran through my body.

David persisted: 'Abraham, you must make your confession. Confess your sins, ask the Almighty's forgiveness.'

'I don't want to pray. I have nothing to confess,' I retorted.

But David would not be diverted. 'You must not forget the Almighty. Never leave Him.'

'I never forgot Him. I never left Him. It is He who left me. It is He who let us all down.'

When I saw that David intended to carry the argument further still, I lost my patience. 'David, don't punish me! Leave me in peace! I couldn't pray, not even if I tried.'

'At least recite the "Shema",' he said doggedly. 'Repeat after me.' David began at the top of his voice. *'Shema Yisrael Adonai Eloheyno Adonai Ekhod.* (This was the prayer in praise of God, recited upon sleeping and waking, and before death: 'Hear, O Israel, the Lord our God the Lord is one.')

'Come on, repeat after me!' he said

'You pray for me, David.'

'I can't. Every Jew must pray for himself.'

'Then my prayers have been answered,' I said. 'I will not hang! I told you, I will be shot.' David looked at me in bewilderment as he continued to pray at the top of his voice. The Gypsy became angry and threatening.

'Shut up, you rotten Jew, shut up!' he shouted.

I shouted back, 'Let him pray! Don't interrupt! He's praying for all of us. For you too!'

The Gypsy became silent.

Whenever I shut my eyes and think of that evening, I am immediately transported to the darkness of the cell. I can see David in his corner, bowing and swaying back and forth in the traditional manner of Jews at prayer. I can still hear David's crying voice:

> Hear our voice, and be gracious, and forsake us not in the hand of our enemies to blot out our name; remember what Thou hast sworn to our fathers, I will multiply your seed as the stars of heaven: — and now we are left a few out of many … O Guardian of Israel, guard the remnant of Israel, and suffer not Israel to perish, who say, 'Hear, O Israel.'

In the cell there was absolute silence. I could hear the blood thumping in my temples and the heavy breathing of everyone around me. Perspiration trickled down my face and back, and my eyes felt as though they were sinking deeper and deeper into my head. There was no air, for the little window under the ceiling stayed shut. I could hear the trolley from the crematorium rattling in the prison yard. They were loading the bodies. Every time a corpse hit the planks my heart missed a beat, sending shivers up my spine.

The sounds of traffic became fainter. I could hear the noise of a motor bike disappearing into the distance, and the tramping of the reinforcements' boots giving way to silence. A hush seemed to be falling over the prison, when suddenly the sounds of Bunker Kapo Jumbo's mumbling voice, and the rattling of the food trolley, were heard in the corridor.

'David, can you hear? They are bringing food.'

I couldn't believe my ears, but it was true: the food trolley stopped and the door opened. The commandant, guarded by two SS men training their submachine guns on us, counted the prisoners before the cell Aelteste reported. The trolley moved up, loaded with loaves of bread and tins of meat. Nineteen loaves and tins were lined up on the floor. The door shut, and we ate like savages.

Was this my last meal, I wondered, as I busily emptied the tin with my bare hands. 'The service in this place is lousy. They don't even provide forks,' I quipped to David. I ate up the lot, eagerly licking off every bit that had stuck to my fingers. We exchanged few words as we gulped our food. 'Why such a feast?' we asked one another. 'Are they going to dispatch us to the Himmel-kommando?'

In the corridor, the noise continued. Soon Jumbo was back, escorted by the guard, and our door was unlocked again. The jail service threw a heap of shoes, pants and jackets into the middle of the cell, which the Gypsy at once began to distribute. My coat had no back, only two fronts and sleeves held together by its collar. My pants were three times the size of my skeletal body. Without a belt I had trouble keeping them on. Jumbo was nervous.

'Hurry up! Hurry up!' he shouted. 'You're all going to the train.'

On the way out I picked up a blanket that was lying in the corner near the main door. In the cold nights it was to be a blessing. Tearing off a square piece, I tied four knots in it and made myself a hat.

Evacuation to the unknown

According to the meticulously kept records of the SS, as well as the evidence from the trials of the war criminals at Essen in 1965-66, here are some of the dates and numbers of victims who were executed during my imprisonment in the Bunker:

On 12 March 1945, fifty Russians, five Poles, two Czechs and one Lithuanian were hanged. On 23 March 1945, twenty-five Russians and five Poles were hanged. In the last few weeks before the evacuation, a total of three hundred prisoners was executed on the gallows.

I could go on and on with dates and numbers. Many of the victims were Jews, even though today they are always referred to as Poles, Russians, Hungarians, Czechs or by the nationality of whatever country they came from. They are never classified as Jews; yet, when they were doomed to destruction, the only reason for it was their Jewishness.

We were lined up in the prison yard. The blood of the executed was still on the ground. I noticed a smoking pipe lying nearby. I picked it up, wiped it on my pants and eventually put it in my mouth. We marched to the railway line under heavy guard. I kept losing my pants; my shoes had no laces and they were too large, so that they continually slipped off my feet. There were approximately two hundred of us from the Bunker, tightly guarded, kept apart from the other prisoners and loaded in two open cattle wagons. We had more room this time than we had had on previous evacuations. Two SS guards were in our wagon, sitting on boxes near the door.

The train rolled on and on. Once again, the rhythmic shaking and clattering of the steel — clatter-boom, clatter-boom, clatter-boom — sounded endlessly as we headed towards an unknown destination. After twenty-four hours of travelling north, the train changed direction and headed south, then suddenly we were travelling north again. Finally, after forty-eight hours, the train pulled into a railyard adjacent to a river. We soon discovered that it was one of the cargo sections of the port of Hamburg. They intended to load us onto boats and let us drift on the sea to be bombed by the Allied air force or blown up by time bombs. Thousands of prisoners met their deaths on such drifting barges.

Suddenly, we heard the powerful roar of approaching aircraft. Wave after wave of US bombers swept over our heads. The train trembled with the vibrations. I had never seen so many planes in one wave, and I began to count. It seemed impossible. They kept coming and coming, wave after wave, in squadron formation. They seemed to cover the sky from east to west, as far as the eye could see. They were coming from beyond the horizon like a cloud of locusts blotting out the sky. There was no beginning or end. The roaring and trembling grew stronger and more frightening. We took off our striped jackets and waved to our friends. The SS were scared, encouraging us to continue. I loved every minute of it. There were no Messerschmitts in the sky, not even a single cloud of the German flak. The Luftwaffe no longer existed. The Allied air force was in full control of the skies over Germany, and the explosions were music to my ears. The vibrations increased to a heavy thunder as the bombs came raining down before my eyes. Our train was trembling. Never before had I been witness to the end of the world.

One of the many trains that followed ours was carrying prisoners in enclosed freight vans. The Allies bombed them to splinters; only a few came out alive. I saw them when they were brought to Bergen-Belsen, badly wounded, with burns to their faces and bodies, their clothing blackened and torn to shreds. Some prisoners were half naked, with their wounds still bleeding. I was surprised to see that others were actually bandaged. In the past, prisoners who were hurt had never been treated.

At the beginning of 1945, the representative of the Jewish World Congress, Hillel Shtorch, a Swedish Jew who, in the years of the Holocaust, devoted all his energies to saving Jews from destruction, eventually succeeded in contacting Doctor Felix Kerstner, Heinrich Himmler's Swedish masseur. Kerstner was trying to persuade Himmler that it would be greatly to his advantage to save the last Jews. This was at the stage when the German army was crumbling under the pressure of the advancing Allied forces who were rapidly closing in on Berlin from all directions. Although the Third Reich was approaching its inevitable end, Hitler, with his fanatical hatred of the Jews, was determined to destroy every last one. He ordered Himmler to blow up each concentration camp together with all the prisoners.

On 5 April 1945, the day I was evacuated from Dora, Hillel Shtorch obtained news from Dr Kerstner: 'Heinrich Himmler assured me that he will spare the survivors at Bergen-Belsen.'

By showing consideration for the last surviving Jews, Himmler tried to appear to be a man with whom the Western allies could negotiate. At the last minute, he tried to manipulate them with this grand gesture, intending to demonstrate that he had the power and the ability to act like a great statesman. But could Himmler be trusted? Was he a statesman? Were the Third Reich's leaders reliable people with whom the Allies could negotiate?

At the time, I was unaware of the questions, let alone the answers. I was also ignorant of my destination and my fate. I could not pray. All that was left to me was to struggle on and hope for a better tomorrow.

10

Bergen-Belsen

THE ROAR OF THE BOMBERS faded away as the last formations dropped their deadly loads, leaving behind a blazing inferno. Explosion after explosion of delayed-action bombs erupted thunderously, long after the aircraft had disappeared from the sky. The earth trembled as though in its final death throes; everywhere I cast my eyes, I saw rubble and dust. Hardly a structure seemed to have survived this, one of the most devastating air raids on Germany during World War II.

Miraculously, as we pulled away from the river bank, leaving the port of Hamburg in flames behind us, our train was in one piece.

Again, the monotonous sound of clattering steel rocked me to sleep as I stood leaning against the wall of the wagon. Many hours passed before the train pulled up for another stop. As the doors of the wagon rolled wide open with a grinding noise that shook me out of my doze, the familiar barking of the SS began.

'*Alle raus! Alle raus! Aussteigen, aussteigen! Los, los! Schnell, schnell! Bewegung, Bewegung!*'

The first to disembark were the two guards, leaving their rucksacks lying unattended near the open door. Immediately, David and I exchanged glances and knew that we had had the identical thought: to steal the loaf of bread that was strapped onto one of the rucksacks. David positioned himself in front of me to conceal what I was about to do; I grabbed the loaf but, no matter how hard I pulled it would not come loose. I was ready to give up when I suddenly caught sight of a rusty razor lying on the floor. Slashing at the leather strap, I seized the bread and jumped, inadvertently kicking a helmet in my haste to get away. The loud noise of its striking the gravel attracted the attention of the SS guard.

I ran frantically, trying to hide the bread under a coat which barely covered my body. Thousands of hungry eyes pierced the thin, striped material with only one idea in mind. A fellow prisoner grabbed me as I brushed past him; we struggled and I fell. I kicked and fought to protect my treasure, and rolled over onto my belly as a swarm of prisoners collapsed on top of me. I thought I was about to suffocate when the pressure abruptly eased. Before I could properly draw my breath, I was hit on the back with tremendous force. An SS man stood over me, battering my body with his submachine gun. Fuming with anger, he shrieked, 'I'll shoot you like a dog! I'll shoot you! So help me God! You thief!'

I stretched out my hands to fend off the barrel of his gun, to protect myself from a death that seemed to be only seconds away.

'Don't, don't!' I pleaded. 'Forgive me. I didn't mean to. I'm not a thief! I'm hungry, that's all. I'm hungry!'

He kept hitting me as I struggled to my knees, trying to protect my face with my forearms. 'Up! Get up!' he shouted, 'On your feet!'

I stood up. I could feel the crushed bread falling off my body. Like a cluster of maddened birds, the prisoners fought over every crumb, trampling one another. Poking me with the barrel of his submachine gun, the German ordered me to go back to where I had run from.

'Please, don't make me go back!' I begged him. 'Let me stay here. Your friend will shoot me — you know he will.'

'It serves you right! You ought to be shot. You're a thief!'

'I swear to God I have never stolen anything from anyone! I am hungry. My father never taught me to steal. He was an honest man. If you were a father and your son were a prisoner of war in Siberia, starving like I am here, and he stole bread, would you call *him* a thief? Would you say he deserved to be shot? Don't you think I am also human? I am hungry in the same way that many decent German prisoners-of-war who are in Soviet Russia must be starving.'

As I pleaded with him in an attempt to soften his heart, I was amazed to see that there were actually tears forming in his eyes. It was the first time I had ever seen an SS man become emotional. He calmed down and began to talk to me like a human being, calling me 'Mein Junge', my boy.

'Be sensible. You've got to go back to the Bunker contingent. You belong there. You can't stay with the others.'

'But your friend will shoot me.'

'No he won't. Leave it to me.'

I followed him back to the Bunker group, which was heavily guarded. He left me at the rear of the column as we marched on. It was my good fortune that the SS man whose bread I had stolen did not recognise me when he next saw me. To him, we all looked alike. Yet I had every reason to fear him. During the evacuation, he had shot two Russian prisoners merely to break the monotony of the exercise. And so I came to my last camp: Bergen-Belsen.

With the last remnants of my energy, I dragged myself from the railway line into Bergen-Belsen. We were taken to the camp of a Waffen-SS Panzer division where the prisoners from the Bunker were locked up in a separate barracks and heavily guarded. From the outset, although we were under constant surveillance, I was anxious to get away because I feared further executions. I was forever scheming to break away from the barracks and lose myself amongst the thousands of prisoners who were milling around in the main part of the camp. Discipline out there was clearly breaking down.

At first, there was not even the slightest chance, but I did not despair; on the contrary, I was on full alert. Early the next morning, I was standing near to the main entrance, waiting for a break, when I heard the Bunker Kommandant call, 'Ten prisoners to fetch the coffee!' I jumped forward, grabbed two buckets, and was right next to the door in an instant. Under guard, we marched to the kitchen but, as we approached, a mob of prisoners blocked the entrance, forcing the SS to clear the way. During the few moments that they were distracted, I dropped the buckets and lost myself amongst the mob. Drawing a deep breath, I experienced one of my happiest moments in concentration camp, actually rejoicing in my new-found 'freedom'.

I was in poor shape, a real Muselmann: skin and bones; body and legs hurting; anthrax wounds constantly oozing pus that kept sticking to my pants so that, whenever I tore them away, my wounds started bleeding again. I was filthy; my prison garb was at its most inadequate with my trousers constantly slipping off my skeletal body. Although I was on the verge of collapse, I still had my pride and could not accept walking around without them, as some prisoners were doing.

In a corner, on a heap of bric-a-brac, I was lucky enough to find a mattress spring. With much effort, I gradually managed to untwist the metal that kept trying to curl back into its original shape. Eventually, and with profound relief, I succeeded in wrapping it around my waist. It was not an ideal solution, however, because the steel wire rubbed my skin until it bled.

Reunion with Mendele

With my pants firmly fastened, I walked back to the kitchen, mingling with the mob. There, I caught sight of a familiar face. Who was this short, fat prisoner, I wondered. He reminded me of someone I had seen in a dream. He was dressed in a beautiful, brown, leather jacket without prison markings, and on his head he wore a round, black cap matching his black pants which were neatly pressed. His shoes were shiny and he had the air of somebody very important. He bore a slight resemblance to my cousin Mendele, but this could not be! The last time I had seen Mendele, he had looked like a Muselmann, virtually at death's door.

I observed him closely thinking, he *looks* like Mendele. Maybe it *is* Mendele, but still I was doubtful. I saw how everybody deferentially cleared a path for him. Such was the unwritten rule in concentration camp, that a prisoner who looked well and was well-dressed was highly respected.

I'll call his name, I thought, and see what happens. He looked in my direction but did not react. I called again, and again he looked up briefly before turning away.

'Mendele, it's me, Abraham!' I cried. 'Don't you recognise me?'

I saw the shock of recognition flood his eyes. 'My God,' he said. 'Where have you been? Can this really be you?'

'I was in Dora,' I told him.

'I searched for you. The boys told me that you left on a transport.'

'But I didn't.'

'Why did I never see you?' he demanded.

'How could you? I was locked up in the Bunker.'

'Why? What did you do?'

'It's a long story, not for now.'

'Where are your barracks?' Mendele asked next.

'I've just run away from the Bunker here,' I replied. 'I have nowhere to go.'

'Come with me,' he said. 'I'll get you into my block.'

Mendele took me along to his barracks. He was friendly with the Blockaelteste and respected by the orderlies. 'This is my cousin,' he told them. 'He stays with me.'

He too, had been evacuated from Dora, but he had managed to take with him a suitcase full of good civilian clothing from the clothing store at Dora. Dressed in this, he had been taken for a man of some special status, and everybody deferred to him.

When I took off my filthy rags, Mendele was shocked at how little there was left of me. I washed, shaved and put on the fresh clothes Mendele gave me. Within minutes, I felt that I had almost been reborn. The feeling was exhilarating, and I found myself taking one deep breath after another in my excitement and relief.

'Now you look like a human being,' said Mendele with a smile. 'Let's go to the kitchen. I have to see some of my contacts. There's always the chance of getting some food.'

A multitude of inmates was swarming around the kitchen, which was guarded by the SS with their submachine guns at the ready. Suddenly, hundreds of prisoners surged forward in an attempted raid on the vegetable store under the kitchen. Without thinking, I joined the mob. The SS immediately opened fire, gunning down those most exposed. I kept running, disregarding everything around me as the bullets hissed past my body. I had one aim: to grab a few potatoes. Diving head first through one of the vents of the cellar, I dug into the opening like a fox, until only my legs stuck out. In the dark, I grabbed what ever I could until my hands were full of potatoes and carrots.

Anxiously I started to wriggle back out and, in my haste, lost everything except for one large carrot which I pushed under my belt. Withdrawing as fast as I could, I found myself stumbling over dead bodies.

Mendele was amazed when I returned to the barracks. 'Have you lost your mind? You must be crazy! You're going to blow it at the last minute. Now is the time to lie low. We may be free at any minute, and you're risking your life for a potato?'

I shrugged; I didn't know what to say. The mob had gone

berserk and so had I. I promised myself never to do anything of that sort again, but I couldn't help rejoicing at the success of my catch.

'Mendele, I've got a carrot — a beauty! A huge one. I've got it under my belt.'

Into the barracks walked a huge Russian POW with the physique of an ape. His head had a shaven strip in the centre and his hair grew long on either side. His nickname was 'Sybiryak' — the Siberian. Some camps shaved their prisoners in this fashion to make them look ugly, and the style had been ironically labelled 'die Lausenstrasse' style, or the Lice Promenade.

The Sybiryak's left arm was bleeding profusely, but this did not seem to concern him. He was far more preoccupied with the cabbage that he held in both hands and was devouring voraciously, even as it became covered in blood from his wound. All eyes focussed on the blood-covered cabbage in the hands of the Russian. The prisoners watched him with passionate envy as he ate. Not until he had consumed the last morsel did he look at his wound.

'Tear a strip off your shirt and bandage your arm or you will die from loss of blood,' a fellow prisoner told him.

'Watch out,' said another, ' or you will get an infection.'

'Never mind,' the Sybiryak said, 'I pissed on it. And I'll piss on it again. There's no problem, the bullet went right through. *Nichevo, nichevo! Buditt kharacho!*' It's nothing, nothing. It will be alright.'

In an instant of heightened clarity, I understood why Napoleon had lost the war, and I knew it was inevitable that the Germans would, too. Even if they had been able to fathom the savage mysteries of the Russian winter, they would never understand, much less overcome, the Russian mentality.

That night, Mendele and I shared the carrot, upsetting the barracks as we crunched in the dark. We could not afford to be too concerned as it was the only food we had had that day.

Servant of the SS

The next morning, we continued our hunt. I followed Mendele to the kitchen in the hope that something would eventually turn up. Suddenly, my old friend, Kapo Killian, the executioner from Dora, appeared.

'You come here,' he called out, pointing his finger at me. Mendele's stratagem was working. He had picked me because of my clothing.

I approached him, clicking my heels as I stood to attention.

'Do you speak German?' he asked.

'Yes, I do.'

'Are you a Gypsy?'

'No, I'm Jewish,' I replied foolishly, not quick enough to realise that a falsehood was urgently required.

He hit me on the face. As I ran, he kicked me in the backside, but allowed me to escape. Later that day, he came across me again. I will never understand how or why he did not recognise me; but, once more he summoned me and, once more he asked the same questions. This time I gave the right answer.

'I am a German Gypsy,' I told him, baffled by the obvious absence of recognition on his part.

'Right, follow me,' he said, leading me into the SS headquarters. 'You're to work here as a "kalifaktor" (a servant-valet). '

He led me into one of the rooms and ordered me to clean it up. I made the bed and polished the boots of an SS officer.

As I was busy tidying up, their owner came in. It was Rudolph Hoess, the former commandant of Auschwitz. I sprang to attention, removed my prison cap and reported my number according to regulations.

'Weitermachen, weitermachen. Carry on. Carry on,' he said, waving his hand airily. He looked calm and composed as he sat at his desk; relaxed, with the air of an executive serenely doing his work, going through papers, making pencil markings as he read.

When he used the phone, I tried to listen in on his conversations. On this occasion, he was ordering large drums of petrol and kerosene to incinerate the dead. He was insisting that the delivery be without delay, anxious to keep the men's camp under his command 'clean'.

Hoess was an expert at incinerating corpses, unlike the commandant of the women's camp, Joseph Kramer, 'the Butcher of Bergen-Belsen', and his infamous assistant, Elsa Koch. They managed to accumulate thirty thousand corpses: for this they were tried for atrocities and crimes against humanity, and were sentenced to death.

I was surprised by Hoess' soft manner of speech. His voice didn't have the aggressive bark of the German military, to which I had become so accustomed; even when he gave orders, he never raised his voice. Had he donned a grey, pin-striped suit, with a white shirt and an elegant tie, he would have been interchangeable with a bank manager. In his SS uniform, however, he terrified me. He had been the managing director of the Third Reich's largest killing industry, priding himself on having stopped the epidemic of typhus at Auschwitz. His cure was gas.

After the war, he stood trial at Krakow, in Poland, where he was sentenced to death and executed at Auschwitz in his kingdom of terror and death. He was hanged on the same gallows he used to hang his victims in the years of his reign.

Because of my incredible good fortune of having found Mendele, I was transformed from a Muselmann to an élite prisoner: my life had been restored to me. Suddenly, I had access to food when thousands of prisoners were starving to death. While preparing for and serving the SS, I stole food whenever I could.

The first night, before returning to my barracks, I hid it under my clothes. The next day, I organised matters differently, taking the food out during the day as I carried rubbish to the tip. This was much safer in the event of an unexpected body search. I carried two baskets, fitting one into the other. The one with the food and cigarette butts, I put down half-way to the tip; and Mendele, walking not far behind me, ran off with it to the barracks, leaving the empty basket for me to collect later. We had to be extraordinarily cautious, but somehow we managed. Although I don't believe in miracles, this was definitely a miracle. As thousands of prisoners died of starvation in Bergen-Belsen, the two of us were lucky enough to have some food.

The SS were drinking heavily. It could be said that the Third Reich was floating on alcohol. I saw it with my own eyes. I have never seen so much schnapps, vodka and all sorts of liquors from every part of Europe — by the crate-load — as I saw in those final days of the camp. I kept pouring the alcohol and washing the glasses till late at night. I was kept busy cleaning the ashtrays, and picking up every butt — the most valuable, the hardest, currency in the camp.

The famine became extreme. Never before had conditions been

so harsh, driving the starving prisoners to cannibalism. Buttocks and thigh muscles were missing from many of the yellow and green corpses. I had never witnessed this in any of the camps before. The SS simply stopped feeding the prisoners. In my seven or eight days as a servant at Belsen, I was never given a piece of bread or a leftover by anyone. They used to throw such items into the rubbish bin, from where I retrieved them once the SS turned their backs. To them I was not human. They would never neglect the feeding of their dogs, but I had to steal every scrap of food and be careful not to be caught. One thing I never touched was the liquor; I was scared I might get drunk.

Within a few days I took on the appearance of a human being again. In the past six years, I had not eaten chocolate, fruit, cake or any of the most select delicacies which the SS had in abundance. Much of it came from the Red Cross parcels meant for the prisoners who, of course, were never given access to a single item from them.

Liberation

It was on 10 April 1945 that the liberating army closed in. For three days and nights, Belsen was at the centre of a heavy artillery barrage. On the fourth and fifth days, we saw long convoys of military ambulances speeding by on the highway. Although they did not look German, we could not work out which army they belonged to. A white flag appeared above the headquarters; the SS put on white armbands and prepared themselves to surrender.

I was cleaning Rudolph Hoess' room when his adjutant knocked on the door, entered, clicked his booted heels together and, with his right hand stretched out, gave the Nazi salute.

'Heil Hitler,' he said. 'Herr Obersturmbannführer, die Engländer sind da.' ('Sir, the British are here.')

Hoess rose, buttoned up the tunic under his chin and put on his army beret, adjusting it on his head as he admired himself in the mirror. He removed his pistol and locked it in the drawer of his metal cupboard, looking calm and composed as always. Without the slightest sign of emotion, he walked out of his room followed by his adjutant who, with a submachine gun slung around his neck, accompanied Hoess to the door. Being curious, I followed.

It was three o'clock in the afternoon on 15 April 1945 when a jeep carrying five British soldiers pulled up. Four of them wore red military caps and black armbands emblazoned with the red letters, MP, on their left arms. It was only later that I learned these letters stood for 'Military Police'. Each of the four wore a white belt extending like a sash from shoulder to waist. This was attached to another belt at the waist from which a large pistol was suspended at one side. Led by a major of the British Intelligence Service, these were the first British soldiers to enter Bergen-Belsen. Flanked by two heavy tanks, with their machine-guns and gunners at the ready, they headed towards the SS headquarters.

Obersturmbannführer Rudolph Hoess marched forward stiffly as if on parade and, clicking his heels, he saluted in an exaggeratedly military style. The British major waved him off contemptuously, his gesture clearly implying, 'Go to hell.'

Two of the military policemen jumped out of the jeep, ran up to Hoess, and grabbed him in a manner that was blatantly disrespectful. At the same time they removed his belt, an action he protested against loudly and vehemently. 'I am a German officer,' he said. 'I demand to be treated with respect, according to the laws of the Geneva Convention!'

His objections made no impression on the English. They held onto his arms and collar as if he were a criminal, and walked him back to his headquarters. Hundreds of prisoners, cheering and cursing, waving their fists, were closing in on him. They would have lynched him but for the English soldiers who gave him protection. They fired their Tommy guns into the ground at our feet, the bullets digging into the earth and sending up a cloud of dust into the air. This effectively halted the multitude, but their anger kept mounting and they continued to wave their fists, booing and shouting, 'Kill him! Kill him! Murderer! Murderer!' He was fortunate to be locked up in the cellar under his headquarters together with the other SS men who had been rounded up and tightly guarded by the British.

The mood of the ex-prisoners became very ugly indeed. Their anger boiled over into active aggression which they vented on the Kapos. Kangaroo courts passed sentences on the spot. Executions were swift. The lynching and revenge killings were ghastly, bloody incidents lasting forty-eight hours. Amongst those killed was Kapo Kutscher from Althammer.

In the midst of the madness, David Garfinkel came running over and grabbed me excitedly.

'Abraham, let's go,' he cried. 'Let's fix up that Czech informer. I saw the bastard! I know where he is. Come on! Let's get him!'

I pulled myself from his grasp and tried to collect my thoughts.

'I agree with you that he's a bastard,' I said. 'Worse, he's a bloody rat! And yes, it's a great shame that he's still alive when so many good people have died. But I want no part of that bloody, crazy spectacle. I'll have no hand in those savage vendettas!'

I stopped speaking. How could I explain that I had seen enough of killing for a hundred lifetimes? I could not be party to initiating more.

David was looking at me strangely. 'Maybe I'm naive,' I said, shrugging my shoulders, 'but I hope that one day he'll pay for his cowardice. I hope that one day he'll come to realise the extent of the evil he committed and suffer with sleepless nights for it for the rest of his life.'

First day with the British

Deciding to go back to headquarters, I pushed my way past the British guards. I had no knowledge of English so I used sign language to communicate, assisted by some of the English soldiers who had a limited knowledge of German. To the sergeant-major in charge of the headquarters, I explained that I had been working there as a cleaner. Like some of the other ex-prisoners milling around, I was eager to retain my job in the hope of earning some food.

The British major from Intelligence who took charge of Bergen-Belsen spoke German well. He gathered the cleaners together and briefly instructed us to collect all the loose weaponry and ammunition that was still in the building. Even today, I sometimes regret that I did not retain Hoess's silver parade belt with his SS dagger. It had a bone handle with golden SS insignias under the German eagle which held the swastika in its claws. All I took was an SS rucksack and a pair of jackboots; the rest I relinquished to the British.

After the weapons were collected, I kept busy with whatever chores I could find, still anxious to retain my position as a cleaner. The sergeant-major who was in charge of the building, however, stopped us. From his gestures I understood that he wanted to give the cleaning jobs to the SS men. He went down to the cellar and brought up two SS officers. One of them was Oberstabsarzt Kurtzke, a high-ranking officer in the medical corps, who had been the chief staff doctor at Dora.

Dr Kurtzke was very nervous and verbose. Combining his German with sign language, he tried to explain to the sergeant-major that he urgently needed to talk to the British commanding officer. Unable to understand a word he spoke, the sergeant-major turned to me, but I could be of no assistance either. Gesticulating and repeating the word, 'commandant' was the extent of my contribution. The sergeant-major became impatient, curtly ordering the SS men to begin cleaning without further ado.

Kurtzke was persistent. 'Please,' he begged me, 'tell the sergeant-major it is very important. I must talk to the British commandant. It is urgent!'

'I can't speak English — you know that. What is it that's so important?' But Kurtzke was not prepared to tell me.

Once the two SS officers had finished wiping the floor of the corridor, they were ordered to clean the toilets. To begin with, they were reluctant, as though offended by such a task, but soon the loud, authoritative tones of the sergeant-major conveyed to them — by volume alone — that they had little choice in the matter. Responding immediately with a combination of panic and excessive politeness, they said '*Jawohl! Jawohl!*' repeatedly, and applied themselves to the toilets with great fervour. Kurtzke continued to plead with the sergeant-major to take him to the commanding officer, which he eventually did. I was not present at the interview which took place between them but, some time later, Kurtzke told me that it had been his actions which had prevented the prisoners of Bergen-Belsen from being poisoned.

'In the first place, I was the one who stopped the distribution of the food laced with strychnine,' he said. 'I'm talking about when we were still in charge of the camp, before the British arrived. And then it was I who informed the commanding officer that the food in the stores was poisoned. If you are still alive, it is thanks to me.'

Much later it was revealed that, in the last hours of the Third Reich, Hitler's order had been: 'Not one Jew shall fall into the hands of our enemies alive,' — an order faithfully obeyed by the SS, the Regular Army, the Home Guard, and the Hitler Youth, who massacred thousands of Jews in the final moments leading up to the Allied invasion. Although Himmler had once promised Dr Kerstner, his Swedish masseur, that he would save the surviving Jews at Bergen-Belsen, he in fact reversed his decision. On 14 April 1945 he issued the following order to the camp commandants at Dachau and Flossenberg:

> *Die Übergabe kommt nicht in Frage. Das Lager ist sofort zu evakuieren. Kein Heftling darf lebendig in die Hände des Feindes fallen.*
> —*Heinrich Himmler*

> There is no question of handing over. The camp must immediately be evacuated. Not one prisoner must fall into the hands of the enemy alive.
> —Heinrich Himmler

Only in rare instances, in the final moments, did the SS shrink from murdering the prisoners — because they, like Kurtzke, had begun to fear the consequences.

First encounters with freedom

The following morning, along with all the other ex-prisoner servants, I went back to headquarters, but we were told that our services were no longer required. That meant an end to the beautiful biscuits and the tea with milk which had tasted so delightful; it was actually the first time in six years that I had had real tea with sugar. Having lost my position as a cleaner, however, had more serious consequences: I had lost my source of food and was now back in camp with the others.

The British had no food for the thousands of starving former inmates who turned to begging from the soldiers for sustenance. With the war still raging, the supply of food was non-existent; the food stores left by the Germans were poisoned, and many days passed before the first food transport arrived, bringing thousands of tins of powdered milk. But, after six years of starvation, our stomachs could not digest such richness. Thousands of ex-inmates were afflicted with chronic diarrhoea almost immediately. Mendele and I did not drink the powdered milk — some inexplicable instinct warned us of its dangerous unsuitability, and saved our lives.

The outbreak of diarrhoea was a major disaster. The British

medical corps, unable to cope with the situation, became panic stricken when they realised that their powdered milk was killing many thousands of ex-prisoners.

More time passed; it was difficult to ascertain exactly how much, but still the food did not arrive. Corpses were strewn all over the camp, and inmates roamed around, aimless and confused, stumbling more than walking. Inside the barracks, we picked our way over dead bodies, too. Friends collapsed before our eyes. One minute they would be leaning weakly against the walls; the next, they would be falling at our feet. There was nobody to assist us, and we seemed to be wading ankle-deep in urine, vomit and excrement. The stench of dead bodies combined with the urine and faeces was sickening: unable to cope with the gruesome scenes that confronted them constantly, many of the British soldiers vomited and fainted. In order to offer us any assistance at all, and to carry out their assigned tasks within the camp, they not only dressed themselves in rubber suits and gloves, but they wore gas masks as well. To us it did not matter; by now we were almost used to the conditions they found so intolerable.

Those of us still in reasonable shape — that is, able to walk — were anxious to break out of the camp in search of food. Near the barbed wire, thousands of former inmates gathered, and the pressure mounted as the days passed and the famine continued. The British were trying to contain everyone within the boundaries of the camp, fearing the spread of an epidemic amongst the German civilian population. In desperation, they called on a battalion of Hungarian infantry, stationed in the vicinity of Bergen-Belsen, and appointed them to guard the camp. Yesterday's allies of the Germans were now pointing their guns at us. As each hour passed, the tension mounted, the mob moving closer and closer to the wire fence. With the help of interpreters, the British sent out appeals over the loudspeakers, pleading with the survivors to be patient, explaining why we were not permitted to leave. Their pleas fell on deaf ears. How long did they expect starving ex-inmates, on the verge of death, to be patient?

The multitude that had gathered at the barbed wire fence, booed, jeered and cursed the Hungarian soldiers. Suddenly, the mob moved forward, flattening the fence completely. The guards fired their guns into the ground, spraying sand and dust into the air. It was then that we realised that they had orders not to shoot. In great excitement, a wave of ex-prisoners rushed past them, stampeding across the surrounding fields like a herd of beasts.

I was amongst them, charging like a wild animal that has broken loose from its cage. (I later calculated that this was the first time in 1,845 days that I was not enclosed behind barbed wires.) I threw myself to the ground and rolled on the grass. The soft, green meadow was sprinkled with daisies and field flowers. I lay on my back, trying to catch my breath. Looking into the blue sky, I suddenly burst out crying, possessed by a force beyond my control, overcome by a feeling of confused intoxication, overwhelmed by excitement.

I had not as yet come to grips with the reality of it. Millions of thoughts seemed to be flashing through my mind, but simultaneously, so that it was hard to grasp any particular one of them individually. Six, long nightmarish years — I knew that much. I felt as if I were going mad. My mind was moving with supersonic speed, spinning crazily between grief and happiness, one thought contradicting the next. I could not believe that I was still alive and, now, free. Nevertheless, out of the chaos and confusion of my brain and my heart, one clear thought was managing to emerge: Lipek. I had to find my brother.

I lay in the grass gathering my strength. After a while, I picked myself up and joined the mob, following it to the nearest German settlement. The village was swarming with thousands of inmates desperately seeking food. Amongst them, I found Bella with a group of Jewish boys, and I promptly joined up with them. Together, we walked from place to place until, in one of the villages, we came across a group of French army officers who had been prisoners-of-war. Never having seen prisoners of a concentration camp before, they were shocked when they saw us. We told them we were Jews from Bergen-Belsen and, although they had heard about the gas chambers and extermination camps, we were the first living witnesses able to confirm the horror stories they had not quite believed before. They were kind and hospitable, inviting us into their quarters and giving us some of their food. We rested there briefly, chatted with them a short while and, when we bade them farewell, they gave us some confectionery and dried fruit for the road.

We moved on. The German population was cold and withdrawn. When they had to communicate with us, their manner was unfriendly and arrogant. When we asked them for food, their response was always: 'We have none ourselves'. When we broke into their cellars and stores, however, we found plenty of food hidden away.

It was getting dark. Having knocked on a few doors and asked the inhabitants to accommodate us for the night, and having been refused a number of times, we eventually forced our way into a house occupied solely by middle-aged women. There were neither children nor men around, and I wondered if they were hiding.

The women were unfriendly towards us; the feeling was mutual, but we behaved correctly. Misinterpreting our politeness for weakness, they became haughty, affecting disdain at our presence, raising their voices and insisting that we leave at once. We stopped being polite and told them that we were there to stay for the night. At this, one woman in her early fifties became very aggressive and loud.

They seemed to be well-to-do, upper-middle class people — all wearing jewellery, which looked rather odd. I realised that they were probably in fear of losing it should they have to leave the premises in haste or evacuate the area; but the sight of their finery provoked me to anger. Pointing to it in disgust I said, 'Your husbands and sons have sent you beautiful presents from their escapades. They robbed, plundered and murdered all over Europe. Aren't you ashamed to wear the stolen jewellery of murdered people?'

I became very aggressive, ordering the old lady to take off her finery and put it on the kitchen table. The manner in which I did it was very convincing. From many years' observation, I had learned how to bark out orders, and my impersonation of a brutal German scared the life out of all of them. Immediately, they began to obey me.

Bella grabbed me angrily. 'You're not going to behave the way they did!' he roared, and we scuffled briefly before I managed to pushed him away. I spoke Polish so the Germans would not understand.

'I'm not going to touch them or take any of their jewellery,' I said. 'I just want to teach them a lesson.'

I lined them all up; there were about eight or nine women in the place, and I barked orders at them at the top of my voice. They became scared and panicky when I ordered them to put all their jewellery on the kitchen table, but they obeyed me anyway. With a sudden swipe of my hand, I sent it flying all over the kitchen.

'You can keep your stolen jewellery!' I shouted, losing my temper, consumed by an extraordinary anger. 'I'm a Jew. I don't touch stolen goods! I don't rob and plunder or murder the way you noble, pure-blooded Germans do.'

Suddenly, the doors were flung open, and a British officer stood before me. Obviously, one of the hidden members of the household had sneaked out and called for help. Now, a patrol of soldiers waited outside while the officer, with stern formality and in reasonably good German asked, 'What are you doing here?'

He could have had no difficulty in identifying us, but I gave him the information he requested, nevertheless. 'We're ex-prisoners from Bergen-Belsen,' I said. 'We're hungry and tired. All we want is some food and a room to rest in overnight. In the morning we'll move on.'

The British officer was unsure of the best way to handle the situation. Calling in his sergeant, he talked it over at some length without seeming to reach a conclusion.

'We didn't ask to be brought to Germany,' I said to the officer. 'They murdered our families. They destroyed our homes. They robbed us of all we possessed. They used us as slaves and didn't even feed us. And now they can't even give us a little food and shelter for a single night.'

The English officer changed his tone and became friendlier, realising that we were in need of help. Then he looked at the jewellery scattered all over the floor.

'What is this?' he asked.

I explained how the women had come by it. 'They can choke on it, for all I care,' I concluded. 'We don't touch stolen goods. All we want is food and a room for the night.'

'Are any of you carrying weapons?' the officer asked.

His soldiers searched us and, finding us to be unarmed, the officer then ordered the women to give us what we needed. They cleared the attic for us, warmed up some coffee, and gave us a few slices of bread with butter. Early the next morning we were glad to leave.

The surrounding district of Bergen-Belsen was rich, the towns and villages bore no marks of war, and the countryside was blossoming. The livestock looked fat and well-tended, and the cattle fed lazily on the meadow. The civilian population was well-dressed. Everywhere I turned I saw prosperity and wealth. Why would people who lived in comfortable, spacious homes and beautiful surroundings be so hostile and war-like? Why did they invade their neighbours while they had everything in abundance in their own land? I could not understand it.

We stopped at a large, deserted farm where I grabbed a bag and filled it with potatoes. In the corner of a barn I noticed a large cage filled with hares. Four of them joined the potatoes in my sack. Walking became difficult for me as they jumped around frantically inside the sack, throwing me off balance. I stopped a Russian ex-POW and asked him to help me, which he did by simply grabbing the hares and disappearing, leaving me with the potatoes. I was lucky: he could have taken the lot.

With great reluctance, I decided to return to the camp. I didn't know what else to do. My first encounter with freedom had not unfolded as I had dreamed it would. While I was not very happy to get back into the cage, the world outside was strange and cold; I felt lost. I did not belong there.

The nightmare of Bergen-Belsen

For many days, before reinforcements of the British troops arrived, Mendele and I existed on a diet of potatoes alone. Then the soldiers came, directly from the front lines after days of heavy battle — unwashed, unshaven, covered in dust and mud. I will never forget the expression on their faces — those battle-toughened men of the Royal Artillery — when they entered Bergen-Belsen. They had seen a lot of blood in their years of war; many of them had lost their nearest of kin and their homes in the air-raids over England. Some of them had lost their closest mates only a few hours before entering the camp. But when they saw the misery of Bergen-Belsen, they broke down and cried. I am still not sure if the sight of their reaction did not scare us more than our condition scared them.

In the first few days, British soldiers rounded up German citizens from the surrounding areas. They brought them to Bergen-Belsen and made them look at the horrors of their own creation. These were the lord mayors and the leading citizens of the neighbouring villages and towns who had applauded Hitler, serving him with enthusiasm and devotion. Now they stood, expression-less and silent, watching the SS troopers under British guard carrying the corpses. I didn't see any of them faint or cry. When asked by the British what they had to say for themselves, all too often their response was, 'This is not our responsibility; we had nothing to do with this.'

Inside Bergen-Belsen, the nightmare continued: ex-prisoners dying by the hundreds, corpses strewn all over the place. In all the years of my captivity, I had seen a lot of dead bodies but never had I seen them lying, piled up in heaps like this. They looked like mountains of broken marble statues. Wherever I turned, glazed eyes stared at me. Twisted faces expressed agony with their wide-open eyes full of horror and pain. Those eyes followed me around wherever I walked, as they still do today, reminding me of where I was, demanding that I tell the world what had been done to them; that I make the world remember. Bergen-Belsen looked like the Valley of Death. Only the vultures in a desert sky were missing to complete this grotesque scene. The whole world around me was dead. My world, my entire world, was in ashes.

In the beginning, until the bulldozers arrived, the mountain of corpses grew, with thirty thousand bodies rotting under the open sky. Within the next couple of weeks, as earth-moving equipment became available, the bodies were shovelled into long ditches, some of which contained five thousand corpses. Others had two or three thousand. Timber plaques with numbers marked the graves. Some graves had no numbers marked to state how many corpses were in them.

Oberstabsarzt Kurtzke

The days after the liberation of Bergen-Belsen continued in tur-moil, confusion and famine. Once again, I encountered Dr Kurtzke, and we recognised one another immediately. Now that I was no longer a prisoner and a cleaner of the SS headquarters at Belsen, Kurtzke's manner was markedly different. He was exceedingly polite, and stressed how very happy he was to see me. In evidence were his most elegant and courtly German manners, bizarrely out of place in these surroundings.

'You remember me?' he asked ingratiatingly. 'It was I who

warned the British commanding officer not to use the poisoned food that was left behind in the stores by the SS. If I had remained silent, you would have all been dead, and Himmler's order would have been successfully carried out.'

At first, Kurtzke was kept under arrest. Shortly afterwards, the British commanding officer allowed him out of prison as a reward for having saved thousands of ex-prisoners from being poisoned. Now he moved around the camp with his medical kit, without a guard, attending to the sick. Not only was he an extremely skilful doctor, he also had an engaging bedside manner: he knew how to make friends. He even managed to win the sympathy of some of the Russian POWs who remembered him from the days of Dora. On various occasions, Mendele and I spoke to him at some length, and he was always eager to assure us that he had never used any of the deadly phenol injections nor had he ever castrated Jewish male prisoners.

Dr Kurtzke was always anxious to impress upon me that he had taken no part in any of the terrible activities in which the other SS doctors had been involved. He was able to reel off great lists of crimes that he had not committed. To this day, however, I cannot help but wonder exactly what it was that Dr Kurtzke did, in his position as Oberstabsarzt, that he expediently neglected to tell me. He had been, after all, a high-ranking officer in the SS medical corps, a volunteer — as were all the members of the SS — and had been thoroughly investigated and scrutinised before being accepted. As the élite of the SS, responsible for the experiments carried out on prisoners whom they used as human guinea pigs, the doctors had to undergo the most rigorous examination procedures of all SS members. It was they who were in charge of the German extermination apparatus.

Rozia and Tobcia are found alive

On 27 April 1945, the British military administration at Bergen-Belsen announced over the loudspeakers that all citizens from France, Belgium, Holland and Luxembourg should assemble in front of British headquarters to collect their food rations and stand by for further orders: they were going home. Mendele and I ran as fast as we could, and were among the first to collect the rations as well as a bonus of two cigars. We lined up to leave for France.

Army lorries pulled up. Quickly, I jumped on and waited for Mendele to jump up alongside me.

'Abraham,' he said suddenly, just as he was about to board, 'I don't think we should go. Maybe some of our family has survived. We must stay back and look for them.'

I argued that we should leave. 'Staying in Belsen will be of no help to anyone. We should get as far away as we can from this God-forsaken country as fast as possible.'

Mendele was adamant. Although his decision had been made in a moment, now he could not be swayed. 'I'm staying here,' he insisted, refusing to join me.

I jumped off the truck. 'If you won't go, neither will I,' I said.

Within the next few days, we discovered that a fifteen-minute walk from our camp would take us to a women's concentration camp. It was a nightmarish place, devastating in its initial impact. Although I had lived with the dead for many months, the sight of the naked and partly dressed female skeletons, roaming around like ghosts, crushed me — maybe just because they were women. Their breasts were empty, shrivelled-up pieces of skin hanging down over their exposed ribs. Their protruding pelvises and stick-like legs barely covered with skin were lacerated with sores. Their entire bodies were covered either with wounds or human excrement. Their hair had been shaven and sold to German mattress manufacturers; they bore no resemblance whatsoever to human beings. Amidst and between the barracks, under the open sky, were mountains of dead bodies.

As we were wandering about the place a woman walked up to us; she had recognised Mendele and proceeded to lead us to a barracks in front of which a living ghost was seated on a box. 'This is your sister, Rozia,' she said, and wandered away.

We stood before her in shock and bewilderment: Rozia was beyond recognition, no longer able to walk. When she caught sight of us, the excitement of it so overwhelmed her that she lost her power of speech, and was only able to gesture with her right hand in the direction of an open door leading into the barracks.

Inside, the smell was unbearable, with the dead and the living lying together on the same bunks, soaking in their own urine. The prisoners had not been able to wash for a long time and, eight days before the British liberated the camp, the Germans had disconnected the water supply completely. Within six hours of the arrival of the British, the camp had running water again, hot showers and soap. For the first time in many months, the prisoners could wash again. It seemed, however, that they had no energy for even the simplest of tasks.

We found Tobcia lying on a bunk, sick with typhus, burning with fever. Because there was no hospital facility to which she could be moved, she was left in that dark, foetid barracks for many days. She became completely bald from her high temperature; although her hair eventually grew back slowly, it took many months of careful nursing before she — and Rozia, who was also very ill — regained any semblance of moderately healthy human beings. I know that both sisters were on the verge of death, but I could see how our unexpected appearance was like an injection of life for them, giving them the will to survive.

As the weeks that followed liberation passed, and my cousins slowly regained their strength, Lipek was constantly on my mind. With great hopes of finding him alive, I was forever enquiring of ex-inmates whether any of them had heard of or seen my brother. My investigations proved futile, however, so I decided to pack my rucksack and search for him myself. Mendele asked me to delay my venture a little longer to give the girls more time to recover.

'Once they are able to take care of themselves,' he said, 'the two of us can search for our brothers together. I can help you find Lipek, and you can help me find Shlomo and Lipman.'

His argument made sense and I agreed to wait; but, within a few days, my hopes of finding Lipek alive were shattered. I learned the news from our school friend, Roza Feldstein, whom I found in the women's camp at Bergen-Belsen.

The search for Lipek is over

'Lipek was brought to Skarzysko-Kamienna Labour Camp in March 1944, with a transport from the Lodz ghetto,' she told me. 'He was assigned to the ammunition factory B, but he wasn't very strong and couldn't cope with the work. He became weaker with every day that passed until he could hardly stand on his feet. They sent him to the sick bay where I was working as a nursing orderly and I did whatever I could to help him. A few days after he was admitted, the camp commandant, Bartenschlager, pointed his finger at your brother on one of his routine selections.

'Now Lipek was a marked man. The next morning they came to get him, and I remember it was the fourteenth of May, 1944, that I stood watching as they took him away. He was barefoot and walked with great difficulty. He turned his head towards me and gave me a sad smile as if to say, 'Goodbye'. They took him to the little wood adjacent to the camp and they shot him. It was seven in the morning. I have not forgotten. I never will. I have seen many executions, but Lipek's ...' Roza suddenly stopped, unable to finish the sentence. 'My brother, Felek, was with the partisans,' she said at last. 'He fell in a gun battle with the Germans.'

Her voice was calm; there seemed to be no sign of emotion in her at all. For moments that seemed to last an eternity, we stood motionless, neither of us wanting to be the first to cry. I turned and ran back to my barracks, bursting into tears long before I could reach my bunk. I buried my face in my blanket, and it was days before I could face the daylight again. I stayed on my bunk until I could cry no longer.

Sometimes, suffering is limitless, inexhaustible, like a dark catacomb that winds along persistently, endlessly. Blow after blow, one disaster followed another. My life was in shreds when I had to endure yet another loss. One day, Srulek Skoczylas, the brother of my childhood friend, Rivek, turned up at Bergen-Belsen by himself. I had not seen him since we had parted at Birkenau. We fell into each others arms, holding one another tightly without uttering a word. I sensed disaster.

It seems that towards the middle of October 1944, at Birkenau BIIe, Rivek, with the help of Dr Pick, had fully recovered from typhus. Pick decided to keep him in the sick bay for a few extra days to give him a little more rest before sending him back to the camp when, one morning, the SS raided the typhus barracks. They loaded the sick onto a lorry and drove them to the gas chamber. As they drove through Compound BIIe, Rivek jumped off the truck and hid, but luck was against him. The entire camp was lined up for roll-call alongside the barracks: every prisoner was checked; every possible place of concealment was searched. After many hours, they found him hiding in a storm-water drain inside the camp. He kicked, scratched and struggled with his last strength as they dragged him to the gas chambers.

My brother's death had been a terrible blow; I owed my life to him, spurred to survival by the promise I had given my mother that I would look for him once the war was over. I knew that the rest of my family had perished, but I had always been so sure that Lipek would somehow endure. When I realised that he had not pulled through, and when, shortly after, the news of Rivek's death followed, I was utterly devastated. I had lost everything and everybody. I was like a naked, leafless twig, hanging on to the old tree of Israel that stood deep in the ashes of six million branches that had gone up in flames.

Five months later, my cousin Lipman turned up, having been liberated on 8 May 1945, somewhere on a highway in the vicinity of the Neuengamme concentration camp. Of my aunt Sarah and uncle Berish Taglicht, I never heard again. Their only son, Joe, survived the war in England and now lives in Jerusalem with his family. Nor did I ever hear again of uncle Laib, my father's brother; his wife, aunt Ethel; and their three children: they all perished, most probably in Treblinka. And we never found out what happened to Mendele's brother, Shlomo. I had had a large family of uncles, aunts and cousins. Many of them, I had never had the pleasure of meeting personally in my childhood, as some of them lived in Warsaw, others in Kielce and Sosnowiec. In the last fifty years, I have not come across any of them; nor have I ever heard any news of them to suggest that they might have survived.

My cousins, the children of uncle David Laib and aunty Chaya, were a unique Jewish family: four members of their family survived. In Poland, almost the entire Jewish population was destroyed. In some villages and towns, hardly a Jew survived to tell us what had happened. In Estonia, Latvia, Lithuania and the Ukraine, entire Jewish communities were wiped out by the Einsatzgruppen. These 'Aktions' were carried out with the help of a great number of the local population who were, and still are, the only living witnesses; they, too, have joined the conspiracy of silence.

From then on, most of the people with whom I have associated have been survivors; and, to this day, hardly any of my friends know who my family was or anything about the home I came from. My life after the Holocaust, with nothing known to cling to, was like starting over on another planet. Everything — people and places — was alien, almost outlandish, in its unfamiliarity. Yet, in its way, it heralded a new beginning, too. My dream was to go to Australia, to live as far away from Europe as possible. I hoped that there I would find a country free from racial and religious prejudice.

Many years have gone by. I often think that I have learned to live with my past, but the pain never goes away. It is hidden deep within me and, as I write these lines, old wounds reopen, making the feelings of loss and bitterness as painful as they were on the day I heard the news of my brother's death.

Bergen-Belsen makes headlines

Before 15 April 1945, Bergen-Belsen was an obscure place in Germany, unknown to the rest of the world. Within hours of its being discovered by the Royal Artillery of the Second British army, it was to gain universal notoriety. Led by General Sir Miles Dempsey, in the course of their last battles with the Third Reich's retreating army, the soldiers stumbled across one of the largest-ever cemeteries, comprising thirty thousand unburied, decomposing corpses that were piled up in the barracks and under the open sky. They were finally buried in mass graves dug out and shovelled in by British army bulldozers. I stood watching, and to this day still wonder who counted the corpses. There could have been any number.

SOS calls were flashed across the whole world. London, Washington, Moscow, Paris: all the capitals were shocked by the horror story of the terrible discovery. Why they were shocked was beyond me. They knew it all along. The British parliament sent out a delegation of its members; a group of congressmen from Washington was dispatched to obtain a first-hand view; and the Red Cross sent a team of organisers. The United Nations mobilised medical assistance, and four hundred volunteer doctors from Belgium came out with a field hospital. But the rescue efforts were too little, too late. Thousands of victims were beyond the point of being saved. Another twenty thousand former inmates died of typhoid, diarrhoea and starvation within the next few weeks.

Every minute was precious and decisive, but many days passed before food supplies eventually arrived. Military reporters, journalists and film crews from all the world's leading newspapers frantically filmed the most gruesome scenes of misery and death ever witnessed. Prisoners half-crazed with famine looked at them with shock and hostility.

'Are we monkeys in a zoo that you came to film? Give us bread!' they cried.

With the help of a crew of camera-men, Sydney Bernstein, head of the British psychological warfare division, tried frantically to capture the horror scenes. These documentaries were later locked up for forty years and never shown to the public — the intention being not to upset the German nation and to assist in stabilising the relationship with them and winning their friendship. It is possibly not surprising that we have so many books and stories written today, telling us that the gas chambers never existed and that the Holocaust was a Jewish invention. There are still many official documents and masses of files locked up in vaults as classified information. They may never be released and we may never know the whole truth. As Peter Fanner, one of the camera-men and film-editors of the Bergen-Belsen documentary, has said, 'Such an attitude can only promote another Holocaust.'

At the time, Bergen-Belsen suddenly appeared in block letters on the front pages of the world's leading newspapers, with pictures illustrating its horrors. It became the *via dolorosa* for fifty thousand victims, at once becoming synonymous with the atrocities committed by the German nation against a defenceless people for their crime of being born Jewish, and a stark manifestation of the dangers of perpetuating into modernity the myth and the slander of deicide. The results of institutionalised anti-Semitism have never been more apparent, perhaps, than in the images that were flashed around the world from Bergen-Belsen.

The British soldiers worked day and night. It took them many months to clean up. Many of the soldiers and medical personnel of the British army fell sick themselves, contracting typhus, some even dying and being buried next to the mass graves. But it seemed that the gluttony of the Bergen-Belsen cemetery was limitless. For months, the more the rescue workers buried, the more corpses piled up: for many, the liberation had come too late.

Polish anti-Semitism

In August 1945, at Bergen-Belsen, I ran into my childhood friends, Janek Lewin and Abraham Jakubowicz, who had just arrived from Lodz. I was the first familiar face they had encountered, and it was with great excitement that we kissed and hugged one another. With them, they brought news from Poland:

On 19 January 1945, Lodz had been liberated by the Sixth Army of the first Byelorussian front. When the Russian army entered the city, eight hundred Jews were still alive — all that was left of the pre-war Jewish population of approximately two hundred and thirty thousand. The eight hundred had been kept by the Germans in a camp within the ghetto perimeter, at 16 Swietego Jakuba Street, to clean up the ghetto. At the Jewish cemetery, the Germans had dug nine large graves, in preparation for yet another mass murder, but they had miscalculated: the Russian army moved faster than anticipated, and the remaining Jewish lives were saved.

The rest of the news was worse: Jews were daily being murdered by Poles in towns and villages around the country. Buses and trains were being stopped in the middle of their journeys, and any Jews aboard were taken off and shot. The last few survivors who came out of the German concentration camps barely alive, as well as the pitifully few remaining Jewish partisans who emerged from the forests, found their homes had been taken over by Poles when they returned to their towns and villages in the hope of finding some family members still alive. Their welcome was hostile; those who did not run away fast enough were murdered. It is impossible to ascertain the number of those who met their deaths upon returning home.

This was in 1945, when the chimney stacks of the crematoria had stopped smoking, and the Holocaust had ceased all over Europe. Only in Poland did the blatant murder of Jews continue unabated for two more years. The Polish people totally erased the last remnants of Jewish life, overploughing and smashing Jewish cemeteries in Sieradz, Szydlowce, Zelechow and many other towns once inhabited by Jews. Jewish tombstones were flung into the streets, private courtyards, building sheds and toilets with their engravings facing outward. At a later stage the Polish government itself spared no effort in making life impossible for the last two hundred and fifty thousand Jews who survived the Second World

War in Russia and came back to Poland.

On 4 July 1946, a terrible pogrom took place in Kielce, in which forty-two Jews were murdered and many wounded. In 1956, those Jews who had not fled the country were sacked from their employment and left without an income. A second, similar action took place in 1967 and a third in 1974. Of a population of 3.5 million Jews that lived in Poland before the Second World War, all that is left today is a tiny fragment: five thousand Jews dispersed all over Poland. Most of them are old and sick. Within fifteen years, Poland will have achieved its aim: it will be *Judenrein*.

Only statistics are available to tell us about the destruction of the Jewish population in villages where the Holocaust took place. The villages are still in existence; most of the Jewish homes are still there; but, in many cases, not one Jew survived. What did survive is a vicious anti-Semitism, a new phenomenon in the post-Holocaust era, especially in Poland: anti-Semitism without Jews.

When I say that I have learned to live with the past, I do not mean that I have learned to control my anger or my bitterness. There are certain incidents and phenomena that I can never forget, much less forgive, and they are branded on my memory — a memory that I sometimes wish was not quite so vivid.

The anti-Semitism of the Poles is unforgettable. I remember as a child before the war, seeing walls covered in anti-Semitic graffiti. The most popular slogan amongst them was *Zydy Do Palestyny* or *Jews to Palestine*. Today, that slogan has been replaced with one that reads *Zydy Do Gazu*, meaning, *Jews to the gas*.

To say that all Poles were involved in the destruction of the Jewish people would be an exaggeration. With hindsight, however, it seems to me that the majority of them were happy to see the Jews destroyed. Many Poles helped the Germans in identifying Jews who hid outside the ghettoes. Perhaps it is not for me to judge, but I cannot escape the notion that the behaviour of the Polish masses facilitated the Holocaust.

I am aware that to hide or help a Jew was a crime punishable by death; I do not judge the Polish people for not having hidden Jews. On the other hand, the Germans never punished anyone for staying home, turning a blind eye or not denouncing Jews. Poles who hid Jews were more in danger of betrayal by their Polish neighbours than they were of being discovered by the Germans. And, finally, the ultimate act of the tragedy was played out in the Polish forests by the last, struggling, armed Jews — the Jewish partisans — who were mercilessly attacked by the Polish underground army, which had determined that the real war was against the Jews.

In Australia, a person who saves the life of another human being is hailed as a hero and officially decorated with a medal. In Poland, those who saved Jewish lives during the Holocaust have never been acknowledged, let alone decorated, by the Polish government. Today, the Poles are trying to create a myth about the humanitarian manner in which they, as a nation came to the rescue of the Jews; but, regrettably, this is not the case.

In one of his letters to me, my schoolfriend, Professor Lucjan Dobroszycki, wrote, 'The darker the night, the brighter the stars.' Indeed, it was a dark night. Dark and long, the sky was covered with heavy clouds. The stars were bright, but so few were visible. Out of a nation of well over thirty million people, only four thousand Poles were involved in saving Jewish lives. Each one of whom was acknowledged by Yad Vashem in Jerusalem and decorated as a hero.

Kristallnacht never happened; nothing happened

During the years of the Holocaust, Germans, young and old, watched living skeletons being dragged along the highways and carted in open cattle trucks across Germany. I will never forget the indifference on their faces — as though we did not exist or, if we did, as though we had no right to. Sometimes they would throw stones and abuse us. None of them ever tried to help.

After the Liberation, the German population had no knowledge of anything. They had never seen the trains; they had never seen synagogues burning nor had they ever plundered Jewish homes and property. Kristallnacht never happened; in fact, nothing had happened. They had neither seen nor heard anything. They were absolutely unaware of what had happened in the ghettoes and in the concentration camps. They only knew what they were told by survivors. Of course, they agreed that things were bad, but they apportioned guilt and blame in varying degrees upon the Führer and the SS. They themselves were absolutely innocent.

The Germans who lived only a few hundred feet from the

barbed wires surrounding Bergen Belsen pretended not to have any idea of what had gone on behind those wires. They pretended not to have noticed the stench of the rotting corpses that travelled for many kilometres when the wind blew in their direction. The German soldiers who lived in the nearby army barracks, however, complained constantly about the unbearable smell that made them sick to the point of vomiting. In the German archives, many letters of complaint from the German army to the SS are filed, with specific references to the reek of decomposing bodies.

Another fallacy which the Germans attempted to perpetrate was that the 'Wehrmacht', the regular German army, did not participate in and had nothing to do with the Holocaust. From the very outset of the war, wherever the German army invaded, the Wehrmacht beat, robbed, humiliated and murdered the Jewish populations. I witnessed this myself, back in Poland, in my city of Lodz, in 1939. In 1941, the German regular army assisted the Einsatzgruppen in the most horrible butcheries in the history of the Holocaust. In Eastern Europe the Einsatzgruppen counted three thousand men only. They could not have had butchered one-and-a-half million Jews without the help of the army. And much of the photographic documentation of German brutality towards the Jews came from the German soldiers and officers themselves. They took countless photographs, obsessive in their need to record.

Richard von Weizsacker, the president of the West German republic, in his address to the West German parliament on 4 May 1985 marking the anniversary of Hitler's fall, reminded the German people of the Holocaust:

> We all, whether guilty or not, must accept our past. Let each of us who experienced the years of dictatorship ask himself today about his own involvement ...
>
> We must understand that there can be no reconciliation without remembering that the experience of millionfold death is part of the inner consciousness of every Jew.

Then he made this appeal, in a sense, a plea to the Germans to accept and come to terms with their past:

> How was it that we remained indifferent to the burning synagogues, the looting, the stigmatisation of the Jews? Whoever opened his eyes

and ears, whoever wanted to find out what was going on, could not but see that the deporting trains were rolling. The 8th May should be reserved for repentance rather than for celebration.

Finally, he quoted an eighteenth-century Jewish mystic who said: 'Seeking to forget prolongs the exile. The secret of redemption is remembrance.'

The Germans burned synagogues and murdered Jews only because they were Jews. And the rest of the world stood by and let it happen, for the very same reason. Murdering Jews and burning synagogues was an old Christian tradition. Pope John XXIII was the first true Christian brave enough to admit the complicity of Christianity in the Holocaust. He states it clearly in his *Act of Reparation* which he wrote shortly before his death.

> We are conscious today that many centuries of blindness have cloaked our eyes so that we can no longer see the beauty of Thy chosen people, nor recognise in their faces the features of our privileged brethren. We realise that the mark of Cain stands on our foreheads. Across the centuries our Brother Abel has lain in blood which we drew or shed tears we caused forgetting Thy love. Forgive us for the curse we falsely attached to their name as Jews. Forgive us for crucifying Thee a second time in their flesh. For we knew not what we did ...

We are entering a new millenium. We are on the threshold of a new age. The future is our children, and they will live as we have taught them. Unless future generations know about the wrongs committed in the past, they will never learn, and will repeat them.

Part Three
REFLECTIONS

11

Fifty years after liberation

WHEN I RECALL the days behind the electrified fences, I often wonder how I went on living. So many times I nearly gave up: when hunger pangs punished my body; when rain and frost chilled the marrow of my bones, and my fingers and toes were paralysed by the cold. Many of my comrades froze to death in temperatures that dropped to twenty, sometimes twenty-five degrees below zero; yet I continued to struggle to stay sane and to stay alive. Half-naked and frozen, I would cry with pain, but my tears simply froze on my cheeks. Every so often, I thought how much easier it would be to touch the high-voltage electrified fence than to go on living. Just one split second and it would be over. But somehow I did not. I could not. Driven by a force beyond my own reason, beyond logic, I had to go on. I found that I wanted very much to live and one day to fulfil my mother's last wish.

I often wonder, how can anyone ever comprehend what went through the minds of the victims who were pushed into the gas chambers? What did my mother and father feel? What did they think in the last seconds of their lives? How do I record and communicate my unspeakable pain as I stood opposite the crematoria, watching the stacks spewing smoke and fire? I lose my ability to think clearly. I feel confused and inept. The words do not exist. Humanity needs to invent a new language, create a new vocabulary, that will convey and express the horrors of the Holocaust. I can't find the words that will describe the nights and days of fear, fire and smoke. Can anyone feel or imagine the anguish and trauma of a dying mother inside the gas chambers? What did she think and feel in the last minutes of her life when desperately pressing her dying baby to her breast? What words do I have at my command which will describe what it was like to watch my own mother and father burn while the rest of the civilised world stood by and let it happen?

How can humanity ever imagine or understand what it is to be a survivor of the Holocaust? Part of us belongs to a world that is dead. We are the last living links with the millions who perished. We are the ashes that still glow with life. We are the living links with Chelmno, Sobibor, Belzec, Babi Yar and Ponary. Perhaps nobody will ever fully understand the world of survivors, for we are people who have inhaled the smell of the burning flesh and bones of our mothers and fathers, our sisters and brothers, children and friends. That smell lives on in our subconscious forever. We were forged in the fires of hell, and welded with an eternal bond to Auschwitz, Treblinka and Belsen.

As I write my story, I wonder if the world really wants to hear what I have to say. It seems to me that there are many who would like the history of the Holocaust to be struck from the record. Some deny it completely: it never happened. To them, the Holocaust is a Jewish invention. They appear to be doing everything possible to confuse and misinform people, and to water down the events of the Holocaust in an attempt to obscure the fact that it was chiefly a Jewish bloodletting. Yet this denial hides the virus of another Holocaust.

The myth of a bloodless Holocaust is being propagated in many ways. It could be felt in the attempt to build a church on the site of Auschwitz. Or it could be heard during Pope John Paul II's remarkable pilgrimage to Treblinka — where, in 1987, he spoke about fourteen nationalities having been murdered by the Germans in 1942-43, but somehow failed to mention that eight hundred and fifty thousand martyrs who perished at Treblinka happened to be Jews. It is a strange sickness, this anti-Semitism, a unique disease. Gentiles suffer from it and, in consequence, we, the Jews, are dying.

As I try to make some sense of the past, what becomes increasingly evident is that the sparks of the burning synagogues in Germany spread right across the world, setting it on fire. London was bombed; Warsaw was reduced to dust; Moscow and Leningrad were set on fire; Dresden was flattened; and Berlin was reduced to a burned-out shell. The fire even managed to reach the most distant continent on earth, setting Darwin aflame. We would do well to remember that it was the German nation which made Hitler. Over aeons, the snake has not changed its nature nor the leopard its spots; I cannot help but wonder whether the German people have been able to alter themselves so radically from what they were only fifty years ago.

Some facts about Auschwitz

In these post-war times, the word 'holocaust' is used daily by the media for any banality, so that it is almost completely trivialised. A large fire or a road accident is described as a 'holocaust'; it has become an everyday word.

Auschwitz was liberated by the Russians on 27 January 1945. The figure of four million murdered victims that appeared on the first commemorative plaque came from figures provided by a Soviet commission which visited the camp one week after its liberation. That commission submitted its findings to the Nuremberg War Crimes Trial.

With the fall of the communist regime in Poland, a commission was established to look into the charges that the Jewish aspect of the tragedy had been diminished. The commission carefully reviewed the records, and concluded that there had indeed been an attempt to diminish the Jewish tragedy. Therefore, they concluded that they had to remove the plaque. They said that the new plaque would respect the full aspect of the Jewish tragedy.[51]

In his article, 'Auschwitz: The Dangers of Distortion', Yehuda Bauer, Professor of Holocaust Studies at the Institute of Contemporary Jewry of the Hebrew University, writes:

> There were never 4 million victims in Auschwitz. According to a painstakingly researched paper by the doyen of French Jewish Holocaust historians, Georges Wellers ('Essai de Determination du nombre de Morts au Camp d'Auschwitz,' *Le Monde Juif*, Fall 1983), which is now accepted as a basis for understanding the horror statistics of Auschwitz, the total number of people who died there, both by gassing in the extermination camp of Birkenau and by starvation, torture, execution or disease in the concentration camp and its satellite camps, was in the neighbourhood of 1.6 million.
>
> A total of 215,409 Poles were brought to Auschwitz. Of these, 3,665 were gassed in the gas chambers; 79,345 died or were murdered in the camp: a total of 83,010 Polish victims. The number of Gypsies who

were gassed is 6,430; 13,825 died in the camp. A total of 11,685 Russians were also gassed.

The figure for Jews murdered by gassing is 1,323,000, with 29,980 dying in the camp; a total of about 1,350,000. [Obviously, these figures, despite their apparent detail, cannot be taken as totally accurate, but they give a general indication — author.] The basis for these figures is the clandestine registration carried out by a group of very courageous men and women who worked as clerks in the camp administration and had a fairly clear picture of what was going on.

One of the reasons for the misinformation disseminated about Auschwitz lies in the fact, demonstrated by a number of authoritative historical research projects, mainly by my colleague Yisrael Gutman, that from the end of 1942 on, Auschwitz ceased to be a predominantly Polish camp.

At that time, Himmler decided to transport the Jews from all the other camps to Auschwitz; parallel to that, [non-Jewish] Poles were gradually shipped out of there to other camps. Himmler's order was not completely carried out, and many Jews remained in the camps they were in at the end of 1942, or to which they were brought later.

The partial execution of the order, however, meant that the three main Auschwitz camps and their satellites received large transports of Jews, most of whom were not gassed on arrival; and from 1943, Auschwitz became a predominantly Jewish camp. Many of the 200,000 Poles brought to Auschwitz died not there but in other camps — but, of course, a majority survived.[52]

Today, Auschwitz is a museum where tens of thousands of tourists from all over the world come to visit the shrine of remembrance of the victims of the Holocaust. When they arrive, Jews find that the one 'Jewish' barracks is always shut, able to be opened by prior arrangement only. As well as this, before the intervention of the Pope, the Polish Catholic Church attempted to build a Carmelite church on what is arguably the site of the largest Jewish cemetery in history.

Attempts have been made to convert the Holocaust into a universal tragedy, a tragedy of humanity where Jews are not even mentioned; or, if so, marginally only. Claims that Auschwitz was a concentration camp mainly for Polish prisoners, and built by them, have been widely disseminated. Apart from the substantial histori-

cal evidence which soundly refutes such falsifications, the follow-
ing passage is an extract from a testimony given by Mark
Jurkowski, a Jew who lived in the town of Auschwitz in pre-war
Poland. It is readily supported by available documentation:

> I came to Australia in early August, 1962.
>
> I was born in Poland in the town of Oswiecim, known today as
> Auschwitz. It was early on the morning of 8 April 1940, the first day of
> Passover that, with two hundred Jewish men, I was lined up in front of
> the Jewish community offices in the town of Auschwitz, waiting to be
> marched off by an SS man to work at the old cavalry barracks on the
> outskirts of town. Every night, we were marched back and released, to
> be picked up again the next morning at the same place and time.
>
> The brutality and beating by the SS were merciless. Each evening,
> we limped back after a long day's work; each evening, we were minus
> a few men who had been killed during the day.
>
> The most savage of the SS was Hauptsturmbannführer Schlechter.
> He was the Chief Building Manager, in charge of converting the army
> camp into a concentration camp which eventually became the infa-
> mous Auschwitz. At the time, none of us was aware of what the
> Germans were up to until the barbed wires completely fenced off the
> camp. On that day, a large detachment of SS men were placed on
> guard around the camp. Later that night, after we were lined up and
> counted many times, an SS officer delivered a speech:
>
> 'You Jews,' he told us, 'are the enemy of the German nation and a
> threat to the security of the State. For this reason you are being
> detained as prisoners of the Third Reich.'
>
> I doubt very much if any others of the first two hundred Jewish
> prisoners who initiated the concentration camp are still alive. I was
> among the three Jewish prisoners who attached the wrought iron sign,
> *ARBEIT MACHT FREI*, above the gates.

Jurkowski managed to escape from Auschwitz in February 1941.
He obtained false documents as a Pole, and fought in the Polish
underground army until the Russian army liberated Poland. At the
time, he was a lieutenant and was incorporated into the regular
Polish army. Promoted to the rank of captain, he continued fighting with the second division. His army unit was among the first of
the troops to reach the outskirts of Berlin in 1945.

Today, Mark Jurkowski from Auschwitz is recognised as a

Polish officer who carried out the highest orders of the Polish army. He was extensively decorated for his brave action in battle against the Germans and for his services in the underground fighting for the liberty of Poland.

The German people in post-war Germany

In 1986, on a visit to Berlin to see a childhood friend, I met a young German writer whom I will call 'Siss'. An intellectual, who looks with a critical eye on her own people and the rest of the world, she said to me, 'My dear Abraham, have no illusions about Germany and the Germans. We have not chosen democracy voluntarily. We have been forced to accept it after our defeat. To us, democracy is a foreign body, a transplant from the Allies. Nothing has really changed since the war — not here, nor in the rest of the world, in particular with regards to anti-Semitism.

'The Russians are the same as always. Their anti-Semitism is as virulent as it was in the days of the pogroms under the Tsar. The Polish hatred against the Jews is still full of anger, even though there are very few Jews left alive today in Poland. The French are as anti-Semitic as ever; the Austrians are no better. And, my dear Abraham ... '

She paused and took a breath, as though unsure whether to continue. I could tell she did not like what she was about to say.

'The Germans are as the Germans always were: they were Nazis long before Hitler was born and will stay so, although he is dead. The term 'Nazi' was born in the Hitler era; however, the idea and the German mentality has always been like that. It is a very old German characteristic. They were always intolerant, nationalistic and aggressive. People change but very, very slowly. The older generation lied. They all worshipped Hitler. Even the old women in the kitchen and the young mothers who nursed their babies — they all enjoyed the loot their sons and husbands sent them from wherever they invaded. My parents were Nazis, and they still are to this very day. It is very sad, but this is the truth about my family and my people. This state of affairs I find very difficult to come to terms with. I may have to leave Germany because I find myself here as a stranger in my own country.'

I listened in silence, finding my gravest fears confirmed by her words. Pointing her finger at the Berlin Wall, she said, 'One day, when this wall comes down and Germany is reunited, we will eventually revert to dictatorship. My people love to be regimented. They never had a revolution. They love to be told what to do, and cannot function without orders from the authorities. They love soldiering, silver buttons and epaulettes. Clicking of the heels and militarism is their second nature. My German people have a great admiration for the army; they love marching to the beat of the drum. Our biggest problem is that, once we start marching, we forget when to stop.'

Reunification is now a fact, and we must wait to see whether her prophecy is realised.

Will they ever learn?

Fifty years have gone by since 15 April 1945, when I was reborn. The last survivors of the Holocaust have commemorated the fiftieth anniversary of their miraculous escape from hell, when the gates of Auschwitz, Buchenwald, Bergen-Belsen and others were liberated by the Allied armies. Since then, after two thousand years, the State of Israel has been established. No more pogroms! No more expulsions! No more Holocausts!

Two generations have been born since. Year after year we, the survivors, commemorate the six million who perished in the gas chambers and in the forests of eastern Europe, mowed down by the machine-guns of the German Einsatzgruppen. These days, I cannot escape the comparisons with Biafra, Pol Pot's 'Kampuchea', Korea, Vietnam. I think of the genocide in Rwanda, and the 'ethnic cleansings' in Bosnia-Herzegovina. Since the collapse of Soviet Russia, I still remember the gulags. I think of Mao's purges and the Cultural Revolution. The world is like a volcanic island, constantly erupting.

I also think of the Turkish families incinerated alive in Germany recently, as the German population stood around watching whilst the police reacted slowly. In the beginning they did not intervene. With the reunification of Germany, it seems that the Nazis are showing their teeth again. Their evil spirit is gaining momentum from day to day. Is Nazism on the way back? Perhaps it was always there.

Today, many young Germans claim, 'We have nothing to do with the past. We are not responsible for what happened before.

Enough is enough! It is time to forget yesterday and get on with tomorrow. It is time to forget Auschwitz! We've heard enough of Bergen-Belsen!' While they claim not to know much about what their fathers and grandfathers did, and rightfully abrogate responsibility for it, some of them seem to be eager to attack foreigners, to burn their homes and hostels — thereby emulating their forefathers to perfection.

Although many young Germans dissociate themselves from the past, one of the very few synagogues in Germany went up in flames at Lubeck the night before Passover — not in Hitler's Germany in 1938, but in the new democratic Germany in 1994.

In Italy, in France and in Hungary, the fascists are on the rise and, with them, so is anti-Semitism. The old disease of which the Gentiles cannot cure themselves grows and spreads like a cancer worldwide.

I think a lot about the future, a future I may not even be part of. Nevertheless, I feel it is my duty to raise the alarm, and to warn younger and future generations to beware. It is happening again!

As a survivor of the Lodz ghetto, Auschwitz-Birkenau, Althammer, Dora and Bergen-Belsen, I turn to you in the name of my mother, my father and brother, and the six million innocent martyrs — for they are all dead and can speak no longer.

Say no to the black plague of Nazism. It brought destruction and misery to tens of millions of people, and devastated most of Europe. Do not forget the Deutsche Wehrmacht and the SS. Young Germans, remember Stalingrad! Remember, or we shall all be doomed to relive our past.

As my thoughts guide my pen along the last lines of my story, I ask myself whether I have told all there is to be told. Will my words help the world to untangle itself from the web in which it is trapped, and from which it seems desperately unable to free itself.

I am only a mortal, an everyday person, one of many millions in this world. My abilities are limited and so are my means, and there is so much to tell. I have so many questions to ask for which I can still find no answers.

We survivors have always had a reputation of being paranoid whenever we discuss the deeply entrenched phenomenon of European anti-Semitism. But much that is occurring there today reveals our 'paranoia' to be based on a palpable reality.

To my mother, Fradl, my father, Shimon, and my brother, Lipek; and to my uncles and aunts, Berish, Sarah, David Laib, and Chaya; and to Shlomo, my cousin, and all my relatives and friends — especially you, my childhood friend, Rivek, and my rabbi, Yitzchak Laib — I want to say how much I regret that you did not live to see the day of liberation. I want you all to know that I have never forgotten you and I never will. In my story you are all alive. You will live forever, and go on telling future generations your story. Hopefully, they will learn, and will never let it happen again. I have learned that man is not infallible; also, that whoever does not learn from the mistakes of the past is a fool. I hope that humanity has learned the lesson of the Holocaust, and that it will stay vigilant and alert, in order never to let the evil of a Hitler hurt civilisation again.

I am a dreamer. So is every Jew, or else we would have disappeared long ago. In the years behind the barbed wires, dreaming preserved my sanity and my love for life.

EPILOGUE

From the ashes of Auschwitz, and the dark abyss of death and evil in Bergen-Belsen, to the ultimate triumph of the human spirit, I started my life again.

Together with my cousin, Mendele Blicblau, I left Germany on 6 November 1945. Disguised as American soldiers, we jumped an empty freight train in the middle of the night and illegally crossed the German border into Belgium. There I met Madeleine, the fifteen-year-old who was later to become my wife. She had returned from the south of France where she had spent the war passing as a non-Jew.

Although I had lost everyone in the Holocaust, Madeleine brought life back into my soul. She was my resurrection. After having lost my parents in Auschwitz and, later, my brother, she showed me that I still had a life to live.

In 1949, I chose to come to Australia rather than follow an acting career in New York (where I had been offered a three-year scholarship to Lee Strasberg's acting school). My landing permit was arranged by Sol Rosenfeld, who had been a neighbour of Mendele's parents in Lodz. After sending for Madeleine, I settled in Melbourne and eventually made a career in the women's fashion industry, designing award-winning garments under the name of 'Champs Elysées Models'. Australia became my new country, where the horizon lit up with a new beginning.

Madeleine bore me a son — 'Shimon Dov', or Simon Bernard — so my father's memory is kept alive and the name of our family will continue. Simon is aware of his name. He knows how his grandfather lived, how he died, and why.

On 12 May 1980, in the prime of her life, Madeleine passed away at the age of forty-nine. Since then, life without her has never been the same. But the sun still rises every morning, and I am here to live every day as it comes.

NOTES

1 Eliezer Berkovits, *Faith After the Holocaust*, Ktav Publishing, New York, 1973, p. 22.

2 Martin Luther, *Von den Juden und inhren Lugern*, (*On the Jews and their Lies*), Wittenburg 1543.

3 Charles Wighton, *Eichmann: His Career and Crimes*, Odhams Press, Long Acre, London, 1961, pp. 89-90.

4 A. Wolf Jasni, *Di geshichte fun yidn in Lodz in di yorn fun der deytshe yidn-oysrotung* (*The History of The Jews in Lodz in the Years of the Holocaust*), Hamenorah, Tel Aviv, 1966, Vol. 2, pp. 68-71. For reasons of authenticity, I have translated Rumkowski's speeches from the Yiddish, as they were recorded in this book.

5 Lucjan Dobroszycki, *The Chronicle of the Lodz Ghetto 1941-1944*, Yale University Press, New Haven and London, 1984.

6 This account is heavily reliant on Lucjan Dobroszycki, *op. cit.*, p. xlii.

7 A. Wolf Jasni, *op. cit.*, p. 19.

8 *Ibid.*, p. 411

9 Israel Tabaksblat, *Khurbn Lodz* (*The Destruction of Lodz*), Tsentral farband fun poylishe yidn in Argentine, Buenos Aires, 1946, p. 62.

10 Norman H Baynes (ed), *The Speeches of Adolf Hitler, April 1922-August 1939*, Oxford University Press, London, 1942, Vol. 1, p. 741.

11 An extract from the Archives du Centre de Documentation Juive Contemporaine, Paris. Document No. XLIX-35, 6 July 1942. Translated from the French.

12 Ilya Ehrenburg and Vasily Grossman, *The Black Book*, Holocaust Library, Walden Press, New York, 1981.

13 Lucjan Dobroszycki, *op. cit.*, pp. 68-9, verifies these suspicions: the mentally ill removed from the Wesola Street Mental Institution had indeed been injected with scopolamine (tranquilliser) the night before. The first truck came for them at 11.00 a.m; the second truck came at 2.00 p.m. [It was said at the time that the patients were then murdered near Lodz in the forests.]

14 Dr Leni Yahill, 'Gassing', in *Holocaust*, Keter Publishing, Jerusalem, 1974, p. 98.

15 Martin Gilbert, *Atlas of the Holocaust*, Michael Joseph in association with the Board of Deputies of British Jews, London, 1982, pp. 80, 83.

16 This and the preceding account of the origins of Chelmno on p. 50 are taken from Lucjan Dobroszycki, *op. cit.*, pp. liv-lv.

17 *Lodz Ghetto*, Viking Penguin, New York, 1989, p. 492.

18 A. Wolf Jasni, *op. cit.*, p. 50.

19 Zdunska Wola *Yizkor Book*, Israel Press, Tel Aviv, 1968, p. 400.

20 A. Wolf Jasni, *op. cit.*, pp. 70-71

21 A. Wolf Jasni, *op. cit.*, p. 175

22 Lucjan Dobroszycki, *op. cit.*, footnote 48, p. 169.

23 *Ibid.*, footnote 70, p. 209.

24 *Ibid.*, footnote 69, p. 208.

25 The text of the entire speech ('Give Me Your Children') can be found in *Lodz Ghetto*, Viking Penguin, New York, 1989, pp. 328-31.

26 Israel Tabaksblat, *op. cit.*, p. 124. I have translated the letter from the original Yiddish version as reported by Tabaksblat, the messenger who carried the document to Rumkowski.

27 Statistics from article by Colin Tatz, Professor of Politics at

Macquarie University, in *Australian Jewish News*, Melbourne edition, 7 Sept. 1990, p. 29.

28 Jacob Celemanski is the author of the book *Mit Mein Farschnittenem Folk* (*With My Destroyed People*) published by Unser Tsait, New York.

29 Emanuel Ringelblum, *Polish-Jewish Relations During the Second World War*, Yad Vashem, Jerusalem, 1974, p. 219.

30 This and the preceding quotations on pp. 99-101 are transcribed from Aviva Ravel, *Faithful Unto Death* (based on the Bund Archives in New York), Arthur Zygielbaum Branch Workman Circle, Montreal, 1980, pp. 167, 169, 170, 172, 174-9.

31 A. Wolf Jasni, *op. cit.*, p. 356.

32 A. Wolf Jasni, *op. cit.*, pp. 356-57.

33 A. Wolf Jasni, *op. cit.*, p. 357.

34 A. Wolf Jasni, *op. cit., loc. cit.*

35 A. Wolf Jasni, *op. cit.*, p. 403.

36 Israel Tabaksblat, *op. cit.*, p. 81.

37 A. Wolf Jasni, *op. cit.*, p. 422.

38 A. Wolf Jasni, *op. cit.*, pp. 422-23.

39 See footnote 47.

40 A. Wolf Jasni, *op. cit.*, Vol II, pp. 454-55.

41 Dr Henry Goldszmit, better known as Janusz Korczak, was a doctor of medicine, child psychologist, pedagogue, poet, writer of children's literature. Korczak was the director of a Warsaw ghetto orphanage on Sliska Street. On 5 August 1942, Korczak joined his children on their last journey to the gas chambers of Treblinka. He chose to go with his children, knowing full well what they were heading for. Korczak could have saved his life by joining his friends outside the ghetto where they had a hiding place for him.

42 There are various versions of Mordechai Chaim Rumkowski's arrival and death at Auschwitz. My version is based on what I heard on my arrival at Auschwitz-Birkenau from the other

inmates who arrived with Rumkowski.

43 The *Australian Jewish News*, 6 May 1994, p. 9 (translated from the Yiddish).

44 The *Australian Jewish News*, 12 Aug. 1994, p. 12 (translated from the Yiddish).

45 The *Australian Jewish News*, 6 May 1994, p. 9 (translated from the Yiddish).

46 Danuta Czech, *Kalendarium Der Ereignisse im Konzentrationslager Auschwitz-Birkenau, 1939-1945, 1 Auflage*, Rowohlt, Reinbek near Hamburg, 1989.

47 Excerpts from the diary of Rudolf Hoess, commandant of Auschwitz extermination camp, from the National Museum in Auschwitz. Manuscript pages: 140-2, 176-7, 229-30, plus typed copies in Polish translation. Published by the Jewish Holocaust Museum, Elsternwick Australia, March 1990, Vol. 7, No. 1, p. 8; June 1990, Vol. 7, No. 2, p. 10; Sept. 1990, Vol. 7, No. 3, p. 4.

48 David S. Wyman, *The Abandonment of the Jews — America and the Holocaust, 1941–1945*, Pantheon Books, New York, 1984, pp. 296-97.

49 Eliezer Berkovits, *op. cit.*, p. 17.

50 Australian Institute of Jewish Affairs, *Briefing*, No. 19, Nov. 1992, p. 2.

51 The *Australian Jewish News*, 10 Aug. 1990, p. 23.

52 *Ibid.*